Computer Networking and Communication Systems

Computer Networking and Communication Systems

Edited by Connor Butler

CLANRYE
INTERNATIONAL
www.clanryeinternational.com

Clanrye International,
750 Third Avenue, 9th Floor,
New York, NY 10017, USA

ISBN: 978-1-63240-948-5

Cataloging-in-Publication Data

Computer Networking and Communication Systems / edited by Connor Butler.
   p. cm.
Includes bibliographical references and index.
ISBN 978-1-63240-948-5
1. Computer networks. 2. Information networks. 3. Network computers. 4. Electronic data processing--Distributed processing. 5. Telecommunication. I. Butler, Connor.
TK5105.5 .C66 2020
004.6--dc23

For information on all Clanrye International publications
visit our website at www.clanryeinternational.com

Contents

Preface

A computer network is defined as a digital telecommunications network in which computing devices share resources using data links between nodes. Data links can be established over cable media or wireless media. Computer networks support a number of services and applications, such as digital audio, digital video and access to the World Wide Web. In a computer network, data is transmitted or received in the form of packets between nodes. Local Area Network, Wide Area Network and Metropolitan Area Network are the three main types of networks. The chief components of computer networks are servers, transmission media, clients, network interface card, network operating system, etc. A communication system is a collection of communication networks, relay stations, transmission systems, tributary stations, and data terminal equipment that are able to interoperate and interconnect. Communication systems can be of different types, depending on the type of media and technology used, and application area, such as optical communication system, radio communication system, tactical communications system, etc. This book discusses the fundamentals as well as modern approaches of computer networking. Also included in it is a detailed explanation of the various concepts and applications of communication systems. This book on computer networking and communication systems is a collective contribution of a renowned group of international experts.

All of the data presented henceforth, was collaborated in the wake of recent advancements in the field. The aim of this book is to present the diversified developments from across the globe in a comprehensible manner. The opinions expressed in each chapter belong solely to the contributing authors. Their interpretations of the topics are the integral part of this book, which I have carefully compiled for a better understanding of the readers.

At the end, I would like to thank all those who dedicated their time and efforts for the successful completion of this book. I also wish to convey my gratitude towards my friends and family who supported me at every step.

Editor

On Internet Traffic Classification: A Two-Phased Machine Learning Approach

Taimur Bakhshi and Bogdan Ghita

Center for Security, Communications and Network Research, University of Plymouth, Plymouth PL4 8AA, UK

Correspondence should be addressed to Taimur Bakhshi; taimur.bakhshi@plymouth.ac.uk

Academic Editor: Tin-Yu Wu

Traffic classification utilizing flow measurement enables operators to perform essential network management. Flow accounting methods such as NetFlow are, however, considered inadequate for classification requiring additional packet-level information, host behaviour analysis, and specialized hardware limiting their practical adoption. This paper aims to overcome these challenges by proposing two-phased machine learning classification mechanism with NetFlow as input. The individual flow classes are derived per application through k-means and are further used to train a C5.0 decision tree classifier. As part of validation, the initial unsupervised phase used flow records of fifteen popular Internet applications that were collected and independently subjected to k-means clustering to determine unique flow classes generated per application. The derived flow classes were afterwards used to train and test a supervised C5.0 based decision tree. The resulting classifier reported an average accuracy of 92.37% on approximately 3.4 million test cases increasing to 96.67% with adaptive boosting. The classifier specificity factor which accounted for differentiating content specific from supplementary flows ranged between 98.37% and 99.57%. Furthermore, the computational performance and accuracy of the proposed methodology in comparison with similar machine learning techniques lead us to recommend its extension to other applications in achieving highly granular real-time traffic classification.

1. Introduction

Traffic classification methods using flow and packet based measurements have been previously researched using various techniques ranging from automated machine learning (ML) algorithms to deep packet inspection (DPI) for accurate application identification. Port and protocol analysis, once the default method for traffic identification is now considered obsolete as most applications use dynamic ports, employ HTTPS or encrypted SRTP or use tunnelling, which makes classification close to impossible. Deep packet inspection (DPI) is useful; however the computational overhead and additional hardware required for packet analysis severely limit its practical implementation for network operators [1]. Moreover, aggregation based traffic monitoring techniques using flow measurements have proliferated in recent years due to their inherent scalability and ease of implementation as well as compatibility with existing hardware using standardized export formats such as NetFlow and IPFIX [2]. However,

despite an increase in use, flow based network monitoring also encountered traffic classification challenges mainly due to frequent obfuscation and encryption techniques employed by many applications [3–5]. Most automated machine learning classification algorithms utilizing NetFlow involve significant processing overhead and sometimes employ sanitized input requiring simultaneous computations on flow records and packet traces to obtain meaningful results [3, 6, 7]. Additionally, popular Internet applications generate convoluted sets of flows representing content specific and auxiliary control flows, making application identification on a per-flow basis even more challenging. The present paper proposed a per-flow C5.0 decision tree classifier by employing a two-phased machine learning approach while solely utilizing the existing quantitative attributes of NetFlow records. Flow records for fifteen popular Internet applications were first collected and unique flow classes were derived per application using k-means clustering. Based on these

TABLE 1: Traffic classification approaches.

Category	Classification methodology	Attribute(s) used	Granularity	Processing time	Sample tools/ML techniques
Port based	Protocol port	Protocol ports	High	Low	Any (custom), PRTG network monitor [55], Nagios [56], Wireshark [48]
Payload inspection	Deep packet inspection	Payload inspection of, for example, first n packets, first packet per direction	High	High	OpenDPI [1], nDPI [45], L7 (TIE) [35]
	Stochastic packet inference	Statistical properties inherent in packet header and payload	High	High	Netzob [57], Polyglot [58], KISS [8]
Behavioural techniques	End-point behaviour monitoring	Identifying host (communication) behaviour pattern	Low	Moderate	BLINC [46], SVM [59], naïve Bayes [60]
	Traffic accounting	Heuristic analysis of inspected packets, flows	High	High	ANTCs [61], naïve Bayes [60], Bayesian network [62]
Statistical approaches	Packet based	Packet and payload size, interpacket arrival time	High	Moderate	kNN [63], Hidden Markov/Gaussian Mixture Models
	Flow based	Duration, transmission rate, multiple flow features	Low	Low	k-means/hierarchical clustering [27], J48 [30], C5.0 [31], BFTree [64], SVM [59]

preclassified flows (the ground-truth data), the C.50 classifier was subsequently trained for highly granular per-flow application traffic classification. The classified applications included YouTube, Netflix, Dailymotion, Skype, Google Talk, Facebook video chat, VUZE and BitTorrent clients, Dropbox, Google Drive and OneDrive cloud storage, two interactive online games, and the Thunderbird and Outlook email clients. The rest of this paper is organized as follows. Section 2 presents related background work in traffic classification and gives an overview of k-means clustering and C.50 algorithm. Section 3 elaborates on data collection, preprocessing, and feature selection methodology. Section 4 details flow clustering using k-means and discusses the derived flow classes. Section 5 evaluates the accuracy of the resulting C5.0 classifier while Section 6 compares the performance and computation overhead of the proposed approach with state-of-the-art ML based classification schemes. Final conclusions are presented in Section 7.

2. Background

The following subsections present a comprehensive overview of state of the art in traffic classification and consider related work in addressing flow level classification challenges using supervised, unsupervised, and cascaded ML techniques. A brief outline of k-means clustering and C5.0 machine learning techniques in the context of traffic classification is detailed afterwards.

2.1. Traffic Classification Methodologies and Related Work. Traffic classification serves as a fundamental requirement for network operators to differentiate and prioritize traffic for a number of purposes, from guaranteeing quality of service to anomaly detection and even profiling user resource requirements. Consequentially a large body of research can

be attributed to traffic classification such as [8–13] along with comprehensive surveys [14–16], which reflect the interest of the networking community in this particular avenue. From a high level methodology perspective, traffic classification research can be broadly divided into port and packet payload based classification, behavioural identification techniques, and statistical measurement based approaches [16]. A summary of the prevalent classification approaches, their traffic feature usage, and associated algorithms is given in Table 1. While port based classification techniques are now considered obsolete given the frequent obfuscation techniques and dynamic range of ports used by applications, packet payload inspection methods remain relevant primarily due to their high classification accuracy. Payload based classifiers inspect packet payloads using deep packet inspection (DPI) to identify application signatures or utilize a stochastic inspection (SPI) of packets to look for statistical parameters in packet payloads. Although the resulting classification is highly accurate it also presents significant computational costs [16–18] as well as being error-prone in dealing with encrypted packets. In comparison, behavioural classification techniques work higher up the networking stack and peruse the total traffic patterns of the end-points (hosts and servers) such as the number of machines contacted, the protocol used, and the time frame of bidirectional communication to identify the application being used on the host [19–22]. Behavioural techniques are highly promising and provide a great deal of classification accuracy with reduced overhead compared to payload inspection methods [9, 13]. However, behavioural techniques focus on end-point activity and require parameters from a number of flows to be collected and analysed before successful application identification. With increasing ubiquity of flow level network monitoring which presents a low-cost traffic accounting solution, specifically utilizing Net-Flow due to scalability and ease of use, statistical classification techniques utilizing flow measurements have gained momentum [2, 8–12, 23]. Statistical approaches exploit application diversity and inherent traffic footprints (flow parameters) to characterize traffic and subsequently derive classification benchmarks through data mining techniques to identify individual applications [24]. Statistical classification is considered light-weight and highly scalable from an operational point of view especially when real-time or near real-time traffic identification is required. While traffic classification in the network core is increasingly challenging and seldom implemented, application flow identification at the edge or network ingress as detailed in [16] allows operators in shaping the respective traffic further upstream. Statistical flow based traffic classifications however, due to minimal number of available features in a typical flow record such as NetFlow, report low classification accuracy and increasingly rely on additional packet payload information to produce effective results [8–12]. The present work picks up from this narrative and solely utilizes NetFlow attributes using two-phased machine learning (ML), incorporating a combination of unsupervised k-means cluster analysis and C5.0 based decision tree algorithm to achieve high accuracy in application traffic classification.

Typical statistical flow level classification can be further subdivided based on the type of ML algorithm being used, that is, supervised or unsupervised. Unsupervised methods alone do not rely on any training data for classification and, while being time and resource efficient, especially with large data sets, encompass significant limitations hampering their wider adoption. Firstly, cluster analysis is mostly done offline and relies on evaluating stored flow records in statistical applications for cluster learning and traffic identification [25, 26]. Secondly, unsupervised clustering quite often also requires additional information from packet-level traces requiring specialized hardware and is therefore considered as an expensive option for network operators [27, 28]. Lastly, once traffic records have been clustered, defining optimal value ranges of classification attributes for real-time systems is seldom easy and highly dependent on the data set used [29].

Supervised ML algorithms in contrast require a comprehensive training data set to serve as primary input for building the classifiers; the completeness of the data set, together with the ability of the method to discriminate between classes, is the decisive factor for the accuracy of the method. Although considered favourable in terms of presenting a discrete rule set or decision tree for identifying applications, supervised training also falls short of presenting a complete solution to classification challenges, as a highly accurate training/test data set (also referred to as ground-truth data) is required prior to further use. To aid in obtaining accurate ground-truth data several ideas have been explored. Separate offline traffic identification systems were used to preprocess and generate training data for online classifiers in [30]. Custom scripts were employed in [31] on researcher machines to associate flow records and packets with application usage. Deep packet inspection was used to obtain application names for labelling training data in [32]. However, obtaining accurate ground-truth data considering only singular application class labels for subsequent training of the supervised ML classifier falls significantly short of recognizing the different

flows generated per application [25–32]. Internet applications generate a convoluted set of flows including both application initiated content specific or auxiliary control flows and other functional traffic such as DNS or multicasts. Per-flow traffic classification hence requires a full appreciation of the peculiar traits and types of flows (classes) generated per application to eliminate the classification system relying on time window analysis or packet derivative information to achieve higher classification accuracy.

To increase the flow classification accuracy, cascaded classification methodologies employing a combination of algorithms as well as semisupervised ML approaches have also been previously explored. Foremski et al. [33] combined several algorithms using a cascaded principle where the selection of chosen algorithm to be applied for each IP flow classification depended on predetermined classifier selection criteria. Jin et al. [23] combined binary classifiers in a series to identify traffic flows while using a scoring system to assign each flow to a traffic class. Additionally, collective traffic statistics from multiple flows were used to achieve greater classification accuracy. Similarly Carela-Español et al. [34] used k-dimensional trees to implement an online real-time classifier using only initial packets from flows and destination port numbers for classification. de Donato et al. [35] introduced a comprehensive traffic identification engine (TIE) incorporating several modular classifier plug-ins, using the available input traffic features to select the classifier(s), merging the obtained results from each, and giving the final classification output. A similar approach was followed in Netramark [36] incorporating multiple classifiers to appraise the comparative accuracy of the algorithms as well as use a weighted voting framework to select a single best classification output. Another prominent ML tool used in traffic classification studies is Weka [37], incorporating a library (Java based) of supervised and unsupervised classifiers which can be readily implemented on test data set to evaluate the accuracy of the results from each methodology. Using multiple classifiers and selecting the best choice for classifying each traffic flow through voting or even combining the results for a final verdict, however, does not specifically consider refining the ground-truth data to fully account for the multiple flow classes (per application) and their subsequent identification. Additionally merging multiple instances of classifiers raises scalability issues with regard to their real-time implementation.

Semisupervised learning techniques on the other hand use a relatively small amount of labelled data with a large amount of unlabelled records to train a classifier [38]. Two ML algorithms, unsupervised and supervised, were combined in [39] and the scheme used a probabilistic assignment during unsupervised cluster analysis to associated clusters with traffic labels. Zhang et al. [40] proposed using a fractional amount of flows labelled through cluster analysis to train and construct a classification model specifically focusing on zero-day application identification. The sole use of cluster analysis to serve as a means for identifying applications and generating training data without either additional manual or automated validation may, however, lead to incorrect traffic labelling. Unmapped flow clusters from unsupervised learning were, for example, attributed to unknown traffic in [39]. Error-prone labelling of flows through cluster analysis using semisupervised approaches may also result in significant misclassification penalties.

Subflow qualification is paramount to fully apply network policies such as guaranteeing application QoS, profiling user activity, and accurately detecting network anomalies. Furthermore, correct subflow identification aids in reducing the over-time degradation of supervised algorithms by accounting for the multiple types of flow classes and their respective parameters per application, reducing the unseen examples. The present approach refines the acquired ground-truth data by segregation of prelabelled application flows through independent unsupervised clustering, thereafter used to train a supervised C5.0 decision tree. The resulting classifier is hence able to recognize the multiple flow classes even from the same application without combining the results from multiple classifiers or using popular voting. This also increases the scalability of the final decision tree which can be implemented as a standalone system at suitable traffic aggregation points in the network capable of real-time traffic classification.

Finally, as noted in [25, 41, 42], given the multitude of classification methodologies, dissimilar traffic traces, and the diversity in flow classification features, benchmarking the performance of classification algorithms is a difficult undertaking. In the present work, the widely used classification tool Weka [36] was employed to yield a qualitative comparison in terms of the accuracy and computational overhead of the proposed design against some state-of-the-art classification methods.

2.2. k-Means Clustering. Flow level clustering requires efficiently partitioning collected flows per application into groups based on exported NetFlow attributes. One of the prominent unsupervised clustering techniques is the k-means clustering algorithm preferred over other methods such as hierarchical clustering, due to its enhanced computational efficiency [10, 32]. k-means minimizes a given number of vectors by choosing k random vectors as initial cluster centres and assigning each vector to a cluster as determined by a distance metric comparison with the cluster centre (a squared error function) as given in (1). Cluster centres are then recomputed as the average (or mean) of the cluster members. This iteration continues repeatedly, ending either when the clusters converge or when a specified number of iterations have passed [27, 43]:

$$J = \sum_{j=1}^{k} \sum_{i=1}^{n} \left\| x_i^j - c_j \right\|^2. \tag{1}$$

In (1), c_j represents cluster centre, n equals the size of the sample space (collected flows), and k is the chosen value for number of unique clusters (flow classes). Hence, using k-means, n flows can be partitioned into k classes. Value of k is of significant importance as it directly influences the number of flow classes affecting overfitting. An intelligent alternative to calculate the optimal number of clusters is by using the Everitt and Hothorn graphical approach [44], discussed and applied in Section 4.

2.3. C5.0 Machine Learning Algorithm. The C5.0 algorithm and its predecessor C4.5 described in [30] attempt to predict a dependent attribute by finding optimal value ranges of an independent set of attributes. At each stage of iteration, the algorithm aims to minimize information entropy by finding a single attribute that best separates different classes from each other. The process continues until the whole sample space is split into a decision tree isolating each class. Hence, in a sample space comprising n application flow classes, if training data is given by preclassified samples given by vector S (2), each sample flow f_n may consist of a j-dimensional vector (3), where z_j represents independent attributes which are used to identify the class in which f_n falls:

$$S = [f_1, f_2, f_3, f_n] \tag{2}$$

$$f_n = [z_1, z_2, z_3, z_j]. \tag{3}$$

C5.0 could therefore be used to build a decision tree utilizing flow attributes z_j of each sample f_n from preclassified training data. C5.0 also includes advanced options for boosting, pruning, and winnowing to enhance accuracy and computational efficiency of the resulting decision tree classifier [31]. The adaptive boosting proposed in [32] generates a batch of classifiers instead of a single classifier and uses vote count from each classifier on every examined sample to predict the final class. Advanced pruning options remove parts of the classification tree representing relatively high error rate at every stage of iteration and once finally for the complete tree to reduce performance caveats. Finally enabling winnowing reduces the feature set required for classification by removing covariates with low predictive ability during classifier training and cross-validation stage.

3. Methodology

To address the challenges of obtaining high quality ground-truth data incorporating flow class segregation and identification in each of the examined applications, our proposed classification technique utilizes unsupervised cluster analysis and supervised classifier training in tandem. A high level overview of the traffic classification scheme is shown in Figure 1 with a description of principal steps as follows.

(i) *Preprocessing.* Internet traffic is collected from end-user machines and marked with application labels accordingly (e.g., Skype and YouTube) using a localized operational packet-level classifier. Application labelled traffic is afterwards exported as flows using a flow exporting utility for unsupervised cluster analysis.

(ii) *Cluster Analysis.* Using unsupervised k-means, flows belonging to individual applications are separately cluster analysed to extract unique subclasses per application, offering a finer granularity of the classification (e.g., YouTube and Netflix flows would be classed as streaming and browsing).

(iii) *Classifier Training.* Flows marked with their k-means clusters, indicating the subclass they belong to, are

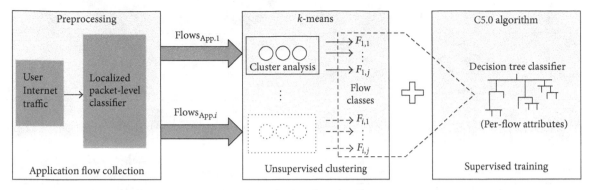

FIGURE 1: Traffic classification scheme.

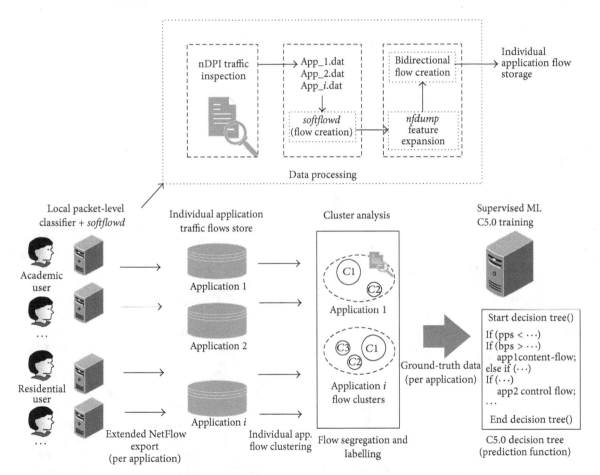

FIGURE 2: Data collection and preprocessing workflow.

afterwards fed to a C5.0 classifier for supervised training, leading to a decision tree.

(iv) *Evaluation.* A separate data set is used for testing the accuracy of the algorithm. For each NetFlow record the trained C5.0 classifies the application and the subclass of the flow based on their respective attributes, ingrained during decision tree creation.

The following subsections detail the methodology used for collecting NetFlow records from user machines, flow customization, k-means clustering, and designing feature sets for the C5.0 classifier.

3.1. Data Collection. To increase the scalability of the resultant classifier in identifying traffic from different network settings, NetFlow records were collected from two environments: (i) typical residential premises using broadband connection and (ii) an academic setting using corporate Internet as depicted in Figure 2. Two PCs were used in each environment for user traffic generation and collection. In order to accurately isolate traffic for each of the fifteen examined applications, a localized extension of packet-level classifier nDPI [45] was used on the researcher's machines, excluding references to application data or the end-point identity of users for anonymity similar to [46, 47]. The nDPI is based on the

TABLE 2: Traffic collection summary.

Traffic class	Application	Bytes ($\times 10^6$)	Flows	Dates	Duration (hrs)
Video streaming	YouTube	16093.87	879641	[09–12]/09/2015	6.89
	Netflix	11586.61	454985	[08–09]/09/2015	5.65
	Dailymotion	11258.12	398412	[15–16]/03/2016	5.31
Video chat/VoIP	Skype	6251.06	1492380	[08–17]/10/2015	9.45
	Gtalk	4584.02	1025260	[14–18]/03/2016	4.25
	Facebook Messenger	7824.13	1158302	[15–21]/03/2016	3.28
P2P torrent	VUZE	131611.31	1318749	[20–23]/09/2015	4.28
	BitTorrent	154138.97	1308881	[20–23]/09/2015	3.56
Cloud storage	Dropbox	211833.57	408677	[11–23]/09/2015	1.56
	Google Drive	158923.52	358426	[20–23]/03/2016	2.31
	OneDrive	186358.21	325854	[21–27]/03/2016	1.81
Online games	8-Ball Pool	953.91	1358425	[10–13]/10/2015	0.35
	Treasure Hunt	1158.28	1592362	[15–22]/03/2016	2.11
Email client	Thunderbird	1401.36	821484	[15–31]/08/2015	2.21
	Outlook	1854.54	698722	[19–31]/03/2016	3.55

libcap and OpenDPI library [48] and is continuously updated to increase the number of applications and protocols that can be successfully identified. Once the traffic from the examined applications was identified and marked with application names, it was converted to the NetFlow format using the *softflowd* utility [49]. A total of approximately 13.6×10^6 flows were collected and marked with application labels. Table 2 presents a summary of collected flows including the bytes, flows, time frame of the traffic collection, and the duration associated with each application. The NetFlow records were afterwards subjected to further preprocessing, that is, feature set expansion using the nfdump utility [50] and creation of bidirectional flows before being exported to individual application storage filers as detailed in the following section.

3.2. Customizing NetFlow Records. NetFlow by default outputs 5-tuple address, port, and protocol connection information ⟨SrcIP, DstIP, SrcPo, DstPo., Proto.⟩ along with the timing and interface relating to each flow. Transmitted and received flows are, however, not correlated by default. Generally considered as lacking an extensive set of attributes, it further extrapolates the use of packet traces for traffic identification as highlighted in [26–29]. To fully explore the prediction ability of NetFlow attributes with the proposed methodology, *nfdump* [50] was used to expand the NetFlow output to display flow duration, number of packets, data rate (bits per second), packet transfer rate (pps), and bytes per packet (Bpp) for each flow; then transmitted and received flows were correlated to output a 17-tuple bidirectional flow as shown by the snippet in Table 3.

3.3. Extracting Flow Classes (k-Means Clustering). Popular applications such as YouTube or Skype generate an intricate set of flows between various web servers and the client depending on their underlying content distribution, load balancing, and authentication schemes [51–54]. While DPI based traffic classification is useful in identifying the respective applications, it does not specifically segregate different

flows generated per application attributed to the primary application content or control signalling, session establishment, embedded webpage advertisements, and so forth. Per-flow classification consequently requires a separation of content specific and supplementary flows to retrieve the different flow classes generated per application for subsequently training and testing the classifier. Flow classification is not possible using supervised ML alone due to lack of information about the flow classes generated by an application, requiring an independent technique for per-application flow segregation. The k-means algorithm was therefore independently applied on paired bidirectional flows generated per application in order to retrieve the respective flow classes. Due to extensive repetition of source and destination IP addresses, port numbers, and protocol information in the collected data, these were deemed scalar entities for analysis and excluded while clustering. The remaining 12 attributes chosen to isolate application specific flows from auxiliary data per application for further analysis comprise transmitted bytes Tx.B., transmitted packets Tx.Pkt., transmitted data rate in bits per second Tx.bps., transmitted packers per second Tx.pps., transmitted packet size in bytes per packet Tx.Bpp., transmitted flow duration Tx.s., received bytes Rx.B., received packets Rx.Pkt., received data rate in bits per second Rx.bps., received packets per second Rx.pps., received packet size in bytes per packet Rx.Bpp., and received flow duration Rx.s. The clustering vector per application could therefore be represented by the following equation:

$$F_{ij} = \left[\text{Tx.B}_{ij}, \text{Tx.pkt}_{ij}, \text{Tx.bps}_{ij}, \text{Tx.pps}_{ij}, \text{Tx.Bpp}_{ij}, \right.$$

$$\text{Rx.s}_{ij}, \text{Rx.B}_{ij}, \text{Rx.pkt}_{ij}, \text{Rx.bps}_{ij}, \text{Rx.pps}_{ij}, \text{Rx.Bpp}_{ij}, \quad (4)$$

$$\left. \text{Rx.s}_{ij} \right].$$

In (4), i and j are unique per application and per flow, respectively. Hence, bidirectional flows represented by vector F_{ij} split into k clusters represent the types of flows per

TABLE 3: 17-tuple bidirectional NetFlow records.

	SrcIP	DstIP	Prot.	SrcPo	DstPo	Tx.B.	Tx.Pkt.	Tx.s.	Tx.bps.	Tx.pps.	Tx.Bpp.	Rx.B.	Rx.Pkt.	Rx.s.	Rx.bps.	Rx.pps.	Rx.Bpp.
12	*Private IP* address	Website/application	TCP	59648	80	1737	10	16.551	839	0	173	2768	10	16.542	1338.0	0	276
13	*Private IP* address	Website/application	TCP	50254	443	763	8	0.073	83616	109	95	4571	7	0.063	580444.0	111	653
14	*Private IP* address	Website/application	TCP	37832	443	397	5	0.078	40717	64	79	3657	4	0.041	713560.0	97	914
15	*Private IP* address	Website/application	TCP	47216	443	2663	12	1.291	16501	9	221	5718	11	1.279	35765.0	8	519
16	*Private IP* address	Website/application	TCP	53509	443	883	10	0.278	25410	35	88	4472	9	0.243	147226.0	37	496

TABLE 4: NetFlow feature sets for C5.0 classifier training.

Set 1	Set 2
Protocol and port information	Protocol and port information
(i) Source and destination port *num*	(i) Source and destination port *labels*
(ii) Protocol (TCP, UDP)	(ii) Protocol (TCP, UDP)

Set 3	Set 4
Flow parameters	Flow parameter ratios
(i) Received and transmitted packets (Rx.Pkts., Tx.Pkts.)	(i) Received packets to transmitted packets (Rx.Pkts./Tx.Pkts.)
(ii) Received and transmitted packet rate (Rx.pps., Tx.pps.)	(ii) Received to transmitted packet rate (Rx.pps./Tx.pps.)
(iii) Received and transmitted data rate (Rx.bps., Tx.bps.)	(iii) Received to transmitted data rate (Rx.bps./Tx.bps.)
(iv) Received and transmitted bytes per packet (Tx.Bpp., Rx.Bpp.)	(iv) Received to transmitted bytes per packet (Rx.Bpp./Tx.Bpp.)
(v) Received and transmitted data (Rx.B., Tx.B.)	(v) Received to transmitted data (Rx.B./Tx.B.)
(vi) Received and transmitted flow duration (Tx.s., Rx.s.)	(vi) Received to transmitted flow duration (Rx.s./Tx.s.)

application. Once segregated, flows per application were subsequently labelled with the respective flow class before data sets for all the fifteen examined applications were combined and split in equal proportions (~50%) for training and testing the C5.0 ML classifier.

3.4. Feature Selection. Feature set selection is of paramount importance for training the classifier, given that these should be predictive and must correctly classify the application traffic. The selected features must also closely link to the flow classes derived from k-means clustering and utilize their NetFlow values to discriminate between different application flows. NetFlow attributes can be broadly grouped by transport layer parameters and network layer traffic statistics for each flow. Both groups were studied for classifier training individually and in combination to examine their efficiency for classification. Additionally, minimizing the set of features for traffic classification also minimizes the processing overhead involved in creating decision trees and reduced classification time. Four sets of features sets were, therefore, devised around transport and network layer features translating for the independent attributes z_j, given in (3) as shown in Table 4. Set 1 included source and destination port numbers along with protocol information. Set 2 used source and destination ports however, rather than using actual port numbers; these were labelled as Known (0–1023) and Unknown (>1023) aiming to evaluate classification accuracy on basic port information alone. Set 3 included 12 flow attributes excluding source and destination IP addresses and port and protocol information while set 4 represented the same as ratios thereby reducing the feature set to 6 covariates with the intention of compressing the size of resulting decision tree even further.

4. Unsupervised Flow Clustering

4.1. Calculating Flow Classes per Application: Value of k. A total of 6.8 million bidirectional flows were cluster analysed independently for each application using the computationally efficient Hartigan and Wong implementation of k-means in R [43]. Since value of k directly influences the number of flow clusters (classes) per application, Everitt and Hothorn

method was employed to determine k number per application [44]. This graphical technique plots *within cluster sum of square values* (wss) against the number of clusters k, with the curve in plot signifying an appropriate number of clusters that fit the input data. The plot of wss versus k of flow records for each application is given in Figures 3–7. Automated scripting calculated the maximum *within cluster variance* between successive values according to Everitt and Hothorn criteria in reaching the optimal cluster number per application and marked the respective flow records with the individual cluster colour. Table 5 details the optimal number of clusters translating for different types of flows classes determined per application along with the "within sum of squares" per cluster to "total sum of square distance" between clusters (wss/total_ss) representing the tightness of these clusters in covering the entire sample space, that is, flow records. A small sample set comprising approximately 1K bidirectional flows from each cluster was afterwards analysed offline to assign the respective flow labels as detailed in the following section.

4.2. Analysis. YouTube access seemed to be solely used for *streaming* (and not content upload) in the present case and the corresponding clusters indicated 3 unique flow classes generated as shown by the graph in Figure 3(a). According to YouTube traffic analysis studies carried out in [51, 52], these were narrowed to three unique flow classes and attributed to content-streaming, website browsing (or video searches), and redirections between YouTube and other Google content distribution servers. Netflix and Dailymotion video streaming similarly showed three flow classes, two for video content-streaming having different download rates corresponding to start of video succeeded by steady buffering stage and a third for user searches. For these applications, video streaming flows were labelled as "streaming" while website searches and server redirections were labelled as "browsing."

The Skype client was used for *video with voice communication* rather than file sharing or instant messaging as per the labelled flow record perusal. Subsequent clustering produced two highly discriminate clusters given by the knee-point of the graph in Figure 4(a). Skype stores user information in a decentralized manner with Skype clients acting as

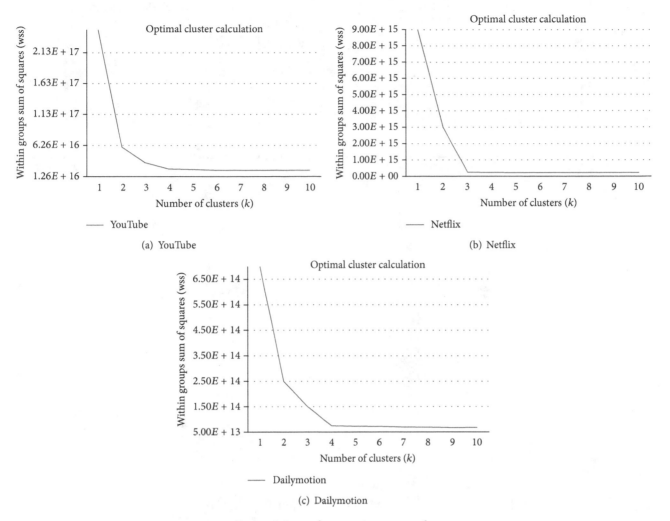

FIGURE 3: Inner-cluster variance versus k.

TABLE 5: Segregated flows per application.

Traffic class	Application	Cluster (k)	wss/total_ss	Content specific flows	Auxiliary flows
	YouTube	3	87.3%	Streaming	Browsing
Streaming	Netflix	3	94.6%	Streaming	Browsing
	Dailymotion	3	95.1%	Streaming	Browsing
	Skype	2	98.8%	Comms.	Comms. Ctrl.
Comms./VoIP	Gtalk	2	97.21%	Comms.	Comms. Ctrl.
	Facebook Messenger	3	92.12%	Comms.	Comms. Ctrl., Browsing
Torrents/P2P	VUZE	3	97.9%	Torrent	Torr.Ctrl.
	BitTorrent	3	91.2%	Torrent	Torr.Ctrl.
	Dropbox	3	89.2%	Up/dwnld.	Browsing
Cloud storage	Google Drive	3	88.15%	Up/dwnld.	Browsing
	OneDrive	3	92.14%	Up/dwnld.	Browsing
Gaming	8-Ball Pool	2	88.4%	Game ctrl.	Game setup
	Treasure Hunt	2	91.98%	Game ctrl.	Game setup
Email	Thunderbird	2	99.14%	Email msg.	Dir. lookups
	Outlook	2	97.45%	Email msg.	Dir. lookups

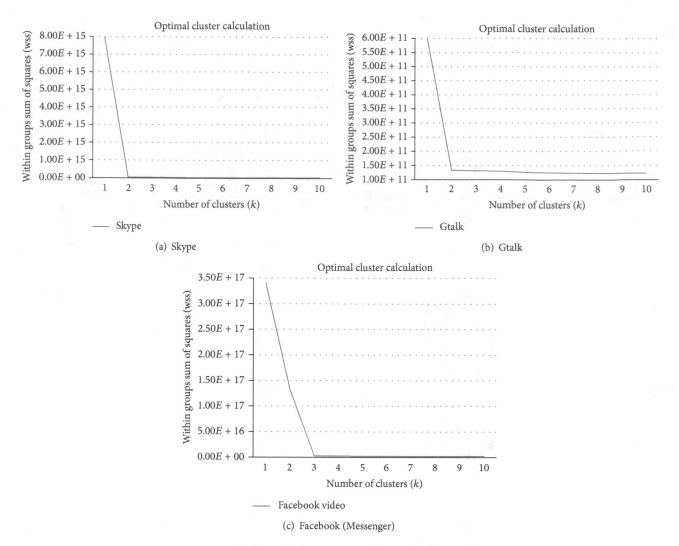

(a) Skype

(b) Gtalk

(c) Facebook (Messenger)

FIGURE 4: Inner-cluster variance versus k.

host nodes that initiate connections with super nodes for registering with a Skype login server and exchanging continuous keep-alive messages [53]. The resulting overlay peer-to-peer network employs both TCP and UDP connections both for communication between host and super nodes and for communication between two hosts running the client application [54, 65]. One flow cluster was hence determined to be directly associated with control features servicing connections and authentication between host and super nodes, having a much lower data volume and receiving rate and a significant number of unidirectional flows compared to the second group. The second flow cluster is comprised of video calls between Skype clients having substantially higher data rate and total data volume. The respective flows were labelled as "Comms. Control" and "Comms." accordingly. The same number of clusters was observed for Gtalk attributed to voice communication and control signalling with the Google content server with the later having a lower traffic footprint with respect to flow transmission duration and the average bit rate of the flows compared to the former. For Facebook Messenger, however, three optimal clusters were observed,

one with a high bit rate and duration similar to the VoIP calls observed in Skype and Gtalk, one for connection establishment, and lastly one for the background live newsfeed being continuously updated on the Facebook page. The clusters were thus accordingly labelled under "Comms." and "Comms. Control" and "Browsing" classes.

For *online cloud storage*, usually requiring low user interactivity as highlighted in [66], the prominent Dropbox storage, Google Drive, and OneDrive were examined. The applications employed file transfers ranging in size from 25 KB to 1.5 GB, frequently in batches of 1, 5, and 10 files. Cluster analysis on generated traffic featured around 3 optimal flow clusters as represented by Figure 5. The three distinct flow clusters after analysis were labelled as one each for file "uploads" and "downloads" and a third for interaction with the hosting website tagged "browsing."

To examine *torrent applications*, the original BitTorrent and VUZE derivative client were used on researcher machines to search and download different combinations of files with sizes ranging from 25 MB to over 1 GB. Cluster analysing these torrent flows resulted in three distinct clusters

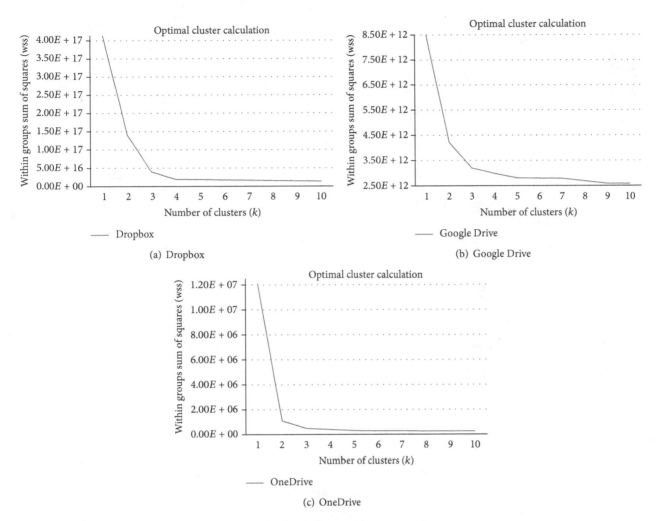

FIGURE 5: Inner-cluster variance versus k.

representing actual file download labelled as "torrent" and later two as "torrent control" responsible for further seeding of downloaded files and communication with other peers.

For online interactive Macromedia Flash player based pool and Treasure Hunt game, two clearly distinct flow classes as depicted in Figures 6(c) and 7(a) responsible for initial "game setup" and continued interactive "game control" constituted all flows.

Lastly the email clients Thunderbird and Outlook were used with three distinct email accounts, Yahoo, Gmail, and a corporate account. Cluster analysis revealed two discrete types of flows shown in Figures 7(a) and 7(b). One flow cluster comprised sending and receiving email messages which in this case could also be easily identified by looking at well-known destination port assignments for SMTP, POP, and IMAP protocols. The second flow class represented "directory lookups" by the client using HTTP and SSL having significantly lower total data volume per flow compared to email messages.

Segregated flows of all applications were labelled with flow classes and combined into a single data set. The next section details the splitting of training and testing data and evaluates the C5.0 ML classifier.

5. C5.0 Decision Tree Classifier

Approximately 6.8 million flows were labelled with appropriate flow classes as a result of k-means cluster analysis, in accordance with Table 4. In order to comprehensively test classifier accuracy, the data set was further split in almost equal percentages (~50%) per flow class for training and testing purposes.

5.1. Classifier Evaluation. C5.0 ML was applied on the training data set using feature sets 1 to 4, with alternate pruning and boosting options. As mentioned earlier, enabling pruning removes parts of the decision tree representing relatively higher error rates than others while adaptive boosting generates a batch of classifiers and uses voting on every examined sample to predict the final class. Classifiers were derived by enabling both options to analyse improvements in predictive ability using the feature sets in Table 4. The resulting prediction accuracy for each attribute set is reported in Table 6. Set 1 included source and destination port numbers along with protocol information and resulted in a maximum accuracy of 41.97% with the maximum allowed boosting factor of 100 and could easily be ruled out for use as standalone feature set for

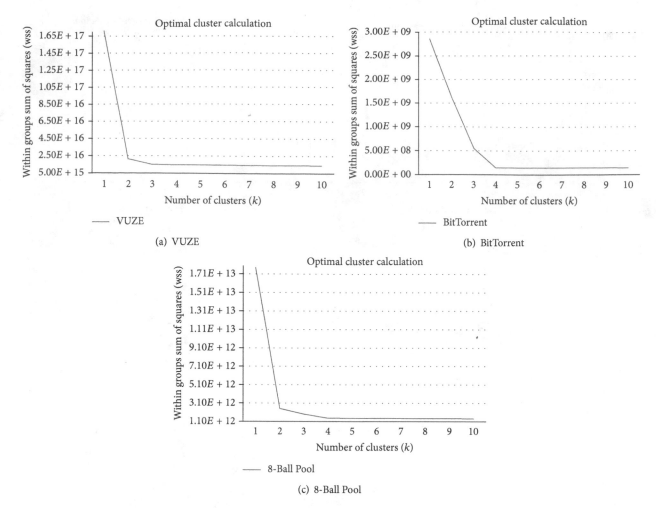

FIGURE 6: Inner-cluster variance versus k.

TABLE 6: Feature sets versus classifier accuracy.

Feature set	Pruning = false			Pruning = true		
	No boost	Boost 10	Boost 100	No boost	Boost 10	Boost 100
Set 1	39.58	40.01	41.34	39.44	40.48	41.97
Set 2	24.29	24.29	24.29	24.29	24.29	24.29
Set 3	82.29	83.24	84.29	82.20	84.97	83.95
Set 4	73.18	75.51	75.70	73.18	72.62	75.03
Sets 1 + 3	91.37	94.39	95.98	92.37	94.52	96.67
Sets 1 + 4	84.48	87.47	86.47	84.48	86.42	86.79
Sets 2 + 3	84.90	86.91	85.71	84.90	85.00	85.61
Sets 2 + 4	74.37	77.07	77.21	74.37	76.83	77.42

classification. Set 2 used port name labelling instead of actual numbers and protocol information, resulting in considerably low accuracy even when compared to set 1 with uniformity in values regardless of boosting at 24.29%. Set 3 included twelve flow attributes and resulted in a significantly improved accuracy of 84.97% with a boost 10. Finally, set 4 incorporating only six flow ratios led to a maximum accuracy of 75.03% with

100 times' boost. In this particular instance disabling pruning resulted in a more accurate classifier at 75.70%. When used in combinations sets 2 and 4 presented lowest accuracy peaking at 77.42% while sets 1 and 4 as well as 2 and 3 resulted in reasonable level of classifier accuracy at 86.79% and 86.91%, respectively. Sets 1 and 3 combined showed a considerable improvement with classification accuracy peaking at 96.67%

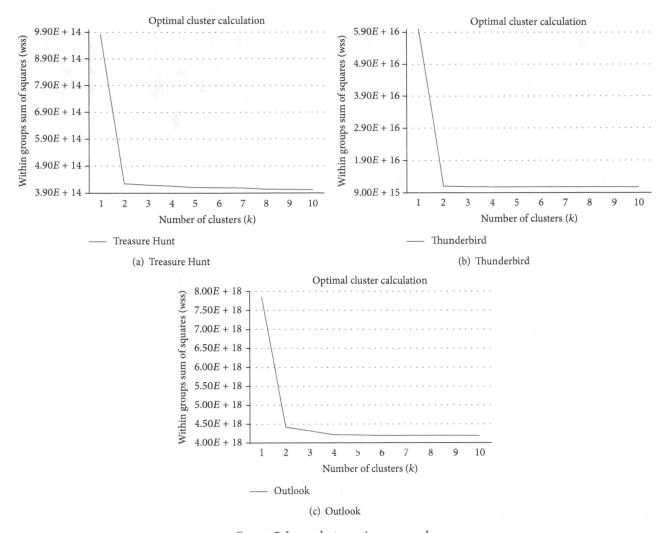

FIGURE 7: Inner-cluster variance versus k.

TABLE 7: Misclassification table for best feature set combination (training stage).

Application classified	(a)	(b)	(c)	(d)	(e)	(f)	(g)	(h)	(i)	(j)	(k)	(l)
(a) Game_setup	156432										229	
(b) Game_ctrl.		257707										
(c) Browsing	32		932493									
(d) Stor_dnld.				63212								
(e) Stor_upld.					56613							
(f) Email_mssg.						257707						
(g) Email_dir.							122343					
(h) Comms.								257552				
(i) Comms_ctrl.								87	561432		157	
(j) Streaming				35						77343		
(k) Torr_ctrl.											203764	
(l) Torrent	89											453142

with a 100-boost while even with a boost 10 or a single classifier (no boost) the prediction results were 94.52% and 92.37%, respectively.

The misclassification table generated during training stage for this best combination (sets 1 and 3) classifier is presented in Table 7. The highest number of discrepancies was observed between "game setup" and "torrent control" classes (229 flows). Due to low predictive ability (estimated during classifier training), only one attribute received packets per second (Rx.pps.) was winnowed during the training

TABLE 8: Flow attribute usage.

Flow attribute usage in selected C5.0 classifier		
Category	Attribute	Percentage use
Protocol and port	Protocol	80.62%
	Destination port	100%
	Source port	100%
Transmitted flow (Tx) attributes	Bytes [Tx.B.]	100%
	Packets [Tx.Pkt.]	100%
	Bits per second [Tx.bps.]	100%
	Packets per sec. [Tx.pps.]	96.25%
	Bytes per package [Tx.Bpp.]	100%
	Duration [Tx.s.]	95.48%
Received flow (Rx) attributes	Bytes [Rx.B.]	100%
	Packets [Rx.Pkt.]	100%
	Bits per sec. [Rx.bps.]	100%
	Bytes per package [Rx.Bpp.]	100%
	Duration [Rx.s.]	98.61%

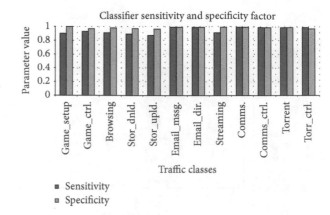

FIGURE 8: Classifier sensitivity and specificity factor per traffic class.

stage. The remaining 14 attributes used to build the resulting classifier along with their percentage use are given in Table 8.

5.2. Confusion Matrix Analysis. The confusion matrix for selected classifier specifying cross-tabulation of predicted classes and observed values with associated statistics between different flow classes is given in Table 9. The highest errors occurred between "game control" and "browsing" flows (60114 or 1.76% of total tested flows), while no misclassification errors were observed between "game setup" and "torrent control" flows as witnessed during training cross-validation stage. The overall accuracy statistics are presented in Table 10. The value for the kappa coefficient [67, 68], which takes into account chance occurrences of accurately classified flows and is generally considered a more robust measure than simple percent agreement calculation, was also significantly high at 95.31%. The overall accuracy rate was also computed along with a 95 percent confidence interval (CI) for this rate (0.9364 and 0.956) and a one-sided test to see if the accuracy is better than the "no information rate," which is taken to be the largest class percentage in the data (P value: accuracy > NIR: $<2.2e - 16$) [69]. McNemar's test P value however was not available due to sparse tables (bidirectional flow vectors having very low or zero attribute values for some flow classes, i.e., Skype control, etc.).

5.3. Sensitivity and Specificity Factor. For a given flow, the classifier's ability to accurately predict the flow class is characterized by classifier sensitivity factor and to differentiate this flow from other flow classes is by its specificity factor. Both parameters are of significant importance and ascertaining a classifier's suitability for both flow identification and discrimination. The sensitivity and specificity bar graph for each flow class for the selected classifier is given in Figure 8. Lowest

sensitivity was recorded for cloud storage flows (87.67–89.89%) among all classes, also evident from Figure 8 due to a higher mismatch between storage download and streaming (1335 or 0.039%) as well as storage upload and browsing flows (4006 or 0.11% of total tested flows). The corresponding specificity values for both storage flow classes, however, being significantly high indicated correct differentiation ability of the classifier for this application and lower sensitivity factor accredited to other application flows being misclassified under this class. Communication and BitTorrent traffic classes showed high sensitivity and specificity values. The selected classifier also showed high accuracy in detecting and differentiating between email messages and directory lookups. The classification accuracy reported per flow class was also greater than 90% for all applications apart from Dropbox which showed 87.67% accuracy due to mismatch with streaming and browsing flows. The specificity values, however, were substantively high without exception across all flow classes ranging between 98.37 and 99.57%. The results represent a highly granular classifier with ability to accurately identify application traffic as well as discriminate between flows generated by same application without employing any complex time window flow and packet analysis. As an added advantage, the approach only used a minor change in output formatting of NetFlow attributes together with basic scripting for creating bidirectional flows. The next section considers some alternate approaches for machine learning based traffic classification and compares their accuracy and computational overhead with the derived classifier.

6. Qualitative Comparison

To undertake a comprehensive qualitative evaluation of the two-phased ML approach, we considered alternate ML classifiers and appraised their viability for per-flow traffic classification in relation to the proposed technique. Weka machine learning software suite (version 3.6.13) was employed to evaluate the eight most commonly utilized supervised machine learning algorithms in comparison with the proposed two-phased approach. The comparison evaluated (i) the classification accuracy of each algorithm and (ii) the computational overhead including the training and testing times to validate

TABLE 9: Confusion matrix calculation for optimal classifier (evaluation stage).

Application classified	(a)	(b)	(c)	(d)	(e)	(f)	(g)	(h)	(i)	(j)	(k)	(l)
(a) Game_setup	156435											
(b) Game_ctrl.		257718	60114									
(c) Browsing	632	25481	932494		4006							
(d) Stor_dnld.				63208								
(e) Stor_upld.					56611							
(f) Email_mssg.						257710						
(g) Email_dir.		3981	2561				122346					
(h) Comms.								257552				
(i) Comms_ctrl.			4587						561433			
(j) Streaming				1335						77341		
(k) Torrent										2078	453143	
(l) Torr_ctrl.		5843	6154									203766

TABLE 10: Overall statistics.

Statistical property	Value
Classifier accuracy	96.67%
95% confidence interval (CI)	(0.9364, 0956)
No information rate	0.3332
P value (Acc > NIR)	$<2.2e-16$
Kappa	0.9531
McNemar's test P value	NA

the results from each classification technique as well as (iii) provide perspectives on the scalability of our two-phased machine learning classifier. The classifiers used the same ratio of training and testing data set pools (marked with respective application class), where 50% of the flows were used for training the respective classifier and the remaining 50% flows were used for testing purposes.

We briefly describe the machine learning algorithms that were evaluated as follows.

J48/C4.5 decision tree constructs a tree structure, in which each node represents feature tests, each branch represents a result (output) of the test, and each leaf node represents a class label, that is, application flow label in the present work [30, 70]. In order to use a decision tree for classification, a given tuple (which requires class prediction) corresponding to flow features walks through the decision tree from the root to a leaf. The label of the leaf node is the classification result. The algorithm was enabled with default parameters (confidence factor of 0.25 and reduced-error pruning by 3-fold) in the Weka implementation of the present experiment to optimize the resulting decision tree.

k nearest neighbours (kNN) algorithm computes the distance (Euclidean) from each test sample to the k nearest neighbours in the n-dimensional feature space. The classifier selects the majority label class from the k nearest neighbours and assigns it to the test sample [63]. For the present evaluation $k = 1$ was utilized.

Naïve Bayes (NB), considered as a baseline classifier in several traffic classification studies, selects optimal (probabilistic) estimation of precision values based on analysis of training data using Bayes' theorem, assuming highly independent relationship between features [60, 71].

Best-first decision tree (BFTree) uses binary splitting for nominal as well as numeric attributes and uses a top-down decision tree derivation approach such that the best split is added at each step [64]. In contrast to depth-first order in each iterative tree generation step [64, 72], the algorithm expands nodes in best-first order instead of a fixed order. Both gain and Gini index are utilized in calculating the best node in tree growth phase. The algorithm was implemented using postpruning enabled and with a default value of 5-fold in pruning to optimize the resulting classifier.

Regression tree representative (REPTree) is a fast implementation of decision tree learning which builds a decision/regression tree using information gain and variance with reduced-error pruning along with backfitting. REPTree uses regression tree logic to create multiple trees and selects the best from all the generated trees. The algorithm only sorts values for numeric attributes once. It was implemented with pruning enabled with the default value of 3-fold.

Sequential minimal optimization (SMO), a support vector classifier trained using a sequential minimal optimization algorithm by breaking optimization problem into smaller chunks, was solved analytically. The algorithm transforms nominal attributes into binaries and by default normalizes all attributes [59, 73]. It was implemented using Weka with normalization turned on along with the default parameters (the complexity parameter $C = 1$ and polynomial exponent $P = 1$).

Decision tables and naïve Bayes (DTNB) is a hybrid classifier which combines decision tables along with naïve Bayes and evaluates the benefit of dividing available features into disjoint sets to be used by each algorithm, respectively [74]. Using a forward selection search, the selected attributes are modeled using NB and decision table (conditional probability table) and at each step, and unnecessary attributes are removed from the final model. The combined model

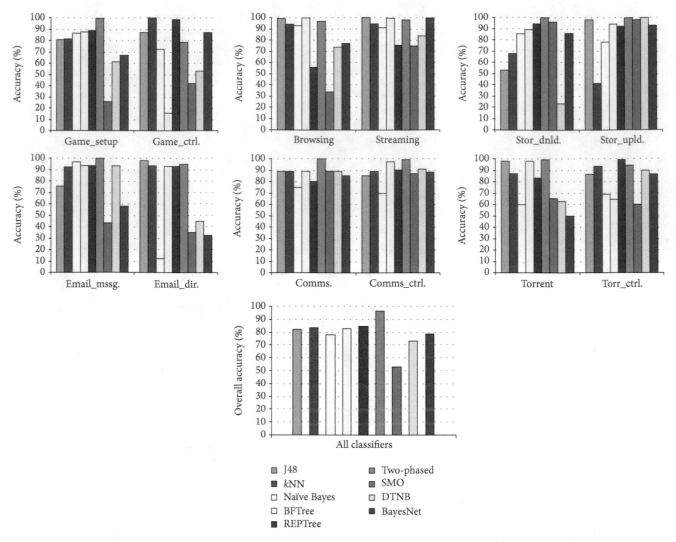

FIGURE 9: Comparative and average overall accuracy of machine learning algorithms for each traffic class.

reportedly [74] performs better in comparison to individual naïve Bayes and decision tables and was implemented with default parameters. The final classifier selected and used 5 attributes (out of 16 using backward elimination and forward selection search).

Bayesian network (BayesNet) is an acyclic directed graph that represents a set of features as its vertices and the probabilistic relationship among features as graph edges [62]. While using Bayes' rule for probabilistic inference, under invalid conditional independence assumption (in naïve Bayes) BayesNet may outperform NB and yield better classification accuracy [75]. The default parameters, that is, SimpleEstimator, were used for estimating the conditional probability tables of BN in the Weka implementation of BN on the training set.

The following subsections highlight a qualitative comparison between the above machine learning classification techniques and the proposed two-phased approach.

6.1. Comparative Accuracy. The respective accuracy of each examined traffic class for multiple classifiers is given in Figure 9. Overall the two-phased approach achieved better per-flow classification in comparison with the alternate techniques, while for few applications (flow types) the classification accuracy was almost equal. For the game setup flows the accuracy is the highest. For game control flows, alternate approaches such as kNN and REPTree provide a better percentage of correctly identified flows. This was considered earlier while evaluating the sensitivity of two-phased classifier and was mainly due to misclassification errors (of game control) with the web browsing flows. kNN and REPTree, however, provide a lower accuracy than two-phased ML for browsing and streaming flows. Similarly, for the streaming application tier, SMO based approach yielded highly accurate results comparable to two-phased machine learning approach while it yielded minimal accuracy when email tier was examined. For the communication application flows, almost all classifiers with the exception of NB (~63%) provided correct classification results (~80%). This was primarily due to the predictive ability of flow parameters for this set of applications. For torrent based flows, J48 decision tree along with BFTree provided almost 99.99% classification results, with BFTree (97.25%) exceeding the two-phased classifier which gave approximately 90.02% flow identification capability of torrent control flows due to mismatch with game control and browsing flows. Therefore, while one approach might be suitable for identifying certain traffic flows, similar high accuracy might not be realized for a different application using the same classifier. In terms of overall accuracy, two-phased ML provided a much more coherent and applicable result at 96.67% with the lowest accuracy attributed to SMO at approximately 53.2% correctly classified records.

6.2. Computational Performance. To evaluate the computational performance of the classifiers, each was independently implemented on a test machine (PC), an Intel based i54310-M processor chipset with two CPUs each at 2.70 GHz and 16 GB of memory. The operating system used a GNU/Linux kernel (3.14.4 x64) and it was verified that no other user processes (apart from the Weka software suite) were consuming CPU cycles or any of the operating system processes were CPU or I/O intensive. The two-phased ML evaluation included the combined cluster analysis and subsequent C5.0 training phase from labelled flows. This was done solely to examine the computational requirements of the unsupervised and supervised machine learning ensemble, excluding the ground-truth acquisition and refinement (i.e., DPI based application flow perusal and subclass marking) which can be done offline and continuously on much greater data sets in a practical network implementation. To give a realistic comparison, the alternate classifiers used the same application labelled flows (ground-truth). The average CPU utilization for each classifier in terms of the flow records and bytes processed (testing) is given in Figure 10. We observed a linear relationship between the CPU utilization and the amount of records processed for all classifiers followed by a steady-state pattern albeit different consumption footprints. The kNN classifier had the highest CPU usage at up to 5.32% with a gradual decrease steadying at 4.21%. NB classifier had the lowest consumption at 1.61% while two-phased ML reported around 4.31% usage. Similarly the average memory usage per classifier in processing flow records and bytes of data is provided in Figure 11. The BFTree algorithm had the highest memory usage at 190.28 MB with the two-phased ML at 175.31 MB. BayesNet had the lowest memory footprint with a steady-state value of approximately 50.14 MB.

The average training and testing times with respect to three different sizes of flow sets (1000, 1 million, and 3 million) for each classifier are depicted in Figure 12. The training time for two-phased classifier was significantly high compared to other classifiers for flow record size of 1000 flows. This was due to the in-tandem processing of the two embedded algorithms used. The training time relationship for most classifiers with respect to the size of training data at larger values of the latter was, however, nonlinear. The training time for J48, for example, for both 1M and 3M flows, was approximately the same averaging at around 59.35 minutes. Similarly, BFTree approximated in between 60.12 minutes for 1M and 63.45 minutes for 3M flows, respectively. Two-phased classifier also reported between 80.87 minutes and 84.51 minutes for the respective flow records in the training phase. This yields

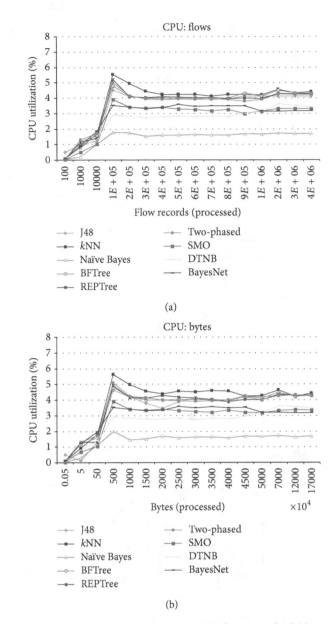

FIGURE 10: CPU utilization percentage: (a) flow records; (b) bytes.

approximately on average 0.88 seconds spent training around 1K flows with a standard deviation (σ) of 1.137 between 1M and 3M flows. Hence, the proposed technique results in better performance in terms of training times in the steady state with relatively larger data sets. However, as noted above it does not specifically consider the time duration involved in offline analysis of optimal cluster labelling following examination of different types of traffic generated per application. The SMO classifier accounted for the highest training times with larger flow records requiring around 140.35 minutes of training 3M flows. SMO, therefore, reported the lowest accuracy while having substantial resource consumption, performing quite marginally compared to other techniques.

Considering the testing timelines, NB followed by J48 classifiers were most efficient in classifying flows at approximately 6.3 minutes and 8.12 minutes, respectively.

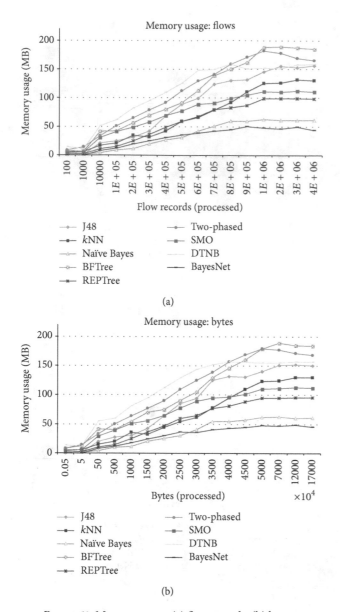

FIGURE 11: Memory usage: (a) flow records; (b) bytes.

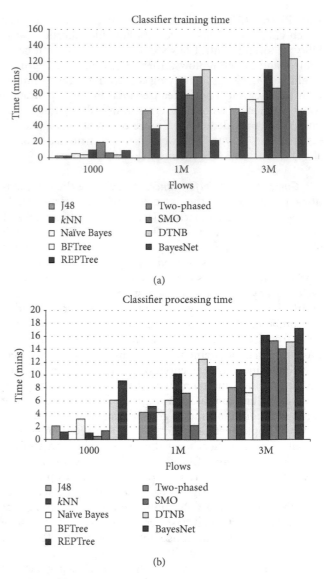

FIGURE 12: Classifier time frames for (a) training and (b) processing time.

Two-phased recorded a linear relationship between the flows tested and the respective processing time frame. Approximately 15.17 minutes was spent in classifying 3M flows, averaging at 0.30 seconds for processing 1K flow records with a standard deviation (σ) of 0.071 between 1M and 3M flows. Thus, given the high accuracy of the two-phased approach the computation performance seems highly applicable in realistic traffic classification scenarios. BN reported the highest 16.91 minutes in testing 3M flows albeit average overall classification performance as depicted in Figure 9. The two-phased approach therefore yields better accuracy across all traffic classes with a comparably smaller computational cost when considered in relation to the examined alternate classification approaches implemented using the Weka platform. However, it may be noted that since Weka is a Java based implementation of the classifiers, the exact computational

overhead reported might be different when a standalone classifier utility for each approach is applied resulting in a more efficient performance.

6.3. *Scalability.* In classification accuracy comparisons among several classifiers it is evident that the prediction ability of a scheme is highly dependent on analysing a correct measure of variation between the selected flow attributes for each traffic class. Traditionally the bidirectional flow features utilized in the present research have shown considerable applicability in multiple classifiers to attain a (somewhat) acceptable degree of traffic identification. However, as highlighted in [14, 16] the wide majority of the classification algorithms are infeasible with respect to their application in the network backbone by ISPs. The reasons for this lack of applicability range from the tremendous amount of traffic generated in the network core to the actual methodology of the approach, for example, sometimes requiring analysis of end-point behaviour for classification [16, 76]. In addition flow based techniques often rely on statistical information from bidirectional traffic (specifically TCP) and placing the traffic measurement or collection point as close to the ingress or the edge of the network as possible to collect the necessary features from outbound as well as inbound flows. An alternate approach to address this limitation [77] details an algorithm for predicting the inbound traffic flow attributes based on the unidirectional transmitted TCP flows. However, in the present case we propose using the former technique of keeping flow measurements as close to the ingress or edge of the network. This technique ensures corroboration between upstream and downstream host traffic to generate bidirectional flow features, minimizing the operational and computational cost of implementing the two-phased classifier.

The proposed two-phased approach is significantly reproducible due to the utilization of NetFlow, ubiquitous in present ISP networking gear. Additionally, the derived classifier reported high efficiency in dealing with voluminous data (flow records) with high level of accuracy, again a basic traffic classification requirement by service providers. The synergetic combination of classifiers in the present case produced comprehensive traffic classification results and a comparatively lower processing overhead while using non-specialized hardware.

7. Conclusion

The present paper used a twofold machine learning approach for traffic classification on a per-flow basis by solely using Net-Flow attributes and without depending on packet derivatives or complex time window analysis. During the unsupervised phase, approximately 6.8 million bidirectional flows for all applications were collected and cluster analysed resulting in 12 unique flow classes. The supervised phase used four different feature sets of NetFlow attributes from the derived flow classes to test and train the C5.0 ML decision tree classifier. The foremost feature set comprising 14 NetFlow attributes reported an average prediction accuracy of 92.37% increasing to 96.67% with adaptive boosting. Sensitivity factor of the classifier was also exceedingly high ranging above 90% with only cloud storage flows (file upload and downloads) reporting relatively low values between 87.67 and 89.89% due to misclassification with general web browsing and streaming flows. The corresponding specificity factor, however, translating for classifier flow discrimination ability ranged between 98.37 and 99.57% across all applications. Furthermore, the substantive accuracy of the present approach in achieving highly granular per-flow application identification and the computational efficiency in comparison with other machine learning classification methodologies paves way for future work in extending this method to include other applications for real-time or near real-time flow based classification.

Competing Interests

The authors declare that there are no competing interests regarding the publication of this paper.

References

[1] T. Bujlow, V. Carela-Español, and P. Barlet-Ros, "Independent comparison of popular DPI tools for traffic classification," *Computer Networks*, vol. 76, pp. 75–89, 2015.

[2] R. Sadre, A. Sperotto, R. Hofstede, and N. Brownlee, "Flow-based approaches in network management: recent advances and future trends," *International Journal of Network Management*, vol. 24, no. 4, pp. 219–220, 2014.

[3] M. Iliofotou, B. Gallagher, T. Eliassi-Rad, G. Xie, and M. Faloutsos, "Profiling-by-association: a resilient traffic profiling solution for the Internet backbone," in *Proceedings of the 6th International Conference on Emerging Networking Experiments and Technologies (Co-NEXT '10)*, Philadelphia, Pa, USA, December 2010.

[4] N. Williams, S. Zander, and G. Armitage, "A preliminary performance comparison of five machine learning algorithms for practical IP traffic flow classification," *ACM SIGCOMM Computer Communication Review*, vol. 36, no. 5, pp. 5–16, 2006.

[5] J. Camacho, P. Padilla, P. García-Teodoro, and J. Díaz-Verdejo, "A generalizable dynamic flow pairing method for traffic classification," *Computer Networks*, vol. 57, no. 14, pp. 2718–2732, 2013.

[6] A. Dainotti, A. Pescapè, and K. C. Claffy, "Issues and future directions in traffic classification," *IEEE Network*, vol. 26, no. 1, pp. 35–40, 2012.

[7] L. Stewart, G. Armitage, P. Branch, and S. Zander, "An architecture for automated network control of QoS over consumer broadband links," in *Proceedings of the IEEE Region 10 International Conference (TENCON '10)*, November 2005.

[8] A. Finamore, M. Mellia, M. Meo, and D. Rossi, "KISS: stochastic packet inspection classifier for UDP traffic," *IEEE/ACM Transactions on Networking*, vol. 18, no. 5, pp. 1505–1515, 2010.

[9] P. Bermolen, M. Mellia, M. Meo, D. Rossi, and S. Valenti, "Abacus: accurate behavioral classification of P2P-TV traffic," *Computer Networks*, vol. 55, no. 6, pp. 1394–1411, 2011.

[10] L. Bernaille, R. Teixeira, and K. Salamatian, "Early application identification," in *Proceedings of the 2nd Conference on Future Networking Technologies (CoNEXT '06)*, Lisboa, Portugal, December 2006.

[11] M. Crotti, M. Dusi, F. Gringoli, and L. Salgarelli, "Traffic classification through simple statistical fingerprinting," *ACM SIGCOMM Computer Communication Review*, vol. 37, no. 1, pp. 5–16, 2007.

[12] A. Dainotti, A. Pescapé, and C. Sansone, "Early classification of network traffic through multi-classification," in *Traffic Monitoring and Analysis*, J. Domingo-Pascual, Y. Shavitt, and S. Uhlig, Eds., vol. 6613 of *Lecture Notes in Computer Science*, pp. 122–135, Springer, Heidelberg, Germany, 2011.

[13] T. Z. J. Fu, Y. Hu, X. Shi, D. M. Chiu, and J. C. S. Lui, "PBS: periodic behavioral spectrum of P2P applications," in *Passive and Active Network Measurement*, S. B. Moon, R. Teixeira, and S. Uhlig, Eds., vol. 5448 of *Lecture Notes in Computer Science*, pp. 155–164, Springer, Berlin, Germany, 2009.

[14] H. Kim, K. C. Claffy, M. Fomenkov, D. Barman, M. Faloutsos, and K. Lee, "Internet traffic classification demystified: myths, caveats, and the best practices," in *Proceedings of the ACM CoNEXT Conference (CoNEXT '08)*, 12 pages, New York, NY, USA, 2008.

[15] W. Li, M. Canini, A. W. Moore, and R. Bolla, "Efficient application identification and the temporal and spatial stability

of classification schema," *Computer Networks*, vol. 53, no. 6, pp. 790–809, 2009.

[16] S. Valenti, D. Rossi, A. Dainotti, A. Pescape, A. Finamore, and M. Mellia, "Reviewing traffic classification," in *Data Traffic Monitoring and Analysis*, vol. 7754 of *Lecture Notes in Computer Science*, pp. 123–147, Springer, 2013.

[17] W. A. Wulf and S. A. McKee, "Hitting the memory wall: implications of the obvious," *Computer Architecture News*, vol. 23, no. 1, pp. 20–24, 1995.

[18] S. Kumar and P. Crowley, "Algorithms to accelerate multiple regular expressions matching for deep packet inspection," in *Proceedings of the Annual Conference of the ACM Special Interest Group on Data Communication (SIGCOMM '06)*, pp. 339–350, Pisa, Italy, September 2006.

[19] T. Karagiannis, A. Broido, M. Faloutsos, and K. C. Claffy, "Transport layer identification of P2P traffic," in *Proceedings of the ACM SIGCOMM Internet Measurement Conference (IMC '04)*, pp. 121–134, Taormina, Italy, October 2004.

[20] T. Karagiannis, K. Papagiannaki, N. Taft, and M. Faloutsos, "Profiling the end host," in *Passive and Active Network Measurement*, S. Uhlig, K. Papagiannaki, and O. Bonaventure, Eds., vol. 4427 of *Lecture Notes in Computer Science*, pp. 186–196, Springer, Heidelberg, Germany, 2007.

[21] K. Xu, Z.-L. Zhang, and S. Bhattacharyya, "Profiling internet backbone traffic: behavior models and applications," in *Proceedings of the 2005 Conference on Applications, Technologies, Architectures, and Protocols for Computer Communications (SIGCOMM '05)*, vol. 35, no. 4, pp. 169–180, ACM, 2005.

[22] M. Iliofotou, P. Pappu, M. Faloutsos, M. Mitzenmacher, S. Singh, and G. Varghese, "Network monitoring using traffic dispersion graphs (TDGs)," in *Proceedings of the 7th ACM SIGCOMM Internet Measurement Conference (IMC '07)*, pp. 315–320, San Diego, Calif, USA, October 2007.

[23] Y. Jin, N. Duffield, J. Erman, P. Haffner, S. Sen, and Z.-L. Zhang, "A modular machine learning system for flow-level traffic classification in large networks," *ACM Transactions on Knowledge Discovery from Data*, vol. 6, no. 1, pp. 1–34, 2012.

[24] A. Moore, D. Zuev, and M. Crogan, "Discriminators for use in flow-based classification," Tech. Rep., University of Cambridge, Cambridge, UK, 2005.

[25] J. Erman, M. Arlitt, and A. Mahanti, "Traffic classification using clustering algorithms," in *Proceedings of the ACM SIGCOMM Workshop on Mining Network Data (MineNet '06)*, pp. 281–286, ACM, New York, NY, USA, September 2006.

[26] L. Yingqiu, L. Wei, and L. Yunchun, "Network traffic classification using K-means clustering," in *Proceedings of the 2nd International Multi-Symposiums on Computer and Computational Sciences (IMSCCS '07)*, pp. 360–365, August 2007.

[27] V. Carela-Español, P. Barlet-Ros, and J. Solé-Pareta, "Traffic classification with sampled NetFlow," Tech. Rep. UPC-DAC-RR-CBA-2009-6, 2009.

[28] D. Rossi and S. Valenti, "Fine-grained traffic classification with Netflow data," in *Proceedings of the 6th International Wireless Communications and Mobile Computing Conference (IWCMC '10)*, pp. 479–483, July 2010.

[29] Y. Wang, Y. Xiang, J. Zhang, W. Zhou, G. Wei, and L. T. Yang, "Internet traffic classification using constrained clustering," *IEEE Transactions on Parallel and Distributed Systems*, vol. 25, no. 11, pp. 2932–2943, 2014.

[30] A. B. Mohammed and S. M. Nor, "Near real time online flow-based internet traffic classification using machine learning

(C4.5)," *International Journal of Engineering*, vol. 3, no. 4, pp. 370–379, 2009.

[31] T. Bujlow, T. Riaz, and J. M. Pedersen, "A method for classification of network traffic based on C5.0 machine learning algorithm," in *Proceedings of the International Conference on Computing, Networking and Communications (ICNC '12)*, pp. 237–241, Maui, Hawaii, USA, February 2012.

[32] O. Mula-Valls, *A practical retraining mechanism for network traffic classification in operational environments [M.S. thesis in Computer Architecture, Networks and Systems]*, Universitat Politècnica de Catalunya, Barcelona, Spain, 2011.

[33] P. Foremski, C. Callegari, and M. Pagano, "Waterfall: rapid identification of ip flows using cascade classification," *Communications in Computer and Information Science*, vol. 431, pp. 14–23, 2014.

[34] V. Carela-Español, P. Barlet-Ros, M. Sole-Simo, A. Dainotti, W. de Donato, and A. Pescape, "K-dimensional trees for continuous traffic classification," in *Traffic Monitoring and Analysis: Second International Workshop, TMA 2010, Zurich, Switzerland, April 7, 2010. Proceedings*, vol. 6003 of *Lecture Notes in Computer Science*, pp. 141–154, Springer, Berlin, Germany, 2010.

[35] W. de Donato, A. Pescape, and A. Dainotti, "Traffic identification engine: an open platform for traffic classification," *IEEE Network*, vol. 28, no. 2, pp. 56–64, 2014.

[36] S. Lee, H. Kim, D. Barman et al., "NeTraMark: a network traffic classification benchmark," *ACM SIGCOMM Computer Communication Review*, vol. 41, no. 1, pp. 22–30, 2011.

[37] M. Hall, E. Frank, G. Holmes, B. Pfahringer, P. Reutemann, and I. H. Witten, "The WEKA data mining software: an update," *ACM SIGKDD Explorations Newsletter*, vol. 11, no. 1, pp. 10–18, 2009.

[38] O. Chapelle, B. Scholkopf, and A. Zien, *Semi-Supervised Learning*, MIT Press, Cambridge, Mass, USA, 2006.

[39] J. Erman, A. Mahanti, M. Arlitt, I. Cohen, and C. Williamson, "Semisupervised network traffic classification," in *Proceedings of the ACM International Conference on Measurement and Modeling of Computer Systems (SIGMETRICS '07)*, San Diego, Calif, USA, June 2007, *Performance Evaluation Review*, vol. 35, no. 1, pp. 369–370, 2007.

[40] J. Zhang, X. Chen, Y. Xiang, W. Zhou, and J. Wu, "Robust network traffic classification," *IEEE/ACM Transactions on Networking*, vol. 23, no. 4, pp. 1257–1270, 2015.

[41] L. Salgarelli, F. Gringoli, and T. Karagiannis, "Comparing traffic classifiers," *ACM SIGCOMM Computer Communication Review*, vol. 37, no. 3, pp. 65–68, 2007.

[42] F. Bakerand, B. Fosterand, and C. Sharp, "Cisco architecture for lawful intercept in IP networks," RFC 3924, IETF, 2004.

[43] J. MacQueen, "Some methods for classification and analysis of multivariate observations," in *Proceedings of the 5th Berkeley Symposium on Mathematical Statistics and Probability*, vol. 1, pp. 281–297, Berkeley, Calif, USA, 1967.

[44] B. S. Everitt and T. Hothorn, *A Handbook of Statistical Analyses Using*, Chapman & Hall/CRC, Boca Raton, Fla, USA, 2006.

[45] Ntopng Traffic Classifier, http://www.ntop.org/products/traffic-analysis/ntop/.

[46] T. Karagiannis, K. Papagiannaki, and M. Faloutsos, "BLINC: multilevel traffic classification in the dark," in *Proceedings of the ACM Conference on Applications, Technologies, Architectures, and Protocols for Computer Communications (SIGCOMM '05)*, pp. 229–240, Philadelphia, Pa, USA, August 2005.

[47] P. Haffner, S. Sen, O. Spatscheck, and D. Wang, "ACAS: automated construction of application signatures," in *Proceeding of the ACM SIGCOMM Workshop on Mining Network Data (MineNet '05)*, pp. 197–202, ACM Press, August 2005.

[48] Libcaplibrary, http://www.tcpdump.org/.

[49] SoftflowDaemon, http://www.mindrot.org/projects/softflowd/.

[50] Nfdump Tool Suite, http://nfdump.sourceforge.net/.

[51] M. Zink, K. Suh, Y. Gu, and J. Kurose, "Characteristics of YouTube network traffic at a campus network—measurements, models, and implications," *Computer Networks*, vol. 53, no. 4, pp. 501–514, 2009.

[52] X. Cheng, J. Liu, and C. Dale, "Understanding the characteristics of internet short video sharing: a youtube-based measurement study," *IEEE Transactions on Multimedia*, vol. 15, no. 5, pp. 1184–1194, 2013.

[53] Skype, "What are P2P Communications?" https://support.skype.com/en/faq/FA10983/what-are-p2p-communications.

[54] S. A. Baset and H. G. Schulzrinne, "An analysis of the Skype peer-to-peer internet telephony protocol," in *Proceedings of the 25th IEEE International Conference on Computer Communications (INFOCOM '06)*, pp. 1–11, Barcelona, Spain, April 2006.

[55] PRTG Network Monitor, https://www.paessler.com/prtg.

[56] Nagios IT Infrastructure Monitoring, https://www.nagios.org/.

[57] G. Bossert, F. Guihéry, and G. Hiet, "Towards automated protocol reverse engineering using semantic information," in *Proceedings of the 9th ACM Symposium on Information, Computer and Communications Security (ASIA CCS '14)*, pp. 51–62, 2014.

[58] J. Caballero, H. Yin, Z. Liang, and D. Song, "Polyglot: automatic extraction of protocol message format using dynamic binary analysis," in *Proceedings of the 14th ACM Conference on Computer and Communications Security (CCS '07)*, pp. 317–329, Alexandria, Va, USA, October 2007.

[59] J. Platt, "Sequential minimal optimization: a fast algorithm for training support vector machines," Tech. Rep. MSR-TR-98-14, Advances in Kernel Methods—Support Vector Learning, 1998.

[60] R. Caruana and A. Niculescu-Mizil, "An empirical comparison of supervised learning algorithms," in *Proceedings of the 23rd International Conference on Machine learning (ICML '06)*, pp. 161–168, ACM, 2006.

[61] W. Li, K. Abdin, R. Dann, and A. Moore, *Approaching Real-Time Network Traffic Classification (ANTCs)*, RR-06-12, Department of Computer Science Research Reports, Queen Mary College, University of London, 2006.

[62] J. Pearl, "Bayesian networks: a model of self-activated memory for evidential reasoning," in *Proceedings of the 7th Conference of the Cognitive Science Society*, UCLA Technical Report CSD-850017, pp. 329–334, University of California, Irvine, Calif, USA, August 1985.

[63] N. S. Altman, "An introduction to kernel and nearest-neighbor nonparametric regression," *The American Statistician*, vol. 46, no. 3, pp. 175–185, 1992.

[64] H. Shi, *Best-first decision tree learning [M.S. thesis]*, University of Waikato, Hamilton, New Zealand, 2007.

[65] T. Sinam, I. T. Singh, P. Lamabam, and N. Ngasham, "An efficient technique for detecting Skype flows in UDP media streams," in *Proceedings of the IEEE International Conference on Advanced Networks and Telecommunications Systems (ANTS '13)*, pp. 1–6, IEEE, Kattankulathur, India, December 2013.

[66] P. Casas and R. Schatz, "Quality of experience in cloud services: survey and measurements," *Computer Networks*, vol. 68, pp. 149–165, 2014.

[67] J. Cohen, "Weighted kappa: nominal scale agreement provision for scaled disagreement or partial credit," *Psychological Bulletin*, vol. 70, no. 4, pp. 213–220, 1968.

[68] J. Carletta, "Assessing agreement on classification tasks: the kappa statistic," *Computational Linguistics*, vol. 22, no. 2, pp. 248–254, 1996.

[69] M. Kuhn, "Building predictive models in R using the caret package," *Journal of Statistical Software*, vol. 28, no. 5, 2008.

[70] J. R. Quinlan, *C4.5: Programs for Machine Learning*, Morgan Kaufmann Publishers, 1993.

[71] G. H. John and P. Langley, "Estimating continuous distributions in bayesian classifiers," in *Proceedings of the 11th Conference on Uncertainty in Artificial Intelligence (UAI'95)*, pp. 338–345, Morgan Kaufmann, 1995.

[72] J. Friedman, T. Hastie, and R. Tibshirani, "Additive logistic regression: a statistical view of boosting," *The Annals of Statistics*, vol. 28, no. 2, pp. 337–407, 2000.

[73] C.-C. Chang and C.-J. Lin, "LIBSVM: a library for support vector machines," *ACM Transactions on Intelligent Systems and Technology*, vol. 2, no. 3, article 27, 2011.

[74] M. Hall and E. Frank, "Combining naive bayes and decision tables," in *Proceedings of the Twenty-First International Florida Artificial Intelligence Research Society Conference*, D. L. Wilson and H. Chad, Eds., pp. 318–319, AAAI Press, Miami, Fla, USA, May 2008.

[75] R. E. Neapolitan, *Probabilistic Reasoning in Expert Systems: Theory and Algorithms*, John Wiley & Sons, New York, NY, USA, 1989.

[76] G. Szabo, I. Szabo, and D. Orinscay, "Accurate traffic classification," in *Proceedings of the IEEE International Symposium on a World of Wireless, Mobile and Multimedia Networks (WoWMoM '07)*, pp. 1–8, IEEE, Espoo, Finland, June 2007.

[77] J. Erman, A. Mahanti, M. Arlitt, and C. Williamson, "Identifying and discriminating between web and peer-to-peer traffic in the network core," in *Proceedings of the 16th International World Wide Web Conference (WWW '07)*, pp. 883–892, Banff, Canada, May 2007.

2

Symmetric Blind Decryption with Perfect Secrecy

Juha Partala

Physiological Signal Analysis Team, The Center for Machine Vision and Signal Analysis, University of Oulu, Oulu, Finland

Correspondence should be addressed to Juha Partala; juha.partala@oulu.fi

Academic Editor: Ziba Eslami

A blind decryption scheme enables a user to query decryptions from a decryption server without revealing information about the plain-text message. Such schemes are useful, for example, for the implementation of privacy-preserving encrypted file storages and payment systems. In terms of functionality, blind decryption is close to oblivious transfer. For noiseless channels, information-theoretically secure oblivious transfer is impossible. However, in this paper, we show that this is not the case for blind decryption. We formulate a definition of perfect secrecy of symmetric blind decryption for the following setting: at most one of the scheme participants is a passive adversary (honest-but-curious). We also devise a symmetric blind decryption scheme based on modular arithmetic on a ring $\mathbb{Z}_{p^2}$, where p is a prime, and show that it satisfies our notion of perfect secrecy.

1. Introduction

Over the past 15 years, data has moved from local storage to centralized data warehouses in the cloud. The accessibility of large amounts of personal data through a public network has given rise to many security and privacy issues [1]. Fortunately, such issues have generally been taken seriously. For example, in many countries, ethical and legal requirements have been imposed on guaranteeing the confidentiality of medical records [2, 3]. However, the implementation of privacy technologies is nontrivial, especially if the data storage has been outsourced to a cloud operator. Sensitive information can often be inferred from simple access patterns either by outsiders or by the operator of the storage. For example, being able to observe a medical doctor to access the medical record of a patient can leak sensitive information. Therefore, such access patterns should be kept hidden both from outsiders and from the party that is administering the records. Oblivious databases [4] and privacy-preserving encrypted file systems [5] are examples of technologies that can be used to hide the access information from the administrator. For such systems, the decryption of data is typically handled by a central decryption server. Such systems can be conveniently implemented using *blind decryption schemes* [6]. Blind decryption is a versatile primitive. It can be used as a building block for many privacy-critical applications,

such as privacy-preserving payment systems [7], key escrow systems, oblivious transfer protocols [8], privacy-preserving systems for digital rights management [9, 10], and private information retrieval [11]. A blind decryption scheme consists of an encryption scheme together with a blind decryption protocol intended to decrypt messages in a privacy-preserving fashion. The meaning of "blind decryption" can be easily described based on the following scenario depicted in Figure 1. Suppose that Alice has obtained several encrypted messages from an encryptor. Alice is entitled to choose and decrypt exactly one of those messages. Suppose that the decryption key k is stored on a decryption server and Alice wishes to have the server decrypt the message for her in such a way that neither the encryptor nor the decryptor learns the message chosen by Alice.

There are suggestions for practical blind decryption based on public-key cryptography [5, 6, 12–14]. It is also possible to implement the blind decryption functionality with other protocols such as secure multiparty computation [15]. However, the resulting schemes would be computationally demanding. For many applications, symmetric primitives are sufficient and computationally more efficient. In addition, they can provide secrecy that is not based on computational assumptions. Oblivious transfer schemes [16, 17] deliver the same functionality directly between the sender and the receiver without the decryption server. However, for noiseless

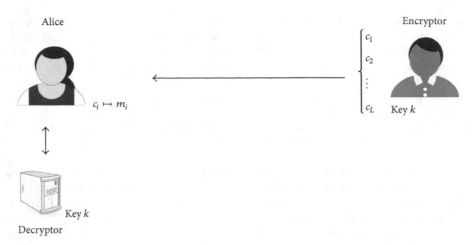

FIGURE 1: Blind decryption. Alice has obtained L ciphertexts from an encryptor and is entitled to choose exactly one of those for decryption. Alice interacts with a decryptor that shares a key k with the encryptor to transform the ciphertext message c_i into a plain-text message m_i. Neither the encryptor nor the decryptor learns the plain-text message chosen by Alice.

channels, information-theoretically secure oblivious transfer is impossible [18]. In addition, blind decryption schemes do not seem to exist, such that the privacy of the user is based on information-theoretic security. Our work aims to fill this shortage. In this paper, we give a meaningful definition of perfect secrecy for the blind decryption scenario. In particular, we formulate perfect secrecy of symmetric blind decryption in a setting in which at most one of the participants is an adversary but adhering to the protocol (at most one of the participants is honest-but-curious). We also propose a symmetric key blind decryption scheme SymmetricBlind which satisfies our definition. The scheme is based on modular arithmetic on a ring $\mathbb{Z}_{p^2}$, where p is a prime. Our main contribution is theoretical. Perfect secrecy requires the key to be changed for each decryption. Therefore, many existing applications of blind decryption which are built on the public-key case in the computational security model are not directly applicable. However, for the first time, we are able to give a meaningful definition of perfect secrecy of blind decryption and to show that blind decryption is possible in the information-theoretic security model. Additional research is needed to show which applications are possible in this model.

The paper is organized as follows. In Section 2, we describe work that is related to ours. Section 3 discusses the fundamental definitions and the preliminaries for the rest of the paper. In Section 4, we formulate three perfect secrecy properties that the blind decryption scheme needs to satisfy. In Section 5, we give a description of a symmetric blind decryption scheme SymmetricBlind. In Section 6, we show that the devised scheme satisfies our definition of perfect secrecy. Finally, Section 7 considers future work and Section 8 provides the conclusion.

2. Related Work

Chaum was the first to consider blindness in the context of digital signatures and privacy-preserving payment systems [7]. He described the first public-key blind signature scheme [19] by utilizing the properties of RSA encryption [20].

The scheme can be also used for encryption and can be therefore considered as the first blind decryption scheme. In the early articles, blind decryption is referred to as "blind decoding." Discrete logarithm based blind signature schemes were suggested in [21–24]. Sakurai and Yamane were the first to consider public-key blind decryption based on the discrete logarithm problem [6]. Their method was based on ElGamal Cryptosystem [25] and related to the blind signature of Camenisch et al. [24]. The method was later applied for the implementation of a key escrow system [12]. Mambo et al. were the first to consider blind decryption that is secure against chosen plain-text attacks by signing the ciphertext messages [26]. The resulting scheme is not capable of public-key encryption, since a secret signing key is required. Green described the first public-key blind decryption scheme [5] that is secure against adaptive chosen ciphertext attacks (IND-CCA2) using bilinear groups. The security of these constructions has been considered computationally either in the random oracle model [11] or using computational indistinguishability and infeasibility assumptions [5].

Oblivious transfer protocols are symmetric primitives that offer functionality similar to blind decryption. For oblivious transfer, there are two participants: a sender and a receiver. For the original definition of oblivious transfer, the sender transmits a message which the receiver gets with probability 1/2. The sender remains oblivious as to whether the receiver actually got the message. This form of oblivious transfer was introduced by Rabin [16]. The concept was later extended by Even et al. [17]. For $\binom{2}{1}$-oblivious transfer, the receiver can choose one from two messages without the sender knowing which of the messages was chosen. A related concept that can be considered as a further generalization is *all-or-nothing disclosure of secrets* [27] for which Alice is willing to disclose at most one secret from a set to Bob without Bob learning information about the rest of the secrets. Alice must not learn which secret Bob chose. Adaptive queries were considered by Naor and Pinkas [28]. They also considered active adversaries and provided security definitions related to the simulatability of the receivers.

Camenisch, Neven, and Shelat extended the work of Naor and Pinkas by defining *simulatable* oblivious transfer [29] and providing practical constructions for such a scheme. There are other suggestions for oblivious transfer based on problems in bilinear groups [30], groups of composite order [31], and the Diffie-Hellman problem [32–37]. These schemes are based on computational assumptions. It is impossible to achieve information-theoretic security for both of the parties using noiseless channels [18]. However, it is possible using noisy channels such as discrete memoryless channels [38] or a trusted initializer (shown by Rivest in 1999; see "unconditionally secure commitment and oblivious transfer schemes using private channels and a trusted initializer"). For the computational security setting, the functionality of oblivious transfer can be also implemented with public-key blind decryption using the method of Dodis et al. [39].

General *multiparty computation* protocols can be also applied to implement blind decryption capabilities. Secure multiparty computation was originally introduced by Yao [40] for the two-party case. The general case for $n \geq 2$ is due to Goldreich et al. [41]. However, secure multiparty computation protocols are computationally intensive in comparison to blind decryption and oblivious transfer.

3. Preliminaries

3.1. Notation. For the set of integers modulo n, we denote $\mathbb{Z}_n = \{[0], [1], \ldots, [n-1]\}$ and equate a congruence class with its least nonnegative representative. That is, we consider $\mathbb{Z}_n = \{0, 1, \ldots, n-1\}$. By the notation $x \bmod n$ we mean the unique $i \in \{0, 1, \ldots, n-1\}$ such that $i \equiv x \pmod{n}$. We denote the uniform distribution on a set X by $U(X)$. If a random variable Z is uniformly distributed on a set X, we denote it by $Z \sim U(X)$. When an element x is sampled from $U(X)$, we denote it by $x \leftarrow U(X)$.

3.2. Symmetric Encryption. A symmetric encryption scheme $\mathsf{SE} = (\mathsf{Gen}, \mathsf{Enc}, \mathsf{Dec})$ with key space $\mathcal{K}$, plain-text space $\mathcal{M}$, and ciphertext space $\mathcal{C}$ consists of three algorithms:

(1) The key generation algorithm $\mathsf{Gen}(s)$: on inputting a security parameter s, Gen outputs a key $k \in \mathcal{K}$

(2) The encryption algorithm $\mathsf{Enc}(k, m)$: on inputting a key $k \in \mathcal{K}$ and a message $m \in \mathcal{M}$, Enc outputs a ciphertext $c \in \mathcal{C}$

(3) The decryption algorithm $\mathsf{Dec}(k, m)$: on inputting a key $k \in \mathcal{K}$ and a ciphertext $c \in \mathcal{C}$, Dec outputs a message $m \in \mathcal{M}$ such that $m = \mathsf{Dec}(k, \mathsf{Enc}(k, m))$

3.3. Blind Decryption. Blind decryption has been considered in the literature for the asymmetric case. However, in this paper, we are interested in the symmetric case that is easily adapted from the asymmetric one [5]. A symmetric blind decryption scheme BlindDecryption consists of a symmetric encryption scheme $\mathsf{SE} = (\mathsf{Gen}, \mathsf{Enc}, \mathsf{Dec})$ and a two-party protocol BlindDec. The protocol BlindDec is conducted between an honest user Alice and the decryption server which we shall call the decryptor. The protocol enables Alice, who is in possession of a ciphertext c, to finish the protocol

with the correct decryption of c. As a result of running BlindDec, Alice on inputting a ciphertext $c = \mathsf{Enc}(k, m) \in \mathcal{C}$ outputs either the message $m \in \mathcal{M}$ or an error message $\perp$. The decryptor, on inputting the key $k \in \mathcal{K}$, outputs nothing or an error message $\perp$. To be secure, the exchanged messages must not leak information to malicious users (the *leak-freeness property* [8]). The property can be formalized based on computational indistinguishability. For every adversary, there has to be a simulator so that the following two games are well defined. For the first game, a probabilistic polynomial time (PPT) adversary A can choose any number L of ciphertexts c_i for $i \in \{1, 2, \ldots, L\}$. It is then given the correct decryptions by executing BlindDec with the decryptor. Finally, A outputs the plain-text message and ciphertext pairs (m_i, c_i) for $i \in \{1, 2, \ldots, L\}$. For the second game, a simulator S chooses any number L of ciphertexts c_i for $i \in \{1, 2, \ldots, L\}$. In this game, the plain-text messages are obtained by querying a trusted party. BlindDecryption is *leak-free* if for every PPT adversary A there is a simulator S such that for every PPT distinguisher D the probability of distinguishing between these two games is negligible [5].

Another important property for secure blind decryption is the *blindness property*. It formalizes the idea that the decryptor must not learn anything about the actual plain-text message. This can be formalized by giving a PPT algorithm D the possibility to choose two ciphertexts c_1, c_2 and giving it oracle access to two instances of BlindDec based on these choices. If the probability of distinguishing these two instances is negligible for every PPT algorithm D, then BlindDecryption satisfies *ciphertext blindness*. For a formal and rigorous definition, see, for example, [5].

3.4. Perfect Secrecy. The notion of perfect secrecy is due to Shannon [42]. Let $\mathsf{SE} = (\mathsf{Gen}, \mathsf{Enc}, \mathsf{Dec})$ be an encryption scheme with key space $\mathcal{K}$, plain-text space $\mathcal{M}$, and ciphertext space $\mathcal{C}$. Let K denote a random variable on the key space induced by Gen. SE satisfies perfect secrecy if, for every random variable M on the plain-text space, every plain-text $m \in \mathcal{M}$, and every ciphertext $c \in \mathcal{C}$,

$$\Pr\left[M = m \mid c = \mathsf{Enc}(K, M)\right] = \Pr\left[M = m\right]. \tag{1}$$

Equivalently, SE satisfies perfect secrecy if and only if, for every random variable M on the plain-text space, every plain-text messages $m_1, m_2 \in \mathcal{M}$, and every ciphertext $c \in \mathcal{C}$,

$$\begin{aligned} &\Pr\left[c = \mathsf{Enc}(K, M) \mid M = m_1\right] \\ &= \Pr\left[c = \mathsf{Enc}(K, M) \mid M = m_2\right]. \end{aligned} \tag{2}$$

4. Perfect Secrecy for Symmetric Blind Decryption

In this section, we formulate a condition for the perfect secrecy of blind decryption. Instead of computational indistinguishability, we consider secrecy of symmetric blind decryption based on the information observed by the parties. In the following, let $\mathsf{SE} = (\mathsf{Gen}, \mathsf{Enc}, \mathsf{Dec})$ together with BlindDec be a symmetric blind decryption scheme with key space $\mathcal{K}$, plain-text space $\mathcal{M}$, and ciphertext space $\mathcal{C}$.

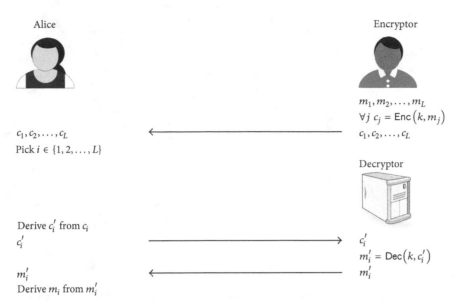

Alice

Encryptor

$m_1, m_2, \ldots, m_L$
$\forall j \; c_j = \mathsf{Enc}\left(k, m_j\right)$

$c_1, c_2, \ldots, c_L$

$c_1, c_2, \ldots, c_L$
Pick $i \in \{1, 2, \ldots, L\}$

Decryptor

Derive c_i' from c_i
c_i'

c_i'
$m_i' = \mathsf{Dec}\left(k, c_i'\right)$

m_i'

m_i'
Derive m_i from m_i'

FIGURE 2: The general blind decryption scenario. Alice chooses a ciphertext c_i and derives a related ciphertext c_i' that she transmits to the decryptor. The decryptor responds with the corresponding plain-text message m_i' from which Alice can recover m_i.

4.1. The Scenario. For the sake of clarity, we do not consider active adversaries. We assume that the parties adhere to the blind decryption protocol and only observe the flow of messages (and possibly deduce information from those messages). Active adversaries could, for example, induce errors to the protocol messages. Such adversarial scenarios are left for future work. In addition, we do not consider the case where the decryptor is colluding with either Alice or the encryptor against the other. Such a case is equivalent to the oblivious transfer scenario and information-theoretic security is impossible for noiseless channels [18]. However, we note that such collusion scenarios are important for certain applications and need to be investigated in the future. We do consider the case where the adversary is impersonating one of the parties, which is a paramount requirement for many applications. For clarity, we also restrict ourselves to the case where Alice decrypts a single message $m \in \mathcal{M}$. Similar to the one-time pad, we assume that a new key is derived after every decryption. However, in our case, there could be several ciphertexts $c_1, c_2, \ldots, c_L$ encrypted under the same key. Nevertheless, once Alice has decrypted one of the messages, we consider that particular key used and a new key, and a new set of ciphertexts is generated.

The scenario is the following. The encryptor chooses a set of L plain-text messages m_i for $i \in \{1, 2, \ldots, L\}$. He encrypts those messages under a key k to obtain ciphertext messages $c_j = \mathsf{Enc}(k, m_j)$ for $j \in \{1, 2, \ldots, L\}$ that he transmits to Alice. Alice chooses one of those messages c_i. To hide the actual ciphertext c_i, we assume that there is a ciphertext transformation space $\mathcal{C}' \subseteq \mathcal{C}$ so that Alice can derive a related ciphertext message $c_i' \in \mathcal{C}'$ that she transmits to the decryptor. The decryptor responds with its decryption $m_i' \in \mathcal{M}$ which Alice transforms to the correct plain-text message m_i. The general scenario has been depicted in Figure 2. The used variables have been collected into Notations for easier reference.

4.2. Security Requirements. As described in Section 3.2, the scheme has to satisfy the following property.

4.2.1. Leak-Freeness. Outsiders must not learn information about the plain-text messages by observing the exchanges.

The easiest way to provide leak-freeness against outsiders is to protect each exchange with an encryption scheme that satisfies perfect secrecy. However, leakage also needs to be addressed considering the protocol participants. Considering each individual party, we can divide leak-freeness as follows.

(1) Leak-Freeness against the Encryptor. Honest-but-curious encryptor must not learn information about the plain-text message obtained by Alice at the end of the protocol by observing the blind decryption messages. The situation is depicted in Figure 3.

(2) Leak-Freeness against Alice. This property ensures that, after obtaining m_i, Alice does not learn information about the remaining $L - 1$ plain texts m_j for $j \neq i$. The situation is depicted in Figure 4.

In contrast to computational security, we cannot define leak-freeness as a distinguishing problem. Instead, we shall consider the probability distributions regarding the exchanged elements. We also want to prevent decryptor from deducing information about the plain-text message m_i.

4.2.2. Blindness against the Decryptor. This property ensures that an honest-but-curious decryption server does not learn the message Alice wants to decrypt. The situation is depicted in Figure 5.

In the computational security setting, there can be multiple applications of the blind decryption protocol for a fixed key. In our case, we want a fresh key for every decryption to achieve perfect secrecy. Therefore, we formulate leak-freeness

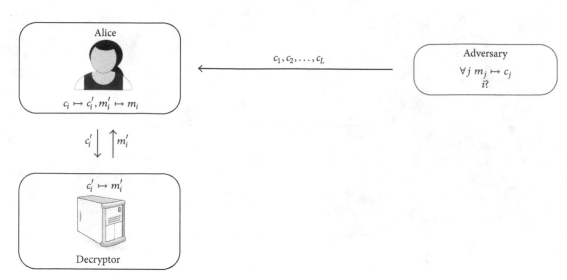

FIGURE 3: Malicious encryptor. The adversary attempts to learn which message was chosen by Alice.

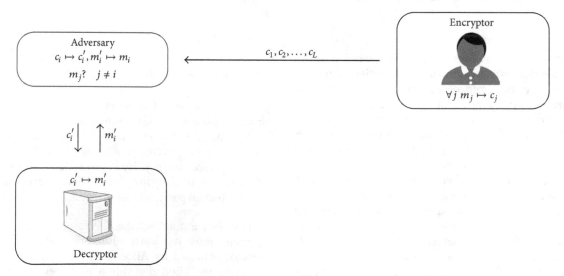

FIGURE 4: Malicious Alice. The adversary attempts to decrypt additional messages.

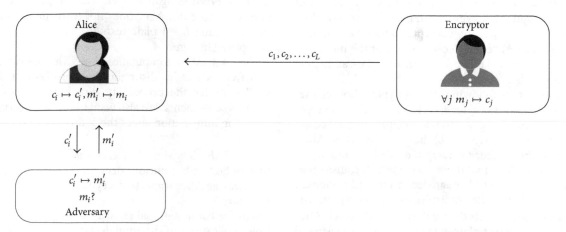

FIGURE 5: Malicious decryptor. The adversary attempts to learn the plain-text message that Alice obtains.

and blindness for a single decryption. However, as was described before, we want to be able to encrypt multiple messages with the same key. For example, in privacy-preserving payment systems, blind decryption is used to enable Alice to choose one (only one) item from a selection of items. This results in a scenario in which there are L plain-text and ciphertext pairs (m_j, c_j) for $j \in \{1, 2, \ldots, L\}$ but there is only a single application of BlindDec.

In the following section, we formulate these conditions based on information. Note that these conditions also provide secrecy against observers that are not participants of the scheme, since the information possessed by such observers is a proper subset of that of any of the participants. The following notation is used. Let K denote the random variable of blind decryption keys on the key space $\mathcal{K}$ induced by Gen. Let M_j for $j \in \{1, 2, \ldots, L\}$ denote the random variables corresponding to the choice of m_i for $j \in \{1, 2, \ldots, L\}$ by the encryptor and let M denote the random variable corresponding to the plain-text m Alice obtains at the end of the scheme. Following the standard practice [43], we assume that K is independent of M and M_j for every $j \in \{1, 2, \ldots, L\}$. Let C' denote the random variable on the ciphertext transformation space $\mathcal{C}'$ for the ciphertext message c' that Alice discloses to the decryptor. Finally, let M' denote the random variable corresponding to the message m' that the decryptor responds with. These variables have been collected into Notations.

4.3. Perfect Leak-Freeness against the Encryptor. We shall first formulate leak-freeness against the encryptor. The blind decryption protocol messages c' and m' should not disclose any information about m_i to the encryptor. Equivalently, the messages should not leak information about i that was chosen by Alice even if the encryptor knows the key k and the right plain-text messages m_j for $j \in \{1, 2, \ldots, L\}$.

Definition 1 (perfect leak-freeness against encryptor). A symmetric blind decryption scheme is *perfectly leak-free against the encryptor* for a single decryption of a maximum of L messages if, for every random variable M, M_j for $j \in \{1, 2, \ldots, L\}$ on the plain-text space and every $m, m', m_j \in \mathcal{M}$ for $j \in \{1, 2, \ldots, L\}$ and every $c' \in \mathcal{C}'$,

$$\Pr\left[M = m \mid C' = c', M' = m', M_1 = m_1, \ldots, M_L = m_L\right]$$
$$= \Pr\left[M = m \mid M_1 = m_1, \ldots, M_L = m_L\right]. \tag{3}$$

Our definition states that an honest-but-curious encryptor can equally easily guess the plain-text message Alice wanted to be decrypted with or without information provided by the blind decryption protocol messages c' and m'. Note that, in the normal scenario, $M = M_i$ for some $i \in \{1, 2, \ldots, L\}$. However, we do not want to restrict the definition to such a case. For example, there could be homomorphic blind decryption schemes for which certain operations could be permitted on the ciphertexts. Note also that the encryptor inherently possesses more information about m than an outsider, since m is dependent on $m_1, m_2, \ldots, m_L$.

4.4. Perfect Leak-Freeness against Alice. In order to be practical, the scheme needs to ensure that Alice is not able to decrypt messages. Therefore, we need to ensure that Alice obtains neither the decryption key nor any information about the decryptions of $c_1, c_2, \ldots, c_L$ without interacting with the decryptor. In addition, after a single application of BlindDec, Alice must not have any information about the remaining $L - 1$ messages. To make the requirement precise, we require that the observation of a single plain-text and ciphertext pair (m_1, c_1) does not leak any information about the decryption of another ciphertext c_2. The property is, in fact, a property of the encryption scheme.

Definition 2 (perfect leak-freeness against Alice). A symmetric encryption scheme SE satisfies *perfect leak-freeness against Alice* for a single decryption if, for every random variable M_1, M_2 on the plain-text space, every $m_1, m_2, m \in \mathcal{M}$, and every $c_1, c_2 \in \mathcal{C}$, such that $c_1 \neq c_2$,

$$\Pr\left[c_1 = \mathsf{Enc}(K, M_1), c_2 = \mathsf{Enc}(K, M_2) \mid M_1 = m_1, M_2\right.$$
$$= m_2\left] = \Pr\left[c_1 = \mathsf{Enc}(K, M_1), c_2 \right. \tag{4}$$
$$= \mathsf{Enc}(K, M_2) \mid M_1 = m_1, M_2 = m\right].$$

The condition states that the probability of obtaining the ciphertext pair (c_1, c_2) is the same whether we encrypt (m_1, m_2) or (m_1, m). That is, observation of the ciphertexts c_1, c_2 does not yield information about the decryption of c_2 even if we know the decryption of c_1.

4.5. Perfect Blindness against the Decryptor. We still need to consider privacy against an honest-but-curious decryptor. It is reasonable to assume that $c_1, c_2, \ldots, c_L$ have been delivered to Alice using a private channel. If the decryptor can observe c_j for $j \in \{1, 2, \ldots, L\}$, it means that he knows the corresponding plain-text messages, since he is in possession of the blind decryption key. Therefore, it is natural to require that the ciphertexts be protected by a separate secure channel between Alice and the encryptor. For the blindness property, we want the server to learn nothing of the actual message m that Alice derives at the end of the blind decryption scheme. In this case, the decryptor knows the correct key k as well as the messages c' and m' exchanged with Alice.

Definition 3 (perfect ciphertext blindness against the decryptor). A symmetric blind decryption scheme satisfies *perfect ciphertext blindness against the decryptor* if, for every random variable M on the plain-text space, every $m, m' \in \mathcal{M}$, and every $c' \in \mathcal{C}'$

$$\Pr\left[M = m \mid C' = c', M' = m'\right] = \Pr[M = m]. \tag{5}$$

The condition states that it is equally easy to guess the correct plain-text message with and without the information possessed by the decryptor. Note that we have assumed that $c_1, c_1, \ldots, c_L$ have been delivered to Alice in perfect secrecy.

4.6. Perfect Secrecy for Symmetric Blind Decryption. Finally, we can state our definition of perfect secrecy based on the properties defined above.

Definition 4 (perfect secrecy of blind decryption). A symmetric blind decryption scheme consisting of a symmetric encryption scheme SE and a blind decryption protocol BlindDec satisfies perfect secrecy for symmetric blind decryption for a single decryption of a maximum of L messages against a single honest-but-curious party if the scheme is perfectly leak-free against the encryptor for a maximum of L messages, SE is leak-free against Alice, and the scheme satisfies perfect ciphertext blindness against the decryptor.

5. A Concrete Blind Decryption Scheme

We shall now devise a blind decryption scheme SymmetricBlind that satisfies Definition 4. We shall implement our scheme using two tiers of symmetric encryption. For the outer tier, we apply a scheme that satisfies ordinary perfect secrecy. Let that scheme be denoted by SE. The outer encryption scheme will hide information about $c_1, c_2, \ldots, c_L$ from the decryptor and also provide secrecy for c' and m' against the encryptor. To achieve perfect blindness and leak-freeness against Alice, we design an inner tier encryption scheme called 2PAD that satisfies a useful transformation property which enables us to construct a blind decryption protocol BlindDec. To sum up, our final construction will consist of two tiers of encryption and a protocol for Alice to query a single decryption from the decryptor. The general overview of the scheme is depicted in Figure 6. It would be possible to implement some of the required privacy properties with multiple applications of the one-time pad. For example, if $c_i = m_i \oplus k_i$, Alice could hide the plain-text message from the decryptor by querying for the decryption of $c'_i = c_i \oplus k'$, where k' is only known to Alice. The correct plain-text message would be obtained from $m'_i = c'_i \oplus k_i = c_i \oplus k' \oplus k_i$ by computing $m'_i \oplus k' = c_i \oplus k_i = m_i$. However, such a protocol would leak i to the decryptor, since i would be needed for decryption. In addition, for a single decryption, the decryptor would have to maintain a set of L keys which would quickly grow to an unmanageable size as L grows. In contrast, the optimal key size for single decryption would be $2|m_i|$, where $|m_i|$ is the bit length of m_i, assuming that each plain-text message is of the same bit length. Therefore, simply applying the one-time pad is not sufficient.

In the following, we first describe our inner encryption scheme 2PAD that will provide perfect leak-freeness against Alice, as well as the required message transformation property. Then, we proceed to the description of a blind decryption protocol utilizing this scheme. Finally, we combine the inner encryption scheme with an outer encryption scheme that satisfies ordinary perfect secrecy and describe the complete blind decryption scheme.

5.1. The Inner Encryption Scheme. We shall first construct an inner encryption scheme called 2PAD with some useful properties. Our inner scheme is based on modular arithmetic on the ring $\mathbb{Z}_{p^2}$, where $p \geq 5$ is a prime. Our plain-text space is $\mathbb{Z}_p$ and every $m \in \mathbb{Z}_p$ is mapped to the ciphertext space $\mathbb{Z}_{p^2}$. To satisfy Definition 2, we want to add an amount of randomness that is at least twice the binary length of m in

the encryption operation. Therefore, the keys of 2PAD will consist of pairs $(x_k, y_k) \in \mathbb{Z}_p \times \mathbb{Z}_p$. Let $b \in \mathbb{Z}_{p^2}$. Then,

$$b \equiv pz' + z'' \pmod{p^2}, \tag{6}$$

where $z', z'' \in \mathbb{Z}_p$. Therefore, we can essentially represent b with two elements of $\mathbb{Z}_p$. Using such a representation, we encrypt a single message $m \in \mathbb{Z}_p$ by first sampling a random element $z \leftarrow U(\mathbb{Z}_p \setminus \{0\})$ and setting $b := (pm + z) \bmod p^2$. Then, we add the key (x_k, y_k) by computing

$$c := \left(px_k b^2 + py_k b + b \right) \bmod p^2$$
$$= px_k z^2 + py_k z + pm + z \tag{7}$$

which is the ciphertext message. To enable blinding, Alice needs to be able to transform c into another ciphertext c'. The encryption operation entails such a transformation property that follows from the congruence

$$px_k b'^2 + py_k b' + b' \equiv px_k b^2 + py_k b + b \pmod{p^2} \tag{8}$$

for every $x_k, y_k \in \mathbb{Z}_p$ and $b, b' \in \mathbb{Z}_{p^2}$ such that $b \equiv b' \pmod{p}$. Let m_1 be a plain text and let $c_1 = px_k b^2 + py_k b + b$ be its encryption with $b = (pm_1 + z) \bmod p^2$. Let c_2 now be any ciphertext under the same key (x_k, y_k) such that $c_2 \equiv c_1 \equiv z \pmod{p}$ and let m_2 be the corresponding plain text. Since $c_2 \equiv c_1 \equiv z \pmod{p}$, we have $c_2 = px_k b'^2 + py_k b' + b'$, where $b' = (pm_2 + z) \bmod p^2$. Now, by (8),

$$c_2 \equiv px_k b'^2 + py_k b' + b' \equiv px_k b^2 + py_k b + b'$$
$$\equiv c_1 - b + b' \pmod{p^2}, \tag{9}$$

from which

$$c_2 \equiv c_1 - pm_1 + pm_2 \pmod{p^2}, \tag{10}$$

which enables us to compute m_2 using c_2, m_1, c_1 without the key (x_k, y_k). Namely, if we know a plain text m_1 and its encryption $c_1 = px_k z^2 + py_k z + pm_1 + z$, we know the decryption m_2 of c_2 for every $c_2 \equiv c_1 \pmod{p}$. The plain text m_2 can be computed by the transformation algorithm Map in Algorithm 1.

Let $z \equiv c_1 \equiv c_2 \pmod{p}$. The algorithm works because

$$\frac{(c_2 - c_1 + pm_1)}{p}$$
$$= \frac{\left(px_k z^2 + py_k z + pm_2 + z - px_k z^2 - py_k z - pm_1 - z + pm_1 \right)}{p} \tag{11}$$
$$= \frac{(pm_2)}{p} = m_2.$$

In order to query the decryptor, Alice can transform a ciphertext c into any c' such that $c' \equiv c \pmod{p}$. The Map algorithm can transform the corresponding plain text m' to the decryption m of c.

Decryption is straightforward knowing the key (x_k, y_y). Its operation, as well as the complete encryption scheme, is described below.

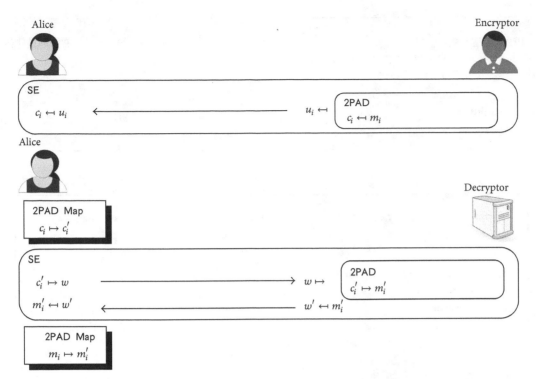

FIGURE 6: General overview of SymmetricBlind. Two tiers of encryption are applied. The outer tier (SE) satisfies ordinary perfect secrecy. The inner tier (2PAD) provides perfect leak-freeness against Alice and has a transformation property enabling perfect blindness against the decryptor.

```
(1) procedure Map(c₁, m₁, c₂)
(2)     If c₁ ≠ c₂ (mod p) output ⊥
(3)     m₂ := ((c₂ − c₁ + pm₁)/p) mod p
(4)     output m₂
(5) end procedure
```

ALGORITHM 1

Definition 5 (2PAD). The symmetric encryption scheme

$$\text{2PAD} = (\text{Gen}_{\text{2PAD}}, \text{Enc}_{\text{2PAD}}, \text{Dec}_{\text{2PAD}}) \quad (12)$$

consists of Algorithms 2, 3, and 4.

The plain-text and ciphertext spaces of 2PAD depend on the chosen prime p; the plain-text space is $\mathbb{Z}_p$, while the ciphertext space is $\mathbb{Z}_{p^2}$. Let us show the correctness of the scheme. That is,

$$\text{Dec}_{\text{2PAD}}(x_k, y_k, \text{Enc}_{\text{2PAD}}(x_k, y_k, m)) = m \quad (13)$$

for every key (x_k, y_k) and plain text m. Let $c = \text{Enc}_{\text{2PAD}}(x_k, y_k, m)$. Then one has

$$c = px_k b^2 + py_k b + b \equiv px_k z^2 + py_k z + pm + z$$
$$\left(\text{mod } p^2\right) \quad (14)$$

and $c \mod p = z$, where $z \in \mathbb{Z}_p$. Now,

$$\text{Dec}_{\text{2PAD}}(x_k, y_k, c) = \frac{(t − z)}{p}$$

$$= \frac{\left(p(-x_k)z^2 + p(-y_k)z + px_k z^2 + py_k z + pm + z − z\right)}{p} \quad (15)$$

$$= \frac{(pm + z − z)}{p} = m.$$

We shall later show that, given a single plain-text and ciphertext pair (m_1, c_1) and a ciphertext c_2 such that $c_2 \neq c_1 \pmod{p}$, we still have information-theoretic security for c_2. That is, 2PAD satisfies perfect leak-freeness against Alice whenever $c_i \neq c_j \pmod{p}$ for $i \neq j$. However, suppose that we have two plain-text and ciphertext pairs $(m_1, c_1), (m_2, c_2)$ such that $c_1 \neq c_2 \pmod{p}$. We can show that the key x_k, y_k can be completely determined from such two pairs.

Proposition 6. *For every plain-text and ciphertext pair* $(m_1, c_1), (m_2, c_2)$ *such that* $c_1 \neq c_2 \pmod{p}$, *there is a unique key* (x_k, y_k) *such that*

$$c_1 = \text{Enc}_{\text{2PAD}}(x_k, y_k, m_1),$$
$$\quad (16)$$
$$c_2 = \text{Enc}_{\text{2PAD}}(x_k, y_k, m_2).$$

```
(1) procedure Gen_2PAD(s)                    ▷ s determines the size for the plaintext space
(2)     Choose a public prime p such that p ≥ 5 and p ≥ 2^s
(3)     x_k ← U(Z_p)
(4)     y_k ← U(Z_p)
(5)     output (x_k, y_k)
(6) end procedure
```

ALGORITHM 2

```
(1) procedure Enc_2PAD(x_k, y_k, m)          ▷ Input consists of a key (x_k, y_k) and a message m ∈ Z_p
(2)     z ← U(Z_p \ {0})
(3)     b := (pm + z) mod p^2
(4)     c := (px_k b^2 + py_k b + b) mod p^2
(5)     output c
(6) end procedure
```

ALGORITHM 3

```
(1) procedure Dec_2PAD(x_k, y_k, c)          ▷ Input consists of a key (x_k, y_k) and a ciphertext c ∈ Z_{p^2}
(2)     z := c mod p
(3)     t := (p(-x_k)z^2 + p(-y_k)z + c) mod p^2
(4)     m := ((t - z)/p) mod p
(5)     output m
(6) end procedure
```

ALGORITHM 4

Proof. Let $z_1, z_2 \in \mathbb{Z}_p$ such that $z_1 \equiv c_1 \pmod{p}$ and $z_2 \equiv c_2 \pmod{p}$. Let also $v_1 = (c_1 - pm_1 - z_1)/p$ and $v_2 = (c_2 - pm_2 - z_2)/p$. Then, we have a system of two equations:

$$v_1 = x_k z_1^2 + y_k z_1,$$
$$v_2 = x_k z_2^2 + y_k z_2, \tag{17}$$

where v_1, v_2, z_1, z_2 are known. Now, let

$$Z = \begin{pmatrix} z_1^2 & z_2^2 \\ z_1 & z_2 \end{pmatrix}. \tag{18}$$

Note that since $z_1, z_2 \not\equiv 0 \pmod{p}$ and $z_1 \not\equiv z_2 \pmod{p}$, we have $z_1^2 z_2 - z_1 z_2^2 \not\equiv 0 \pmod{p}$ and Z is invertible modulo p. Therefore, the equation pair has a unique solution:

$$(v_1 \ v_2) \cdot Z^{-1} = (x_k z_1^2 + y_k z_1 \ \ x_k z_2^2 + y_k z_2) \cdot Z^{-1}$$

$$= (x_k \ y_k) \begin{pmatrix} z_1^2 & z_2^2 \\ z_1 & z_2 \end{pmatrix} \cdot Z^{-1} = (x_k \ y_k). \tag{19}$$

☐

Due to the transformation algorithm Map, we require that if Bob sends L ciphertext messages $c_1, c_2, \ldots, c_L$ to Alice, we have $c_i \not\equiv c_j \pmod{p}$ for every $i \neq j$. Otherwise, it would be trivial for Alice to derive the decryptions of all of the ciphertexts from a single plain-text and ciphertext pair. Therefore, the maximum number of ciphertext messages under the same key is determined by $L \leq p - 1$.

5.2. Blind Decryption Protocol. Next, we give a description of a blind decryption protocol based on the transformation algorithm Map.

Definition 7 (BlindDec). Suppose that the encryptor and the decryptor share a key $(x_k, y_k) = \text{Gen}_{2PAD}(s)$ intended for a single decryption by Alice. Furthermore, let Alice have an encrypted message $c = \text{Enc}_{2PAD}(x_k, y_k, m)$ that is not known to the decryptor. Finally, suppose that the prime p is public knowledge. Let the protocol BlindDec be defined by the following exchange between Alice and the decryptor:

(1) Alice: compute $c' := c \bmod p$ and transmit it to the decryptor

(2) Decryptor: reply with $m' = \text{Dec}_{2PAD}(x_k, y_k, c')$

(3) Alice: compute the plain-text message $m = \mathsf{Map}(c', m', c)$

Let us quickly check the correctness of BlindDec. Let $z \equiv c' \equiv c \pmod{p}$. Then, $c = px_k z^2 + py_k z + pm + z$, where m is the plain-text message. The decryptor replies with

$$m' = \frac{\left(p(-x_k)z^2 + p(-y_k)z + z - z\right)}{p} \tag{20}$$

$$= (-x_k)z^2 + (-y_k)z.$$

But now Alice can compute

$$\mathsf{Map}\left(c', m', c\right) = \frac{\left(c - z + pm'\right)}{p}$$

$$= \frac{\left(px_k z^2 + py_k z + pm + z - z + pm'\right)}{p} \tag{21}$$

$$= \frac{\left(px_k z^2 + py_k z + pm - px_k z^2 - py_k z\right)}{p} = \frac{(pm)}{p}$$

$$= m,$$

which is the correct plain-text message.

5.3. The Complete Blind Decryption Scheme. As was mentioned earlier, the communication between Alice and the encryptor has to be protected in order to prevent the decryptor from obtaining the plain-text messages corresponding to $c_1, c_2, \ldots, c_L$. If the decryptor can observe these ciphertext messages, it can freely decrypt all of them, since it knows the correct key. Therefore, we need to apply an outer encryption scheme that hides the ciphertext messages. The same solution is the easiest way to provide perfect leak-freeness against the encryptor, since it enables us to simplify the secrecy conditions. In our case, we want to protect both of these exchanges with an outer tier of encryption which provides perfect secrecy. Let $\mathsf{SE}_n = (\mathsf{Gen}_n, \mathsf{Enc}_n, \mathsf{Dec}_n)$ be any symmetric encryption scheme that satisfies perfect secrecy such that the plain-text and ciphertext space is $\mathbb{Z}_n$. We will be applying SE_n with both $n = p^2$ and $n = p$ together with 2PAD to provide the required leak-freeness and blindness properties. The outer tier is composed in the following way. Alice and the encryptor share a set of keys $k_1, k_2, \ldots, k_L$. The encryptor protects each ciphertext message by computing $u_j = \mathsf{Enc}_{p^2}(k_j, c_j)$ for $j \in \{1, 2, \ldots, L\}$. It sends $u_1, u_2, \ldots, u_L$ to Alice. Similarly, Alice and the decryptor share a pair of keys k_C, k_P that are used to protect c' and m'. Alice sends $w = \mathsf{Enc}_p(k_C, c')$ to the decryptor that responds with $w' = \mathsf{Enc}_p(k_P, m')$. The resulting scheme SymmetricBlind is defined as follows.

Definition 8 (SymmetricBlind). Let $\mathsf{SE}_n = (\mathsf{Gen}_n, \mathsf{Enc}_n, \mathsf{Dec}_n)$ be a symmetric encryption scheme such that the plain-text and ciphertext space is $\mathbb{Z}_n$ and let SE_n satisfy perfect secrecy. Let Alice and the encryptor share a set of keys $k_1, k_2, \ldots, k_L$. Let Alice and the decryptor share a pair of keys k_C, k_P

Alice	Encryptor
	Choose $m_1, m_2, \ldots, m_L$
	$\forall j:$
	$c_j = \mathsf{Enc}_{2\mathsf{PAD}}(x_k, y_k, m_j)$
	such that
	$c_j \not\equiv c_{j'} \pmod{p} \; \forall j \neq j'$
	$\forall j: u_j = \mathsf{Enc}_{p^2}(k_j, c_j)$
$u_1, u_2, \ldots, u_L \quad \longleftarrow$	$u_1, u_2, \ldots, u_L$
$\forall j \; c_j = \mathsf{Dec}_{p^2}(k_j, u_j)$	
Pick i	
$c' = c_i \bmod p$	
$w = \mathsf{Enc}_p(k_C, c')$	*Decryptor*
$w \qquad\qquad \longrightarrow$	w
	$c' = \mathsf{Dec}_p(k_C, w)$
	$m' = \mathsf{Dec}_{2\mathsf{PAD}}(x_k, y_k, c')$
	$w' = \mathsf{Enc}_p(k_P, m')$
$w' \qquad\qquad \longleftarrow$	w'
$m' = \mathsf{Dec}_p(k_P, w')$	
$m_i = \mathsf{Map}(c', m', c_i)$	

Box 1

intended for a single blind decryption by Alice. Also let the encryptor and the decryptor share a blind decryption key $(x_k, y_k) = \mathsf{Gen}_{2\mathsf{PAD}}(s)$, where $2^s \geq L + 1$, which is intended for single blind decryption by Alice. SymmetricBlind is determined by Box 1.

Note that we require that the parameter s determining the size of the plain-text space satisfy $2^s \geq L + 1$ to ensure that the generated prime p satisfies $L \leq p - 1$ and the scheme supports at least the encryption of L messages.

6. Security of SymmetricBlind

We shall now consider the security of SymmetricBlind. We proceed to show that the devised scheme satisfies the three conditions formulated in Section 4: perfect leak-freeness against the encryptor, perfect leak-freeness against Alice, and perfect blindness against the decryptor.

6.1. Perfect Leak-Freeness against the Encryptor

Proposition 9. SymmetricBlind *satisfies perfect leak-freeness against the encryptor for a single decryption of a maximum of $L \leq p - 1$ messages, where p is determined by* $\mathsf{Gen}_{2\mathsf{PAD}}(s)$.

Proof. The claim follows directly from the observation that the encryptor sees only w and w'. By the description of SymmetricBlind, c' and m' are protected by encryption satisfying perfect secrecy and thus do not leak information to the encryptor. $\qquad\square$

It is easy to see that the outer tier of encryption is necessary. Suppose that the outer encryption scheme was not applied. Then c' would leak $c_i \bmod p$ which would betray i to the encryptor.

6.2. Perfect Blindness against Decryptor. We shall now prove that the decryptor does not get information about the plaintext message.

Proposition 10. SymmetricBlind *satisfies perfect blindness against the decryptor for a single blind decryption.*

Proof. Since $c_1, c_2, \ldots, c_L$ are protected with perfect secrecy, we only need to show that

$$\Pr\left[M = m \mid C' = c', M' = m'\right] = \Pr\left[M = m\right], \quad (22)$$

where C' and M' are the random variables associated with the messages c' and m', respectively. Let X, Y denote the random variables corresponding to the key elements $(x_k, y_k) \leftarrow \text{Gen}(s)$, respectively. The reply m' from the decryptor is completely determined by the key (x_k, y_k) and the element $c' = c_i \bmod p$, since $m' = (-x_k)c'^2 + (-y_k)c'$. Therefore,

$$\Pr\left[M = m \mid C' = c', M' = m'\right]$$
$$= \Pr\left[M = m \mid X = x_k, Y = y_k, C' = c'\right]. \quad (23)$$

Let us consider C'. By the description of the scheme, we have $C' = C_i \bmod p$, where i is the chosen index of Alice. But, for every i, we have, by the description of Enc_{2PAD}, that $C_i \bmod p \sim U(\mathbb{Z}_p \setminus \{0\})$. Therefore, C' is independent of X and Y and

$$\Pr\left[M = m \mid X = x_k, Y = y_k, C' = z\right]$$
$$= \Pr\left[M = m \mid X = x_k, Y = y_k, C' = z'\right] \quad (24)$$

for every $z, z' \in \mathbb{Z}_p \setminus \{0\}$ and

$$\Pr\left[M = m \mid X = x_k, Y = y_k\right]$$
$$= \sum_{z \in \mathbb{Z}_p \setminus \{0\}} \Pr\left[M = m \mid X = x_k, Y = y_k, C' = z\right]$$
$$\cdot \Pr\left[C' = z \mid X = x_k, Y = y_k\right] = \frac{1}{p-1} \quad (25)$$
$$\cdot \sum_{z \in \mathbb{Z}_p \setminus \{0\}} \Pr\left[M = m \mid X = x_k, Y = y_k, C' = z\right]$$
$$= \Pr\left[M = m \mid X = x_k, Y = y_k, C' = z\right]$$

for any $z \in \mathbb{Z}_p$. By our assumption, M is independent of X and Y and therefore we have

$$\Pr\left[M = m \mid X = x_k \cap Y = y_k\right] = \Pr\left[M = m\right], \quad (26)$$

which shows our claim. $\square$

The proof shows that the decryptor (with the knowledge of the key (x_k, y_k) and c' and m') does not gain any information about the plain-text message m assuming that c_j

for $j \in \{1, 2, \ldots, L\}$ have been delivered to Alice in perfect secrecy. Considering the secrecy against the decryptor, it would suffice to send c' without the additional level of encryption. However, the additional level is necessary to achieve leak-freeness against the encryptor.

6.3. Perfect Leak-Freeness against Alice. We shall now consider an honest-but-curious Alice and show that the observation of a single plain-text and ciphertext pair (m_1, c_1) does not yield information about the decryption of c_2 for $c_2 \not\equiv c_1 \pmod{p}$.

Proposition 11. SymmetricBlind *satisfies perfect leak-freeness against Alice for a single decryption of a maximum of $L \leq p - 1$ ciphertexts.*

Proof. By the description of SymmetricBlind, the ciphertext messages $c_1, c_2, \ldots, c_L$ are of different congruence class modulo p. Let M_1, M_2 be random variables over the plain-text space $\mathbb{Z}_p$. Let X, Y denote the random variables corresponding to the key elements $(x_k, y_k) = \text{Gen}_{2PAD}(s)$. We have to show that

$$\Pr\big[c_1 = \text{Enc}_{2PAD}\left(X, Y, M_1\right), c_2$$
$$= \text{Enc}_{2PAD}\left(X, Y, M_2\right) \mid M_1 = m_1, M_2 = m_2, c_1$$
$$\not\equiv c_2 \pmod{p}\big] = \Pr\big[c_1 = \text{Enc}_{2PAD}\left(X, Y, M_1\right), c_2 \quad (27)$$
$$= \text{Enc}_{2PAD}\left(X, Y, M_2\right) \mid M_1 = m_1, M_2 = m, c_1$$
$$\not\equiv c_2 \pmod{p}\big]$$

for every $m_1, m_2, m \in \{0, 1, 2, \ldots, p-1\}$ and $c_1, c_2 \in \mathbb{Z}_{p^2}$ such that $c_1 \not\equiv c_2 \pmod{p}$. Given a valid assignment for m_1, c_1 and c_2, it suffices to show that

$$\Pr\big[c_1 = \text{Enc}_{2PAD}\left(X, Y, M_1\right), c_2$$
$$= \text{Enc}_{2PAD}\left(X, Y, M_2\right) \mid M_1 = m, M_2 = m_2, c_1 \quad (28)$$
$$\not\equiv c_2 \pmod{p}\big] = \frac{1}{p^2}$$

for every $m \in \mathbb{Z}_p$. By Proposition 6, for every plain-text and ciphertext pair $(m_1, c_1), (m, c_2)$ such that $c_1 \not\equiv c_2 \pmod{p}$, there is a unique key (x_k, y_k). Therefore,

$$\Pr\big[c_1 = \text{Enc}_{2PAD}\left(X, Y, M_1\right), c_2$$
$$= \text{Enc}_{2PAD}\left(X, Y, M_2\right) \mid M_1 = m_1, M_2 = m, c_1 \quad (29)$$
$$\not\equiv c_2 \pmod{p}\big] = \Pr\left[X = x_k, Y = y_k\right].$$

By the definition of Gen_{2PAD}, X and Y are independent and we have

$$\Pr\left[X = x_k, Y = y_k\right] = \Pr\left[X = x_k\right] \cdot \Pr\left[Y = y_k\right]$$
$$= \frac{1}{p^2}. \quad (30)$$

$\square$

We have now established the perfect secrecy of SymmetricBlind according to Definition 4.

TABLE 1: Parameter examples for SymmetricBlind.

p	Decryptor key length [bits]	Plain text length [bits]	Ciphertext length [bits]
5	12	3	5
7	12	3	6
11	16	4	7
23	20	5	10
101	28	7	14
1009	40	10	20
5003	52	13	25
20011	60	15	29
$2^{31} - 1$	124	31	62
$2^{61} - 1$	244	61	122
$2^{127} - 1$	508	127	254

6.4. The Parameters. An optimal encryption scheme, with plain-text space $\mathcal{M}$, that satisfies perfect leak-freeness against Alice for a single decryption needs $2\log_2|\mathcal{M}|$ bits of randomness for a key. 2PAD achieves exactly this bound, since the plain-text space is $\mathbb{Z}_p$ and a single key (x_k, y_k) contains $2\log_2 p$ bits of randomness. Assuming that messages and keys are represented by binary strings, we need $2\lceil \log_2 p \rceil$ bits of key to encrypt messages of length $\lfloor \log_2 p \rfloor$. For a single decryption with SymmetricBlind, the decryptor needs to store the key elements $x_k, y_k \in \mathbb{Z}_p$, as well as the keys k_C, k_P. The keys k_C, k_P are used to encrypt messages of $\mathbb{Z}_p$. Therefore, $\lceil \log_2 p \rceil$ bits for each of these keys suffice for perfect secrecy. In total, the decryptor needs to store key material of $4\lceil \log_2 p \rceil$ bits for a single decryption of a message of bit length $\lfloor \log_2 p \rfloor$. Since the ciphertext space is $\mathbb{Z}_{p^2}$, the ciphertext's length in bits is approximately twice the plain text's length. Depending on the length of the plain-text messages and the needed maximum number of encryptions $L \le p - 1$, we should therefore choose the smallest possible p, since its bit size has no effect on the security of the scheme. Table 1 lists some possible choices for p and the resulting key, plain text, and ciphertext lengths in bits. Note that for long plain-text messages the maximum number of messages L is practically unlimited.

7. Future Work

There are two main drawbacks of the construction presented in this paper. First, we have not considered active adversaries. Similar to the one-time pad, we have only considered such adversaries that observe the flow of messages. For practical scenarios, we need to consider adversaries that actively induce errors into the protocol flow. However, such considerations are most naturally conducted in the computational infeasibility model which has been used, for instance, in [5]. In the active adversaries setting, it would also be natural to consider the security of the devised scheme in the framework of computational indistinguishability such that the truly random keys are exchanged with pseudorandom bit strings. In particular, the computationally hard version of our scheme

yields efficient practical implementation. The computational security model is also more appealing considering applications due to the limitations induced by the information-theoretic model. For example, in the information-theoretic security model, private information retrieval requires an amount of communication that is at least the size of the database [44]. Similarly, in SymmetricBlind, a fresh key is needed for each decryption resulting in limitations regarding existing applications. For example, applications that require adaptive queries cannot be instantiated with SymmetricBlind, since a fresh key would be required for each query. We leave it for future research to consider SymmetricBlind and its possible generalizations and applications in the computational security model.

The second drawback is that we have only considered the case of a single adversary. While it does not make sense to consider a scenario where Alice is colluding with the encryptor against the decryptor, the scenario where the encryptor and the decryptor are colluding is an important one. For many scenarios, Alice cannot be certain whether the encryptor and the decryptor are in fact separate entities. However, if they are a single entity, the scenario is identical to oblivious transfer. We cannot achieve information-theoretic security in such a case [18]. For example, it is easy to see that our construction fails for colluding encryptor and decryptor. If that is the case, we effectively remove the outer layer of encryption, which means that $c' = c_i \bmod p$ leaks i to the adversary. To provide security against colluding encryptor and decryptor, we would need to detect such collusion or to turn to computational assumptions. We leave the question as an open problem for future research. Another interesting question for future work is to consider the case where we do not apply the outer layer of encryption from the encryptor to Alice. Thus far, we have defined perfect blindness so that the decryptor has absolutely no information about the plain-text message. However, we could relax the requirement so that, similar to leak-freeness against the encryptor, the information is conditioned on the plain texts $m_1, m_2, \ldots, m_L$. In other words, we could relax the requirement so that the decryptor may observe the selection (and the corresponding plain-text messages) given to Alice. Such relaxation is natural in the oblivious transfer case where the encryptor and the decryptor are the same entity. We could then define blindness as a property requiring only that the selection i be hidden. It is again easy to see that our scheme without the outer layer of encryption fails such a property. If $c_1, c_2, \ldots, c_L$ are not protected, then $c' = c_i \bmod p$ leaks i. Similarly, attempting to convert SymmetricBlind into an oblivious transfer scheme using the method of Dodis et al. is impossible, since SymmetricBlind requires that the parties be truly separate. The unification of encryptor and decryptor leaks i even in the computational security model [39]. We leave this consideration also for future work.

8. Conclusion

In this paper, we give a definition of perfect secrecy for symmetric blind decryption in the setting where one of the parties may be malicious but adhering to the protocol of the scheme. We consider neither active adversaries nor the setting where two of the participants are colluding against the third. We construct a symmetric blind decryption scheme SymmetricBlind and show that it satisfies our definition of perfect secrecy. The scheme is based on two layers of encryption, where the inner layer utilizes a novel encryption scheme 2PAD given in this paper. 2PAD is based on modular arithmetic with $\mathbb{Z}_{p^2}$ as the ciphertext space, $\mathbb{Z}_p$ as the plaintext space, and $\mathbb{Z}_p \times \mathbb{Z}_p$ as the key space, where $p \geq 5$ is a prime. The security of SymmetricBlind is shown information-theoretically and does not depend on the size of p. For a fixed blind decryption key, SymmetricBlind supports a single blind decryption from a selection of $L \leq p-1$ messages. For a single decryption of a message of bit length $\lfloor \log_2 p \rfloor$, the decryption server needs to store key material of $4\lceil \log_2 p \rceil$ bits.

Notations

Variables

$\mathcal{K}$:	Key space
$\mathcal{M}$:	Plain-text space
$\mathcal{C}$:	Ciphertext space
$\mathcal{C}'$:	Ciphertext transformation space
k:	Blind encryption/decryption key
L:	The number of messages encrypted under a single blind decryption key
$m_1, m_2, \ldots, m_L$:	Plain-text messages chosen by the encryptor
$c_1, c_2, \ldots, c_L$:	Ciphertext messages obtained by encrypting with the blind encryption key
c or c_i:	Ciphertext message chosen by Alice
c' or c_i':	Transformed ciphertext message chosen by Alice
m' or m_i':	Decryption of c' under the blind decryption key
m or m_i:	The plain-text message Alice obtains at the end of the scheme.

Random Variables

K:	Random variable on $\mathcal{K}$ induced by Gen
$M_1, M_2, \ldots, M_L$:	Random variables corresponding to the choice of $m_1, m_2, \ldots, m_L$ by the encryptor
C':	Random variable on $\mathcal{C}'$ induced by Alice using BlindDec
M':	Random variable on $\mathcal{M}$ induced by decryption of C' by the decryptor
M:	Random variable corresponding to the plain-text message m Alice obtains at the end of the scheme.

Acknowledgments

Financial support from Infotech Oulu Graduate School and the following foundations is gratefully acknowledged: Finnish Foundation for Technology Promotion, the Nokia Foundation, Tauno Tönning Foundation, Walter Ahsltröm Foundation, and the Finnish Foundation for Economic and Technology Sciences (KAUTE).

References

[1] B. Thuraisingham, "Big data security and privacy," in *Proceedings of the 5th ACM Conference on Data and Application Security and Privacy (CODASPY '15)*, pp. 279-280, ACM, New York, NY, USA, March 2015.

[2] Office for Civil Rights, United State Department of Health and Human Services, Medical privacy. national standards of protect the privacy of personalhealth-information, 2013, http://www.hhs.gov/ocr/privacy/hipaa/administrative/privacyrule/index.html.

[3] European Parliament, Directive 95/46/EC of the European Parliament and of the Council of 24 october 1995 on the protection of individuals with regard to the processing of personal data and on the free movement of such data, 1995, http://eur-lex.europa.eu/.

[4] S. Coull, M. Green, and S. Hohenberger, "Controlling access to an oblivious database using stateful anonymous credentials," in *Public key cryptography—PKC 2009*, S. Jarecki and G. Tsudik, Eds., vol. 5443 of *Lecture Notes in Computer Science*, pp. 501–520, Springer, Berlin, Germany, 2009.

[5] M. Green, "Secure blind decryption," in *Public Key Cryptography—PKC 2011*, D. Catalano, N. Fazio, R. Gennaro, and A. Nicolosi, Eds., vol. 6571 of *Lecture Notes in Computer Science*, pp. 265–282, Springer Berlin Heidelberg, Berlin, Germany, 2011.

[6] K. Sakurai and Y. Yamane, "Blind decoding, blind undeniable signatures, and their applications to privacy protection," in *Information Hiding*, R. Anderson, Ed., vol. 1174 of *Lecture Notes in Computer Science*, pp. 257–264, Springer, Berlin, Germany, 1996.

[7] D. Chaum, "Blind signatures for untraceable payments," in *Advances in Cryptology*, D. Chaum, R. Rivest, and A. Sherman, Eds., pp. 199–203, Springer, Boston, Mass, USA, 1983.

[8] M. Green and S. Hohenberger, "Blind identity-based encryption and simulatable oblivious transfer," in *Advances in cryptology—ASIACRYPT 2007*, K. Kurosawa, Ed., vol. 4833 of *Lecture Notes in Computer Science*, pp. 265–282, Springer, Berlin, Germany, 2007.

[9] R. Perlman, C. Kaufman, and R. Perlner, "Privacy-preserving DRM," in *Proceedings of the 9th Symposium on Identity and Trust on the Internet (IDTRUST '10)*, pp. 69–83, Association for Computing Machinery, Gaithersburg, Md, USA, April 2010.

[10] L. L. Win, T. Thomas, and S. Emmanuel, "Privacy enabled digital rights management without trusted third party assumption," *IEEE Transactions on Multimedia*, vol. 14, no. 3, pp. 546–554, 2012.

[11] C. P. Schnorr and M. Jakobsson, "Security of signed ElGamal encryption," in *Advances in cryptology—ASIACRYPT 2000*, vol. 1976 of *Lecture Notes in Computer Science*, pp. 73–89, Springer, Berlin, Germany, 2000.

[12] K. Sakuraii, Y. Yamane, S. Miyazaki, and T. Inoue, "A key escrow system with protecting user's privacy by blind decoding," in

Information Security, E. Okamoto, G. Davida, and M. Mambo, Eds., vol. 1396 of *Lecture Notes in Computer Science*, pp. 147–157, Springer, Berlin, Germany, 1998.

[13] Y. Sameshima, "A key escrow system of the RSA cryptosystem," in *Information Security*, E. Okamoto, G. Davida, and M. Mambo, Eds., vol. 1396 of *Lecture Notes in Computer Science*, pp. 135–146, Springer, Berlin, Germany, 1998.

[14] L. T. Phong and W. Ogata, "New identity-based blind signature and blind decryption scheme in the standard model," *IEICE Transactions on Fundamentals of Electronics, Communications and Computer Sciences*, vol. E92.A, no. 8, pp. 1822–1835, 2009.

[15] A. C.-C. Yao, "How to generate and exchange secrets," in *Proceedings of the 27th Annual Symposium on Foundations of Computer Science*, pp. 162–167, Toronto, Canada, October 1986.

[16] M. O. Rabin, "How to exchange secrets with oblivious transfer," TR-81, Aiken Computation Lab, Harvard University, Cambridge, Mass, USA, 1981.

[17] S. Even, O. Goldreich, and A. Lempel, "A randomized protocol for signing contracts," *Communications of the Association for Computing Machinery*, vol. 28, no. 6, pp. 637–647, 1985.

[18] I. Damgård, J. Kilian, and L. Salvail, "On the (im)possibility of basing oblivious transfer and bit commitment on weakened security assumptions," in *Proceedings of the 17th International Conference on Theory and Application of Cryptographic Techniques (EUROCRYPT '99)*, vol. 1999, pp. 56–73, Springer, Berlin, Germany.

[19] D. Chaum, "Security without identification: transaction systems to make big brother obsolete," *Communications of the ACM*, vol. 28, no. 10, pp. 1030–1044, 1985.

[20] R. L. Rivest, A. Shamir, and L. Adleman, "A method for obtaining digital signatures and public-key cryptosystems," *Communications of the Association for Computing Machinery*, vol. 21, no. 2, pp. 120–126, 1978.

[21] D. Chaum and T. Pedersen, "Wallet databases with observers," in *Advances in Cryptology—CRYPTO' 92*, vol. 740 of *Lecture Notes in Computer Science*, pp. 89–105, Springer, Berlin, Germany, 1993.

[22] T. Okamoto, "Provable secure and practical identification schemes and corresponding signature schemes," in *Advances in Cryptology—CRYPTO '92*, E. Brickell, Ed., vol. 740 of *Lecture Notes in Computer Science*, pp. 31–53, Springer, Berlin, Germany, 1992.

[23] P. Horster, M. Michels, and H. Petersen, "Meta-Message recovery and Meta-Blind signature schemes based on the discrete logarithm problem and their applications," in *Advances in Cryptology—ASIACRYPT'94*, J. Pieprzyk and R. Safavi-Naini, Eds., vol. 917 of *Lecture Notes in Computer Science*, pp. 224–237, Springer, Berlin, Germany, 1995.

[24] J. L. Camenisch, J.-M. Piveteau, and M. A. Stadler, "Blind signatures based on the discrete logarithm problem," in *Advances in Cryptology—EUROCRYPT '94*, A. De Santis, Ed., vol. 950 of *Lecture Notes in Computer Science*, pp. 428–432, Springer, Berlin, Germany, 1995.

[25] T. ElGamal, "A public key cryptosystem and a signature scheme based on discrete logarithms," *IEEE Transactions on Information Theory*, vol. 31, no. 4, pp. 469–472, 1985.

[26] M. Mambo, K. Sakurai, and E. Okamoto, "How to utilize the transformability of digital signatures for solving the oracle problem," in *Advances in Cryptology—ASIACRYPT '96*, K. Kim and T. Matsumoto, Eds., vol. 1163 of *Lecture Notes in Computer Science*, pp. 322–333, Springer, Berlin, Germany, 1996.

[27] G. Brassard, C. Crépeau, and J.-M. Robert, "All-or-nothing disclosure of secrets," in *Proceedings of the Advances in Cryptology (CRYPTO '86)*, vol. 263, pp. 234–238, Springer, Santa Barbara, Cali, USA, 1987.

[28] M. Naor and B. Pinkas, "Oblivious transfer with adaptive queries," in *Advances in Cryptology—CRYPTO 99*, M. Wiener, Ed., vol. 1666 of *Lecture Notes in Computer Science*, pp. 573–590, Springer, Berlin, Germany, 1999.

[29] J. Camenisch, G. Neven, and a. shelat, "Simulatable adaptive oblivious transfer," in *Advances in Cryptology—EUROCRYPT 2007*, M. Naor, Ed., vol. 4515 of *Lecture Notes in Computer Science*, pp. 573–590, Springer, Berlin, Germany, 2007.

[30] M. Green and S. Hohenberger, "Universally composable adaptive oblivious transfer," in *Advances in Cryptology—ASIACRYPT 2008*, J. Pieprzyk, Ed., vol. 5350 of *Lecture Notes in Comput. Sci.*, pp. 179–197, Springer, Berlin, Germany, 2008.

[31] S. A. Jarecki and X. Liu, "Efficient oblivious pseudorandom function with applications to adaptive OT and secure computation of set intersection," in *Theory of Cryptography*, O. Reingold, Ed., vol. 5444 of *Lecture Notes in Computer Science*, pp. 577–594, Springer, Berlin, Germany, 2009.

[32] K. Kurosawa and R. Nojima, "Simple adaptive oblivious transfer without random oracle," in *Advances in cryptology—ASIACRYPT 2009*, M. Matsui, Ed., vol. 5912 of *Lecture Notes in Computer Science*, pp. 334–346, Springer, Berlin, Germany, 2009.

[33] K. Kurosawa, R. Nojima, and L. T. Phong, "Efficiency-improved fully simulatable adaptive OT under the DDH assumption," in *Proceedings of the 7th International Conference on Security and Cryptography for Networks (SCN '10)*, vol. 6280, pp. 172–181, Springer, Amalfi, Italy, September 2010.

[34] M. Green and S. Hohenberger, "Practical adaptive oblivious transfer from simple assumptions," in *Theory of Cryptography*, Y. Ishai, Ed., vol. 6597 of *Lecture Notes in Computer Science*, pp. 347–363, Springer, Berlin, Germany, 2011.

[35] K. Kurosawa, R. Nojima, and L. T. Phong, "Generic Fully Simulatable Adaptive Oblivious Transfer," in *Applied Cryptography and Network Security*, J. Lopez and G. Tsudik, Eds., vol. 6715 of *Lecture Notes in Computer Science*, pp. 274–291, Springer, Berlin, Germany, 2011.

[36] B. Zhang, H. Lipmaa, C. Wang, and K. Ren, "Practical fully simulatable oblivious transfer with sublinear communication," in *Financial Cryptography and Data Security*, A.-R. Sadeghi, Ed., vol. 7859 of *Lecture Notes in Computer Science*, pp. 78–95, Springer, Berlin, Germany, 2013.

[37] V. Guleria and R. Dutta, "Efficient adaptive oblivious transfer without q-type assumptions in UC framework," in *Information and Communications Security*, L. C. K. Hui, S. H. Qing, E. Shi, and S. M. Yiu, Eds., vol. 8958 of *Lecture Notes in Computer Science*, pp. 105–119, Springer International Publishing, New York, NY, USa, 2015.

[38] C. Crépeau, K. Morozov, and S. Wolf, "Efficient unconditional oblivious transfer from almost any noisy channel," in *Security in Communication Networks*, C. Blundo and S. Cimato, Eds., vol. 3352 of *Lecture Notes in Computer Science*, pp. 47–59, Springer, Berlin, Germany, 2005.

[39] Y. Dodis, S. Halevi, and T. Rabin, "A cryptographic solution to a game theoretic problem," in *Proceedings of the 20th Annual International Cryptology Conference (CRYPTO '00)*, M. Bellare, Ed., vol. 1880 of *Lecture Notes in Computer Science*, pp. 112–130, Springer, Santa Barbara, Calif, USA, August 2000.

[40] A. C. Yao, "Protocols for secure computations," in *Proceedings of the 23rd Annual Symposium on Foundations of Computer Science (SFCS '08)*, pp. 160–164, November 1982.

[41] O. Goldreich, S. Micali, and A. Wigderson, "How to play any mental game," in *Proceedings of the 19th Annual ACM Conference on Theory of Computing (STOC'87)*, pp. 218–229, IEEE Press, New York, NY, USA, May 1987.

[42] C. E. Shannon, "Communication theory of secrecy systems," *The Bell System Technical Journal*, vol. 28, no. 4, pp. 656–715, 1949.

[43] J. Katz and Y. Lindell, *Introduction to Modern Cryptography*, Chapman & Hall, Boca Raton, Fla, USA, 2007.

[44] B. Chor, O. Goldreich, E. Kushilevitz, and M. Sudan, "Private information retrieval," *Journal of the ACM*, vol. 45, no. 6, pp. 965–982, 1998.

[45] J. Partala, Symmetric blind decryption with perfect secrecy, CoRR, 2015, http://arxiv.org/abs/1510.06231.

3

SEMAN: A Novel Secure Middleware for Mobile Ad Hoc Networks

Eduardo da Silva[1,2] and Luiz Carlos Pessoa Albini[1]

[1]*Department of Informatics, Federal University of Parana (UFPR), 81531970 Curitiba, Brazil*
[2]*Department of Informatics, Catarinense Federal Institute (IFC), 89245000 Araquari, Brazil*

Correspondence should be addressed to Eduardo da Silva; eduardo@ifc-araquari.edu.br

Academic Editor: Tzonelih Hwang

As a consequence of the particularities of Mobile Ad Hoc Networks (MANETs), such as dynamic topology and self-organization, the implementation of complex and flexible applications is a challenge. To enable the deployment of these applications, several middleware solutions were proposed. However, these solutions do not completely consider the security requirements of these networks. Based on the limitations of the existing solutions, this paper presents a new secure middleware, called Secure Middleware for Ad Hoc Networks (SEMAN), which provides a set of basic and secure services to MANETs aiming to facilitate the development of distributed, complex, and flexible applications. SEMAN considers the context of applications and organizes nodes into groups, also based on these contexts. The middleware includes three modules: service, processing, and security. Security module is the main part of the middleware. It has the following components: key management, trust management, and group management. All these components were developed and are described in this paper. They are supported by a cryptographic core and behave according to security rules and policies. The integration of these components provides security guarantees against attacks to the applications that usethe middleware services.

1. Introduction

Mobile Ad Hoc Networks (MANETs) are very attractive in several scenarios, as [1] soldiers carrying out information on a battlefield; people sharing information during a meeting; attendees using notebooks in an interactive conference; rescuers working after disasters. MANETs are dynamically established without any fixed infrastructure or centralized administration, and their operation is held by the nodes themselves [2].

On the other hand, these characteristics also impose several challenges, and the major ones are related to security. In addition to conventional wireless communication problems, the dynamic topology facilitates action of adversaries, making MANETs susceptible to both passive and active attacks [2]. In a passive attack, an unauthorized adversary tries to discover or to use system information without interaction with the network, while in an active one, the adversary tries to break into the system aiming to affect its operation [3]. Due to these particularities, the development of applications for MANET is not an easy task [4].

In general networks, to support the resolution of heterogeneity, scalability, and resource sharing problems and to allow the implementation of more complex and flexible applications, middleware solutions have been successfully used [5]. These solutions aim to provide interoperability and other services, as distribution of functionality, scalability, load balancing, and fault tolerance [6].

Several middleware solutions have also been proposed to support applications and services on MANETs. These solutions are message-oriented [7] and were classified, in a previous work [4], on tuple space-based, P2P-based, context-based, cross-layer, and application-oriented solutions. A complete analysis and comparison of these middleware solutions can be found in [4].

To support MANETs characteristics, a middleware must be lightweight in terms of the amount of processing, memory, and bandwidth consumption, to maintain its overhead as small as possible. Further, it must self-adapt to the dynamic environment and handle unpredictable message loss. Considering the security requirements of MANETs and since the middleware handles all the communication between a client and an application, it must also considers the security requirements [6]. However, middleware solutions do not consider, or consider only partially, the security requirements of the MANETs. As a consequence, security can be considered the main drawback of the solutions reported on [4]. Thus, the need for developing a middleware arises which considers the security challenges of MANETs and contains a set of components to provide secure services to applications.

This paper proposes a new Secure Middleware for Mobile Ad Hoc Networks, called SEMAN (*Secure Middleware for Mobile Ad Hoc Networks*). The middleware is based on groups, which are formed considering the context information. Group members exchange information which can be used on decision making and services provisioning. SEMAN has a security module which aims to ensure the system confidentiality and the resistance to following malicious attacks: selfish, byzantine, impersonation, and Sybil. The contributions of this paper are the new architecture of a secure middleware for MANETs; the design of a context-based group management and definition of strategies to the secure group communication; the integration of trust management and evaluation services; and an identity-based key management scheme integrated with the SEMAN cryptographic core.

The remaining of the paper is composed of six sections. Section 2 presents the network and the attack model. Section 3 introduces SEMAN: Secure Middleware for Mobile Ad Hoc Networks. Section 4 details the security model of SEMAN and how it can ensure security for middleware clients. Section 5 presents a scheme for secure group communication based on key agreements. Section 6 presents the integration of the security components to provide security to applications on different scenarios. Finally, Section 7 presents the conclusions and some research directions.

2. Network and Attack Model

The proposed middleware considers an asynchronous network composed of n mobile nodes, denoted by $N_1, \ldots, N_n$. The description of SEMAN considers the notation presented as follows:

$\mathbb{G}_1$: cyclic additive group with order p,

$\mathbb{G}_2$: cyclic multiplicative group with order p,

e: bilinear pairing in which $e : \mathbb{G}_1 \times \mathbb{G}_1 \to \mathbb{G}_2$,

$H_1(x)$: hash function in which $H_1(x) = \{0,1\}^* \to \mathbb{G}_1^*$,

$H_2(x)$: hash function in which $H_2(x) = \mathbb{G}_2 \to \mathbb{Z}_p^*$,

$N_{\mathscr{F}}$: founder nodes,

N_i: identification of node i,

SK_i: private key of node i,

PK_i: private key of node i,

MSK: master private key of system,

MPK: master public key of system,

MSK_i: share of master private key hold by node i.

It is assumed that only trust nodes participate in group initialization phases.

SEMAN aims to protect the network against some malicious attacks as selfish, byzantine, impersonation, and Sybil. Even though SEMAN may be effective against other attacks, they were not considered in this paper.

(i) Selfish Attacks. A node presents a selfish behavior either as a consequence of a malicious and intentional act or to save its own resources. But regardless the reason, the selfish behavior may compromise the network activities and any decision-making scheme which needs the cooperation of nodes. To guarantee the security against a selfish behavior, SEMAN group operations are structured considering the secret sharing (t over n) technique, in which $n - (t + 1)$ nodes may be unavailable, or present a selfish behavior, and the system is able to attend the requests. Further, trust management component provides information about the behavior of nodes in a context. Thus, if a node is selfish and does not participate on group activities, the other nodes will be aware of this behavior through the trust management component.

(ii) Byzantine Attacks. A malicious node may perform a byzantine attack against the system, issuing false information or making decisions on behalf of a group. Thus, a byzantine attack may compromise the reliability of the middleware operations. The strategy to organize nodes into groups using secret sharing technique t-over-n increases the system protection against these attacks. Then, a malicious node must compromise, at least, other t nodes to perform any malicious activity on behalf of a group, making its actions more difficult and limited. Also, similar to selfish attack, the trust management provides ways for nodes to inform other ones if they detect some byzantine behavior. Thus, based on trust information, byzantine nodes can be isolated.

(iii) Impersonation Attacks. An attacker may steal the identity of a node and compromise the system reliability issuing false information on behalf of this node. A key management service is implemented to prevent this kind of attack against the system. All secure services provided by the middleware use cryptography. By using the key management, the middleware ensures that an identity belongs to the node that is using it. Thus, an attacker needs to compromised the entire key management component to be success on this kind of malicious action. Also, a secure communication service provided by the group management is implemented which increases the reliability of SEMAN against impersonation attacks, ensuring that only members of a closed group are able to decrypt a message sent to this group.

(iv) Sybil Attack. In a Sybil attack, a malicious node creates a false identity and gets the authorization of other nodes to have this false identity accepted in the system. Then, system reliability is affected, since a unique node may perform several activities on behalf of a group. Similar to impersonation attack, key management helps to prevent the action of a Sybil attacker. As the identity of a node is certified by the key management, it is necessary that an attacker compromises the

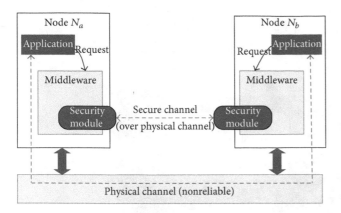

FIGURE 1: Reliable communication using a secure middleware.

key management scheme to be able to create a false identity and issue a valid public/private key pair to this new identity. Also, the secure communication of the group management component increases the reliability of SEMAN against this attack. As the secure communication service ensures that only the members of a closed group are able to decrypt a message sent to a group, it prevents a node from creating a false identity and from using this identity to receive messages sent to a group that it is not a member of.

This section presented the network characteristics addressed in this work and the attack model considered. Four kinds of attacks and how they may compromise the network behavior, performance, and operations were described.

3. Secure Middleware for Mobile Ad Hoc Networks

This section describes the SEMAN, the new context-based middleware that utilizes a group approach to support decision making related to security. Based on [4], context-based solutions are more suitable for MANETs. Further, the group approach facilitates the nodes organization on the contexts and security-related decision making. Figure 1 illustrates how applications may use the middleware to perform a reliable communication over an unreliable physical channel.

SEMAN provides support to secure and reliable communications between multiple nodes in scenarios susceptible to malicious attacks. It is composed of distributed modules and a set of group-based cryptographic operations. To support middleware operations, nodes with similar requirements form groups. These groups, called context groups, are self-organized and dynamically formed with no user interaction, considering only applications profiles and requirements. Services are provided and utilized by the applications in a context and, consequently, they are made available to nodes that belong to groups of this context.

SEMAN is composed of a communication interface, a catalog, and three modules: services, processing, and security, as illustrated in Figure 2. Applications requests may be sent either to the middleware or to lower layers. Without loss of generality, only the former scenario is considered in this

paper. All message exchanges between the middleware and the applications are performed by using the communication interface, which classifies messages and deliveries them to the correct module or application.

The catalog is composed of a nonvolatile memory and is responsible for keeping all pending requests and security information about applications and nodes, like cryptographic keys, trust information, credential, and so forth. It is important to ensure the resistance in, at least, three scenarios: (i) node crash; (ii) network disconnection; and (iii) long delays in service provisioning. These situations may result either from a malicious action or from the dynamic behavior of MANETs.

The next subsections present the main characteristics and functionalities of the three modules and their components.

3.1. Services Module. The services module is responsible for keeping a list and details of all services and applications hosted by the node to other nodes. It encompasses the resource management, mobility management, and distributed storage. All these components are accessed by internal and external applications.

3.1.1. Resource Management. A service that provides information about location and availability of resources, as nodes, remote services, and contents, is very important for MANETs [8]. This service must consider the following restrictions: (i) mitigate the communication overhead, avoiding unneeded updates about available resources; (ii) be independent of nodes geographical position; and (iii) be independent of routing protocol. This component must consider the resources discovery and allocation, as well as their location management.

Resource management must offer, at least, four subcomponents, as depicted in Figure 3: allocation, registration, discovery, and location of resources. Each subcomponent requests and provides information to processing and security modules. For example, the security module provides information about nodes and applications authorization, while the resource allocation subcomponent provides information about the use of resources to the processing module.

Information about resources is locally stored and available to all local applications that use the middleware services. Also, this information can be available to other nodes, considering their context and permissions. The control access is maintained by security module and is based on context group formation.

3.1.2. Mobility Management. This component is particularly important, since mobile nodes can move and change their geographical positions unpredictably, affecting the performance of distributed applications. Besides nodes mobility, this service must consider the applications mobility, which can migrate from a node to another. To provide an effective service to applications, it contains three subcomponents, as depicted in Figure 4: location management, transfer management, and disconnection management.

Location management must provide information about nodes physical location to applications. Thus, it is assumed

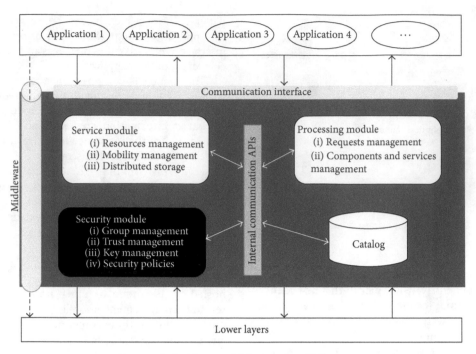

FIGURE 2: Architecture of the secure middleware.

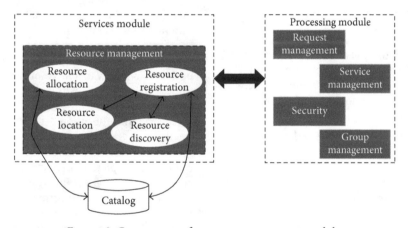

FIGURE 3: Components of resource management module.

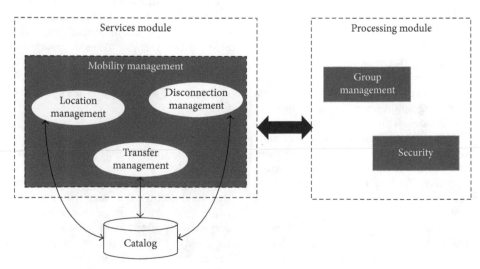

FIGURE 4: Components of mobility management module.

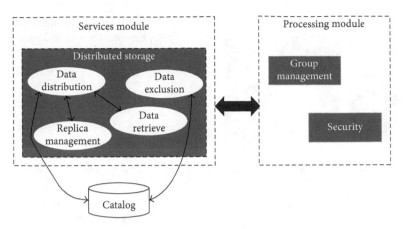

FIGURE 5: Components of distributed storage component.

that members of a group keep their location up-to-date in this group. Transfer management must allow mobile applications to keep the connection during a migration. It aims to mitigate the delay of applications transfers and to eliminate applications losses resulting from the migration. Finally, disconnection management must provide information about the reachability or disconnections of nodes that provide services through SEMAN.

3.1.3. Distributed Storage. This component allows nodes to store their information in a distributed, secure, dynamic, and self-organized way. It does not depend on any specific node availability and must be highly resistant to malicious attacks. Its main objective is to distribute context information to nodes of a group related to this context. This context information is fragmented into the network, and the absence of some nodes should not affect the stored data retrieval.

It is composed of four subcomponents, illustrated in Figure 5: data distribution, data retrieve, replica management, and data exclusion. All these components have a relationship with security and group management modules.

Data distribution is responsible for disseminating information to remote nodes. Data retrieve handles the access requests and locates remote data. Replica management is responsible for keeping enough active replicas to ensure the information availability and the data consistency. Exclusion data guarantees that when requested, data will be excluded from all remote nodes in which it is stored.

3.2. Processing Module. Processing module is responsible for keeping the central operation of SEMAN. It is composed of requests management and services and components management.

3.2.1. Requests Management. This component is responsible for keeping a registration of all services requests made to the middleware. It keeps the registration of both pending and attended requests.

An application is able to use, simultaneously, one or more services provided by the middleware. Due to the dynamic characteristics of MANETs, applications may not be aware of

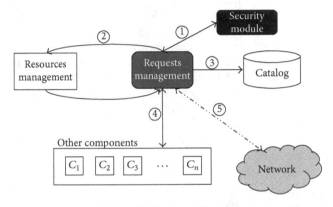

FIGURE 6: Services requests.

which services are being provided in a given time or which nodes are hosting these services. Figure 6 depicts how a service request is operated by SEMAN. Upon receiving a request, the request management component gets the security parameters with the security module. Then, it must check the availability of the requested service with the resource management component. If the service is provided by the middleware, it stores the information about the request into the catalog, performs the required communications with other components, and sends the request to the corresponding nodes.

As services may be provided by more than one node, SEMAN might

(1) request the service to all nodes that provide it, increasing the service availability and reducing the reply time;

(2) distribute the requests among nodes that provide it, making a load balance; or

(3) choose the more reliable node based on previous experiences.

During the service provisioning, the middleware may provide mechanisms to prevent malicious attacks. It must authenticate and authorize applications. Also, all messages exchanged with the middleware must be ciphered, to prevent eavesdropping.

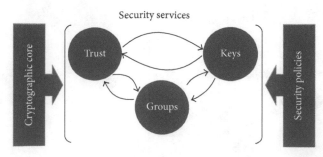

FIGURE 7: Security module diagram.

3.2.2. Services and Components Management. This component has a simple but essential function to the middleware operation. It is responsible for keeping a registration of all services and components provided by SEMAN. When a user wants to make a service available, through the middleware, this services must be previously registered. All relevant information of the new service, as security policies and context, must be stored into catalog. Then, other nodes can be informed about the availability of the new service.

This component must provide primitives to the registration of new services, as well the query of provided services. Similarly, for each registered component, it is necessary to store information about access strategies and services requirements.

3.3. Conclusion. This section presented an overview of SEMAN, its modules, and main characteristics. All next section will detail the security operations and module and how they will provide security to the middleware applications.

4. Security Module

This module is the central point of SEMAN. Its components, as depicted in Figure 7, include key management, trust management, and group management. These components operate with cryptographic operations and security policies components, which provide basic security primitives to the module.

Security services use a context-based group approach. All management operations and decision making are based on information provided by other members of the context group. Thus, nodes cooperate among themselves to increase the reliability of available services. However, the use of all components is not mandatory.

4.1. Cryptographic Core. To ensure that messages are not prone to eavesdropping, all messages must be ciphered. Though any cryptographic mechanism can be used, identity-based ones seem to be more suitable for MANETs [9]. Symmetric schemes impose a high cost to manage pairwise secret keys, and when compared with traditional certificate-based asymmetric schemes, identity-based cryptography (IBC) presents at least three advantages [10]:

(1) does not require certificates, mitigating certificates storage, distribution, and verification cost;

(2) makes easy noninteractive key agreement, reducing communication and processing overhead;

(3) removes the requirement of destination public keys authentications before message sending.

Another advantage to use IBC on MANETs is that they have a simple key management and a reduced storage cost, if compared with other methods. On IBCs, the identity of a user, as e-mail or IP, is used to derive the node public key. Thus, all nodes are able to disclose the public key of other nodes without data exchange. However, IBCs present a drawback. Private key is generated and available by an entity known as Private Key Generator (PKG). This characteristic imposes an implementation challenge, since PKG can be a single point of failure. To mitigate the impact of a central PKG, in this work the PKG is distributed over the network.

4.2. Cryptographic Operations. SEMAN considers the use of identity-based cryptography. Any IBC can be used, depending on middleware requirements. Without loss of generality, the Boneh and Franklin scheme is employed [11].

The main algorithms to perform cryptographic operations and to support the secure communication between nodes are composed of configuration and extraction and encryption and decryption. The former two are detailed on Section 4.4, which discusses the key management, since they are related to system initialization and key issuing.

The encryption and decryption algorithms are presented as follows. Let $k \in \mathbb{Z}^+$ be a security parameter from security module and $\mathbb{G}$ a generator of BDH parameter.

(1) *Encryption*: to encrypt M using a public key of node i, follow the next steps:

  (a) calculate $\text{PK}_i = H_1(N_i)$;
  (b) choose a random $r \in \mathbb{Z}_q^*$;
  (c) generate the encrypted text $C = \langle rP, M \oplus H_2(g_i^r) \rangle$ in which $g_i = \hat{e}(N_i, \text{PK}_i) \in \mathbb{G}_2^*$.

(2) *Decryption*: let $C = \langle U, V \rangle$ be the encrypted text using the public key of node i. To decrypt the message the private key SK_i is necessary. The following formula shows as text may be decrypted:

$$V \oplus H_2\left(\hat{e}\left(\text{SK}_i, U\right)\right) = M. \tag{1}$$

The proof of these algorithms can be found in [11].

4.3. Trust Management. Though cryptography may be used to ensure communication security, it does not provide information about the reliability of the nodes [12]. Further, many cryptographic mechanisms, such as key management [13, 14], rely on some degree of preestablished trust between nodes. However, trust in any kind of open network is very difficult to be valued and has received a lot of attention from the security community [15].

In a previous work [16, 17], TRUE was presented to evaluate the trust between pairwise communicating nodes. TRUE uses the concept of trust chains formed between nodes by

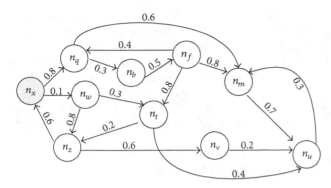

FIGURE 8: Example of trust chain G_{tr}^x from node n_x.

direct monitoring and recommendations of physical neighbors. It supports applications in an autonomous and dynamic way, while keeping the ability to resist malicious attacks. In this approach, each node creates in a self-organized strategy a trust network based on context, to provide trust information represented by a direct graph $G_{tr} = (V_{tr}, E_{tr})$, in which vertexes V_{tr} are the nodes and edges E_{tr} are the trust relationships between them. The trust network, or trust graph, contains all trust information which a node has about other nodes in a context. This information, or evidences, is gathered via direct interaction or by recommendations, considering the system security policies. The trustworthiness of a node is always locally computed, with no kind of message exchange, based on the trust network. In the next subsection are briefly presented the operation of the TRUE and its procedures and an evaluation of the proposed service.

4.3.1. Building Context-Based Trust Networks. When joining the system, each node N_i creates its own trust network $G_{tr}^i = (V_{tr}^i, E_{tr}^i)$ in a self-organized way. Initially, nodes have knowledge only about nodes with which they have direct trust relations, and only such data is stored in the trust network. Then, in predetermined time intervals (ΔT_{ex}), nodes exchange trust evidences with their physical neighbors, propagating trust values through the network in an epidemic behavior [18, 19].

During trust information exchange, each node evaluates the relevance of the received evidences by calculating the trustworthiness of the sender. Then, it decides whether it accepts or not such evidences, based on local policy rules. If it accepts the trust evidences, then it incorporates the received information on its context-based trust network. Otherwise, trust evidences are discarded.

4.3.2. Trust Evaluation. To evaluate the trust on node N_u, node N_x must either have a direct connection with node n_u in G_{tr}^x or it finds at least one trust chain (TC) from N_x to N_u in G_{tr}^x. Trust chains represent a transitive trust from N_x to N_u. The trust network graph G_{tr}^x is depicted in Figure 8. As node N_x can find several different trust chains between itself and N_u in G_{tr}^x, each chain is denoted as $TC_{(N_x, N_u)}^i$.

If N_x has a direct trust with N_u, only this value is considered on trust evaluation. Otherwise, it tries to find a trust

path in G_{tr}^x. Upon finding a chain, node N_x must compute its trust. Consider N_1 to N_m as the m intermediary nodes in the ith trust chain, denoted as $TC_{(N_x, N_u)}^i$; (2) estimates the trustworthiness of $TC_{(N_x, N_u)}^i$:

$$TC_{(N_x, N_u)}^i = TV_{(N_x, N_1)} \times \prod_{j=1}^{m-1} TV_{(N_j, N_{j+1})} \times TV_{(N_m, N_u)}. \quad (2)$$

Returning to Figure 8, there are several chains between n_x and n_u, for example,

(1) chain ($N_x \rightarrow N_q \rightarrow N_m \rightarrow N_u$), trust chain value $TC_{(N_x, N_u)}^1 = 0.8 \times 0.6 \times 0.7 = 0.336$;

(2) chain ($N_x \rightarrow N_q \rightarrow N_b \rightarrow N_f \rightarrow N_m \rightarrow N_u$), trust chain value $TC_{(N_x, N_u)}^2 = 0.8 \times 0.3 \times 0.5 \times 0.8 \times 0.7 = 0.067$.

Furthermore, nodes can use a threshold value for each edge of the trust chain (β value). If at least one edge of the trust chain has a trust value below this threshold, the chain is discarded. After calculating the trust value for all chains, the trust value $TV_{(N_x, N_u)}$ can be calculated applying a weighted mean as follows:

$$TV_{(N_x, N_u)} = \frac{\sum_{i=1}^k \left(TC_{(N_x, N_u)}^i \times \left(1/\left| TC_{(N_x, N_u)}^i \right| \right) \right)}{\sum_{i=1}^k \left(1/\left| TC_{(N_x, N_u)}^i \right| \right)}. \quad (3)$$

The weighted mean reduces the impact of transitivity in trust chains. In fact, the greater the chain, the less reliable it is. Thus, this method aims to privilege small chains, following a social perspective.

4.4. Key Management. SEMAN employs identity-based cryptography (IBC) [20] to perform its cryptographic operations, which requires an entity acting as a Private Key Generator (PKG). As the PKG knows the master private key, it is able to decrypt or sign messages on behalf of any client, without any active attack and without being detected. This problem is known as key escrow. These issues have been considered the main drawback that leads to the low adoption of IBC outside closed environments [21]. Boneh and Franklin suggested distributing the PKG to handle these problems using secret sharing schemes (n, t), in which n nodes form a distributed PKG (D-PKG) and only a subset of $t + 1$ nodes is able to compute the master private key [11].

Several identity-based key management schemes have been designed for MANETs and most of them consider the distribution of the PKG [9]. However, proposed schemes do not consider all characteristics of these networks.

In a previous work [22], the Identity-based Fully Self Organized (iFUSO) key management service was presented, which can be integrated with SEMAN. The iFUSO considers an asynchronous network composed of n nodes, represented by $N_1, N_2, \ldots, N_n$, in which malicious nodes can compromise at most t nodes and $t < n$. It considers that only trusted nodes participate in the system initialization. Nodes which initialize the system are called founding nodes, denoted by $N_{\mathscr{F}}$.

These nodes form the distributed PKG (D-PKG) in a fully distributed way. No node knows the master private key, since it is distributed in t-over-n threshold scheme. Also, to adapt to the dynamism of the network, iFUSO allows nodes to join or leave the D-PKG.

To prevent the system from cryptanalysis attacks, the iFUSO provides a way to update public and private keys of nodes, similar to [23, 24]. The key update may occur either periodically according to a predetermined interval, or reactively when the number of revoked nodes reaches a threshold value. Nodes are able to update their public keys autonomously and their private key by requesting to the D-PKG. Further, the iFUSO supports both implicit and explicit revocations.

4.4.1. Initialization.

The iFUSO must be initialized by a set of m founding nodes ($N_{\mathscr{F}}$), which must be able to securely exchange information to initialize the system. As the first step of the initialization, nodes must determine

(1) the system size n and the security threshold t;

(2) p, q: two large prime numbers, in which q divides ($p-1$);

(3) $\mathbb{G}_1$: a cyclic additive group with order p;

(4) a generator $g \in \mathbb{G}_1$;

(5) $\mathbb{G}_2$: a cyclic multiplicative group with order p;

(6) the pairing type making sure that there exists a bilinear paring $e : \mathbb{G}_1 \times \mathbb{G}_1 \to \mathbb{G}_2$ of the chosen type;

(7) $\mathscr{G} = \langle e, \mathbb{G}_1, \mathbb{G}_2 \rangle$.

This step can be performed jointly by nodes which are initializing the group, or proposed by one node to the others.

To initialize the system, founding nodes set up the D-PKG, generating the master public key and its corresponding master private key. The D-PKG is built in a distribute t-over-n way among the n founding nodes.

4.4.2. New Members Joining the D-PKG.

In a MANET it is very important for a D-PKG to be highly dynamic and decentralized, and new nodes must be able to join the distributed PKG at any time. Thus, these nodes must receive a share of MSK, computed by at least t members of the D-PKG.

If a new node N_k wants to join the D-PKG, it must contact at least t members of the D-PKG to get the corresponding information from these nodes. The join of new nodes to the D-PKG must follow the following:

(1) node N_k selects t members of D-PKG, denoted by Ω;

(2) node N_k requests each node of Ω to be accepted as a member of the D-PKG;

(3) each node $N_j \in \Omega$ sends a piece of information $f(j,k) = S_j^k$ back to N_k;

(4) after receiving t replies, N_k can compute its polynomial share MSK_k using a Lagrange interpolation.

4.4.3. Issuing Node Private Key.

The iFUSO is composed of a number of continuous, nonoverlapping key update phases, denoted by p_Δ, in which Δ represents the phase index. As in [23], each p_Δ is associated with a unique binary phase string denoted as str_Δ. For each N_i, its public key is represented by $\text{PK}_i = H_1(N_i)$ while the corresponding private key is represented by $\text{SK}_i = (\text{PK}_i)^{\text{MSK}}$. Recalling that in the iFUSO no node knows MSK, which is generated and stored in a fully distributed way. To retrieve its private key SK_i, node N_i must request the D-PKG for it and to wait for at least t replies. Thus, the following steps must be executed:

(1) N_i must select at least t nodes from the D-PKG. This set of nodes is denoted by Ψ. To minimize the requesting time, the Ψ has all nodes of the D-PKG;

(2) N_i requests its share of SK_i to each node in Ψ;

(3) each node $N_j \in \Psi$ sends back to N_i a share of the private key $\sigma_i^j = (\text{PK}_i)^{\text{MSK}_j}$;

(4) upon receiving at least t replies, N_i computes its private key SK_i as

$$\text{SK}_i = \prod_{k \in \Psi} \left(\sigma_i^k \right)^{\lambda_k}, \tag{4}$$

in which $\lambda_k = \prod_{k \in \Psi} (k/(k-i))$ are appropriate Lagrange coefficients.

4.4.4. Key Renewing.

To prevent attacks against the distributed PKG and potential threats resulting from compromised keys, a technique similar to the one proposed in [23], known as key update or key renewing, is employed. Security solutions based on key update are common practices on MANETs [25–27]. In the iFUSO, a new key update phase p_{i+1} starts after a predetermined time threshold. As all nodes must update their keys, if the members of the distributed PKG do not update the key of a given node N_a, it is (implicitly) considered revoked.

Each node N_a can autonomously update its public key $\text{PK}_{a,p_i} = (H_1(N_a), H_1(\text{str}_i))$, in which $\text{str}_i = \text{str}_{i-1} + 1$. On the other hand, generating the phase private key involves at least t members of the D-PKG. A given node N_z, member of the D-PKG, sends a request to at least $t-1$ other members of the D-PKG.

4.4.5. Key Revocation.

The iFUSO also provides techniques to verify if the public key of a node is revoked. Key revocations must be handled within the system, as nodes must be able to immediately verify the status of a public key [28]. Almost all key management schemes for MANETs consider the key revocation based on expiration time [29]. However, this is not sufficient since nodes must be able to revoke keys before expiration, as consequence of a compromise key or malicious behavior.

Thus, iFUSO supports both implicit and explicit revocations. If any node is not allowed to recover the common private key during a given phase p_i, then it is neither able to encrypt nor able to decrypt any information during this phase and is considered implicitly revoked.

On the other hand, the explicit revocation of the *i*FUSO is based on a list of revoked nodes stored by nodes themselves. Upon detecting the misbehavior of node N_a, node N_b generates a signed accusation message against N_a, which must be sent to the D-PKG. To avoid the interception of the accusation message, it is sent via broadcast encryption. This technique, besides decreasing the communication cost of revocation, increases the security since the malicious nodes are not able to read the accusation message.

Upon receiving an accusation message against N_a from N_b, a member of the D-PKG, will drop it if N_b has been previously revoked. Otherwise, it saves the accusation message. To prevent false accusations against legitimate nodes, a node N_a is diagnosed as compromised just when the accusations against it reach a revocation threshold γ in a predetermined time window. The value of γ defines the trade-off between the false accusations tolerance and the compromise detectability. Once the revocation threshold is reached, a key revocation against node N_a is generated and published.

4.5. Group Management.

This section presents how the group management must be carried out to support the activities of SEMAN. It this paper, a group is a set of nodes sharing common interests and willing to cooperate on activities related to this interest. This "common interest" is also called *context*. Context information must be frequently updated and made available to other nodes, to allow the efficient organization of groups [30].

Due to several varieties of services provided by a middleware, many kind of distinct groups may be formed, with different mobility pattern, lifetime, organization strategies, internal politics, and joining rules characteristics. However, independent of group characteristics, system must provide resources management to allow the creation and update of existing groups and their profiles.

To support several kinds of applications, with strong and light security restrictions, two group management techniques are used: *yellow pages* and *closed groups*. Yellow pages groups, or open groups, provide primitives allowing nodes to freely form groups and to avail services related to its context. As these groups are open, they do not consider the trustworthiness of their members. Thus, these groups are indicated to services that require a lower trust level or when applications themselves are responsible for this task.

Closed groups use trust management information at their formation. Thus, all services provided by members of a closed context group obey the preestablished security requirements. Also, both internal and external group secure communication are allowed.

4.5.1. Storage Information about Existing Groups.

In SEMAN, context groups are considered services available in the network. Information about the existence of groups and their main features must be available to nodes that want to participate in these groups or to enjoy services provided by them. To this end, it is important that the middleware provides ways to manage this information and make it available during its operations. Many architectures were proposed to organize the service provisioning on MANETs. An initial study about

these architectures can be found in [31]. Solutions can be classified into with directories and without directories.

In the first approach, information about groups is stored in a directory which can be centralized or distributed. Nodes which store information about directories are called server nodes. Every time a node wants to provide a data, it finds out some server node and requests the storage of this data. On the other hand, a node that wants to use this data needs only to contact a server node and gets a list of nodes which are providing it.

In the second approach, information about groups is not stored in a directory and must be propagated or requested when needed. Thus, when a node wants to provide a service in the network, it diffuses this information, in order to reach the higher number of nodes. It can be employed by global or controlled flooding techniques. When a node wants to use a service and it does not have local information about this service, it requests such an information in the network, via global or controlled flooding.

There is not a consensus about which strategy is more suitable for MANETs. Group discovery is considered good when presenting a high availability, keeping a low communication cost and small delays. Thus, if the network has just few service requirements, a strategy without directories with on demand queries would be more suitable. On the other hand, a network with many services but with few queries would generate unnecessary communications to keep information about these services.

Any one of these architectures may be used on SEMAN. In this work, the use of a fully distributed directories architecture is considered. When a new group is created, its information is disseminated in the network. All nodes locally store information about groups. Thus, every time a node needs information about a group, it may get it locally, without delays or additional costs.

4.5.2. Yellow Pages.

The first group formation strategy in the SEMAN is called *yellow pages*. This technique, based in the traditional yellow pages, works as a directory of services, fully open and dynamic. Group formation is directly related to some kind of provided service. When a node wants to provide a service, it informs the middleware, which propagates this information to all other nodes, to make them aware of the new service.

When another node wants to use a service, it requests to the middleware a list of nodes which are providing the service. Based on this list, the node may request or not the service considering information from the trust management module.

This kind of approach is important in providing services without a high level of security. Any node can freely participate in a group and provide a given service. Client applications can, therefore, determinate the trust level they want in a service. Thus, the middleware, based on information provided by the trust management module can select the more trustworthy nodes which are providing the service.

Formation of an Open Group. Before initiating a group, a node needs to certify that there is no other group with the same characteristics of the new one. To this, it queries its local directory. If the group already exists, the node joins this group (Section 4.5.2). Otherwise, it creates the new group.

When a node wants to form a new context group, it defines all main features of this group, as identifier, mobility pattern, context information, service provided, and initial nodes. Other information may be included to make the group management easier. Then, it disseminates this information through the network, as discussed in Section 4.5.1.

Joining and Leaving an Open Group. When a node wants to participate in an open group G_α, it needs to create a message informing that it is providing the same services as described in the group G_α profile. Then, it must disseminate this information through the network, in order that all nodes be aware that it is providing such services. Note that there is no strategy to block the participation of nodes on open groups. Any node may send a message informing that it is participating in this group.

Similarly, when a node wants to leave a group, it just creates a message informing that it is leaving the group and disseminates this information through the network. However, as this message is not mandatory, or nodes may leave unpredictably and involuntary the network, is necessary some technique are necessary to ensure the consistency of nodes participating in a group. Thus, the node which has created the group, or the older one, periodically performs queries to members, checking their availability. So, at the end of a cycle, a list of available nodes is disseminated into network. It is important that checking interval be not so small in order to prevent a high communication overhead.

Using Secure Services of Open Groups. Open groups do not provide native secure communication methods between members or to service requests. As nodes are able to freely join groups, the group key establishment is difficult. But this does not block that services provided by open groups require ciphered and signed message requests.

When a node wants to request any service to members of an open group, it makes a request directly to these nodes, by using either unicast or multicast messages. If it wants to use ciphered messages, it may use the security primitives provided by the middleware for communication between nodes, supported by cryptographic operations and key management components.

4.5.3. Closed Groups.

While some services may be supported by an open group management scheme, other services require a more controlled management. In this case, the middleware provides a dynamic closed group management service to applications. These groups are formed based on applications context, interest, and security requirements.

An example of closed groups is the key management described in Section 4.4 and in [22], which requires a high trustworthy and restrict service. This section describes the closed group management operations, as group formation, new members joining, and leaving.

Closed Group Formation. As previously assumed, groups are formed based on applications context. Each node is able to autonomously promote the formation of a group without a central entity or a group manager. During the group formation, the creator node must only specify the group profile and security requirements.

A group may be composed of a set of nodes, with a unique assumption: these nodes must be able to securely exchange information to initialize the group. Then, to start a group nodes must determinate

(1) group size n and the security threshold t;

(2) p and q: two large prime numbers, in which q divides $(p-1)$;

(3) $\mathbb{G}_1$: a cyclic additive group of order p;

(4) generator $g \in \mathbb{G}_1$;

(5) $\mathbb{G}_2$: a cyclic multiplicative group of order p;

(6) the paring type to ensure that exists a bilinear paring $e : \mathbb{G}_1 \times \mathbb{G}_1 \to \mathbb{G}_2$ to the choose paring;

(7) $\mathcal{G} = \langle e, \mathbb{G}_1, \mathbb{G}_2 \rangle$.

These values must be defined by all nodes through an agreement approach or may be proposed by a founder node to the other ones. After that, each founder node must have the following public elements:

(1) prime numbers p and q;

(2) generator g and cyclic additive group $\mathbb{G}_1$;

(3) cyclic multiplicative group $\mathbb{G}_2$;

(4) $\mathbb{Z}_q^*$: an elliptic field with order q;

(5) $H_1(x)$: a *hash* function in which $H_1(x) = \{0,1\}^* \to \mathbb{G}_1^*$;

(6) $H_2(x)$: a *hash* function in which $H_2(x) = \mathbb{G}_2 \to \mathbb{Z}_p^*$.

To initialize the group, nodes must generate a public identification of this group and a signature. This signature is distributed between group members by using a threshold cryptographic scheme (m, t) among the m founder nodes, as follows:

(1) Each node N_i chooses a bivariate symmetric polynomial function $f_i(x, y)$ over $\mathbb{Z}_q^*$ in which the two variables x and y must be at most order t. The polynomial function is described as

$$f_i(x, y) = \sum_{k=0}^{t} \sum_{j=0}^{t} a_{k,j}^i x^k y^j, \tag{5}$$

in which $a_{k,j}^i \in \mathbb{Z}_q^*$, $a_{k,j}^i = a_{j,k}^i$, and $a_{0,0}^i = z_i$.

(2) Each N_i computes $f_l^i(x)$ for all N_l founder nodes as

$$f_l^i(x) = f_i(x, l) = \sum_{k=0}^{t} \sum_{j=0}^{t} a_{k,j}^i x^k l^j. \tag{6}$$

Then, N_i securely sends $f_l^i(x)$ to N_l.

(3) Each node N_i computes its share of the signature Sign_i:

$$\text{Sign}_i = f_i(x) = \sum_{j=1}^{n} f_i^j(x) = \sum_{j=1}^{n} f_j(x, i) = f(x, i). \quad (7)$$

(4) Signature Sign is not known by any node but is defined as

$$\text{Sign} = \sum_{N_i \in m} \text{Sign}_i \bmod q. \quad (8)$$

Each node N_i, after computing its share Sign_i, publishes g^{Sign_i}. When nodes receive t shares, they are able to compute the group identity as $\text{ID} = \sum_{i=1}^{t} g^{\text{Sign}_i}$. Then, the group identity ID can be published to all other nodes.

After group formation, nodes which want to collaborate in a specific context or interest must search a group and request its participation in this group. As each group is set with its profile and security requirements, nodes themselves may decide whether available groups attend their own interests.

Joining. As describe in Section 4.5.3, each closed group has its profile and requirements. Thus, nodes themselves may decide on participating or not of a group. If a node N_x wants to join a group G_α it must request to G_α members the participation authorization. To be able to join G_α, N_x needs the approval of at least t members. The following steps must be performed:

(1) node N_x chooses t nodes of group G_α, denoted by Ω;

(2) node N_x requests each node of Ω to be accepted as member of group G_α;

(3) each node $N_j \in \Omega$ sends an information share $f(j, k)$ back to node N_k;

(4) upon receiving t replies, N_x may compute its polynomial share Sign_x by using Lagrange interpolation:

$$\text{Sign}_k = S_k(x) = \sum_{j=1}^{t} \lambda_j S_j^k = \sum_{j=1}^{t} \lambda_j f(j, k) = f(x, k). \quad (9)$$

After computing Sign_x, N_x is able to participate in all group operations.

Members Exclusion. When a node does not attend anymore the security or trust requirement of a group, it must have its participation revoked. To this, signed accusation messages are employed with a list of revoked associations. When a given node N_x has a number of accusations higher than a threshold γ, it has its association revoked. The value of γ is a group parameter, defined on its creation profile.

When a node N_a, based on information provided by trust management, believes that N_x does not satisfy anymore the group requirements, it issues a signed accusation message and sends it to all other group members. To thwart excluded nodes from receiving this message, the signed accusation message must be unknown by them. Thus, a variant of

the identity-based broadcast encryption proposed on [32] is used.

Let $\mathscr{E}$ be the set of excluded nodes; then node N_a generates the parameters for the broadcast encryption:

(1) $\forall i \in \mathscr{N} \setminus \mathscr{E}$ computes $\text{PK}_i = H_1(N_i)$;

(2) it randomly selects $r \in \mathbb{Z}_p^*$ and $\forall i \in \mathscr{N} \setminus \mathscr{E}$ computes $s_i = H_2(\widehat{e}(\text{PK}_i^r, \text{MPK}))$;

(3) it randomly selects $k \in \mathbb{Z}_p^*$ and computes a message encrypting key $K = \widehat{e}(g, g)^k$;

(4) it randomly selects $\alpha \in \mathbb{Z}_p^*$;

(5) it computes $\text{Hdr} = (C_1, C_2, C_3)$ in which

$$C_1 = g^r;$$
$$C_2 = (g^\alpha)^k; \quad (10)$$
$$C_3 = \left\{ c_i = \left(g^{1-1/\alpha}\right)^{1/s_i} \right\}_{N_i \in \mathscr{N} \setminus \mathscr{E}}.$$

After that, N_a has the key K and Hdr and uses K to encrypt the accusation message K, generating C_K. Finally, N_z broadcasts the ciphered message (Hdr, C_K).

When a nonrevoked node N_b receives this message, it is able to retrieve the accusation message K encapsulated in the header Hdr, using its private key SK_b, as follows:

(1) computes $s_i = H_2(\widehat{e}(\text{SK}_b, C_1))$;

(2) retrieves c_i from C_3 and computes

$$\widehat{e}\left(C_2^{-1}, c_i^{s_i}\right) \times \widehat{e}(g, C_2)$$
$$= \widehat{e}\left(\left((g^\alpha)^k\right)^{-1}, \left(\left(g^{1-1/\alpha}\right)^{1/s_i}\right)^{s_i}\right) \times \widehat{e}g, (g^\alpha)^k \quad (11)$$
$$= \widehat{e}(g, g)^{-k(\alpha-1)} \times \widehat{e}(g, g)^{k\alpha} = K.$$

With K, node N_b is able to decrypt the encrypted message C_K, extracting the accusation message K. Upon receiving γ accusations, each node creates an association revocation register and stores it locally in a revoked associations list. This list may be made publicly available to all nodes, in order that external member be aware that N_x is no longer authorized to provide service in name of the group.

4.6. Conclusion. This section presented the security module and its components. Cryptographic operations, trust management, group management, and key management components were detailed. Also, how these components will ensure security to the middleware was explained.

5. Secure Group Communication

To allow secure group communication, the use of a group key agreement protocol is proposed. This kind of protocol allows that a group of users exchange information over an insecure and public communication channel and agree on a secret key to be used to derive a session key. Then, the session key can be used to ensure requirements as authentication, confidentiality, and integrity.

The group key agreement approach is attractive to dynamic networks since it does not require the presence of a central controller or a leader. In this case, all users generate the key session. Thus, no node is able to control or to predict the session key. This kind of approach has been widely employed in distributed and collaborative applications, as file sharing, distributed computing, and audio and video conferences, among others.

Several proposals to session group key establishment can be found in the literature [33–35]. Any scheme that makes use of identity-based approach may be easily employed in the SEMAN. Without the loss of generality, the scheme proposed by Zhang et al. in [35] is assumed. An advantage of this scheme is that it allows outside group nodes to send ciphered messages to group members. This makes the secure service request to closed groups easier.

In the key agreement, members of a group G_α issue signed messages. The union of all signed messages issued by them form a group encryption key, called GEK_α, which may be public. However, only members of the group are able to derive the group decryption key GDK_α. The next subsections present the key agreement operations and the group encryption and decryption key generation.

5.1. Agreement. A given node N_i, with the private key SK_i and member of group G_α, must perform the following steps to carry out the key agreement:

(1) to choose a random number $\eta_i \in \mathbb{Z}_q^*$;

(2) to compute $r_i = g^{\eta_i}$;

(3) to choose a random number $k \in \mathbb{Z}_q^*$;

(4) to compute $g_1 = g^k$;

(5) for all $1 \le j \le n$, to compute $f_j = H_2(N_j)$, in which $H_2(x)$ is a hash function;

(6) for all $1 \le j \le n$, to compute $z_{i,j} = \text{SK}_i f_j^{\eta_i}$;

(7) to publish $\sigma_i = (r_i, \varrho_i, \{z_{i,j}\}_{j \in \{1,\dots,n\}, j \ne i})$.

In this case, ϱ_i is the identity-based signature on value r_i. Element $z_{i,j} = \text{SK}_i f_j^{\eta_i}$ is not published, but kept secret by node n_i.

5.2. Encryption Key Generation and Use. To get a group encryption key, a node firstly checks the n tuple of signature message $(r_1, \varrho_1), \dots, (r_n, \varrho_n)$. If all signatures are valid, then it computes

$$w = \prod_{i=1}^{n} r_i,$$

$$Q = \hat{e}\left(\prod_{i=1}^{n} H_1(N_i), g_1\right). \tag{12}$$

Then, it sets the group encryption key as $\text{GEK} = (w, Q)$. To encrypt a message M, any node, member or not of the group, generates a ciphered text as follows:

(1) selects $\rho \in \mathbb{Z}_q^*$;

(2) computes $c_1 = g^\rho$, $c_2 = w^\rho$, and $c_3 = M \oplus H_3(Q^\rho)$;

(3) generates the ciphered text $c = (c_1, c_2, c_3)$.

After the ciphered text c generation, it can be sent through the network and only members of destination group are able to decrypt the transmitted message.

5.3. Decryption Key Generation and Use. Each node N_i checks the n tuples of signed messages $(r_1, \varrho_1), \dots, (r_n, \varrho_n)$. If all signatures are valid, node N_i computes $\text{GDK} = \prod_{j=1}^{n} z_{j,i}$ and makes the following verification:

$$\hat{e}(\text{GDK}_i, g) \overset{?}{=} \hat{e}(f_i, w) \cdot Q. \tag{13}$$

If the equation is correct, node N_i accepts the key GDK as decryption group key. Otherwise, it aborts the procedure.

When a node N_i, member of group, receives a ciphered message $c = (c_1, c_2, c_3)$, it uses the decryption key GDK as

$$M = c_3 \oplus H_3\left(\hat{e}(\text{GDK}, c_1)\hat{e}(f_i^{-1}, c_2)\right). \tag{14}$$

5.4. Conclusion. This section presented how to provide a secure group communication through SEMAN. How nodes may use cryptographic services to make an agreement and provide secure group communication to applications was discussed.

6. Components Integration in Different Scenarios

Policy management component is responsible for supporting the security module integrating the trust, key, and group management components. Thus, the development of strategies is fundamental to provide security in several scenarios in which applications may be provided by SEMAN.

This section discusses some cases, which show how the middleware may be used in different scenarios. Security parameters described to each scenario are configured on the security policy component, part of the security module. It is important to point out that several scenarios can be found in a unique network. Some applications may be better suitable to open scenarios, while other ones require a more rigorous security control. SEMAN allows the configuration of these different scenarios, since applications and nodes are organized into context, with profiles and security parameter set according to provided services.

Three scenarios are presented:

(i) *open*: indicated to applications which do not require a high security control;

(ii) *partially restrict*: indicated to applications which require an intermediary security support but do not require a rigid control on their operations;

(iii) *restrict*: indicated to applications which require a high security level on their operations.

To each presented scenario, distinct security policies are indicated. Table 1 illustrates how security components

Table 1: Security policies for distinct scenarios.

	Trust	Key	Groups
Restrict	Block evidence exchanges with nonreliable nodes	Allow the service to be provided to each distinct group t value greater than $n/2$	Prioritize closed group creation Trust restriction to group joining
Partially restrict	Trust values of α and β between 0.4 and 0.6	A unique system to all the middleware t value greater than $n/2$	Prioritize closed group creation Allow the service providing in closed groups
Open	Trust values of α and β less than 0.4	A unique system to all the middleware Small t value Great interval between updates	Most part of provided services in open groups

may be set to proposed scenarios. However, these scenarios parameters and politics are not static, and new environments and configurations may be proposed and configured by middleware users.

Next subsections detail these scenarios and how security components may be integrated in the service provisioning to applications. Each scenario discusses how SEMAN can ensure the desired security and the communication overhead imposed by it. However, the measurement of this kind of overhead is a complex task, since these values depend on several factors: group size, update interval, threshold values, and others. Then, a more realist approximation of the overhead is a future work.

6.1. Open Scenarios. A first scenario that SEMAN may be employed is an open environment, which requires a less rigorous security control. Several applications may provide services in an open scenario. An example is the data and file distributed storage service. In this case, users may share, for a while, data or files that do not require a high level of confidentiality and availability, as video or audio files.

(1) *Trust management*: adopting TRUE, values of α and β may be small, less than 0.4. Then, middleware will consider more nodes reliable on evaluated context. As a consequence, more nodes will be considered reliable to provide services in this context.

(2) *Key management*: using *iFUSO*, values of t may also be small, less than $m/2$, in which m is the members of D-PKG. Also, update interval may be high. Then, system overhead is reduced while the service is offered to users considering the defined parameters.

(3) *Group management*: in open scenarios, services may be provided in open groups, and users themselves can query the trust management component to decide by the use or not of the offered services.

Note that, in this scenario, a unique great group may be used to the key management of the entire middleware. Then, all applications which need cryptographic services use the same service.

To all other services provided in the network, the trust management may provide trust information on the context of these services. For example, a resource localization service have a different context than a distributed storage. Nodes

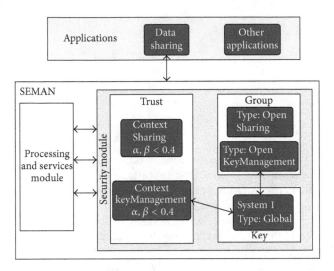

Figure 9: Open scenario.

which provide these services may be organized into open groups, but their users may use trust values to choose the best servers to their requirements.

Figure 9 illustrates a possible configuration of the security module to satisfy applications in an open scenario. In this case, the "data sharing" application requests services to the middleware. Services and processing modules reply application requests and, if necessary, make queries to the security module. In this scenario, trust management provide two contexts: "sharing" and "KeyManagement." Both have α and β values lower than 0.4.

The context KeyManagement is queried by the key management system for key issuing, revocation, and update. Though trust management values will be considered in the key issuing, threshold values to the acceptance are small. Thus, any node may request participation as a D-PKG member, making the group open, but the private master key is issued only if this node satisfies a minimal trust requirements.

The other context is called Sharing and may be queried by applications on the acceptance or not of services provided by members of an open group named "Sharing." Note that any node is able to participate in this group. If necessary, group members or client applications may query the global key management system to check the identity authenticity of any group member.

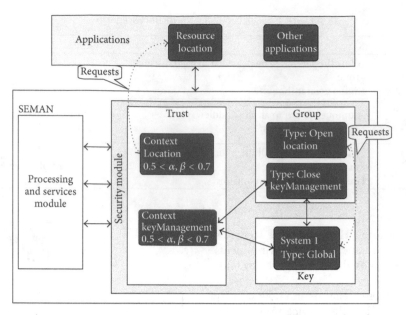

FIGURE 10: Partially restrict scenarios.

With these configurations, middleware provides just some security guarantees to applications. Applications which perform queries to trust management may receive unreliable information, since system is susceptible to false accusation attacks. The key management is vulnerable to impersonation attacks, since an attacker needs to compromise a small number of D-PKG members to be accepted and to receive its own private key or even to be a D-PKG member.

6.2. Partially Restrict Scenarios. A second scenario is a partially restrict scenario, in which an intermediary security control is necessary. A service example which can be classified as partially restrict is the resource localization. In this case, it is important to provide guarantees of nodes authenticity, but at same time it does not need to block any node to provide a service to applications.

In this case, security parameters and threshold values may be set with more restrictions than previous scenario. Hereafter, some suggestions are presented:

(1) *trust management*: using TRUE, α and β values may be between 0.5 and 0.7. Then, middleware will exchange information with nodes that have an intermediary trust evaluation in the context. As a consequence, the communication overhead will be smaller than previous scenario, while it keeps a higher control of transmitted information;

(2) *key management*: with *iFUSO*, t value for the master key sharing should be higher than $m/2$, to prevent network partitioning attacks. Further, key update intervals may not be large, to block unreliable nodes to be on the system for a long time;

(3) *group management*: in this scenario, some applications may be provided in closed groups, but the majority may be organized into open groups. Thus,

even all nodes being able to join a group and to provide services in this context, client applications may use trust management information to select the best node to request a service.

Note that in this scenario, a unique group may be used to the middleware-wide key management. Thus, all applications which need cryptography use the same service. As on open scenarios, the trust management must have information of a context which will be queried by key management, for example key-management. For all other provided services, the trust management may provide trust information on their own context.

Figure 10 illustrates how SEMAN components may be integrated to satisfy security requirements on partially restrict scenarios. "Resource location" application requests services to the middleware, which are received by the services and processing modules. When necessary, some queries are made to the security module. Two contexts are envisaged: KeyManagement and Location. On both contexts, trust management α and β values are between 0.5 and 0.7.

As in open scenarios, KeyManagement context is queried by the key management for key issuing, revocation, and update. However, only nodes of the closed group named "KeyManagement" are accepted to be members of the D-PKG. Thus, the participation of nodes as D-PKG members is more restrictive, making the system more reliable. Also, α and β parameters of the KeyManagement context may be increased, to ensure more security to key management and to client applications.

The other context is called Location and may be queried by application itself in the acceptance or not of services provided by members of group named "Location." As in the open groups, any node may be member of this group and, if necessary, client applications may query the global key management to check the identity authenticity of a node.

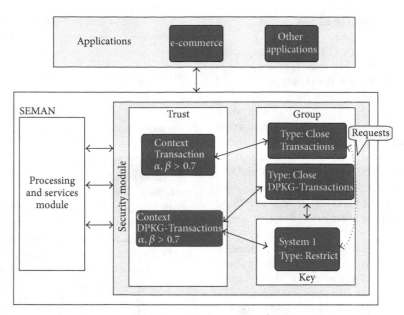

FIGURE 11: Restrict scenarios.

With these configurations the system should be protected against impersonation attacks. Also, higher α and β values make the propagation of false accusations against a node reputation more difficult. Thus, the middleware ensures, to users, the authenticity of nodes which are participating in these groups.

6.3. Restrict Scenarios. The third scenario is a restrict environment, in which a more rigorous security control is necessary. This context considers the applications which cannot be compromised in face of attacks. These applications perform, in general, essential tasks to users and, if affected by malicious attacks, may compromise the integrity of provided services. Examples are the e-commerce or financial transactions. These services may receive the guarantee from the middleware that they are protected against malicious attacks.

In this case, security parameters and threshold values must be set with many restrictions. The following are some suggestions:

(1) *trust management*: if TRUE is adopted, α and β values must be higher than 0.7. Then, middleware will exchange information only with reliable nodes in related context. As a consequence, less nodes will be able to join groups of this context;

(2) *key management*: with *i*FUSO, t values for master key sharing must be higher than $m/2$. Further, update phase interval cannot be high. Then, the system overhead is increased, but services provided will ensure security against malicious attacks;

(3) *group management*: in restrict scenarios, applications must be provided in closed groups, with a more restrictive control on group joining.

Note that for this kind of scenario, different key management group may be used, for each application. Thus, more restrictive applications may have their own context-related key management. This blocks malicious nodes, even the ones not participating in the group that is providing a service, to be a D-PKG member. On the other hand, a global key management scheme may be implemented to provide service to groups with less restrictive applications. For all other services, the trust management may provided trust information on the services context.

Figure 11 illustrates the integration of SEMAN components on restrict scenarios. E-commerce application requests services to middleware. Requests are received by the services and processing modules that if necessary query the security module. Two contexts are envisaged: DPKG-Transaction and Transaction. On both contexts, trust management has α and β values higher than 0.7.

The DPKG-Transaction is queried by the key management of closed group "Transaction." To this, group management allows the formation of a closed group called "DPKG-Transaction," which has only the nodes that satisfy the requirements to be a D-PKG member. These D-PKG members make queries to the closed group "Transactions" to check nodes reliability and issue private keys to them.

The other context is called Transactions and it is queried by members of closed group with same name, which are responsible for the acceptance or not of a new member, or by the exclusion of a current member. Unlike previous scenarios, to participate in a group, nodes need to satisfy the trust requirements defined by group policies, increasing the system security and protection against malicious attacks.

6.4. Hybrid Scenarios. Three distinct scenarios of security module configuration were presented. However, in practice, each application which is using the middleware services may present a different scenario. For example, at the same time, middleware may provide services to applications that require a high level of security and also to an open one. Thus, SEMAN security policies must be directed to applications and services contexts which use the security module.

A recommendation to the use of SEMAN in these scenarios is the setting of a global key management, which satisfies all services. Thus, the entire network is supported by a unique D-PKG and all users have a unique public/private key pair to use on all applications. Trust management must offer information about users in two contexts: key-management and key-management-dpkg.

Trust information about first context (key-management) is used by key management when D-PKG members perform users private key issuing, update, or revocation. In this case, users with trust value in this context less than a threshold (that must be high) will not have their keys issued or update by D-PKG members.

Trust information of the second context (key-management-dpkg) is used by D-PKG members on decisions about the acceptance or not of new D-PKG member. These restrictions must be higher than the key issuing restrictions. For example, a node can be authentic and has the right to have its private key issued by a D-PKG. However, it cannot be reliable enough to be member of D-PKG.

With a secure key management, middleware ensures the protection of cryptographic operations against malicious attacks and the authenticity of members. Thus, each application may be provided inside a context of closed or open groups, which requires a high level of reliability or allows that services to be provided by any node. Thus, each application will be protected against malicious actions depending of its own policies.

6.5. Conclusion. This section presented a study of some scenarios which SEMAN may be employed to satisfy applications requirements.

7. Conclusions and Future Directions

This paper proposed secure context-based middleware, called SEMAN, which employs a group approach to support security making decisions. The middleware architecture and an overview of its operations were discussed. Also, how SEMAN services must be provided and how group approach may be applied to ensure the security were presented.

SEMAN has three modules: services, processing, and security. The first two are responsible for providing services and for requests management. Security module is responsible for ensuring the security to applications that use the services provided by SEMAN. This module is composed of trust, key, and group management components. All these components were detailed, focusing on how they can be used to ensure the security to applications.

Security module components are integrated through policies management which is responsible for security parameters of each provided service. Further, all activities are supported by identity-based cryptographic operations. The integration of these components was discussed in distinct scenarios, in which some configuration suggestions were presented to satisfy applications requirements.

TABLE 2: Expected communication overhead.

	Trust	Key	Groups
Restrict	Low	Low	High
Partially restrict	Medium	Low	Medium
Open	High	Very low	Low

SEMAN provides security against selfish, impersonation, Sybil, and byzantine attacks. But other attacks can be found on MANET and may affect the middleware efficacy. At the end, some scenarios in which SEMAN may be employed were presented. These scenarios are classified into open, partially restrict, and restrict. Table 2 illustrates the expected overhead in each presented scenario. SEMAN does not impose a high communication overhead. Key management, for example, needs more messages exchanges during a group creation and update. However, key updates do not occur frequently.

Group management presents an overhead that depends on the way groups are organized. Closed groups have higher overhead than open ones. However, even closed groups have a higher communication cost only during group formation. Further, secure group communication allows multicast messages, decreasing the quantity of individual messages.

Trust management imposes a higher communication overhead when groups are open and, then, α and β values are smaller. However, even this higher quantity of messages is performed just among neighbor nodes, not affecting the entire network. Then, security module of SEMAN can be used to ensure the security requirements of application while not imposing a high communication overhead to network.

To increase the system reliability, new services can be integrated to SEMAN and may be performed in future work, as integrating with analysis tools of external environment, to help automatic and dynamic configuration of security policies; proposing the integration of SEMAN with other certificateless public key cryptography; implementing and evaluating the middleware in real scenarios; and designing an accounting scheme integrated with trust management to impede that denial of service attacks overhead the system with false control messages. Further, a study should be performed in order to reduce de requirements of exponential and pairing computations. Authors suggest the use of certificateless public key cryptography, or other alternative models, comparing their computational cost.

Competing Interests

The authors declare that they have no competing interests.

Acknowledgments

This study is partially funded by CNPq, Grants 448004/2013-6.

References

[1] B. Wu, J. Chen, J. Wu, and M. Cardei, "A survey of attacks and countermeasures in mobile ad hoc networks," in *Wireless Network Security*, Y. Xiao, X. S. Shen, and D.-Z. Du, Eds.,

Signals and Communication Technology, chapter 12, pp. 103–135, Springer, New York, NY, USA, 2007.

[2] P. Papadimitratos and Z. J. Haas, "Securing mobile ad hoc networks," in *The Handbook of Ad Hoc Wireless Networks*, chapter 21, pp. 457–481, CRC Press, Boca Raton, Fla, USA, 2005.

[3] R. Shirey, *RFC 2828: Internet Security Glossary*, EUA, Marina del Rey, Calif, USA, 2000, http://www.ietf.org/rfc/rfc2828.txt.

[4] E. da Silva and L. C. P. Albini, "Middleware proposals for mobile ad hoc networks," *Journal of Network and Computer Applications*, vol. 43, pp. 103–120, 2014.

[5] P. A. Bernstein, "Middleware: a model for distributed system services," *Communications of the ACM*, vol. 39, no. 2, pp. 86–98, 1996.

[6] J. Al-Jaroodi, I. Jawhar, A. Al-Dhaheri, F. Al-Abdouli, and N. Mohamed, "Security middleware approaches and issues for ubiquitous applications," *Computers and Mathematics with Applications*, vol. 60, no. 2, pp. 187–197, 2010.

[7] S. Hadim, J. Al-Jaroodi, and N. Mohamed, "Trends in middleware for mobile ad hoc networks," *Journal of Communications*, vol. 1, no. 4, pp. 11–21, 2006.

[8] I. Chlamtac, M. Conti, and J. J.-N. Liu, "Mobile ad hoc networking: imperatives and challenges," *Ad Hoc Networks*, vol. 1, no. 1, pp. 13–64, 2003.

[9] E. da Silva, A. L. dos Santos, L. C. P. Albini, and M. N. Lima, "Identity-based key management in mobile ad hoc networks: techniques and applications," *IEEE Wireless Communications*, vol. 15, no. 5, pp. 46–52, 2008.

[10] H.-Y. Chien and R.-Y. Lin, "Improved ID-based security framework for ad hoc network," *Ad Hoc Networks*, vol. 6, no. 1, pp. 47–60, 2008.

[11] D. Boneh and M. Franklin, "Identity-based encryption from the weil pairing," in *Advances in Cryptology—CRYPTO 2001*, J. Kilian, Ed., vol. 2139 of *Lecture Notes in Computer Science*, pp. 213–229, Springer, London, UK, 2001.

[12] X. Li, J. Slay, and S. Yu, "Evaluating trust in mobile ad hoc networks," in *Proceedings of the Workshop of International Conference on Computational Intelligence and Security (CIS '05)*, Springer, Xi'an, China, 2005.

[13] J. van der Merwe, D. Dawoud, and S. McDonald, "A survey on peer-to-peer key management for mobile ad hoc networks," *ACM Computing Surveys*, vol. 39, no. 1, article 1, Article ID 1216371, 2007.

[14] M. Nogueira, G. Pujolle, E. Silva, A. Santos, and L. Albini, "Survivable keying for wireless ad hoc networks," in *Proceedings of the IFIP/IEEE International Symposium on Integrated Network Management (IM '09)*, pp. 606–613, IEEE Communications Society, Long Island, NY, USA, June 2009.

[15] M. Blaze, J. Feigenbaum, and J. Lacy, "Decentralized trust management," in *Proceedings of the 17th IEEE Symposium on Security and Privacy (SP '96)*, pp. 164–173, Oakland, Calif, USA, May 1996.

[16] M. Misaghi, E. da Silva, and L. C. P. Albini, "Distributed self-organized trust management for mobile ad hoc networks," in *Networked Digital Technologies*, R. Benlamri, Ed., vol. 293 of *Communications in Computer and Information Science*, pp. 506–518, Springer, 2012.

[17] E. da Silva, M. Misaghi, and C. P. Luiz, "True: a trust evaluation service for mobile ad hoc networks resistant to malicious attacks," *Journal of Digital Information Management*, vol. 10, no. 4, pp. 262–271, 2012.

[18] J. W. Mickens and B. D. Noble, "Modeling epidemic spreading in mobile environments," in *Proceedings of the 4th ACM Workshop on Wireless Security (WiSe '05)*, pp. 77–86, ACM, Cologne, Germany, September 2005.

[19] X. Zhang, G. Neglia, J. Kurose, and D. Towsley, "Performance modeling of epidemic routing," *Computer Networks*, vol. 51, no. 10, pp. 2867–2891, 2007.

[20] A. Shamir, "Identity-based cryptosystems and signature schemes," in *Advances in Cryptology*, G. R. Blakley and D. Chaum, Eds., vol. 196 of *Lecture Notes in Computer Science*, pp. 47–53, Springer, New York, NY, USA, 1985.

[21] A. Kate and I. Goldberg, "Distributed private-key generators for identity-based cryptography," in *Security and Cryptography for Networks*, J. A. Garay and R. De Prisco, Eds., vol. 6280 of *Lecture Notes in Computer Science*, pp. 436–453, Springer, Berlin, Germany, 2010.

[22] E. da Silva and L. C. P. Albini, "Towards a fully self-organized identity-based key management system for MANETs," in *Proceedings of the 9th International Conference on Wireless and Mobile Computing, Networking and Communications (WiMob '13)*, pp. 717–723, Lyon, France, October 2013.

[23] Y. Zhang, W. Liu, W. Lou, and Y. Fang, "Securing mobile ad hoc networks with certificateless public keys," *IEEE Transactions on Dependable and Secure Computing*, vol. 3, no. 4, pp. 386–399, 2006.

[24] H. Luo, J. Kong, P. Zerfos, S. Lu, and L. Zhang, "URSA: ubiquitous and robust access control for mobile ad hoc networks," *IEEE/ACM Transactions on Networking*, vol. 12, no. 6, pp. 1049–1063, 2004.

[25] L. Zhou and Z. J. Haas, "Securing ad hoc networks," *IEEE Network*, vol. 13, no. 6, pp. 24–30, 1999.

[26] J. Kong, P. Zerfos, H. Luo, S. Lu, and L. Zhang, "Providing robust and ubiquitous security support for mobile ad-hoc networks," in *Proceedings of the International Conference on Network Protocols (ICNP '01)*, pp. 251–260, Washington, DC, USA, November 2001.

[27] S. Yi and R. Kravets, "MOCA: mobile certificate authority for wireless ad hoc networks," in *Proceedings of the 2nd Annual PKI Research Workshop (PKI '03)*, National Institute of Standards and Technology (NIST), Gaithersburg, Md, USA, 2003.

[28] K. Hoeper and G. Gong, "Key revocation for identity-based schemes in mobile ad hoc networks," in *Ad-Hoc, Mobile, and Wireless Networks*, T. Kunz and S. S. Ravi, Eds., vol. 4104 of *Lecture Notes in Computer Science*, pp. 224–237, Springer, 2006.

[29] V. Daza, P. Morillo, and C. Ràfols, "On dynamic distribution of private keys over MANETs," *Electronic Notes in Theoretical Computer Science*, vol. 171, no. 1, pp. 33–41, 2007.

[30] O. Courand, O. Droegehorn, K. David et al., "Context aware group management in mobile environments," in *Proceedings of the 14th IST Mobile and Wireless Communications Summit*, Nokia Research Center, Dresden, Germany, 2005.

[31] C. N. Ververidis and G. C. Polyzos, "Service discovery for mobile ad hoc networks: a survey of issues and techniques," *IEEE Communications Surveys & Tutorials*, vol. 10, no. 3, pp. 30–45, 2008.

[32] J. Hur, C. Park, and S. O. Hwang, "Privacy-preserving identity-based broadcast encryption," *Information Fusion*, vol. 13, no. 4, pp. 296–303, 2012.

[33] D. Augot, R. Bhaskar, V. Issarny, and D. Sacchetti, "An efficient group key agreement protocol for ad hoc networks," in *Proceedings of the 6th IEEE International Symposium on a World*

of Wireless Mobile and Multimedia Networks (WoWMoM '05), pp. 576–580, Washington, DC, USA, June 2005.

[34] B. E. Jung, "An efficient group key agreement protocol," *IEEE Communications Letters*, vol. 10, no. 2, pp. 106–107, 2006.

[35] L. Zhang, Q. Wu, B. Qin, and J. Domingo-Ferrer, "Provably secure one-round identity-based authenticated asymmetric group key agreement protocol," *Information Sciences*, vol. 181, no. 19, pp. 4318–4329, 2011.

4

Performance Analysis of the Effect of Nonlinear Low Noise Amplifier for Wideband Spectrum Sensing in the Poisson Field of Interferers

Bipun Man Pati and Attaphongse Taparugssanagorn

Telecommunications, Asian Institute of Technology, P.O. Box 4, Klong Luang, Pathumthani 12120, Thailand

Correspondence should be addressed to Bipun Man Pati; bemaanpati@gmail.com

Academic Editor: Rui Zhang

A cognitive radio (CR) device likely consists of a low-cost low noise amplifier (LNA) due to the mass-production reason. Nevertheless, the operation of a low-cost LNA becomes highly nonlinear causing intermodulation (IM) interference. The most important task of CR devices is to sense the wideband spectrum to increase opportunistic throughput. In noncooperative secondary networks, the IM interference usually can be ignored for the narrowband spectrum sensing, while the IM interference needs to be taken into account along with interference from other CR devices in the wideband case. Our contribution is to study the effects of a nonlinear LNA for the second case in environments modeled by Poisson field of interferers reflecting more realistic scenario. As shown in the simulation results, the performance of the receiver is degraded in all the cases due to the nonlinearity of LNA. The adaptive threshold setting based on the multivariate Gaussian mixture model is proposed to improve the receiver performance.

1. Introduction

The number of wireless devices is growing constantly. One common reason is the increasing mobile penetration; that is, the costs of access and devices, for example, smart phones and tablets, are coming down. No matter what the device is, it utilizes radio frequency (RF) spectrum as its channels for its communications. As a result, RF spectrum plays a very important role in wireless communications. The current RF allocation, which is used by the federal communications commission (FCC), defines specific RF bands for specific uses. For example, there are RF bands allocated for cellular communications, military communications, marine, amplitude modulation (AM)/frequency modulation (FM), and so forth. This method of frequency allocation results in heavy utilization of some RF bands and very poor utilization of some other RF bands [1]. Hence, the efficient utilization of RF spectrum is a major challenge in today's wireless communication systems.

CR is a software defined radio (SDR) that has the ability to sense the environment and adjust its RF parameters to provide opportunistic access to secondary user (SU) on the frequency band of primary user (PU). In the context of CR, PUs or licensed users are those who have legacy right for the frequency band and SUs are those who opportunistically access the frequency band of PU. Since CRs are secondary users, one of the requirements of CR is to reliably detect the existence of PU in a given frequency band before actually utilizing that band for communication purpose. The other requirement is that when utilizing the frequency band of PU, it is very important for CR that they do not interfere with the PU. This requirement leads to the spectrum sensing as the first and most crucial task of CR.

The CR front-end can support either narrowband or wideband spectrum sensing. In narrowband spectrum sensing, a very narrowband of spectrum is sensed to decide if what is sensed is really signal with noise or just noise. If the band consists of signal with noise the secondary user is prohibited to use that band and is allowed if the band consists of only noise. While in the present CR performs narrowband spectrum sensing, in the long run, the CR needs to perform sensing over wide range of frequency increasing the overall opportunistic throughput [2]. Wideband spectrum sensing senses spectral opportunities in a wide range of frequency. Determining spectral holes in wideband spectrum can be done using channel by channel scanning approach [3]. But this method of detecting spectrum holes requires an RF front-end with many tunable narrow band-pass filters. This results in higher implementation complexity. As a result, a direct conversion receiver (DCR) has become very common as receiver for wideband spectrum sensing. Although superheterodyne receiver is also an alternative solution, several advantages of DCR, for instance, the circumvention of the image problem, no use of image filter, and surface acoustic wave (SAW) filter [4], over the superheterodyne technique make it suitable for CRs. Therefore, the DCR is generally preferred over the superheterodyne receivers.

A received signal in wideband spectrum sensing has high dynamic range; as a result, the receiver operates at the nonlinear region. This causes nonlinear distortion and adversely affects the sensing decision of the spectrum sensing algorithms. The components that give rise to the nonlinearity property in the DCR are an RF filter, an LNA, and a mixer. The nonlinear distortion is caused by IM and cross-modulation (XM) terms that occur when the signal passes through the nonlinear components of the receiver. These terms might fall within the region of the desired signal in case of the wideband spectrum sensing. It is noted that these IM distortion (IMD) terms cannot be filtered out as in the narrowband sensing case since these terms overlap with the PU signal being sensed. Among other components in the DCR, the most significant source of nonlinearity is LNA [5].

With regard to interference modeling in a CR application, the interference from a CR network to a PU network has received a lot more attention in the literature [6, 7]. This is obvious since the CR users must not interfere with the PU. The study of interference from PUs to a CR network has been reported in a number of papers [8, 9]. In [9], they study the interference to a CR network due to several PUs and derive outage probability distribution for the entire CR network. It does not consider the effect of the intranetwork interference on a single CR sensing node. The performance of only a single spectrum sensing node due to the intranetwork interference in noncooperative environment was studied in [10]. However, this paper assumed that all the interfering signals are colocated spectrally and did not take into account the effect of nonlinearity presented in the CR. The effect of receiver nonidealities has been studied in a number of papers [11–13]. These studies consider narrowband spectrum sensing and assume that the receiver operates in the linear region. References [14, 15] consider wideband spectrum sensing and study the effect of third-order nonlinearity due to LNA in the performance degradation of the energy detector and the cyclostationary detector. These papers study only the effect of IMD terms in the frequency band. However, in noncooperative CR network considering wideband spectrum

sensing the frequency band contains interfering signal from other CRs in addition to IMD terms.

In [10] authors studied the effect of intranetwork interference in noncooperative environment assuming that the interfering signals are colocated spectrally which is good but it does not cover the situation where the interfering signal may be located on separate frequency bands. Furthermore, it does not consider the effect of strong in-band interfering signal on the sensing node due to the nonlinearity of LNA in DCR. A more realistic study would be to consider the situation where CRs may be transmitting either on either separate frequency bands or same frequency band considering the effect of strong in-band interfering signal. References [14, 15] investigated effect of IMD on the performance of sensing node but they do not consider the scenario where the subband of interest may be degraded further by other interfering signals in a noncooperative environment which would be more realistic; for example, the subband at which the sensing node is detecting the PU signal is degraded not only by IMD but also by the interfering signal from other CRs in a noncooperative network.

Our contribution is to study the performance of detector in wideband spectrum sensing in noncooperative environment considering the effect not only of IMD but also due to the interfering signal from other CRs which has not been investigated before in [10, 14, 15]. We investigate the performance of energy detector for wideband spectrum sensing considering the effect of nonlinearity in LNA. In particular, we focus on a noncooperative environment. We consider a more realistic scenario in a noncooperative network where the interfering signals are generated based on the Poisson point process. The Poisson model enables the statistical characterization of network interferer taking into account the spatial distribution as well as the density of the interfering nodes. We model the interference in a wideband spectrum sensing at a particular subband not only by the IMD terms but also due to the interfering signals from other CRs. The model presented provides more realistic viewpoint for studying the performance of detector in a noncooperative network that has not yet been studied in the literature. We identify two more realistic scenarios in such noncooperative network and derive the expression for false alarm and detection probability making use of the central limit theorem (CLT) for each of the two scenarios. By relaxing our model in the distribution of interference and IMD terms we model a very realistic scenario present in a noncooperative network. Finally, we proposed an adaptive threshold setting method that is based on modeling the noise after the nonlinear LNA using multivariate Gaussian mixture model. We investigated by modeling the noise signal after LNA; using the multivariate Gaussian mixture model the performance of detector is enhanced.

The rest of the paper is organized as follows. In Section 2, we describe the system model for noncooperative network along with the interferer and LNA nonlinearity model. In Section 3, we first derive the expression for the detection and the false alarm probabilities considering various cases and then provide the simulation results for those cases. We also discuss the adaptive threshold setting based on multivariate

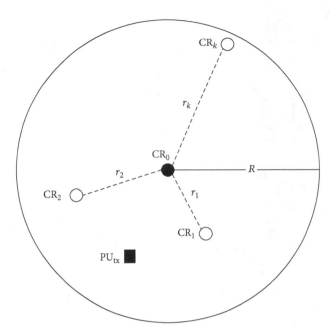

FIGURE 1: System model.

Gaussian mixture model for improving the performance in case of LNA nonlinearity. Finally, conclusions are drawn in Section 4.

2. System Model

The system under consideration is shown in Figure 1. We consider a circular geographical area with the radius R containing K number of CRs, a central CR (CR_0), and a PU. The distance between CR_0 and Kth CR (CR_K) is denoted by r_K. The distance between CR_0 and PU can be varied as required. The PU is the licensed user and has higher priority for transmission than CRs. However, the network policy allows CRs to use the spectrum with the condition that they must not cause harmful interference to the PU.

2.1. Interferer Modeling. The spatial distribution of network interferers is modeled as a Poisson point process in a two-dimensional circular plane. The spatial density of interfering nodes is denoted by λ_{IN} in the number of CRs per unit area. The probability that k number of nodes interfere at any particular time follows the Poisson distribution as expressed in (1). The interfering nodes are defined as the set of terminals which transmit within the frequency band of interest during the sensing time and hence effectively contribute to the total interference.

$$\Pr(K = k) = \frac{(\mu(A))^k e^{-\mu(A)}}{k!}, \tag{1}$$

where $\mu(A) = \lambda_{IN} \pi R^2$.

The distribution of a CR around the circular area is considered to be uniform. Hence, the distribution of r is given by

$$f_R(r) = \begin{cases} \dfrac{2r}{R^2}, & \text{for } 0 < r < R, \\ 0, & \text{otherwise.} \end{cases} \tag{2}$$

2.2. Modeling Nonlinearity due to LNA. During the sensing time interval of CR_0, the other CRs transmit data in various frequency bands. This is plausible because the CR network is noncooperative; that is, one CR may not know the status and location of the other CRs. If CR_0 is close to some other CRs, then strong interference in-band signal is dominated by CR_0. This strong in-band signal forces the LNA to operate in the nonlinear region. As a result, the spurious frequency components, such as IM and XM, occur with some other bands that are possibly in the band of interest. The even-order nonlinearity terms are outside the frequency range while the odd-order nonlinearity terms remain within the frequency range. The complex baseband equivalence of the wideband signal after the nonlinear LNA is written as follows [18]:

$$y[n] = f(x[n]) + w_a[n], \tag{3}$$

where $x[n]$ is the received complex baseband equivalent wideband signal and $w_a[n]$ is the additive white Gaussian noise (AWGN) after the LNA.

The complex baseband equivalent wideband signal in (3) is written as

$$x[n] = s[n] + \sum_{k=1}^{K} (c_k[n]) + w_b[n], \tag{4}$$

where $s[n]$ is the PU signal, $c_k[n]$ is the signal from kth CR, and $w_b[n]$ is the AWGN before LNA.

Since the third-order nonlinearity often dominates over the higher order nonlinearity components, a memoryless polynomial model up to the third-order is used to model the effect of nonlinearity due to the LNA. The third-order memoryless polynomial model consists of the nonlinear coefficients up to the third-order. Thus, $f(x[n])$ in (3) can be written as

$$f(x[n]) = \beta_1(x[n]) + \beta_2(x[n])^2 + \beta_3(x[n])^3, \tag{5}$$

where β_1, β_2, and β_3 are the coefficients of the memoryless polynomial model.

Considering only odd-order nonlinearity in (5) and using (3), the final expression for the signal is given by

$$y[n] = \beta_1(x[n]) + \beta_3(x[n])^3 + w_a[n]. \tag{6}$$

The values for β_1, β_2, and β_3 are related to the circuit specification parameters. β_1 is the small signal gain and its typical value is 35 dB, the value of β_2 can be calculated using the second-order intercept point (IP2) coefficient, and the value of β_3 can be calculated using (7) [16].

$$A_{\text{IP3}} = \sqrt{\frac{4\beta_1}{3\beta_3}}, \tag{7}$$

$$P_{\text{IP3}} = 20 \log_{10} A_{\text{IP3}} + 10 \text{ dBm}, \tag{8}$$

where A_{IP3} and P_{IP3} are the amplitude and power at third-order intercept point (IP3) of the LNA.

3. Spectrum Sensing Method

A cyclostationary detection (CD) performs spectrum sensing by correlating the received signal with its frequency shifted version. The frequency by which the signal is to be shifted is called a cyclic frequency. The cyclic frequency is a function of cyclic feature, for instance, the signal modulation type, its symbol rate, and the carrier frequency. Depending upon the presence or the absence of the cyclic feature, the decision is made to determine the presence or absence of PU signals. A CD takes advantage of the fact that noise is a wide sense stationary (WSS) process with no correlation, whereas the modulated signals are cyclostationary with their spectral correlation and their Fourier transform, the cyclic spectral density (CSD) [8]. The CSD of the received signal is computed as

$$\sum_{\tau=-\infty}^{\infty} R_y^\alpha (\tau) \exp\left(-j2\pi f\tau\right), \tag{8}$$

where the cyclic autocorrelation function (CAF) $R_y^\alpha(\tau)$ is given by

$$R_y^\alpha (\tau) = E\left[y\left(n+\tau\right) y^* \left(n-\tau\right) \exp\left(-j2\pi\alpha n\right)\right], \tag{9}$$

where α is the cyclic frequency which is assumed to be known or it can be extracted and be used for identifying the transmitted signal.

An energy detection (ED) is the special case of the CD with the lag and the cyclic frequency both equal to zero. Therefore, the test statistics under the ED is given by

$$R_y^0 (0) = \frac{1}{N} \sum_{n=0}^{N-1} |y[n]|^2. \tag{10}$$

Let λ_{ED} be the threshold to be compared; then the probability of false alarm P_{fa} and the probability of detection P_d under those two mentioned cases are given by

$$P_{fa} = \Pr\left\{R_y^0 (0) > \lambda_{\text{ED}} \mid H_0\right\}, \tag{11}$$

$$P_d = \Pr\left\{R_y^0 (0) > \lambda_{\text{ED}} \mid H_1\right\}. \tag{12}$$

3.1. P_d and P_{fa} without LNA Nonlinearity and Interference. When the observation interval N is sufficiently large, the test statistics for ED can be approximated as a Gaussian distribution [19] due to the central limit theorem (CLT). The test statistics can then be approximated by

$$f_{R|H_0} (r) \sim \mathcal{N}\left(\sigma_n^2, \frac{2\sigma_n^4}{N}\right), \tag{13}$$

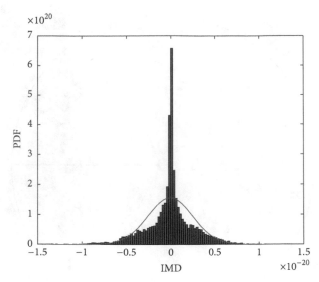

FIGURE 2: Third-order IMD term distribution.

where σ_n^2 is the noise variance and $\mathcal{N}(a,b)$ is a Gaussian distribution with mean a and variance b.

$$f_{R|H_1} (r) \sim \mathcal{N}\left(\sigma_y^2, \frac{2\sigma_y^4}{N}\right), \tag{14}$$

where $\sigma_y^2 = \sigma_s^2 + \sigma_n^2$ is the total variance of signal plus noise and σ_s^2 is the signal variance.

Using (12) and (14) we derive P_d as (15) and using (11) and (13) we derive P_{fa} as (16):

$$P_d = Q\left(\sqrt{\frac{N}{2}}\left(\frac{\lambda}{(\sigma_n^2 + \sigma_s^2)} - 1\right)\right), \tag{15}$$

where the signal to noise ratio (SNR) is defined as σ_s^2/σ_n^2, and

$$P_{fa} = Q\left(\frac{\lambda - \sigma_n^2}{\sigma_n^2/\sqrt{N/2}}\right), \tag{16}$$

where $Q(\cdot)$ is the Q-function. Under H_0 hypothesis, for a fixed P_{fa}, the threshold is derived as

$$\lambda_{\text{ED}} = \sigma_n^2 \left(1 + \frac{Q^{-1}\left(P_{fa}\right)}{\sqrt{N/2}}\right), \tag{17}$$

where $Q^{-1}(\cdot)$ is the inverse Q-function. λ_{ED} in (17) indicates that the threshold estimation is dependent on the noise variance, the signal variance, the number of the samples, and the required false alarm probability.

3.2. Distribution of IMD Terms. The IMD is common and critical in the wideband spectrum sensing. The distribution of IMD term plays a vital role in the detection performance of any detector. The fitting of the IMD distribution with the stable distribution yields the following parameters: α close to 1, β close to 0, and γ and δ equal to 0. For simplicity, we approximate this distribution as a Gaussian distribution. The effect of IMD on the performance of detector is shown through several graphs in Section 3. The distribution of IMD term is shown in Figure 2.

TABLE 1: Simulation parameters for non-Poisson field of interferer.

Parameters	Values
SNR	$-15:30$ dB
SBR (signal to blocker ratio)	$-24:-30$ dB
IMD	$2:10$ dB
β_1	56.23 [16]
β_3	-7497.33 [16]
ρ (noise power uncertainty)	0.001 dB [17]

3.3. P_d and P_{fa} with LNA Nonlinearity.

It is assumed that the signal, the IMD term, and the noise are all mutually statistically independent and tend to a Gaussian distribution for large N. Using the CLT we approximate the test statistics under two hypotheses as

$$f_{R|H_0}(r) \sim \mathcal{N}\left(\sigma_n^2 + \sigma_{\text{imd}}^2, \frac{2\left(\sigma_n^2 + \sigma_{\text{imd}}^2\right)^2}{N}\right), \quad (18)$$

where σ_n^2 is the noise variance and σ_{imd}^2 is the IMD term variance.

$$f_{R|H_1}(r) \sim \mathcal{N}\left(\sigma_y^2, \frac{2\sigma_y^4}{N}\right), \quad (19)$$

where $\sigma_y^2 = \sigma_s^2 + \sigma_n^2 + \sigma_{\text{imd}}^2$ is the total variance with the signal, the noise, and the IMD term.

Using (12) and (19) we derive P_d as (20) and using (11) and (18) we derive P_{fa} as (21):

$$P_d = Q\left(\sqrt{\frac{N}{2}}\left(\frac{\lambda_{\text{ED}}}{\left(\sigma_n^2 + \sigma_s^2 + \sigma_{\text{imd}}^2\right)} - 1\right)\right), \quad (20)$$

where the signal to IMD ratio (SIMDR) is defined as $\sigma_s^2/\sigma_{\text{imd}}^2$, and

$$P_{fa} = Q\left(\frac{\lambda_{\text{ED}} - \left(\sigma_n^2 + \sigma_{\text{imd}}^2\right)}{\left(\sigma_n^2 + \sigma_{\text{imd}}^2\right)/\sqrt{N/2}}\right). \quad (21)$$

Under hypothesis H_0, for a fixed P_{fa}, the threshold is derived as

$$\lambda_{\text{ED}} = \left(\sigma_n^2 + \sigma_{\text{imd}}^2\right)\left(1 + \frac{Q^{-1}\left(P_{fa}\right)}{\sqrt{N/2}}\right). \quad (22)$$

λ_{ED} in (22) indicates that the threshold estimation is dependent on the noise variance, the SNR, the number of the samples, the required false alarm probability, and the IMD variance.

3.4. Simulation Results with and without LNA Nonlinearity.

Table 1 lists the system parameters used in the simulations for the case of the nonlinearity in LNA.

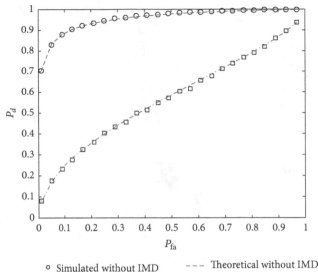

FIGURE 3: P_{fa} versus P_d with SNR at -15 dB, IMD of 10 dB, and $N = 1000$.

Legend:
○ Simulated without IMD --- Theoretical without IMD
□ Simulation with IMD --·- Theoretical with IMD

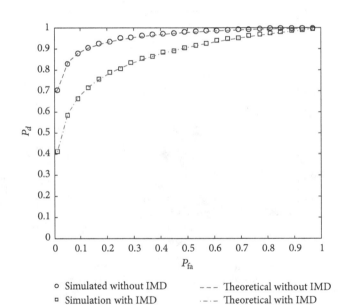

FIGURE 4: P_{fa} versus P_d with SNR at -15 dB, IMD of 2 dB, and $N = 1000$.

Legend:
○ Simulated without IMD --- Theoretical without IMD
□ Simulation with IMD --·- Theoretical with IMD

Receiver Operating Characteristic Curve for ED. The receiver operating characteristic (ROC) curve is obtained by plotting P_{fa} along the x-axis versus P_d along the y-axis. We vary the value of P_{fa} from 0.01 to 1 with an increment of 0.01 at each step. Keeping SNR at -15 dB and IMD at 10 dB and the observation interval at $N = 1000$, the ROC curve obtained is shown in Figure 3. If we reduce the power of IMD term to 2 dB, we obtain the ROC curve as shown in Figure 4; the improvement in ROC curve is seen.

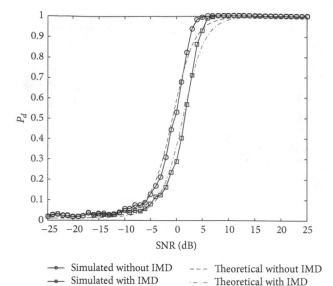

FIGURE 5: P_d versus SNR with IMD of 2 dB and $N = 15$.

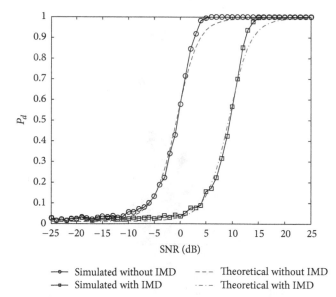

FIGURE 6: P_d versus SNR with IMD of 10 dB and $N = 15$.

The other plot, which is significant, to visualize the performance of the detector is P_d versus SNR. The plot of P_d versus SNR at IMD of 2 dB at $P_{fa} = 0.01$ and observation interval $N = 15$ is shown in Figure 5. Now, to analyze the effect of IMD, we plot the same graph keeping all the parameters constant and increase IMD to 10 dB; the plot obtained is shown in Figure 6. Comparing to the graphs plotted in Figures 5 and 6, it is concluded that when the IMD is low, the required P_d can be achieved at the low SNR. However, when IMD increases the same P_d is achieved at the high SNR.

3.5. Spectrum Sensing under Nonlinear LNA considering Interference.

The received signal from each of the interfering nodes is given by (23). Interfering signals are considered independent of each other. The power of kth interferer at a distance of r_k with respect to the central CR (CR_0) is $P_k = r_k^{-\gamma}$, where γ is the path loss exponent. The complex baseband equivalence wideband signal received by the CR_0 from other CRs is given by

$$c[n] = \sum_{k=1}^{K} \sqrt{P_k} c_k[n], \tag{23}$$

where $c_k[n]$ is the baseband signal from CR_K.

As shown in system model, the CR_0 is sensing the wideband of spectrum; we suppose that there are in total M subchannels that are sensed by the central CR. The received signal by the central CR depends on whether the network is cooperative or noncooperative. In this paper we discuss noncooperative network. Under cooperative network, there is no effect of interference or nonlinearity, since when a CR is sensing spectrum, the other CRs are considered to be quite. This scenario can be modeled as the case of spectrum sensing previously discussed. As mentioned earlier, in a noncooperative network, CRs have no idea about the location and the status of the other CRs. Hence, one CR interferes with the other CR resulting in the degradation of spectrum sensing. For the narrowband spectrum sensing, the effect of nonlinearity is not relevant but the effect of interferer from the other CRs is relevant. However, in the case of the wideband spectrum sensing, the effect of nonlinearity due to the LNA should also be considered in addition to interference from the other CRs. Under the noncooperative case the following two scenarios are possible:

(i) All the CRs transmit on separate frequency bands.

(ii) A number of CRs transmit on the same frequency band.

CR Transmission on Separate Frequency Bands. When all the CRs transmit on separate frequency band, the received complex baseband equivalent wideband signal before the LNA under two hypotheses is given by

$$x[n] = \begin{cases} w_b[n] + \displaystyle\sum_{k=1}^{K} c_k[n], & H_0, \\ \\ w_b[n] + s[n] + \displaystyle\sum_{k=1}^{K} c_k[n], & H_1. \end{cases} \tag{24}$$

We assume that there are M channels available; without loss of generality we can say that $M = K$. The received signal now passed through the LNA. Depending upon the power of the received signal, if any of the received signal powers is larger than the power at IP3, the LNA behaves nonlinearly.

The baseband output signal from the LNA considering only the IMD term and the intranetwork interference under two hypotheses is then obtained by using (6) and (24) and is expressed as

$$
y[n] = \begin{cases} w_a[n] + \beta_1 \sum_{k=1}^{K} c_k[n] + \dfrac{3\beta_3}{2} \sum_{k=1}^{K-1} c_k^*[n]\, c_{k+1}^2[n], & H_0, \\[4mm] w_a[n] + \beta_1 \left(s[n] + \sum_{k=1}^{K} c_k[n] \right) + \dfrac{3\beta_3}{2} \sum_{k=1}^{K-1} c_k^*[n]\, c_{k+1}^2[n], & H_1. \end{cases}
\tag{25}
$$

The received signal at a particular SOI for the first case under two hypotheses is given by

$$
y_{\mathrm{SOI}}[n]
$$
$$
= \begin{cases} w_a[n] + \left(\beta_1 c_z[n] + \dfrac{3\beta_3}{2} c_x^*[n]\, c_y^2[n] \right), & H_0, \\[4mm] w_a[n] + \left(\beta_1 (s[n] + c_z[n]) + \dfrac{3\beta_3}{2} c_x^*[n]\, c_y^2[n] \right), & H_1, \end{cases}
\tag{26}
$$

where c_x and c_y are the interferers whose third-order IMD falls in the SOI, c_z is the interfering signal at SOI, $x, y, z \in K$, and $x \neq y \neq z$.

CR Transmission on the Same Frequency Band. We assume that N number of channels out of M are being allocated by K number of users and are uniformly used by K CRs. Therefore, in each channel, there are $\lfloor K/N \rfloor$ number of CRs, where $\lfloor \cdot \rfloor$ denotes the floor operation. Then, the received complex baseband equivalent wideband signal under two hypotheses is written as

$$
y[n] = \begin{cases} w_b[n] + \sum_{i=1}^{N} \sum_{j=1}^{\lfloor K/N \rfloor} c_{ij}[n], & H_0, \\[4mm] w_b[n] + s[n] + \sum_{i=1}^{N} \sum_{j=1}^{\lfloor K/N \rfloor} c_{ij}[n], & H_1, \end{cases}
\tag{27}
$$

where c_{ij} is the interfering signal where i and j are just the index variable, $i \in M$, $j \in K$.

When $M = N$, we have a similar case to the previous one in which each CR transmits in separate band. Now if we focus on a particular SOI after proper digital filtering, sampling at rate $1/T_s$, and downconversion to intermediate frequency f_{IF}, we further investigate the three following cases:

(i) Noise only case.

(ii) Noise with IMD.

(iii) Noise with IMD plus interferer.

(iv) Noise with interferer.

The first case represents basic hypothesis problem; the fourth case has been already analyzed in the literature. Our focus is on the second and third case. The second case is previously discussed in Section 3.3. For the third case, the signal at the output of the LNA is given by

$$
y_{\mathrm{SOI}}[n] = \begin{cases} w_a[n] + \left(\beta_1 \sum_{j=1}^{\lfloor K/N \rfloor} c_{zj}[n] + \dfrac{3\beta_3}{2} \sum_{j=1}^{\lfloor K/N \rfloor} c_{xj}^*[n]\, c_{yj}^2[n] \right), & H_0, \\[4mm] w_a[n] + \left(\beta_1 \left(s[n] + \sum_{j=1}^{\lfloor K/N \rfloor} c_{zj}[n] \right) + \dfrac{3\beta_3}{2} \sum_{j=1}^{\lfloor K/N \rfloor} c_{xj}^*[n]\, c_{yj}^2[n] \right), & H_1, \end{cases}
\tag{28}
$$

where c_{xj} and c_{yj} are the interfering signal whose third-order IMD term falls in the SOI; c_{zj} are the interfering signal in the SOI.

P_d and P_{fa} under LNA Nonlinearity in Poisson Field of Interferer. It is assumed that the signal, the IMD term, the noise, and the interference are all mutually statistically independent. We model the interference as the Gaussian distribution. Using the CLT in the test statistics,

we approximate the test statistics under two hypotheses as

$$
f_{R|H_0}(r)
$$
$$
\sim \mathcal{N}\left(\sigma_n^2 + \sigma_{\mathrm{imd}}^2 + \sigma_i^2,\ \frac{2\left(\sigma_n^2 + \sigma_{\mathrm{imd}}^2 + \sigma_i^2\right)^2}{N} \right),
\tag{29}
$$

where σ_i^2 is the interference variance.

And

$$f_{R|H_1}(r) \sim \mathcal{N}\left(\sigma_y^2, \frac{2\sigma_y^4}{N}\right), \qquad (30)$$

where $\sigma_y^2 = \sigma_s^2 + \sigma_n^2 + \sigma_{\text{imd}}^2 + \sigma_i^2$.

After some derivation, we can derive P_d and P_{fa} as

$$P_d = Q\left(\sqrt{\frac{N}{2}}\left(\frac{\lambda_{\text{ED}}}{(\sigma_n^2 + \sigma_s^2 + \sigma_{\text{imd}}^2 + \sigma_i^2)} - 1\right)\right), \qquad (31)$$

where the signal to interference ratio (SIR) is defined as σ_s^2/σ_i^2;

$$P_{fa} = Q\left(\frac{\lambda_{\text{ED}} - (\sigma_n^2 + \sigma_{\text{imd}}^2 + \sigma_i^2)}{(\sigma_n^2 + \sigma_{\text{imd}}^2 + \sigma_i^2)/\sqrt{N/2}}\right). \qquad (32)$$

Under H_0 hypothesis, for a fixed P_{fa}, the threshold is derived as

$$\lambda_{\text{ED}} = (\sigma_n^2 + \sigma_{\text{imd}}^2 + \sigma_i^2)\left(1 + \frac{Q^{-1}(P_{fa})}{\sqrt{N/2}}\right). \qquad (33)$$

λ_{ED} in (33) indicates that the threshold estimation is dependent on the SNR, the number of the samples, the required false alarm probability, the IMD variance, and the interference variance.

3.6. Simulation Results.
The interfering CRs are generated randomly according to the Poisson distribution with density $\lambda_{\text{IN}} = 100,000$ persons/km². The distance between PU and CR₀ d_{PU} can be varied. We show result at the distance $d_{\text{PU}} = 600\,\text{m}$. Later, we show the result at $d_{\text{PU}} = 500\,\text{m}$ that shows that the results have the same trend when d_{PU} varied. Moreover, if λ_{IN} is increased, the effect of interference is more severe and vice versa given that the distance between PU and CR₀ is kept unchanged in both the simulations. The effect of varying number of samples is discussed later. Since the theoretical derivation is carried out without the effect of shadowing, the environment effect has been removed in the simulated plot. Hence, the theoretical and simulated curves are the same. This also provides the validation of the simulated and the theoretical results. The plot obtained is shown in Figure 7.

3.7. Effect of Varying Number of Samples.
The simulations in this part are for the importance of the sensing time (interval); that is, it improves the performance of the ED. Sensing time plays an important role in improving the performance of the ED. We plot the effect of the observation interval (N) on P_d. P_d depends upon N. This is due to the fact that increasing N results in the increase in the effective SNR or SIMDR [15, 20]. It is noted that the receiver operating under the high input power experiences more severe nonlinearity behavior. Therefore, the plots obtained in Figures 8, 9, and 10 are further extended negatively, implying a large sensing time, to get the desired P_d. The plot in Figure 8 is plotted with parameters SNR = 3 dB, SBR = −23.98 dB, SIR = −16.47 dB,

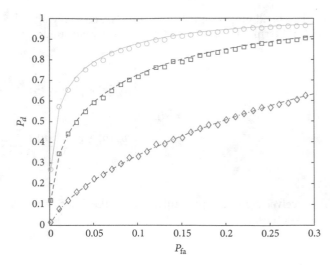

— Theoretical without IMD
--- Theoretical with IMD
·--· Theoretical with IMD and interferers
○ Simulated without IMD
□ Simulated with IMD
◇ Simulated with IMD and interferers

FIGURE 7: P_d versus P_{fa}.

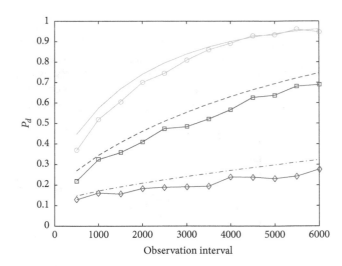

— Theoretical without IMD and interference
--- Theoretical with only IMD
·--· Theoretical with IMD and interference
—○— Simulated without IMD and interference
—□— Simulated with only IMD
—◇— Simulated with IMD and interference

FIGURE 8: Effect of sensing time on the performance of ED at $P_{fa} = 0.1$.

SIMD = −14.86 dB, $P_{fa} = 0.1$, and PU at 600 m. In order to gain insight into the theory, the following simulations are done for a variety of different cases. Keeping all the other parameters unchanged, we adjust the value of P_{fa} to visualize its effect on the performance. Figure 9 is plotted for $P_{fa} = 0.05$. The result clearly indicates the fact that when P_{fa} is decreased, the overall curve shifts towards low P_d at low

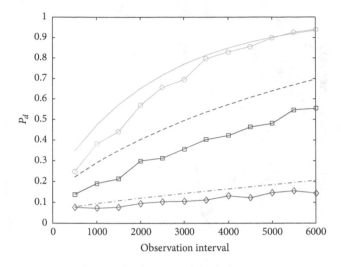

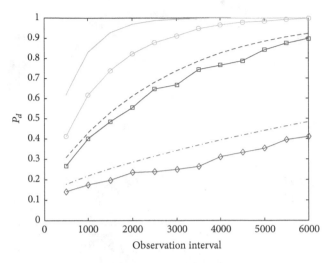

FIGURE 9: Effect of sensing time on the performance of ED at $P_{\text{fa}} = 0.05$.

FIGURE 11: Observation interval versus P_d with PU at 500 m.

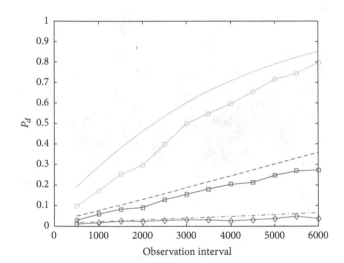

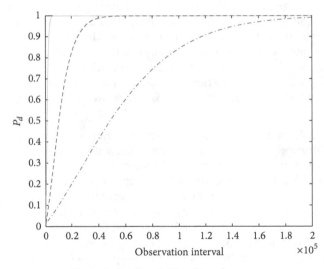

FIGURE 12: Observation interval versus P_d at $P_{\text{fa}} = 0.01$.

FIGURE 10: Effect of sensing time on the performance of ED at $P_{\text{fa}} = 0.01$.

observation interval. Figure 10 is plotted for $P_{\text{fa}} = 0.01$. It is seen that the overall curve shifts towards much lower P_d at lower observation interval.

The theoretical curves and the simulated ROC curves in Figures 8, 9, and 10 are somewhat different from the simulated curves because the simulated results are plotted considering

the effect of environment, that is, shadowing. Hence, the theoretical results can be considered as the upper bound of the performance. Figure 11 shows the situation when the PU distance is decreased to 500 m while keeping all the other parameters unchanged for $P_{\text{fa}} = 0.1$. In order to get the estimation of the total observation time interval required to achieve the required P_d, we plot the theoretical curves to visualize the upper bound on N. Figure 12 is plotted for $P_{\text{fa}} = 0.01$ to determine the required P_d in different scenarios. Figure 12 clearly shows that the observation interval in the

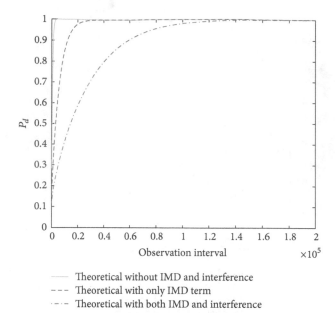

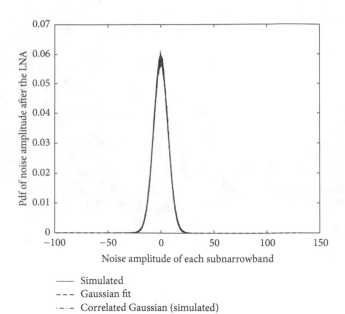

FIGURE 13: Observation interval versus P_d at $P_{\mathrm{fa}} = 0.1$.

FIGURE 14: Pdf of the noise amplitude after nonlinear LNA.

case of the interference from the secondary network considered together with the IMD term is much larger than the one in the case with the IMD term only. This large observation interval required for detection in the case of interference from secondary network may lead to impractical CR. Intuitively, if the requirement of the false alarm probability is increased to $P_{\mathrm{fa}} = 0.1$, the sensing time is reduced for a particular value of the detection probability as shown in Figure 13.

3.8. Simulation Result for Threshold Selection with LNA Nonlinearity. The actual distribution of the statistic of threshold is determined by the correlated Gaussian sequence instead of the white Gaussian sequence. This is due to the nonlinearity of LNA acting on the white Gaussian noise in the absence of PU signal. Figure 14 shows the fitting of the simulated Gaussian noise after the LNA with the correlated Gaussian sequence. The simulated plot in Figure 14 shows that the correlated Gaussian probability density function (pdf) fits the pdf of the nonlinear filtered noise better than the uncorrelated Gaussian pdf [18]. If the threshold is selected based only on Gaussian process for all the subbands, then the performance of ED is degraded. However, it is noted that this happens only when we consider the effect of nonlinearity. When we consider the nonlinearity of LNA, the output of the LNA is not just the white noise sequence but the summation of correlated non-Gaussian and Gaussian process which is approximated using multivariate Gaussian mixtures. Figure 15 depicts the threshold statistics considering the output of the LNA with the multivariate Gaussian mixture. It is clearly seen that the threshold is well approximated by the multivariate Gaussian mixture rather than the Gaussian process which happens to be constant for each frequency band.

As shown in Figure 16, the selected threshold level brings the probability of threshold being exceeded, when only noise is present. The value matches the target P_{fa} that is set to

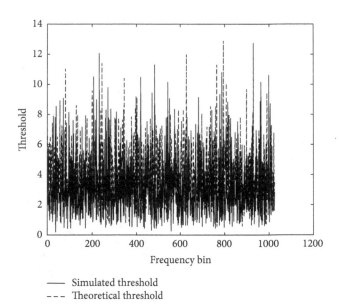

FIGURE 15: Approximation of simulated threshold value with multivariate Gaussian mixture.

0.1. Due to a finite number of samples being used in the simulation, the probability of threshold being exceeded in the presence of only noise cannot exactly be equal to the target P_{fa}. The similar simulation for the case of the target P_{fa} set to 0.01 is shown in Figure 17.

4. Conclusion

The effect of nonlinearity due to the LNA was first considered to visualize its impact on the spectrum sensing. It was seen that the effect of the LNA nonlinearity degrades the performance of ED. It was also examined that the performance of ED depends upon various factors, that is, SNR, the power

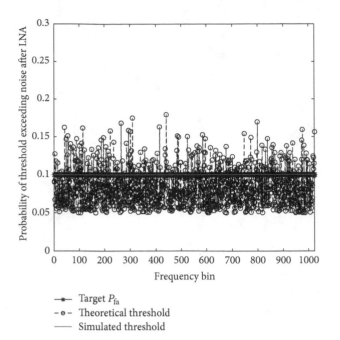

FIGURE 16: Probability of threshold being exceeded only in presence of noise at $P_{fa} = 0.1$.

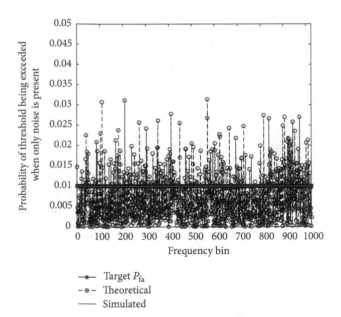

FIGURE 17: Probability of threshold being exceeded only in presence of noise at $P_{fa} = 0.01$.

of IMD, and interfering signal, and the observation interval. In reality, the sensing time in which the CR is required to sense the channel is the fundamental limit that needs to be considered for providing a good quality of service to the users as well as for practical implementation of CR devices.

The analysis in the wideband spectrum sensing along with the effect of interference generated from the other CRs in the secondary network was then performed. For simplicity, the approximations while performing theoretical

analysis were based on the assumption of Gaussian distribution but simulations were carried out with and without the shadowing effect. The effect of shadowing was clearly seen in the simulation results. The main contribution of this paper was to analyze the performance degradation in spectrum sensing due to inherent nonlinearity of an LNA in the Poisson field of interferer considering intranetwork interference, which models the more realistic scenarios than the ones in the existing literatures [10, 15]. It was also shown that the noise model after LNA is more accurate by using the multivariate Gaussian mixture model. A fixed threshold setting for the entire wideband seems to be inappropriate resulting in performance degradation. Therefore, an adaptive threshold setting based on the multivariate Gaussian mixture model was proposed to increase the overall performance of the CR.

Competing Interests

The authors declare that they have no competing interests.

Acknowledgments

The first author would like to thank Asian Development Bank-Japan Scholarship Program (ADB-JSP) for providing him with the grant for pursuing his M.E. degree in Asian Institute of Technology.

References

[1] M. Marcus, J. Burtle, B. Franca, A. Lahjouji, and N. McNeil, *Report of the Unlicensed Devices and Experimental Licenses Working Group*, Federal Communications Commission, Spectrum Policy Task Force, 2002.

[2] H. Sun, A. Nallanathan, C.-X. Wang, and Y. Chen, "Wideband spectrum sensing for cognitive radio networks: a survey," *IEEE Wireless Communications*, vol. 20, no. 2, pp. 74–81, 2013.

[3] A. Sahai and D. Cabric, "Spectrum sensing: fundamental limits and practical challenges," in *Proceedings of the IEEE International Symposium on New Frontiers in Dynamic Spectrum Access Networks (DySPAN '05)*, 2005.

[4] B. Razavi, "Design considerations for direct-conversion receivers," *IEEE Transactions on Circuits and Systems II: Analog and Digital Signal Processing*, vol. 44, no. 6, pp. 428–435, 1997.

[5] M. Allen, J. Marttila, M. Valkama, S. Makinen, M. Kosunen, and J. Ryynanen, "Digital linearization of direct-conversion spectrum sensing receiver," in *Proceedings of the 1st IEEE Global Conference on Signal and Information Processing (GlobalSIP '13)*, pp. 1158–1161, Austin, Tex, USA, December 2013.

[6] Z. Chen, C.-X. Wang, X. Hong, J. Thompson, S. A. Vorobyov, and X. Ge, "Interference modeling for cognitive radio networks with power or contention control," in *Proceedings of the IEEE Wireless Communications and Networking Conference (WCNC '10)*, Sydney, Australia, April 2010.

[7] M. Derakhshani, T. Le-Ngoc, and M. Vu, "Interference and outage analysis in a cognitive radio network with beacon," in *Proceedings of the 25th Biennial Symposium on Communications (QBSC '10)*, pp. 261–264, IEEE, Ontario, Canada, May 2010.

[8] N. Mayekar and A. M. Wyglinski, "Interference performance evaluation of secondary users in cognitive radio networks," in

Proceedings of the IEEE 81st Vehicular Technology Conference (VTC Spring '15), 2015.

[9] Q. Liu, Z. Zhou, C. Yang, and Y. Ye, "Outage probability analysis for cognitive radio network caused by primary users," in *Proceedings of the 3rd IEEE International Conference on Communications and Networking in China (ChinaCom '08)*, pp. 1323–1326, Hangzhou, China, August 2008.

[10] A. U. Makarfi and K. A. Hamdi, "Efficiency of energy detection for spectrum sensing in a Poisson field of interferers," in *Proceedings of the IEEE Wireless Communications and Networking Conference (WCNC '12)*, pp. 1023–1028, April 2012.

[11] M. Valkama, M. Renfors, and V. Koivunen, "Advanced methods for I/Q imbalance compensation in communication receivers," *IEEE Transactions on Signal Processing*, vol. 49, no. 10, pp. 2335–2344, 2001.

[12] J. Verlant-Chenet, J. Renard, J.-M. Dricot, P. De Doncker, and F. Horlin, "Sensitivity of spectrum sensing techniques to RF impairments," in *Proceedings of the IEEE 71st Vehicular Technology Conference (VTC-Spring '10)*, Taipei, Taiwan, May 2010.

[13] V. Syrjälä, M. Valkama, N. N. Tchamov, and J. Rinne, "Phase noise modelling and mitigation techniques in OFDM communications systems," in *Proceedings of the 2009 Wireless Telecommunications Symposium (WTS '09)*, Prague, Czech Republic, April 2009.

[14] E. Rebeiz, A. S. H. Ghadam, M. Valkama, and D. Cabric, "Suppressing RF front-end nonlinearities in wideband spectrum sensing," in *Proceedings of the 8th International Conference on Cognitive Radio Oriented Wireless Networks and Communications (CROWNCOM '13)*, pp. 87–92, July 2013.

[15] E. Rebeiz, A. S. Hagh Ghadam, M. Valkama, and D. Cabric, "Spectrum sensing under RF non-linearities: performance analysis and DSP-enhanced receivers," *IEEE Transactions on Signal Processing*, vol. 63, no. 8, pp. 1950–1964, 2015.

[16] B. Razavi, *RF Microelectronics*, University of California, Los Angeles, Calif, USA; Pearson Education, Upper Saddle River, NJ, USA, 2012.

[17] R. Tandra and A. Sahai, "SNR walls for signal detection," *IEEE Journal on Selected Topics in Signal Processing*, vol. 2, no. 1, pp. 4–17, 2008.

[18] A. Taparugssanagorn, K. Umebayashi, J. Lehtomaki, and C. Pomalaza-Raez, "Analysis of the effect of nonlinear low noise amplifier with memory for wideband spectrum sensing," in *Proceedings of the 1st International Conference on 5G for Ubiquitous Connectivity (5GU '14)*, pp. 87–91, Levi, Finland, November 2014.

[19] A. Gorcin, K. A. Qaraqe, H. Celebi, and H. Arslan, "An adaptive threshold method for spectrum sensing in multi-channel cognitive radio networks," in *Proceedings of the 17th International Conference on Telecommunications (ICT '10)*, pp. 425–429, April 2010.

[20] K. Hamdi and K. B. Letaief, "Power, sensing time, and throughput tradeoffs in cognitive radio systems: a cross-layer approach," in *Proceedings of the IEEE Wireless Communications and Networking Conference (WCNC '09)*, Budapest, Hungary, April 2009.

5

A Persistent Structured Hierarchical Overlay Network to Counter Intentional Churn Attack

Ramanpreet Kaur,[1,2] Amrit Lal Sangal,[1] and Krishan Kumar[3]

[1]*Department of Computer Science and Engineering, National Institute of Technology, Jalandhar, Punjab, India*
[2]*Department of Information Technology, Jaypee University of Information Technology, Solan, Himachal Pradesh, India*
[3]*Department of Computer Science and Engineering, Shaheed Bhagat Singh State Technical Campus, Ferozepur, Punjab, India*

Correspondence should be addressed to Ramanpreet Kaur; ahluwalia.raman1@gmail.com

Academic Editor: Rui Zhang

The increased use of structured overlay network for a variety of applications has attracted a lot of attention from both research community and attackers. However, the structural constraints, open nature (anybody can join and anybody may leave), and unreliability of its participant nodes significantly affect the performance of these applications and make it vulnerable to a variety of attacks such as eclipse, Sybil, and churn. One attack to compromise the service availability in overlay network is intentional churn (join/leave) attack, where a large number of malicious users will join and leave the overlay network so frequently that the entire structure collapses and becomes unavailable. The focus of this paper is to provide a new robust, efficient, and scalable hierarchical overlay architecture that will counter these attacks by providing a structure that can accommodate the fleeting behaviour of nodes without causing much structural inconsistencies. The performance evaluation showed that the proposed architecture has more failure resilience and self-organization as compared to chord based architecture. Experimental results have demonstrated that the effect of failures on an overlay is proportional to the size of failure.

1. Introduction

In the past two decades, structured overlay networks have emerged as a suitable architecture for implementation of various content sharing and internet service support system applications. An overlay network is defined as a layer of virtual network topology on the top of physical network, where a large number of users are pooled in order to share their resources and to provide distributed points of service. The significant scale, fault tolerance, and cost advantages of overlay networks make them very popular in the present internet scenario. Although these structures are very efficient and popular, they are not developed by keeping security in mind and are susceptible to many attacks. They can serve as a vehicle for attackers on the internet as they are vulnerable to many attacks because of the fleeting behaviour of nodes forming the overlay network.

There are two types of overlay networks available: structured and unstructured overlay networks. The structured overlay networks impose constraints on the structure of the overlay. So, if a significant number of nodes join and leave the network at an extremely rapid rate the overhead (maintenance messages) associated with this dynamism can become significant, thus degrading the performance of the system. This requirement makes structured overlay network more sensitive to the fleeting behaviour of nodes. The sensitivity of participants serves as a weapon for attackers to launch churn attack in order to bring the entire overlay structure down. An ideal overlay network should be fault-tolerant and self-organized against the dynamic behaviour of nodes (also known as churn). However, the initial design of overlay structures does not take into consideration the notorious fleeting behaviour of their nodes and thus has the limited fault tolerance and self-organization.

Security is an important issue that needs to be considered when choosing architecture to design an overlay system. Since overlay nodes are potentially unreliable and expected to behave in malicious ways, thus providing an acceptable level of security in overlay based applications is quite challenging. Till date, researchers [1–8] have uncovered the various security issues in structured overlay networks. The major security issues include eclipse attack (colluding nodes attempt to partition the network) [9–12], Sybil attack (where nodes forge identities) [13–15], and churn attack [6, 16–18]. Although a lot of research has been done on eclipse and Sybil attacks, surprisingly churn induced attacks are not widely studied. Most of the proposed structures [19–24] guarantee the performance of structured overlays in controlled environments only and do not consider induced dynamics of malicious peers. Although some researchers [25–29] have studied the criticality of peer dynamics and churn induced attacks, none of the proposed work can cope with these attacks without affecting the openness of overlay networks. So, in this paper, we design a new robust structured hierarchical overlay architecture that will counter these attacks by providing a structure that can accommodate the fleeting behaviour of nodes without causing much structural inconsistencies. In this architecture certain nodes (highly stable nodes with always on characteristic) have assigned special roles to manage the arrangement of less stable and new nodes. The proposed architecture is a robust, self-modifying, and scalable structure based on a hierarchical combination of chord and robust m-child family tree with its nodes spread over multiple peers. A peer can be mapped to a node based on hash based uniform mapping.

From the above analysis, it is clear that, in a dynamic large scale network, the problem of node dynamicity must be addressed without causing routing inconsistency. In this paper, we propose structured hierarchical overlay architecture by using a super peer concept [30–35]. In the proposed approach, we use a combination of ring and robust m-child family tree and explore the dynamicity handling by localizing the effect of churn attack in subtree and cause minimum structural or routing inconsistencies. The use of robust m-child family tree architecture is powerful not just because it supports key based lookup, but because they work even when the network is highly dynamic with nodes constantly joining and leaving the network. That is, robust m-child family tree structure can handle the churn attack scenario without causing much structural inconsistencies as most updates and structural transformations (new key is always inserted at the leaf node) of robust m-child family trees are limited to the leaves and lower levels of the tree. In the proposed hierarchical design, super peer nodes are selected based on some predefined performance criteria such as performance and reliability. These super peer nodes will serve as a root node for individual m-child family trees and will be arranged in ring architecture according to their peer IDs.

As we explain in this paper, the proposed architecture has the following advantages over basic chord architecture:

(i) The proposed architecture provides more stability, as dynamic population changes in this architecture have limited interference to a tree rather than to the whole network. So, this architecture provides "isolation of churn" as node join or leave within a tree will not affect the top level chord overlay.

(ii) Most of the available tree structures suffer from lack of redundancy and therefore their structure is sensitive to single node and link failures. In the robust m-child family tree this limitation is overcome by storing additional pointers to parent and uncles along with the child information to make it robust to node and link failures.

(iii) The m-child family tree structure ensures that new unreliable node will always join as the leaf node and as we know in the tree topology the effect of failure is much higher for nodes close to the root node. So, our proposed tree structure is robust to churn attack where an attacker will trigger a large number of new nodes to join and leave the overlay in a short time span, because all these nodes irrespective of their node ID values will always join as leaf nodes and minimize the topology changes resulting from the new nodes joining and leaving the overlay.

(iv) In order to ensure fault tolerance, each super peer node has a backup node, which periodically pings the super peer and makes checkpoints on its status.

The remainder of this paper is organized as follows. Section 2 introduces the basic concepts and the most important contributions in this area. In Section 3, we provide abstract system model and adversarial model. Section 4 introduces our proposed structured hierarchical overlay network model. In Section 5, we discuss the basic algorithms for the proposed overlay architecture. Section 6 outlines the design of our experiments and covers the results and discussions.

2. Background and Related Work

In this section, we first introduce the basic concepts to aid the better understanding of our research work. Then, we discuss the important research contributions in the field of robust structured overlay networks that can handle a large fraction of malicious peers that frequently join/leave the overlay network to consume most of the network bandwidth for structure management purposes and make the network unstable.

2.1. Basic Concepts. Before discussing the value of proposed architecture, we first introduce the hierarchical overlay networks and then examine the churn, both as legitimate and as malicious behavior. This section will highlight the need of robust overlay architectures to maintain the health and security of the overlay networks in the face of churn.

2.1.1. Structured Hierarchical Overlay Networks. Structured overlay networks are a self-organized, distributed architecture of a large number of heterogeneous and unreliable machines arranged in a specialized structure to share a set of resources with reasonable performance guarantees. In traditional structured overlay networks all the participants are considered equal in the sense that they share the same set of responsibilities and use the same set of rules for determining the lookup routes for the messages [38]. Searching is one of the most important services provided by the structured overlay networks. The desired features of searching are high quality query results, minimum query overhead, high routing efficiency, and resilience to node failures. Structured overlay networks have poor searching performance in dynamic environments, where nodes join and leave the overlay network frequently. To capture the heterogeneity of overlay participants and to improve the performance and scalability, overlay networks utilize the multiple levels of hierarchy in the form of hierarchical overlay networks. In these architectures, different overlay participants are given different roles (super peers and regular nodes) based on their reliability and capability. Structured hierarchical overlay networks use only structured topology at each level. The main aim behind the use of hierarchical overlay networks is to group the overlay nodes logically and each group then utilizes its intragroup overlay protocol for maintenance and lookup operation. This logical grouping of nodes is done in the top layer overlay network, where one or more nodes have been assigned the responsibility of super nodes and act as the gateway to the next level of nodes.

2.1.2. Churn. The correctness and the performance of structured overlay networks mainly depend on its up to date routing table entries that together form an overlay topology with specific structural constraints (e.g., ring structure in the chord overlay network). But, due to their open nature in the real world, where nodes may join or leave the overlay network at any time, this continuous dynamism of peer participants in the form of continuous joining, leaving, and failure from the overlay network is known as churn. Churn has significant impact on the performance of structured overlay networks as it may generate a considerable traffic to accommodate the rebalancing of data among overlay participants and to update the routing table entries accordingly. Thus, significant churn may result in blocking of the normal search operation and result in lookup failures or inconsistent lookups. The most common causes of node's unavailability are network failures, mobility, overload, crashes, or a nightly-shutoff schedule.

2.1.3. Churn: Inherent Weakness to Intentional Attack. Churn is studied as a dynamic legitimate behaviour of overlay participants that degrade the overlay network performance; until 2004, it has been regarded as a potential security threat by Linga et al. [39] to attack the availability of the overlay network. Due to the open nature of overlay networks, it is very difficult to avoid the participation of malicious nodes. Thus, researchers should concentrate on the development of robust overlay networks that can tolerate churn attack while still providing the services to the overlay users.

(1) Different Models of Churn Attack: Random and Strategic. Churn can be exploited as a tool to attack the availability of overlay network by generating peers, joining and leaving the network quickly in order to corrupt the functionality of the overlay network. Churn attack is a peer to peer version of Denial of services (DoS) attacks in which malicious peers frequently join and leave the overlay network to induce a large amount of communication and processing overhead to make it incapable of serving legitimate overlay participants.

These efforts of malicious attackers can be categorized into two main categories based on attacker's capability: random churn attack and strategic churn attack.

Random Intentional Churn Attack. An attacker can exploit the churn effect by triggering the fast join/leave of a number of slave nodes to destabilize the routing infrastructure. This attack is a type of DDoS attack on overlay networks and its impact can be amplified by Sybil nodes.

Strategic Churn Attack. An intelligent adversary can plan a strategic attack against structured overlay network by continuously attacking its weakest part or pinpointing the attack to specified targets only. Such an attacker learns the topology of the overlay by inserting a crawler and then plans its attack accordingly to partition the overlay network.

Churn attacks are an artificially induced churn with potentially high rates to cause bandwidth consumption due to overlay maintenance. This leads to the worst case of denial of service or service degradation. Cooperative web caching [39] is an attractive application of structured overlay networks to eliminate the use of proxy servers by storing metainformation in the overlay nodes. However, this application is vulnerable to churn attack as an attacker can easily mount a distributed denial of service attack by crippling the sharing mechanism. For this, attackers can pose extreme stress in the form of maintenance overhead generated by a large number of concurrent nodes join/leave procedures, which otherwise are considered nonmalicious. In this paper, we have proposed an efficient structured hierarchical overlay network to survive churn attack.

2.2. Related Work. Churn is an attractive tool for an adversary to destabilize the structured overlay network [39]. In this attack, a large number of malicious users will join and leave the network frequently in order to increase the bandwidth consumption due to overlay maintenance. The state-of-the-art structured overlay network architecture [20, 24, 40–43] considers churn as a legitimate node behaviour and provides simple maintenance mechanisms with significant recovery time to handle a set of node failures [44–46]. Researchers have been aware of this attack for quite a while [2, 6–8, 17] and various solutions have been presented to thwart this attack [25, 27, 47–49] but until recently no solution can provably cope with this attack without compromising the openness of the overlay network. Moreover, most of the proposed solutions [27, 48] are static as they can handle only bounded number of node failures. Kuhn et al. [27] have proposed an efficient but a complex architecture to counter an intelligent adversary by continuously shifting newly joined nodes to less sparse areas. In contrast, our proposed technique is simpler and addresses more realistic random intentional churn attack by allowing the new nodes to join as a leaf node thereby isolating the effect of leave of malicious nodes without affecting the rest of the overlay. A large number of researchers are currently working on structuring the overlay networks in a hierarchical manner [31, 33–35, 37, 50–54] in order to achieve better efficiency, performance, maintenance cost, and load balancing. In [53], Rocamora and Pedrasa have

TABLE 1: Comparison of performance of different overlay architectures.

Technique	Topology	Join	Leave	Hops
CHORD [24]	Flat	$O(\log^2 n)$	$O(\log^2 n)$	$O(\log n)$
Pastry [20]	Flat	$O(\log^2 n)$	$O(\log^2 n)$	$O(n \log n)$
TLS [36]	Flat	$O(\log n)$	$O(\log n)$	$O(\log n)$
BATON [19]	Flat	$O(6 \log n)$	$O(\log n)$	$O(\log n)$
Chordella [37]	Hierarchical	$O(\log^2 N)$	$O(\log^2 N)$	$O(\log n)$
		In case of super peer failure, where N is the number of super peers		
This paper	Hierarchical	$O(m^2 - m + 1)$	$O(2) + 2O(m(m-1))$	$O(\log n)$

evaluated the hierarchical DHTs in the churn scenario of mobile nodes and clearly state the effectiveness of hierarchical DHTs as compared to flat DHTs. However, they have not considered the effect of malicious adversary, who maliciously triggers a large number of join requests for limited lifetime to bring the entire system down.

Table 1 summarizes the comparison of performance of different overlay networks and our proposed architecture. In this table, we have compared the performance of different state-of-the-art flat and hierarchical structured overlay networks in terms of lookup hop count and cost of join and leave in the form of messages sent per join/leave event. The major advantage of our proposed work is that the cost of insertion and deletion will not increase with the increase in the network size as the nodes do not need to make its place in the overlay structure; rather they will always join as leaf nodes. The cost of node join or leave will depend on the degree of m-child family tree as it will define the number of redundant pointers to the target node.

3. Model

3.1. System Model. A dynamic structured overlay network is composed, at any time, of a finite set n of nodes due to continuous arrival and departure of overlay nodes. These nodes have assigned a unique identifier derived by using the standard SHA [55] on the IP address of a node from a k-bit identifier space. Each node of the tree will store a range of values by splitting this range into four equal parts and maintain m-child pointers to store the address of the subtree responsible for storage of these ranges. The nodes are organized into trees, and each tree has its autonomous overlay network with a reliable root node. The overall overlay tree organization is provided by top level chord [24] based overlay network. Each tree has its root node (super peer) in the top level overlay network. Super peer nodes act as a gateway between different trees to provide intertree communication. The top layer overlay (chord) is responsible for overall connectivity of different peers. So, chord ring is formed with more stable and powerful nodes. The tree nodes will communicate with each other through message passing using the hierarchical overlay network. This message passing is possible by maintaining a neighbourhood table at each node and this table will define the topology of the lower tier overlay network. The neighbourhood table of each

node will store the address of its immediate descendants, its parent, and its uncles (siblings of its parent). The top level overlay will determine the tree responsible for the key and then the responsible tree will use its overlay to determine the specific node responsible for the desired key. The routing mechanism of our tree structure is similar to searching in a tree. The dynamicity of envisioned system will cause topological inconsistencies and communication failure due to invalid entries in the neighbourhood table. Our envisioned system is robust to the joining of a new node as the new node will always join as the leaf node of the appropriate subtree based on its node ID. So, the joining of a new node and its unreliable behaviour will not affect the rest of the structure of the tree. But, the uninformed leave of a tree node causes disconnection of its descendants from the rest of the tree. So, an efficient recovery mechanism should be in place to fix the network. That is why dynamicity can be used by an attacker as a weapon to collapse the entire structure of overlay networks. The communication failure caused by these topological inconsistencies is the focus of this paper.

3.2. Adversary Model. A fundamental issue faced with an open system is that any new node can join the network at any time and existing nodes can leave the network without informing. The attacker can exploit this dynamic behaviour of nodes, to launch an availability attack against structured overlay networks. In our work, we consider an adversary A_{adv} that can launch a churn attack against the overlay network by performing frequent join and leave of a number of nodes per unit time and results in a drastic change in the population of an overlay. Here, node population n comprises nodes currently participating in overlay $n = (j_1, j_2, \ldots, j_n)$. In this model, we assume that nodes will depart or crash without notice, hence causing communication failure due to invalid neighbourhood table entries. In the intentional churn attack model the attacker will generate a polynomial number of join requests from a large number of nodes with random node IDs and enforce a limited lifetime of each node. The main aim of joining attacker is to ruin the whole system. In our model external adversary controls the churn, but not the behaviour of internal nodes. In traditional DHTs, these newly joined nodes will take their place in the DHT and after an enforced time they all will leave the overlay to break the entire structure and make the overlay network unable to serve queries.

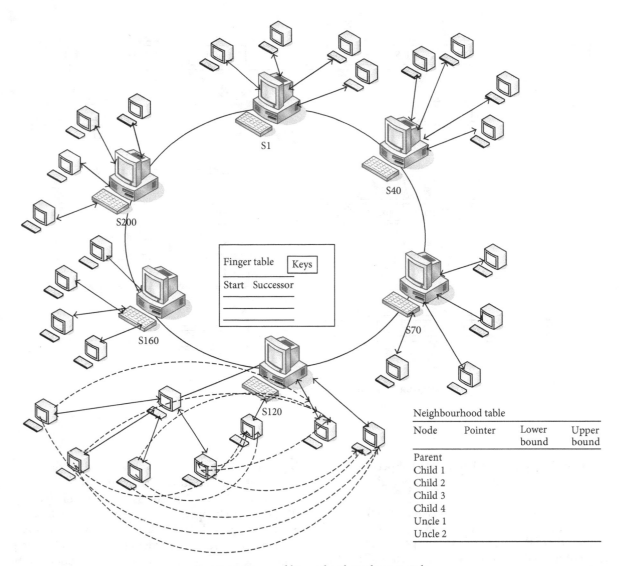

Finger table | Keys

Start   Successor

Neighbourhood table

Node	Pointer	Lower bound	Upper bound
Parent			
Child 1			
Child 2			
Child 3			
Child 4			
Uncle 1			
Uncle 2			

FIGURE 1: Proposed hierarchical overlay network.

4. Proposed Robust m-Child Family Tree Based Structured Hierarchical Overlay Network Architecture

In a structured overlay system, finding an efficient and scalable solution for content discovery in the presence of massive churn is a challenging problem. In this section, we present a robust and fault-tolerant structured hierarchical overlay structure to counter churn attack. The basic mechanism behind our approach is to give a noncritical role to newly joined nodes so that their failure will have no or short range effect. Figure 1 represents the structure of the proposed overlay network.

The proposed architecture is built on a two-tier hierarchical architecture, where the higher tier consists of super peer nodes representing ring nodes and forming the root of the family tree and lower tier represent the remaining family tree. The key idea behind using family tree structure is to create a scalable and robust overlay network, where each node

can store at the max N files. Every family tree has a super peer as its root node. Local peers in the same family tree are connected to other family trees through their root node and are arranged. In case of a query message, the local node will calculate the given key using uniform mapping rule. If a key lies in its own jurisdiction, it will find the node responsible; otherwise query will be moved upward until it finds the node responsible or it reaches the root node. At the root node, it will check whether required key lies in the local m-child family tree or not. If it lies there, then request will be sent to local m-child family subtree; otherwise root will find the super peer responsible for holding the key and forward the query to appropriate super peer in the ring topology.

Definition 1. Each regular peer p will be a member of local m-child family tree with root node S_n (member of the layer 1 chord ring), if S_n is the first node whose ID is followed by the ID of the peer p.

To provide a better understanding of the proposed hierarchical model, we first provide an overview of working of

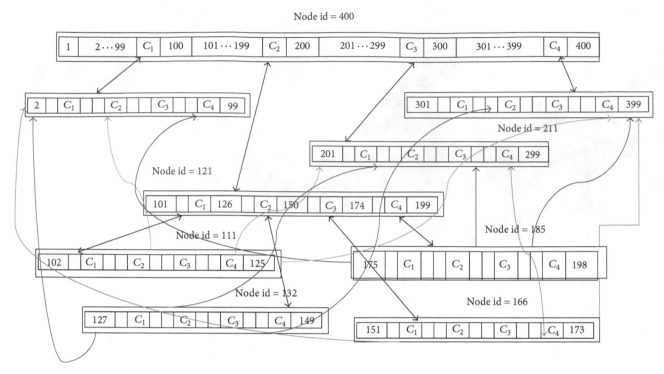

FIGURE 2: Anatomy of robust m-child family tree.

robust m-child family tree and how overlay peers will be organized into robust m-child family tree topology.

4.1. Basic m-Child Family Tree.

We consider trees that store a finite set K of keys in the range $(K_i, K_{i+1}, \ldots, K_n)$, where K_i is the node ID of the root node (super peer) and K_{n+1} is the node ID of immediate successor of the root node in the top layer chord ring as shown in Figure 2. Each node N of the tree contains a sequence of keys K_i split into four equal ranges separated by pointers $c[x]$ referring to its child node. For the leaf nodes all the child pointers are null.

Initially, all the keys are stored by the root node. As a new node joins the tree, it will be added as a leaf node of a subtree based on its node ID value. The child pointer of the parent node will be updated accordingly and the parent will delegate the key storage responsibility of appropriate range (the range in which joining node's ID is falling) to its child node. The values of keys of separate ranges are stored in each subtree.

4.2. Anatomy of Robust m-Child Family Tree.

The creation and maintenance of family tree structure is quite simple. This tree structure fulfils the property that insertions are restricted to be as leaf nodes. So, new nodes can join or leave the data structure without causing much inconsistency and make this system suitable for dynamic environments by decreasing the cost of insertion and deletion. In the proposed architecture, family tree with the fixed root and additional robust pointer structure and robust representation of stored keys is used. An m-child family tree is the one in which a tree can have m children.

Definition 2 (proposed m-child family tree). This is a self-modifying, multiway structure of order m, where each node N is defined as a tuple of $[(\text{Range}_1, C_1), (\text{Range}_2, C_2), (\text{Range}_3, C_3), \ldots, (\text{Range}_m, C_m), \text{bool}, U[x], p]$, where Range_i is the set of key values stored by the specific subtree in the ascending order ($1 \le i \le m$), C_i is the pointer from node N to its child ($1 \le i \le m$), bool is a Boolean variable, which will be true if N is a leaf node and false otherwise, and p and $U[x]$ are the pointers from the node t to its parent and uncle (parent's sibling), respectively. The values of keys separate the ranges stored in each subtree.

The robust pointer structure and new insertion as leaf node make this structure suitable for implementation of overlay network in which new nodes are usually unreliable. In robust m-child family tree structure nodes promptly react to node failure to maintain connectivity.

The structured hierarchical overlay network implements the network as a combination of chord and robust m-child family tree. The information sharing between different peers will be implemented using this combination, where chord network will identify the m-child family tree responsible for storage of a particular range of data and this m-child family tree will then find the particular node responsible for it. This m-child family tree is the basic data structure for a structured hierarchical overlay network with a hash table distributed on it. There is a node in an m-child family tree for each peer in the system. An m-child family tree has spread its nodes over different peers and these values are mapped to hash of an IP address of these peers.

5. Proposed Structured Hierarchical Overlay Network Algorithms

In this section, we introduce different algorithms for creating, maintaining, and querying an m-child family tree based hierarchical structured overlay network that derives its characteristics from the working of general real time family tree structure. Our goal is to create an m-child family tree rooted on super node to store a range of values on different nodes in an effective, fault-tolerant, and efficient manner. In this architecture, top level chord architecture is formed by most reliable (high expected life time) nodes and reduces the expected number of hops and failures.

5.1. Super Peer Selection. In order to create the hierarchical overlay, first, we need to select top layer overlay nodes. More stable nodes will be selected as super peers to minimize the churn effects in the top layer overlay. Various researchers [33–35, 56] have proposed different techniques to select stable peers and designate them as super peers of hierarchical overlays.

In our architecture, we have used a gradient search algorithm [35] to discover highly stable peers for the top layer chord overlay network. In this algorithm peer's uptime is used as a metric to compute the stability of the peer to check whether the node is the suitable candidate to take the responsibility of a super peer. Each super peer node will maintain two tables: finger table for top layer chord overlay and routing table for local m-child family tree. The routing table at each node of m-child family tree will store entries for its immediate descendants and its parent and uncles (siblings of the parent node).

5.2. Tree Creation. The initialization of m-child family tree involves the steps mentioned in algorithm explained in Algorithm 1.

In our algorithm; we first designate the top layer chord overlay node (super peer) as the root node of the m-child family tree. As we know, every chord node with ID m is responsible for the storage of a range of keys between m and M, where $M + 1$ is the ID of its immediate successor in the chord overlay. So, we divide this range into separate chunks, so that layer 2 overlay nodes that have to join the overlay network will choose their subtree according to their ID in the appropriate chunk. As already specified in Section 4, every m-child family tree node is a tuple of $[(\text{Range}_1, C_1), (\text{Range}_2, C_2), (\text{Range}_3, C_3), \ldots, (\text{Range}_m, C_m), \text{bool}, U[x], p]$, so we have to set the pointers for the child, parent, and uncle nodes of the root nodes. Initially they all are NULL pointers and their corresponding entry will be made in the neighbourhood table of the node. These pointers and neighbourhood table will be updated as the new nodes will join the overlay network.

5.3. Peer Join. In order to join an overlay, a requesting node must know at least one peer, who is already registered in the overlay network. That registered peer can be a super peer or

```
Create_Tree(T)  {
    (1)  x = allocate_node()
    (2)  Parent = NULL
    (3)  x[n] = Range(m, M)
    (4)  Set Root(T) = x
    (5)  Divide_in_chunk(x[n], t, ch[p])
    (6)  Repeat for i = 1 to t
    (7)  c[i] = Null
    (8)  Uncle[i] = Null
    (9)  End for
    (10) Return
}
Divide_in_chunk(x[n], t, ch[p])  {
    (1)  ch.size = roundoff(n/t)
    (2)  Repeat for i = 1 to t
    (3)  size = m + ch.size
    (4)  ch[i] = Range(m ⋯ size)
    (5)  m = size
    (6)  end for
}
```

ALGORITHM 1: M-child family tree creation.

a lower tier peer. The steps of joining process are explained with the help of an algorithm in Algorithms 2 and 3.

5.3.1. Impact of Node Join. The impact of joining of a node on the performance of the proposed architecture is negligible. Because, regardless of the ID of joining node, it will always be inserted as a leaf node and its parent will delegate its load to this newly joined node and set its pointer accordingly. So, all the routing table entries will be correct and thus queries can be routed to appropriate nodes without disruption.

Theorem 3. *In a proposed network of N nodes, the expected number of hops for a join operation is $O(\log n)$, where n is the total number of nodes in the overlay and $(O(1) + O(m(m - 1)))$ neighbourhood tables get updated after this join operation, where m is the degree of m-child family tree.*

5.4. Maintenance of Failure of Peers and Super Peers. Maintenance of the proposed approach is mainly of two types: intratree and intertree maintenance. Intratree maintenance handles the impact of normal (informed leave) or abnormal failure on the structure of B-tree. Intertree maintenance aims to preserve super peer's chord structure in the event of super peer failure or informed leave.

5.4.1. Intertree Maintenance (Top Layer Maintenance). In order to withstand churn attack, top layer overlay architecture is made up of highly stable super peer. In order to provide reliability, each super peer is associated with a backup node. In case of informed leave, super peer will inform the backup node about its status and delegate the responsibility. Whereas, in order to handle failure of super peer, a background periodic stabilization process is used. In this stabilization process,

```
Join (n₁, n₂) {
// node n₁ wants to join the overlay network and knows a node n₂ that is currently a member of overlay network.
    (1)  If n₂ is a super node(top layer node), then
    (2)  If host tree is responsible for n₁, then
    (3)  Go to step (6).
    (4)  Else
    (5)  T = Find_Tree(n₁)
         // joining node perform a tree lookup, which is routed in the top level overlay to the super node responsible for the key.
    (6)  n₁.Join_Tree(T)
    (7)  else   // if n₂ is not a super node
    (8)  n₂.Forward_Request(root) // node n₂ will forward the n₁'s join request to its root
    (9)  if root node(host tree) is the super node responsible for the key, then
    (10) n₁.Join_Tree(T)
    (11) else   //if root node(host tree) is not responsible for the key
    (12) T = Find_Tree(n₁)
    (13) n₁.Join_Tree(T)
    (14) Return.
    }
n₂.Find_Tree (n₁) {
// node n₂ will find the super node responsible for node n₁
    (1) T = (n₂, successor)
    (2) if n₁ ∈ T
        // super node responsible for the key is found
    (3) return T
    (4) else
        // forward the query to next node of the ring
    (5) T.Find_Tree (n₁)
}
n₂.Forward_Request (n₁, Root) {
// Forward the join request from node n₂ to the root of the tree
    (1) If (n₂ is not a root node), then
    (2) n₂ = parent(n₂)
    (3) n₂.Forward_Request(k₁, Root)
    (4) else
    (5) Root = n₂
    (6) return
}
```

ALGORITHM 2: Peer join operation in proposed architecture.

backup node will ping the corresponding node after regular interval and take its responsibility in case of failure detection.

5.4.2. *Intratree Maintenance (Tier 2 Maintenance).* Intratree maintenance mechanism is responsible for maintaining the structure of robust m-child family tree in case of node failure or informed leave. In a general tree structure with the loss of the parent node the descendants will be disconnected from the tree. But, in case of an m-child family tree structure after parent loss, they will connect to their grandparents through their uncle (each node will store its parent's address) and grandparent will delegate the parent's responsibility to the appropriate grandchild. In case of failure of nodes, the periodic stabilization mechanism will detect the node failure and take the following corrective measures:

(1) Every child will perform a periodic check to find whether its parent is alive or not. So, child node will identify the node failure.

(2) After failure identification, the child will contact its uncle to inform the grandparent about the failure of their parent node x.

(3) After receiving intimation about failure, a grandparent will apply the informed leave mechanism to arrange the graceful leave of its failed child.

The informed leave mechanism is explained as shown in Algorithm 4.

5.4.3. *Impact of Node Failure.* The impact of failure of nodes lying on m-child family tree is very little in the local subtree only. When a lower tier node fails either its parent or child nodes will trigger a recovery mechanism similar to informed leave mechanism to restore their network connectivity with the rest of the overlay. Each node will also maintain pointers to their uncles, so that in case of cascade failures in a single subtree they can restore the connectivity by contacting their common alive parent with other subtrees (rooted at the same super peer) by contacting their uncle. The additional sets

```
n₁.Join_Tree (T) {
Input: Tree T has a root R(Super peer),
: R is responsible for a range of keys (m to M), where m is the minimum key value and M
is the maximum key value
: Range is divided into 4 almost equal chunks: (ch[1], ch[2], ch[3] and ch[4])
        (1)  Repeat for i = 1 to 4
        (2)  If n₁ ∈ ch[i], then
        (3)  If c[i] == NuLL, then
        (4)  Set c[i] = n₁
        (5)  Delegate ch[i] values to node n₁.
        (6)  parent = T
        (7)  L = parent(T)    // L is the grandparent of newly joined node
        (8)  Initialize_fingers (n₁, L)    // initialize all the child, parent and uncle's pointer values
        (9)  break
        (10) Else
        (11) Set T = c[i]
        (12) break.
        (13) End For.
        (14) n₁.Join_Tree(T)
        (15) Return
}
Initialize_fingers (n₁, L) {
        (1) Divide_in_chunk(x[n], 4, ch[4])
        (2) Repeat for i = 1 to 4
        (3) c[i] = Null
        (4) U[i] = L(c[i])
        (5) End for
}
```

ALGORITHM 3: Peer join operation in the responsible tree of the proposed architecture.

```
Leave(n₁) {
        // node n₁ wants to leave the overlay network.
        (1)  If n₁ is a leaf node, then
        (2)  n₁ delegates its range to its parent and inform its leaving to all neighbours.
        (3)  Else      // n₁ is not a leaf node
        (4)  PR = Predecessor(n₁)    // predecessor of the node in its local subtree
        (5)  PTR = Parent(PR)
        (6)  PT = Parent(n₁)
        (7)  PR delegates its load to PTR
        (8)  N₁ delegates its load to PR.
        (9)  PT now points to PR and node n₁ can leave now.
        (10) Return
}
```

ALGORITHM 4: Peer leave mechanism of proposed architecture.

of links maintained in neighbourhood table apart from the standard links of overlay aid robustness of the proposed architecture.

Theorem 4. *The maintenance operation for failed node n_1 will affect $O(\log t)$ nodes with $(O(2) + 2O(m(m-1)))$ neighbourhood tables updates, where t is the number of nodes in a subtree rooted on parent of failed node and m is the degree of m-child family tree.*

5.5. Lookup Algorithm. Any node from top tier or lower tier can issue a lookup request. In the second case, query should first be forwarded to the connected super peer in order to process it. Super peer will find the tree responsible for answering it, by routing the lookup request in the top tier chord overlay. After successfully finding the tree responsible, the root node will search for the node actually responsible for storing the key as shown in Algorithms 5 and 6.

Key_Lookup (n_1, k_1) {
    // lookup algorithm for key k_1 issued by node n_1
    (1) If n_1 is a super node of tree T, then
    (2) If (n_1 can answer query) then
// if issued query lies in local tree
    (3) Node = k_1.Search_Tree(T)
    (4) Else   // if n_1 cannot answer the query
    (5) $T = n_1$.Find_Tree(k_1)
    // query is routed in the top layer overlay to find the super node responsible for the key
    (6) Node = k_1.Search_Tree(T)
    // find the node responsible for the storage of key k_1 in tree T
    (7) Else
    // n_1 is not a super node
    (8) If (n_1 can answer query) then
// if issued query lies in local sub tree range
    (9) $T = n_1$
    (10) Node = k_1.Search_Tree(T)
    (11) Else // if query is not in local subtree
    (12) n_1.Forward _Request(k_1, root)
    // node n_1 will forward the key lookup request to its root
    (13) Go to step (2).
    (14) Return }
n_1.Find_Tree (k_1) {
    // node n_1 will find the super node responsible for node k_1
    (1) $T = (k_1,$ successor)
    (2) if ($k_1 \in T$)
    // super node responsible for the key is found
    (3) return T
    (4) else
    // forward the query to next node of the ring
    (5) T.Find_Tree (k_1)   }
n_1.Forward_Request (k_1, Root) {
    // Forward the request from node n_1 to the root of the tree
    (1) If (n_1 is not a root node), then
    (2) $n_1 = $ parent(n_1)
    (3) n_1.Forward_Request(k_1, Root)
    (4) else
    (5) Root = n_1
Return }

Algorithm 5: Key lookup operation in proposed architecture.

k_1.Search_Tree (T) {
    //After finding the responsible tree, query will be forwarded towards the appropriate child of tree
    (1) If k_1 lies on the root node, then
    (2) Return k_1
    (3) Else // if key lies on one of its child
    (4) Repeat for $i = 1$ to 4
    (5) if ($k_1 \in$ ch[i]), then
    (6) $T = c[i]$
    (7) Break
    (8) End for
    (9) k_1.Search_Tree(T)
    (10) Return.
}

Algorithm 6: Key lookup operation in the responsible tree of the proposed architecture.

TABLE 2: Simulation parameters.

Type	Parameters	Values				
Simulation parameters	Network Size	Max 10000				
	Churn generator	Multiple churn generators (no churn initially, Pareto churn for normal failure, and lifetime churn for intentional attack)				
	Mean node lifetime	For lifetime churn (churn attack)	1600 s	1300 s	1000 s	700 s	400 s
		For Pareto churn	2,000 s			
Common architecture parameters	Fix finger delay	120 s				
	Stabilization delay	60 s				
	Successor list size	4				
Node distribution	Percentage of super peers	5				
	Percentage of regular peers	95				
	Percentage of malicious peers in regular peers for churn attack scenario only	10	20	30	40	50
Degree of m-child family tree	For basic proposed architecture	2		**4**		6

Theorem 5. *In a proposed network of N nodes, the search for key k_1 is carried out in $O(\log N)$ steps.*

6. Experiments and Results

To prove and verify the proposed hierarchical structure, the omnet++ based overlay simulation framework OverSim [57] is used. The OverSim is an event based simulator with a layered architecture to provide a common API for application development. Its simulation framework is suitable for the design, evaluation, and comparison of different overlay network models at a large scale with support of different underlay networks. The new overlay modules are declared using NED language and their behaviour is customized using C++. The OverSim architecture provides a variety of underlay networks varying from simple underlay to more real IPV4 underlay.

6.1. Experimental Settings. The main parameters of our simulation are listed in Table 2. The simulations are performed using and updating the existing chord architecture in the OverSim simulator. All simulations are conducted on a network of varying size from 500 to 10000 nodes; each node assigned random 160-bit node ID. The network size defines the total number of overlay nodes in the simulation. In our proposed architecture, we have three types of nodes: super peer nodes (stable nodes in chord ring), regular peers (legitimate peers in tree topology), and malicious nodes (nodes with a short life span). As most of the existing analytical and numerical results indicate the presence of a small number of stable nodes in an overlay network, thus, in our proposed architecture, layer 1 overlay comprises about 5% of the total overlay population [58] and the remaining 95% of population comprises a mix of regular and malicious peers for different churn attack scenarios as specified in Table 2.

The selection of *churn generator* is mainly based on the type of churn behaviour simulation. For legitimate churn behaviour, a Pareto churn model is used, which will generate heavy tailed session times similar to real results from many real time peer to peer systems. But, if an attacker wants to insert many short lived peers in the overlay network, then the lifetime churn generator is the most appropriate churn attack generator as it is based on the Weibull distribution, which is known to be best for modelling a variety of life behaviour. The level of churn is simulated by varying the values of mean node lifetime between 400 seconds and 1,600 seconds. A shorter lifetime means a higher level of churn [16].

The *stabilization delay* and the *fix finger delay* refer to the duration between periodic ping to make sure that the neighbour and the exponential neighbours (finger table entries) are alive and successor table and finger table pointers are up to date. Each node on the chord ring maintains a successor list of size 4. The value of these parameters is chosen based on the most recent studies for the performance of chord based overlay networks.

The *degree of m-child family tree* describes the maximum number of children for a node. The fixed value of degree of proposed m-child family tree based overlay architecture used in the experimental settings is emphasized in bold typeface.

6.2. Simulation Results. Two things are evaluated here: first proving that the hierarchy introduced in the proposed architecture added value in terms of performance and scalability; second, proving the robustness of the proposed architecture to the intentional churn attack.

6.2.1. Performance of Proposed Hierarchical Architecture. To evaluate the performance of proposed hierarchical overlay architecture, we simulate it with nodes having legitimate churn behaviour. The following parameters are used for performance assessment of the proposed structure.

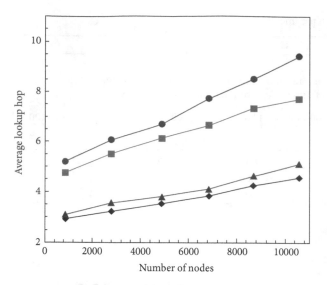

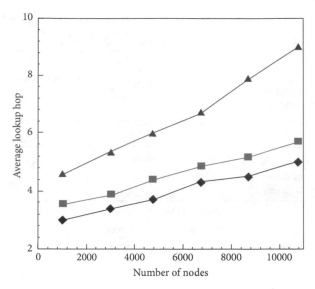

FIGURE 3: Comparison of different overlay network architectures with varying population.

FIGURE 4: Average lookup hop count with different degree of family tree.

(i) Average Lookup Hop Count. The average search hop count measures the performance of a system as the number of average hops needed for search. Figure 3 represents the performance of different overlay networks with respect to different overlay network sizes. The results clearly show that the proposed hierarchical architecture has better results as compared to other architectures due to stable super peer based top layer and the divide and conquer principle for message forwarding in the appropriate subtree with the use of tree based architecture in layer 2. From Figure 3, it is clear that the tree based architectures with fault tolerance capability (redundant pointers) such as BATON [19] perform better than chord architecture [24] due to underlying divide and conquer approach, but lack of redundancy in multiway trees [59] will make the situation worse by failure of the whole subtree in case of the parent failure. We also measure the average hop count by varying the degree of m-child family tree with $m = 2, 4, 6$, respectively, with respect to same set of participants as shown in Figure 4. From Figure 4, it is evident that the lookup hop count is reduced by increasing the degree of m-child family tree. Because, by increasing the degree of m-child family tree, the height of the tree will be reduced and ultimately it will decrease the number of hops to search a particular key. Thus, these results verify our first claim that our proposed architecture is efficient as compared to existing architectures in terms of minimum lookup delay. However, with the increase in the degree of m-child family tree, the number of pointers to be maintained at each node will also increase. Thus, designers have to select the degree of m-child family tree by taking this additional overhead in consideration.

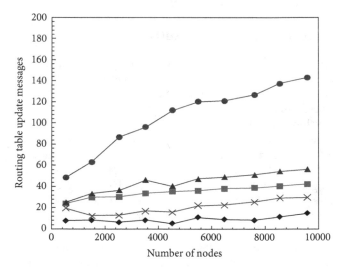

FIGURE 5: Average stabilization messages for single node join/leave.

(ii) Stabilization Messages for Single Node Join and Failure. The purpose of this set of experiments is to measure the overhead caused by the open and dynamic behaviour of overlay network nodes. Figure 5 presents the average number of stabilization messages required for a single join and leave operation. Our experiment confirms that the overhead associated with join operations in proposed architecture is quite low as compared to other systems as a new node always

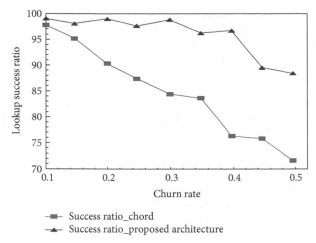

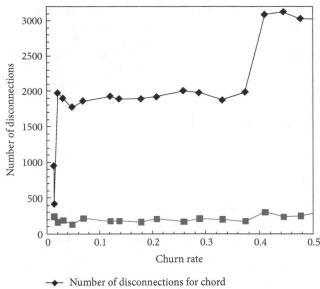

FIGURE 6: Lookup success ratio with varying levels of churn attack.

FIGURE 7: Effects of varying levels of churn on overlay network structure.

has to join as a leaf node and needs to update the pointer of its parent node and uncles (sibling of the parent node), whereas, in case of BATON [19] and multiway tree [59], a new node can join at any position based on its node ID and has to update a large number of pointers to their parent node, siblings, child nodes, and so forth. The join operation of BATON [19] architecture is more costly as compared to multiway tree [59] due to its need to store a large number of redundant pointers for fault tolerance. Moreover, as compared to other architectures, the proposed architecture partitions the overlay into multiple suboverlays and in turn reduces the number of routing table updates per node in case of join and failure.

6.2.2. Robustness of Proposed Hierarchical Architecture. In order to evaluate the effect of the intentional churn attack, we performed simulations starting with a number of honest peers only. We implemented a simple churn attack, where a significant number of nodes are added and removed from the network in each round. In our simulation model first intentional churn attack begins after the super peer topology has been constructed and has stabilized with the tree nodes. The performance of our proposed architecture is expected to remain consistent under intentional churn attack where a significant number of nodes are added and removed from the system within short time duration. We also evaluate the robustness of the proposed architecture under varying levels (represents the percentage of nodes that join/leave the system at each round) of churn attack.

(i) Lookup Success Ratio under Churn Attack. In this set of experiments, we measure the ability of proposed approach to achieve robust lookup operations despite the presence of heavy intentional churn attack. The robust lookup is realized by forcing the unreliable new nodes to get inserted at leaf levels. Figure 6 clearly represents the robust behaviour of proposed architecture: for 25% churn, lookup success ratio is almost 98% and for 50% churn 88% of the queries are correctly answered.

These results clearly indicate the robustness of the proposed architecture under intentional churn attack as our

architecture can provide lookup performance guarantees even when 50% of nodes are malicious.

(ii) Number of Disconnections under Churn Attack. It is the number of peers that lose their connections to the rest of the overlay due to churn attack. The experimental results show that the proposed architecture remains well connected under churn attack. Figure 7 shows that the proposed architecture reduces the large number of disconnections as compared to chord [24] overlay network under varying levels of churn attack. The number of disconnections will be reduced due to the isolation of the churn property of hierarchical network; along with this, our attack model usually triggers the malicious users to join the overlay network in rounds and all these malicious users will join as leaf nodes of the suboverlay. Thus, it will not impact the working of legitimate nodes and results in less number of disconnections.

7. Conclusion

The overlay networks emerge as a popular platform for the construction of large scale distributed systems; however the attackers can unleash the various attacks against overlay networks by exploiting their open nature. We presented a robust hierarchical overlay network to counter the intentional churn attack by adding the newly joined nodes at the leaf levels only with limited connectivity. The proposed architecture offers more stability, lookup efficiency, and less maintenance overhead by using more reliable peers at the top layer chord ring and regular peers inside m-child family tree at layer 2. The m-child family tree architecture reduces the lookup and maintenance message overhead by using divide and conquer principle for message forwarding in the appropriate subtree. But, this efficiency comes at a cost of retaining redundant uncle pointers at each node and incorporation of some sort of centrality in the distributed overlay architecture. Our simulation results demonstrate the effectiveness of the proposed hierarchical architecture to counter different churn attack levels without affecting the performance and connectivity of live peers with minimum maintenance message overhead.

Competing Interests

The authors declare that they have no competing interests.

References

[1] J. Buford, H. Yu, and E. K. Lua, *P2P Networking and Applications*, USA Morgan Kuafmann, 2009.

[2] M. Srivatsa and L. Liu, "Vulnerabilities and security threats in structured overlay networks: a quantitative analysis," in *Proceedings of the 20th Annual Computer Security Applications Conference (ACSAC '04)*, pp. 252–261, December 2004.

[3] L. Ganesh and B. Y. Zhao, "Identity theft protection in structured overlays," in *Proceedings of the 1st International Conference on Secure Network Protocols (NPSEC '05)*, pp. 49–54, IEEE, Washington, DC, USA, 2005.

[4] R. Kaur, A. L. Sangal, and K. Kumar, "Secure Overlay Services (SOS): a critical analysis," in *Proceedings of the 2nd IEEE International Conference on Parallel, Distributed and Grid Computing (PDGC '12)*, pp. 457–462, December 2012.

[5] E. K. Lua, J. Crowcroft, M. Pias, R. Sharma, and S. Lim, "A survey and comparison of peer-to-peer overlay network schemes," *IEEE Communications Surveys and Tutorials*, vol. 7, no. 2, pp. 72–93, 2005.

[6] E. Sit and R. Morris, "Security considerations for peer-to-peer distributed hash tables," in *Proceedings of the 1st International Workshop on Peer-to-Peer Systems (IPTPS '01)*, pp. 261–226, London, UK, 2002.

[7] D. S. Wallach, "A survey of peer-to-peer security issues," in *Proceedings of the International Conference on Software Security: Theories and Systems*, pp. 42–57, Berlin, Germany, 2002.

[8] B. Pretre, *Attacks on peer-to-peer networks [Ph.D. thesis]*, Department of Computer Science Swiss Federal Institute of Technology (ETH), Zürich, Switzerland, 2005.

[9] A. Singh, T.-W. Johnny Ngan, P. Druschel, and D. S. Wallach, "Eclipse attacks on overlay networks: threats and defenses," in *Proceedings of the 25th IEEE International Conference on Computer Communications (INFOCOM '06)*, Barcelona, Spain, April 2006.

[10] A. Singh, M. Castro, P. Druschel, and A. Rowstron, "Defending against eclipse attacks on overlay networks," in *Proceedings of the 11th Workshop on ACM SIGOPS European Workshop (EW '11)*, Leuven, Belgium, September 2004.

[11] D. Germanus, S. Roos, T. Strufe, and N. Suri, "Mitigating eclipse attacks in peer-to-peer networks," in *Proceedings of the IEEE Conference on Communications and Network Security (CNS '14)*, pp. 400–408, San Francisco, Calif, USA, October 2014.

[12] F. D. López-Fuentes, I. Eugui-De-Alba, and O. M. Ortíz-Ruiz, "Evaluating P2P networks against eclipse attacks," in *Proceedings of the Iberoamerican Conference on Electronics Engineering and Computer Science*, vol. 3, pp. 61–68, Guadalajara, Mexico, May 2012.

[13] Z. Trifa and M. Khemakhem, "Mitigation of sybil attacks in structured P2P overlay networks," in *Proceedings of the 8th International Conference on Semantics, Knowledge and Grids (SKG '12)*, pp. 245–248, Beijing, China, 2012.

[14] K. Aberer, A. Datta, and M. Hauswirth, "Efficient, self-contained handling of identity in peer-to-peer systems," *IEEE Transactions on Knowledge and Data Engineering*, vol. 16, no. 7, pp. 858–869, 2004.

[15] H. Rowaihy, W. Enck, P. McDaniel, and T. La Porta, "Limiting sybil attacks in structured P2P networks," in *Proceedings of the 26th IEEE International Conference on Computer Communications (INFOCOM '07)*, pp. 2596–2600, May 2007.

[16] R. Kaur, A. L. Sangal, and K. Kumar, "Analysis of different churn models in chord based overlay networks," in *Proceedings of the Recent Advances in Engineering and Computational Sciences (RAECS '14)*, pp. 1–6, March 2014.

[17] Y.-K. Kwok, "Autonomic peer-to-peer systems: incentive and security issues," in *Autonomic Computing and Networking*, pp. 205–236, Springer, New York, NY, USA, 2009.

[18] B. Awerbuch and C. Scheideler, "Towards a scalable and robust DHT," *Theory of Computing Systems*, vol. 45, no. 2, pp. 244–260, 2009.

[19] H. V. Jagadish, B. C. Ooi, and Q. H. Vu, "BATON: a balanced tree structure for peer-to-peer networks," in *Proceedings of the 31st International Conference on Very Large Data Bases (VLDB '05)*, pp. 661–672, September 2005.

[20] A. Rowstron and P. Druschel, "Pastry: scalable, decentralized object location and routing for large-scale peer-to-peer systems," in *Proceedings of the 18th IFIP/ACM International Conference on Distributed Systems Platforms (Middleware '01)*, Heidelberg, Germany, 2001.

[21] K. Hildrum, J. D. Kubiatowicz, S. Rao, and B. Y. Zhao, "Distributed object location in a dynamic network," in *Proceedings of the 14th Annual ACM Symposium on Parallel Algorithms and Architectures*, pp. 41–52, Winnipeg, Canada, August 2002.

[22] C. Rhea, *Open DHT: a public DHT service [Ph.D. thesis]*, University of California, Berkeley, Calif, USA, 2005.

[23] M. Castro, M. Costa, and A. Rowstron, "Performance and dependability of structured peer-to-peer overlays," in *Proceedings of the International Conference on Dependable Systems and Networks*, pp. 9–18, July 2004.

[24] I. Stoica, R. Morris, D. Liben-Nowell et al., "Chord: a scalable peer-to-peer lookup protocol for Internet applications," *IEEE/ACM Transactions on Networking*, vol. 11, no. 1, pp. 17–32, 2003.

[25] S. Rhea, D. Geels, T. Roscoe, and J. Kubiatowicz, "Handling churn in a DHT," in *Proceedings of the USENIX Annual Technical Conference*, Boston, Mass, USA, June 2004.

[26] D. Stutzbach and R. Rejaie, "Understanding churn in peer-to-peer networks," in *Proceedings of the 6th ACM SIGCOMM on Internet Measurement Conference (IMC '06)*, pp. 189–202, October 2006.

[27] F. Kuhn, S. Schmid, and R. Wattenhofer, "Towards worst-case churn resistant peer-to-peer systems," *Distributed Computing*, vol. 22, no. 4, pp. 249–267, 2010.

[28] Z. Liu, R. Yuan, Z. Li, H. Li, and G. Chen, "Survive under high churn in structured P2P systems: evaluation and strategy," in *Proceedings of the 6th International Conference on Computational Science*, pp. 404–411, Reading, UK, May 2006.

[29] F. Kuhn, S. Schmid, and R. Wattenhofe, "A self-repairing peer-to-peer system resilient to dynamic adversarial churn," in *Proceedings of the 4th International Conference on Peer-to-Peer Systems*, pp. 13–23, Berlin, Germany, 2005.

[30] J. Liang, R. Kumar, and K. W. Ross, "The kazaa overlay: a measurement study," *Computer Networks Journal, Elsevier*, vol. 49, no. 6, 2005.

[31] B. Yang and H. Garcia-Molina, "Designing a super-peer network," Tech. Rep., Stanford University, Stanford, Calif, USA, 2002, http://infolab.stanford.edu/~byang/pubs/superpeer.pdf.

[32] S.-J. Zhou, *Study on the distributed routing algorithm and its security for Peer-to-Peer computing [Ph.D. thesis]*, University of Electronic Science and Technology of China, Chengdu, China, 2004.

[33] L. Garces-Erice, E. Biersack, P. Felber, K. Ross, and G. Urvoy Keller, "Hierarchical peer-to-peer systems," in *Euro-Par 2003 Parallel Processing: 9th International Euro-Par Conference Klagenfurt, Austria, August 26–29, 2003 Proceedings*, vol. 2790 of *Lecture Notes in Computer Science*, pp. 1230–1239, Springer, Berlin, Germany, 2003.

[34] W. Nejdl, M. Wolpers, W. Siberski et al., "Super-peer-based routing and clustering strategies for RDF-based peer-to-peer networks," in *Proceedings of the 12th International Conference on World Wide Web (WWW '03)*, pp. 536–543, Budapest, Hungary, May 2003.

[35] J. Sacha, J. Dowling, R. Cunningham, and R. Meier, "Discovery of stable peers in a self organizing peer-to-peer gradient topology," in *Proceedings of the 6th IFIP WG 6.1 International Conference on Distributed Applications and Interoperable Systems (DAIS '06)*, pp. 70–83, Athens, Greece, June 2006.

[36] F. Buccafurri and G. Lax, "TLS: a tree-based DHT lookup service for highly dynamic networks," in *Proceedings of the OTM Confederated International Conferences, CoopIS, DOA, and ODBASE*, Agia Napa, Cyprus, October 2004.

[37] S. Zöls, Q. Hofstätter, Z. Despotovic, and W. Kellerer, "Achieving and maintaining cost-optimal operation of a hierarchical DHT system," in *Proceedings of the IEEE International Conference on Communications (ICC '09)*, pp. 1–6, June 2009.

[38] R. Kaur, A. L. Sangal, and K. Kumar, "Modelling and simulation of adaptive neuro-fuzzy based intelligent system for predictive stabilization in structured overlay networks," *Engineering Science and Technology, an International Journal*, 2016.

[39] P. Linga, I. Gupta, and K. Birman, "A churn-resistant peer-to-peer web caching system," in *Proceedings of the 2nd International Workshop on Peer-to-Peer Systems (IPTPS '04)*, February 2004.

[40] M. Castro, M. Costa, and A. Rowstron, "Performance and dependability of structured peer to-peer overlays," Tech. Rep., Microsoft Research, 2003.

[41] K. Hildrum, J. D. Kubiatowicz, S. Rao, and B. Y. Zhao, "Distributed object location in a dynamic network," in *Proceedings of the 14th Annual ACM Symposium on Parallel Algorithms and Architectures (SPAA '02)*, pp. 41–52, August 2002.

[42] S. Rhea, D. Geels, T. Roscoe, and J. Kubiatowicz, "Handling churn in a dht," Tech. Rep. ucb/csd-3-1299, UC Berkeley, Computer Science Division, Berkeley, Calif, USA, 2003.

[43] J. Saia, A. Fiat, S. Gribble, A. R. Karlin, and S. Saroiu, "Dynamically fault-tolerant content addressable networks," in *Proceedings of the 1st International Workshop on Peer-to-Peer Systems (IPTPS '02)*, Cambridge, Mass, USA, March 2002.

[44] P. Brighten Godfrey, S. Shenker, and I. Stoica, "Minimizing churn in distributed systems," in *Proceedings of the Conference on Applications, Technologies, Architectures, and Protocols for Computer Communications*, pp. 147–158, 2006.

[45] F. E. Bustamante and Y. Qiao, "Designing less-structured P2P systems for the expected high churn," *IEEE/ACM Transactions on Networking*, vol. 16, no. 3, pp. 617–627, 2008.

[46] X. Meng, X. Chen, and Y. Ding, "Using the complementary nature of node joining and leaving to handle churn problem in P2P networks," *Computers and Electrical Engineering*, vol. 39, no. 2, pp. 326–337, 2013.

[47] B. Y. Zhao, J. Kubiatowicz, and A. D. Joseph, "Tapestry: an infrastructure for Fault-tolerant wide-area location and routing," Tech. Rep. UCB/CSD-01-1141, Computer Science Division, UC Berkeley, Berkeley, Calif, USA, 2001.

[48] X. Li, J. Misra, and C. G. Plaxton, "Active and concurrent topology maintenance," in *Proceedings of the 18th International Conference on Distributed Computing (DISC '04)*, pp. 320–334, Amsterdam, Netherlands, 2004.

[49] M. El Dick, E. Pacitti, R. Akbarinia, and B. Kemme, "Building a peer-to-peer content distribution network with high performance, scalability and robustness," *Information Systems*, vol. 36, no. 2, pp. 222–247, 2011.

[50] Z. Trifa and M. Khemakhem, "A novel replication technique to attenuate churn effects," *Peer-to-Peer Networking and Applications*, vol. 9, no. 2, pp. 344–355, 2016.

[51] D. Korzun and A. Gurtov, "Hierarchical architectures in structured peer-to-peer overlay networks," *Peer-to-Peer Networking and Applications*, vol. 7, no. 4, pp. 359–395, 2014.

[52] T. Koskela, E. Harjula, O. Kassinen, and M. Ylianttila, "Robustness of a P2P community management system based on two-level hierarchical DHT overlays," in *Proceedings of the 16th IEEE Symposium on Computers and Communications (ISCC '11)*, pp. 881–886, July 2011.

[53] J. M. B. Rocamora and J. R. I. Pedrasa, "Evaluation of hierarchical DHTs to mitigate churn effects in mobile networks," *Computer Communications*, vol. 85, pp. 41–57, 2016.

[54] P. Ganesan, K. Gummadi, and H. Garcia-Molina, "Canon in G major: designing DHTs with hierarchical structure," in *Proceedings of the 24th International Conference on Distributed Computing Systems (ICDCS '04)*, pp. 263–272, March 2004.

[55] FIPS 180-1, *Secure Hash Standard*, US Department of Commerce/National Technical Information Service (NIST), Springfield, Va, USA, 1995.

[56] B. Yang and H. Garcia-Molina, "Designing a super-peer network," Tech. Rep., Designing a Super-Peer Network, 2002, http://wwwdb.stanford.edu/~byang/pubs/superpeer.pdf.

[57] I. Baumgart, B. Heep, and S. Krause, "OverSim: a flexible overlay network simulation framework," in *Proceedings of the IEEE Global Internet Symposium (GI '07)*, pp. 79–84, Anchorage, Alaska, USA, May 2007.

[58] B. Mitra, F. Peruani, S. Ghose, and N. Ganguly, "Brief announcement: measuring robustness of superpeer topologies," in *Proceedings of the 26th Annual ACM Symposium on Principles of Distributed Computing (PODC '07)*, pp. 372–373, ACM, August 2007.

[59] H. V. Jagadish, B. C. Ooi, K.-L. Tan, Q. H. Vu, and R. Zhang, "Speeding up search in peer-to-peer networks with a multi-way tree structure," in *Proceedings of the ACM SIGMOD International Conference on Management of Data*, pp. 1–12, ACM, June 2006.

6

Fast Channel Navigation of Internet Protocol Television using Adaptive Hybrid Delivery Method

Timothy T. Adeliyi and Oludayo O. Olugbara (iD)

ICT and Society Research Group, Durban University of Technology, Durban, South Africa

Correspondence should be addressed to Oludayo O. Olugbara; oludayoo@dut.ac.za

Academic Editor: Mohamed El-Tanany

The Internet protocol television brought seamless potential that has revolutionized the media and telecommunication industries by providing a platform for transmitting digitized television services. However, zapping delay is a critical factor that affects the quality of experience in the Internet protocol television. This problem is intrinsically caused by command processing time, network delay, jitter, buffer delay, and video decoding delay. The overarching objective of this paper is to use a hybrid delivery method that agglutinates multicast- and unicast-enabled services over a converged network to minimize zapping delay to the bare minimum. The hybrid method will deliver Internet protocol television channels to subscribers using the unicast stream coupled with differentiated service quality of experience when zapping delay is greater than 0.43 s. This aids a faster transmission by sending a join message to the multicast stream at the service provider zone to acquire the requested channel. The hybrid method reported in this paper is benchmarked with the state-of-the-art multicast stream and unicast stream methods. Results show that the hybrid method has an excellent performance by lowering point-to-point queuing delay, end-to-end packet delay, and packet variation and increasing throughput rate.

1. Introduction

The demand for a higher bandwidth has been overwhelming in recent years because of the deployment of a broadband converged network and delivering service paradigm. Convergence is the capability of the Internet to act as a single foundation for various functions that traditionally had their own platform [1]. The service paradigm is rapidly evolving and expanding to a true triple-play service represented by voice, Internet, and video [2]. The Internet Protocol Television (IPTV) is a key broadcasting service in a converged network that has brought immense potential to give network providers the capacity to expand their market value and revenue generated by increasing the number of subscribers [3].

IPTV in a converged network is a technique that aggregates data, voice, and digital television on a single-network infrastructure line to give subscribers a packed broadband service experience and helping with the utilization of broadband services [4]. IPTV is based on a multicast system for transmitting video across the Internet Protocol (IP) infrastructure because not all channels can be sent to the subscriber home

gateway as a result of the limited network bandwidth [5, 6]. IPTV is the future of TV broadcasting because it offers a real-time video service by transmitting varieties of video contents over a converged network.

The Digital Subscriber Line (DSL) is a dominant network infrastructure for delivering IPTV services in a converged network. DSL access line employs a twisted copper cable between the Digital Subscriber Line Access Multiplexer (DSLAM) in the last mile and the customer premise. Asymmetric Digital Subscriber Line (ADSL) is a type of DSL that has a maximum bitrate of 8 Mb/s and can only support one High Definition Television (HDTV) channel at a time while ADSL2 and Very-high-bit-rate Digital Subscriber Line (VDSL), respectively, support up to 24 Mb/s and 50 Mb/s [7]. An IPTV stream requires about 2–4 Mb/s sustained bandwidth per Standard Definition (SD) stream, using the MPEG4 compression standard with high definition increasing the bandwidth demand to 7–8 Mb/s per stream [8, 9].

The Quality of Service (QoS), which is an important metric frequently used to measure network performance is required in order to guarantee end-to-end IPTV deployment over a converged network and to provide Quality of Experience (QoE) assurance to subscribers. QoS is essential for providing a seamless IPTV service that aids QoE for subscribers. A satisfactory level of the service provided by a network provider is determined by the QoE perceived by subscribers [10]. The lower the QoE, the higher the level of dissatisfaction and the chances of subscribers abandoning such a service. QoE is composed of a variety of metrics frequently used to measure satisfaction by subscribers. The metrics include network performance parameters such as the end-to-end delay and jitter as well as the service quality parameters such as cost, reliability, availability, and usability [11].

However, when compared to the traditional cable and terrestrial broadcasting services, zapping delay becomes the deterrent to the widespread use of IPTV. Zapping delay problem sets in when a change of channel takes 0.43 seconds or more [8, 12, 13] that affects the QoE perceived by subscribers. Zare et al. [14] explain zapping delay as a problem that occurs when a subscriber desires to change a channel, but has to wait several seconds for the desired channel to be made available. The problem gets heightened when network delay and jitter occur such that the channel selected by a subscriber experiences more than 2 second delay when compared to the same channel aired on the traditional broadcasting service.

In view of this, we propose the use of an adaptive hybrid delivery method that agglutinates multicast and unicast methods to address the zapping delay problem in the IPTV over a converged network. In literature, many adaptive network methods have been proposed to address the zapping delay problem over a converged network. The methods include the Data-Centric Network Architecture (DCNA) that supports both data-centric and host-centric applications in order to address the Internet challenges. The DCNA approach is based on the inclusion of a shim layer between the application layer and the transport layer with appropriate interfaces to efficiently connect these layers [15]. Furthermore, a collaborative Internet architecture using the Smart Identifier NETworking (SINET) was proposed to completely eliminate resource location, data content, and user network restrictions. Consequently, the SINET method was designed to absorb all kinds of traffic dominance while compliantly meeting the various future IPTV requirements such as the vehicular network that provides inordinate prospects to address many of the challenging issues facing the current Internet architecture [16, 17].

2. Related Work

There are various methods developed over the years for improving zapping delay in IPTV. Zapping delay is usually caused by command processing time, network delay, buffer delay, multicast leave and join times, processing time in the display device, size of video buffer in encoder, and video decoding delay [14, 18]. In this section, we discuss some of these methods such as the substituting multicast-based IPTV service with the unicast-based IPTV service. A multicast-based IPTV service comes with some intrinsic downfalls in that all network devices deployed within the network must support the Internet Group Management Protocol (IGMP) [19].

However, troubleshooting multicast service is complex, which further heightens the incurred cost of implementation.

In sharp contrast, Jackson et al. [20] explained that the substitution of multicast service with unicast service is not viable because as the number of subscribers increases, the required bandwidth increases. Consequently, it becomes more expensive for the QoE required by the subscribers. Nikoukar et al. [21] proposed a method that sends adjacent channel alongside the channel requested by a subscriber. They assumed that subscribers are likely to watch an adjacent channel to the requested channel. However, this method did not solve the zapping delay problem because if a subscriber does not switch to the adjacent channel, it forfeits the purpose. Lee et al. [22] improved on this method by adding channel popularity with adjacent-based prefetching. This method is used in prefetching the contents of adjacent channels before they are requested. It differentiates the channels prefetched using up and down direction buttons on the Set-Top-Box (STB) remote control based on channel popularity. However, the disadvantage of this method is that the bandwidth load becomes high, causing overload, and it ends up not reflecting the desired channel a subscriber would likely watch.

A new method that predicts the desired channel that a subscriber might likely watch was proposed to address the downside of the channel popularity with adjacent-based prefetching method [22]. This method provides Intelligent Fast Channel Switching (IFCS) based on the behavior of a subscriber. It predicts channel traffic in advance for the subscriber who wishes to watch the channel in the next few moments. Moreover, it analyzes the behaviors of subscribers and obtains their preferences of watching channels to reduce the waiting time of the subscribers [23].

In spite of the number of literature studies addressing the zapping delay problem in recent years, there seems to be no sufficient literature covering IPTV zapping delay in a converged network. This gap intrinsically served a strong motivation for this study. In response to this gap, our proposed method addresses the overall problem of zapping delay by using an adaptive hybrid delivery for fast channel navigation.

3. IPTV Architecture

IPTV in a converged network is a service that uses the IP protocol to deliver multicasting contents to subscribers via a broadband connection. The IPTV architecture spans across four zones as shown in Figure 1. The customer premise where we find devices such as TV, STB, PC, IP Phone, and ADSL router presents IPTV contents to a subscriber. The network provider zone allows a connection between the consumer premise and service provider zone. The service provider zone is responsible for providing services to subscribers. The content provider zone owns or is licensed to air contents and encoded video [24].

3.1. Multicast. IP multicast is a one-to-many method for simultaneously delivering content to a group of nodes instead of one. IP multicast is required to provide IPTV services by joining the multicast group through a channel

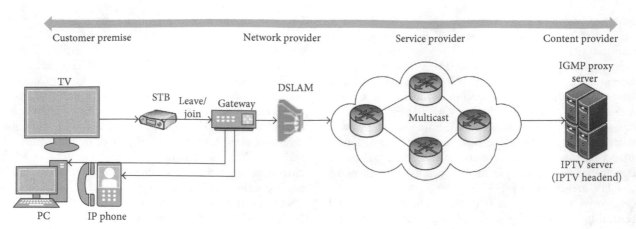

FIGURE 1: IPTV architecture over a converged network.

request initiated from the remote control of the subscriber's set-up box. This multicast service saves bandwidth at both the core and access networks because there is a high probability that multiple subscribers would likely watch the same program at the same time [25, 26].

IPTV channels are distributed to subscribers through the network provider by multicast service rather than broadcast service in order to reduce bandwidth load [27]. The IGMP is used for management purposes, allowing IPTV subscribers to report group memberships to any neighboring routers that are multicast enabled to manage multicast video streams at the service provider zone [28]. The STB performs the process of sending IGMP multicasting tree when an IPTV subscriber switches between channels using a remote control. The leaving group sends a leave message to the edge router at the service provider zone on receiving the IGMP leave message. The edge router will react by sending a specific multicast video stream and terminate the specific multicast channel while the join group message is used to obtain a new channel. After waiting for the IPTV content of the requested channel to be delivered, the STB waits for a decodable frame, called an Intra-coded frame (I-frame). The requested channel is ready to be displayed on the TV set once the requested channel is delivered to the STB of the subscriber [22, 29].

3.2. Unicast.

The unicast service is a one-to-one connection method that conventionally uses the Real-Time Streaming Protocol (RTSP) and Real-Time Protocol (RTP) to recover lost packets. It accelerates a channel change by delivering IPTV contents at a higher rate than the streaming rate of video [30]. A unicast service requires a dedicated zapping server to transmit a unicast burst when a subscriber initiates a channel change request. This stream is sent at a higher bitrate than the usual bitrate that allows the playout buffer to be quickly filled, making a channel readily available to a subscriber [31]. It can significantly reduce the waiting and the buffering time for I-frame, which is the first decodable video frame made available to a subscriber [32, 33].

The downside of a unicast stream is that there is a burst load on the bandwidth imposing significant input and output demands on the video servers. This is heightened

because of the huge requests from subscribers coupled with the variation of the unicast packet rate of transmission and ability to the recover lost packet. Chase [5] summarizes that IP multicast is used as a countermeasure because it provides huge bandwidth efficiency over the unicast delivery.

3.3. Zapping Delay.

In the traditional terrestrial TV broadcasts, all channels are being broadcasted once to a viewer, making channel changes almost immediately. This instantaneous change of channel involves the TV receiver tuning to a specific carrier frequency, demodulating the content, and displaying it on the TV screen [21, 34]. Terrestrial viewers through their experiences expect channel requests to be instantaneous because zapping delay in this system is less than 0.20 s. However, zapping delay occurs in IPTV when the channel change time is above 0.43 s because one requested channel is sent to a subscriber at a time due to high bandwidth consumption that deters the widespread use of IPTV service [35]. In addition, the problem occurs when an IPTV subscriber desires to change a channel but needs to wait until the target channel is available [36]. Zapping delay is considered one of the most important parameters of QoE that defines the acceptability of how subscribers would perceive IPTV contents and services. This is intrinsically caused by command processing time (T_c), network delay (T_n), buffer delay (T_b), and video decoding delay (T_v) [6] as shown in Figure 2. The zapping delay factor (T_z) is expressed as follows:

$$T_z = T_c + T_n + T_b + T_v. \tag{1}$$

The first factor that causes zapping delay in IPTV is the command processing time, which is the time required to examine the header of a frame in order to determine where to direct the frame [37]. The command processing time causes a delay that ensues at the instance a subscriber initiates a channel change request. That is, the time it takes the IGMP leave group message to leave the current channel while the IGMP joint group message is initiated through the multicast network service at the service provider zone to request for the desired channel.

Thereafter is the network delay, which is the time it takes for the requested channel to arrive after the initiation of the

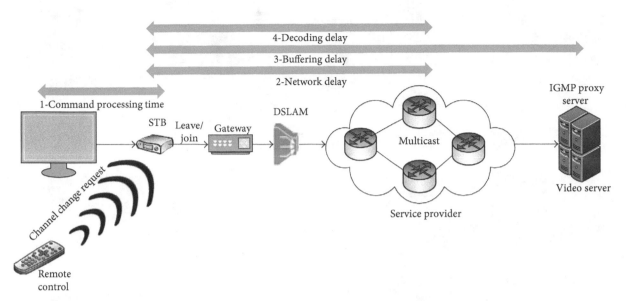

FIGURE 2: Factors of zapping delay in a converged network.

IGMP join group message. The buffering delay arises from buffering video frames after the arrival of the first I-frame. It is the time it takes to repair and retransmit content in order to provide reliability when packets are lost. This buffering is designed to help overcome the intrinsic problems caused by reordering and fluctuations of packets by the unavailability of content resulting from packet loss ratio (PLR), end-to-end delay, network jitter, and throughput rate [38, 39]. Packet loss is bound to occur if the network parameter for receiving IPTV traffic is not appropriately coupled with the different transmission rate. Consequently, PLR is the corrupted, lost, or excessively delayed packets divided by the total number of packets expected at the STB of a subscriber as follows [38]:

$$\text{PLR} = \left(\frac{\text{lost}_{\text{packet}}}{\text{lost}_{\text{packet}} - \text{received}_{\text{packet}}} \right). \quad (2)$$

The end-to-end delay is the time taken for a packet to be transmitted across a network from the IPTV headend to the STB. It is computed as follows [39]:

$$D_{\text{E-E}} = N \left(d_{\text{proc}} + d_{\text{queue}} + d_{\text{tran}} + d_{\text{prop}} \right), \quad (3)$$

where N is the network parameter between the IPTV headend and subscribers, customer premise zone, d_{proc} is the processing delay, d_{queue} is the queuing delay, d_{tran} is the transmission delay, and d_{prop} is the propagation delay.

The network jitter in IPTV is defined as a variation in the end-to-end delay of receiving video stream. At the IPTV headend, video streams are sent in a continuous stream with the packets spaced evenly apart. It is numerically determined as follows [38]:

$$D_{\text{jitter}} = t_{\text{actual}} - t_{\text{expected}}, \quad (4)$$

where t_{actual} is the actual time it takes for the IPTV packet to be received by a subscriber and t_{expected} is the expected time it takes for the IPTV packet to get to the subscriber.

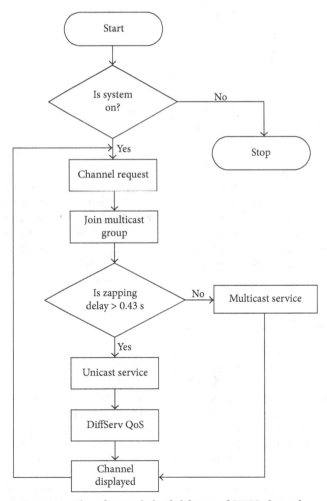

FIGURE 3: The adaptive hybrid delivery of IPTV channels.

The throughput (B_{w}) is the ratio of network capacity (N_c), that is, the network bandwidth over the cumulated load (W) of the average amount of IPTV traffic that passes

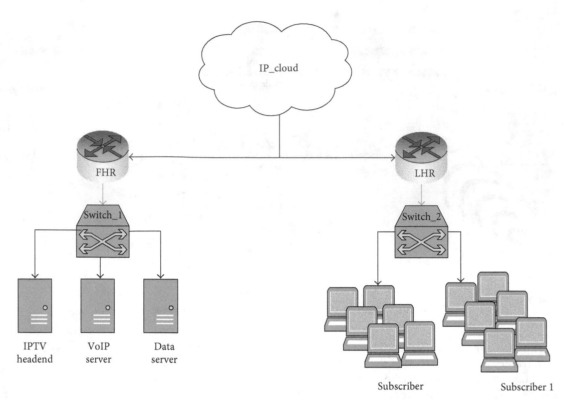

FIGURE 4: The OPNET simulation model of a converged network.

through to the STB. It is determined numerically as follows [39]:

$$B_{w} = \left(\frac{N_{c}}{W} \right). \tag{5}$$

Finally, a video decoding delay is the time it takes for a compressed video to be decoded, which is achieved by using I-frames. It is related to the encoding structure, and the maximum video decoding delay is the length of a group of pictures [40]. IPTV contents are compressed by encoding multicast video stream over IP network where the video streams are divided into groups of pictures [41].

4. Methodology

The essential steps of our adaptive hybrid delivery method that agglutinates multicast and unicast to minimize zapping delay in a converged network are shown in Figure 3. Once zapping delay occurs, a unicast method with Differentiated Service (DiffServ) QoS will be used to deliver IPTV contents from a multicast group to subscribers. This method addresses the requirements of delay, jitter, and real-time sensitive traffic during short periods of congestion. The overprovisioning of bandwidth will help to minimize the long-term average level of congestion within the converged network [42]. It is imperative to use DiffServ QoS to fairly prioritize bandwidth from the unicast stream when zapping delay set in because different services run on a converged network. DiffServ admission control solves the scalability issues and provides IPTV subscribers with a consistently high-quality video with a responsively reduced channel

TABLE 1: Parameters for simulating converged network.

Network	Converged network
IP backbone	IP cloud
Link model	PPP DS3
Server model	Ethernet server
No of servers	3
No of subscribers	20
Link bandwidth (core)	44.736 Mbps
Link bandwidth (access)	100 Mbps
Traffic type of service	IPTV–(streaming video) VoIP, HTTP, FTP, Database

zapping delay time. In addition, it reduces bandwidth consumption by policing IPTV traffic to ensure that it conforms to the service level agreement [43].

As shown in Figure 3, a decision is needed as to when to provide a hybrid stream and a multicast stream for a channel request. This is accomplished when the channel request is received and zapping delay is greater than 0.43 s. The hybrid stream is used for content delivery while a dedicated bandwidth is allocated using the DiffServ for an IPTV content in order to avoid delay and jitter. However, if zapping delay is less than 0.43 s, the channel content stream will be delivered with a multicast stream. The adaptive hybrid delivery method for channel navigation can reduce the problem of zapping delay during IPTV content delivery. Moreover, it can optimize the usage of network bandwidth while providing a resilient quality of service to subscribers. In addition, it can aid bandwidth saving and reduce zapping delay as channel request over the converged network must provide a real-time service.

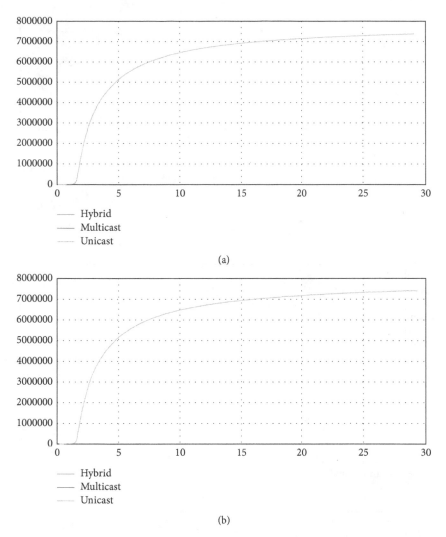

FIGURE 5: (a) IPTV traffic received. (b) IPTV traffic sent.

5. Simulation Experiment and Results

To simulate a realistic hybrid delivery method that will produce an accurate result within an acceptable timeframe, we have used the Optimized Network Engineering Tool (OPNET) Modeler 14.5. The OPNET is an application software that provides a comprehensive Integrated Development Environment (IDE) for the specification, simulation, analysis, and evaluation of the performance of communication networks [44]. The performance of the adaptive hybrid delivery method has been compared with the performances of the state-of-the-art multicast and unicast methods within the OPNET IDE.

Qing and Cong [45] explain that the OPNET modeler provides different levels of modeling, depending on the requirements of the simulation. The graphic user interface of OPNET modeler establishes an overall environment called a project. The operator can develop several network scenarios from a project in order to evaluate and analyze the performance of that network in different "what-if" scenarios. The modeler has to be configured as shown in Figure 4 in order to obtain desirable results. For the simulation experiment, we created a converged network with two routers, which are first hop router and last hop router connected to the cloud with a digital signal level 3 T-carrier link of 44.736 Mbit/s data circuit. The first hop router is connected to the converged network service with the IPTV headend, VoIP server, and data server.

Table 1 shows the network parameters used to configure the converged network topology in Figure 4. This topology has servers equipped for transmitting video, voice, and data services to subscribers. The Protocol Independent Multicast Dense Mode (PIM_DM) was added to the network node model for the simulation of the multicast stream. This has helped to efficiently generate, process, and deliver multicast packet within the converged network [46]. Furthermore, multicast services were enabled on all nodes in order to support efficient multicast stream delivery. The application model of the OPNET was configured to generate and process unicast stream for the simulation of the unicast steam. The OPNET configuration for the simulation of a converged network runs for the duration of 15 min in order to improve the processing speed.

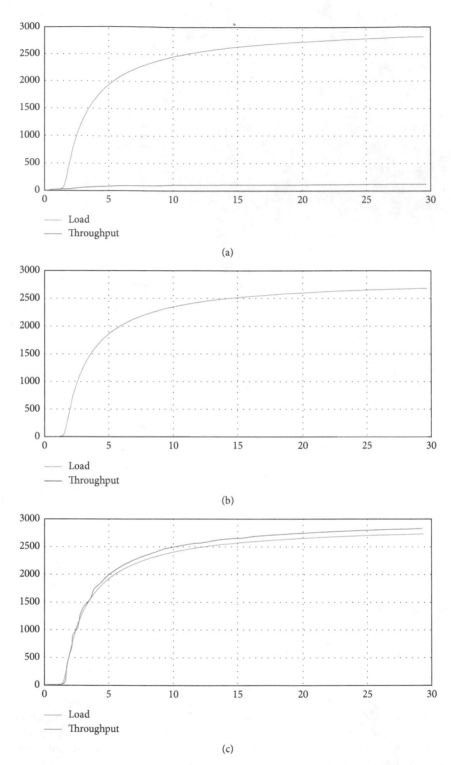

FIGURE 6: (a) Unicast (load versus throughput). (b) Multicast (load versus throughput). (c) Hybrid (load versus throughput).

Figure 5 shows the IPTV traffic received from the headend and traffic sent to 12 subscribers. Specifically, Figure 5(a) shows the IPTV traffic received by the headend from the subscribers for multicast, unicast, and our hybrid methods. All these methods received the same amount of traffic over a period of time. At the same time, the traffic sent by the IPTV headend to subscribers as shown in Figure 5(b) has the same traffic value for all methods. This provides a fair comparison of the simulated methods.

Figures 6(a) and 6(b) depict the IPTV traffic load from the headend versus the throughput rate for the traffic delivered to subscribers for the unicast and multicast methods, respectively. Although the throughput of the unicast method was higher than that of multicast, the downside effect is that it

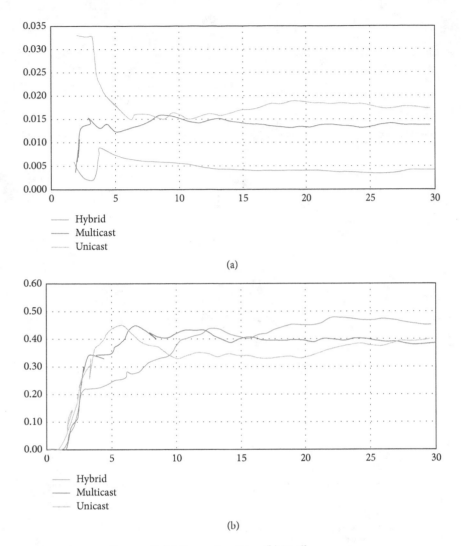

FIGURE 7: (a) Processing time. (b) Traffic request.

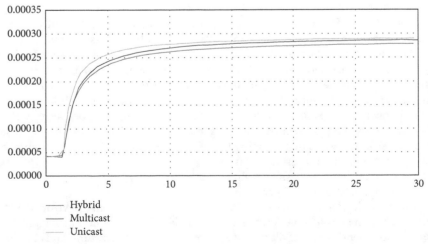

FIGURE 8: End-to-end delay.

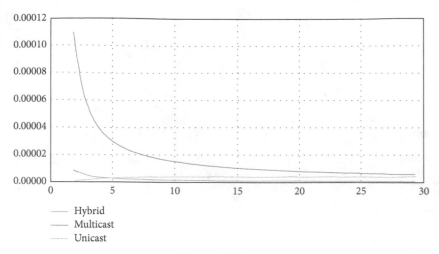

FIGURE 9: Jitter.

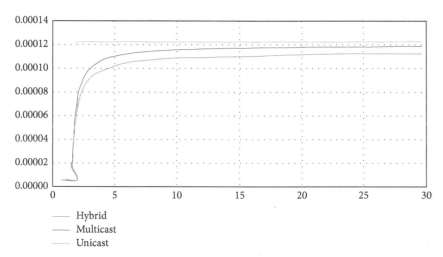

FIGURE 10: Queuing delay.

consumes excessive network resources while multicast has resource allocation challenge [25, 26]. However, Figure 6(c) illustrates the throughput rate of our hybrid method for the traffic delivered to subscribers, which is higher than the load. This result indicates that the hybrid method outclassed the state-of-the-art methods, which is possible by concomitantly taking the advantages of both unicast and multicast methods.

Figure 7(a) shows the performance result of the IPTV headend processing time in responding to requests from subscribers. The comparative result shows that our proposed hybrid method, when compared with the unicast and multicast methods, has the lowest processing time despite having a higher traffic request per second as shown in Figure 7(b). Consequently, our hybrid method efficiently shares network resources evenly without affecting the network performance.

Figure 8 illustrates the end-to-end delay of all packets received at the IPTV headend. The result shows that although our hybrid method has the highest traffic request, the end-to-end delay is low when compared with the results of the unicast and multicast state-of-the-art methods.

In Figure 9, the packet delay variation (jitter) of our hybrid method is significantly less when compared to the unicast and multicast methods. This would help to reduce the zapping delay problem in IPTV.

The queuing delay in Figure 10 is the time it takes the IPTV packet to wait in a queue until it is forwarded to the IPTV subscriber. The hybrid method has the least waiting time when it comes to delivering packets. This can reduce the network delay time and zapping delay in order to increase the perceived quality of experience by a subscriber.

6. Conclusion

In this paper, we have developed and evaluated an adaptive hybrid delivery method that agglutinates the state-of-the-art multicast and unicast methods for fast channel navigation in Internet protocol Television over a converged network. The simulation results show that the hybrid delivery method has a better performance by lowering point-to-point queuing delay, end-to-end packet delay, jitter, and network throughput. The use of the hybrid delivery method reported in this paper can provide efficient, resilient, and reliable IPTV video distribution to subscribers. Moreover, it provides a mechanism for reducing the zapping delay often experienced by IPTV subscribers during channel navigation.

References

[1] M. Jo, T. Maksymyuk, R. L. Batista, T. F. Maciel, A. L. De Almeida, and M. Klymash, "A survey of converging solutions for heterogeneous mobile networks," *IEEE Wireless Communications*, vol. 21, no. 6, pp. 54–62, 2014.

[2] J. Choi, A. S. Reaz, and B. Mukherjee, "A survey of user behavior in VoD service and bandwidth-saving multicast streaming schemes," *IEEE Communications Surveys and Tutorials*, vol. 14, no. 1, pp. 156–169, 2012.

[3] H. Joo, C. Yoon, T.-W. Um, and H. Song, "A novel fountain code-based mobile IPTV multicast system architecture over WiMAX network," *Journal of Visual Communication and Image Representation*, vol. 23, no. 1, pp. 161–172, 2012.

[4] B. Saranya, C. Balasubramaniam, and S. S. L. DuraiArumugam, "Survey on massive multimedia content delivery in push-based wireless converged network," *International Journal of Innovative Research in Advanced Engineering (IJIRAE)*, vol. 2, no. 1, pp. 139–143, 2015.

[5] C. J. Chase, "Broadcast interactive television system," Google Patents, 2016.

[6] B. Dekeris and L. Narbutaite, "IPTV channel zap time analysis," *Elektronika ir Elektrotechnika*, vol. 106, no. 10, pp. 117–120, 2015.

[7] A. Chatterjee, U. K. Roy, and N. Pahari, "Advancement of fixed net tele communication and different services," *Communications on Applied Electronics*, vol. 6, no. 1, pp. 14–22, 2016.

[8] R. Ferro, C. Hernández, and G. Puerta, "Rating prediction in a platform IPTV through an ARIMA model," *International Journal of Engineering and Technology*, vol. 7, no. 6, pp. 2018–2029, 2016.

[9] J. G. Oh, Y. J. Won, J. S. S. Lee, and J. T. Kim, "A convergence broadcasting transmission of fixed 4K UHD and mobile HD services through a single terrestrial channel by employing FEF multiplexing technique in DVB-T2," *Electrical Engineering*, vol. 99, no. 3, pp. 1021–1042, 2017.

[10] J. Lai and B. E. Wolfinger, "A method to improve the channel availability of IPTV systems with users zapping channels sequentially," in *Proceedings of International Conference on Wired/Wireless Internet Communications*, pp. 76–89, Santorini, Greece, June 2012.

[11] H. J. Kim and S. G. Choi, "A study on a QoS/QoE correlation model for QoE evaluation on IPTV service," *Advanced Communication Technology (ICACT)*, vol. 2, pp. 1377–1382, 2010.

[12] M. S. K. Manikandan, P. Saurigresan, and R. Ramkumar, "Grouped frequency interleaved ordering with pre-fetching for efficient channel navigation in internet protocol television," *Multimedia Tools and Applications*, vol. 75, no. 2, pp. 887–902, 2016.

[13] Y. Shin, S. Seol, and K. Lee, "A study on quality of experience of controlling a device remotely in an IoT environment," in *Proceedings of Ubiquitous and Future Networks (ICUFN)*, pp. 699–702, Milan, Italy, July 2016.

[14] S. Zare, S. Mohammad Hosseini Verki, and A. Ghaffarpour Rahbar, "Channel-zapping time in IPTV: challenges and solutions," in *IPTV Delivery Networks: Next Generation Architectures for Live and Video-on-Demand Services*, pp. 151–183, John Wiley & Sons, Hoboken, NJ, USA, 2018.

[15] H. Luo, H. Zhang, M. Zukerman, and C. Qiao, "An incrementally deployable network architecture to support both data-centric and host-centric services," *IEEE Network*, vol. 28, no. 4, pp. 58–65, 2014.

[16] W. Quan, Y. Liu, H. Zhang, and S. Yu, "Enhancing crowd collaborations for software defined vehicular networks," *IEEE Communications Magazine*, vol. 55, no. 8, pp. 80–86, 2017.

[17] H. Zhang, W. Quan, H. C. Chao, and C. Qiao, "Smart identifier network: a collaborative architecture for the future Internet," *IEEE Network*, vol. 30, no. 3, pp. 46–51, 2016.

[18] A. A. Khosroshahi, S. Yousefi, and A. G. Rahbar, "IPTV channel switching delay reduction through predicting subscribers' behaviors and preferences," *Multimedia Tools and Applications*, vol. 75, no. 11, pp. 6283–6302, 2016.

[19] M. Škrbic, N. Šecic, and M. Varatanovic, "A unicast-based IPTV service control," in *Proceedings of Systems and Networks Communications (ICSNC)*, pp. 278–282, Nice, France, August 2010.

[20] D. L. Jackson, R. A. Hansen, and A. H. Smith, "Multicast delivery of IPTV over the Internet," *GSTF Journal on Computing (JoC)*, vol. 1, no. 1, pp. 164–169, 2014.

[21] A. Nikoukar, I. S. Hwang, A. T. Liem, and J. Y. Lee, "Mitigating the IPTV Zap time in enhanced EPON systems," *Journal of Optical Communications and Networking*, vol. 8, no. 6, pp. 451–461, 2016.

[22] S. Lee, H. Moon, H. Bahn, T. Kim, and I. S. Kim, "Popularity and adjacency based prefetching for efficient IPTV channel navigation," *IEEE Transactions on Consumer Electronics*, vol. 57, no. 3, pp. 1135–1140, 2011.

[23] A. A. Beyragh and A. G. Rahbar, "IFCS: an intelligent fast channel switching in IPTV over PON based on human behavior prediction," *Multimedia Tools and Applications*, vol. 72, no. 2, pp. 1049–1071, 2014.

[24] S. Zeadally, H. Moustafa, and F. Siddiqui, "Internet protocol television (IPTV): architecture, trends, and challenges," *IEEE Systems Journal*, vol. 5, no. 4, pp. 518–527, 2011.

[25] S. Almowuena, M. M. Rahman, C. H. Hsu, A. A. Hassan, and M. Hefeeda, "Energy-aware and bandwidth-efficient hybrid video streaming over mobile networks," *IEEE Transactions on Multimedia*, vol. 18, no. 1, pp. 102–115, 2016.

[26] M. Condoluci, G. Araniti, A. Molinaro, and A. Iera, "Multicast resource allocation enhanced by channel state feedbacks for multiple scalable video coding streams in LTE networks," *IEEE Transactions on Vehicular Technology*, vol. 65, no. 5, pp. 2907–2921, 2016.

[27] L. C. Yeh, C. S. Wang, C. Y. Lin, and J. S. Chen, "An innovative application over communications-asa-service: network-based multicast IPTV audience measurement," in *Proceedings of Network Operations and Management Symposium (APNOMS)*, pp. 1–7, Busan, Korea, September 2011.

[28] J.-L. Collet, F.-X. Drouet, S. C. M. M. Lebrun, and G. Marmigere, "Method and apparatus for workload management of a content on demand service," Google Patents, 2011.

[29] C. Y. Lee, C. K. Hong, and K. Y. Lee, "Reducing channel zapping time in IPTV based on user's channel selection behaviors," *IEEE Transactions on Broadcasting*, vol. 56, no. 3, pp. 321–330, 2010.

[30] R. Jana, V. Aggarwal, X. Chen, V. Gopalakrishnan, K. Ramakrishnan, and V. Vaishampayan, "System for consolidating heterogeneous data centers through virtualization of services," Google Patents, 2016.

[31] V. Sgardoni and A. R. Nix, "Raptor code-aware link adaptation for spectrally efficient unicast video streaming over mobile broadband networks," *IEEE Transactions on Mobile Computing*, vol. 14, no. 2, pp. 401–415, 2015.

[32] J. Lai, J. C. Li, A. Abdollahpouri, J. Zhang, and M. Lei, "A fairness-based access control scheme to optimize IPTV fast channel changing," *Mathematical Problems in Engineering*, vol. 2014, Article ID 207402, 12 pages, 2014.

[33] F. M. Ramos, J. Crowcroft, R. J. Gibbens, P. Rodriguez, and I. H. White, "Reducing channel change delay in IPTV by predictive pre-joining of TV channels," *Signal Processing: Image Communication*, vol. 26, no. 7, pp. 400–412, 2011.

[34] H. S. Kim, I. Kim, K. Han, D. Kim, J. S. Seo, and M. Kang, "An adaptive buffering method for practical HTTP live streaming on smart OTT STBs," *KSII Transactions on Internet and Information Systems (TIIS)*, vol. 10, no. 3, pp. 1416–1428, 2016.

[35] F. M. Ramos, "Mitigating IPTV zapping delay," *IEEE Communications Magazine*, vol. 51, no. 8, pp. 128–133, 2013.

[36] J. Ryu, B. Lee, K. T. Kim, and H. Y. Youn, "Reduction of IPTV channel zapping time by utilizing the key input latency," in *Proceedings of 11th Consumer Communications and Networking Conference (CCNC)*, pp. 263–268, Las Vegas, NV, USA, January 2014.

[37] R. Li, M. Li, H. Liao, and N. Huang, "An efficient method for evaluating the end-to-end transmission time reliability of a switched Ethernet," *Journal of Network and Computer Applications*, vol. 88, pp. 124–133, 2017.

[38] D. H. Kim, J. H. Huh, and J. D. Kim, "Analysis of broadcast packet loss for unequal loss protection in Wi-Fi broadcasting system," in *Proceedings of 5th International Conference on IT Convergence and Security*, pp. 1–4, Kuala Lumpur, Malaysia, August 2015.

[39] D. A. Manzato and N. L. da Fonseca, "A survey of channel switching schemes for IPTV," *IEEE Communications Magazine*, vol. 51, no. 8, pp. 120–127, 2013.

[40] H. Joo, H. Song, D.-B. Lee, and I. Lee, "An effective IPTV channel control algorithm considering channel zapping time and network utilization," *IEEE Transactions on broadcasting*, vol. 54, no. 2, pp. 208–216, 2008.

[41] X. Tian, Y. Cheng, and X. Shen, "Fast channel zapping with destination-oriented multicast for IP video delivery," *IEEE Transactions on Parallel and Distributed Systems*, vol. 24, no. 2, pp. 327–341, 2013.

[42] A. Maraj and A. Shehu, "Analysis of different parameters that affect QoS/QoE for offering multi-IPTV video simultaneously in TK," *Journal of Communication and Computer*, vol. 9, pp. 1412–1423, 2012.

[43] A. Bahnasse, F. E. Louhab, H. A. Oulahyane, M. Talea, and A. Bakali, "Novel SDN architecture for smart MPLS Traffic Engineering-DiffServ Aware management," *Future Generation Computer Systems*, vol. 87, pp. 115–126, 2018.

[44] J. Qaddour and Y. Polishetty, "Modeling and performance analysis of a converged network," in *Proceedings of International Conference on Wireless and Mobile Communications (ICWMC)*, pp. 23–27, Barcelona, Spain, November 2016.

[45] L. Qing and L. Cong, "Efficient cluster routing design under the environment of internet of things based on location," in *Proceedings of Intelligent Transportation, Big Data & Smart City (ICITBS)*, pp. 318–323, Fujian, China, December 2016.

[46] A. Golechha, S. Karanje, and J. Abraham, "Comparative study of multicasting protocols based on average end-to-end delay," in *Proceedings of International Conference on Computing, Analytics and Security Trends (CAST)*, pp. 58–61, Pune, India, December 2016.

7

IoT in Action: Design and Implementation of a Building Evacuation Service

Selahattin Gokceli, Nikolay Zhmurov, Gunes Karabulut Kurt, and Berna Ors

Department of Electronics and Communication Engineering, Istanbul Technical University, Istanbul, Turkey

Correspondence should be addressed to Selahattin Gokceli; gokcelis@itu.edu.tr

Academic Editor: Sabrina Gaito

With the development of sensor technologies, various application areas have emerged. The usage of these technologies and exploitation of recent improvements have clear benefits on building applications. Such use-cases can improve smart functions of buildings and can increase the end-user comfort. As a similar notion, building automation systems (BAS) are smart systems that target to provide automated management of various control services and to improve resource usage efficiency. However, buildings generally contain hardware and control services from a diverse set of characteristics. The automated and central management of such functions can be challenging. In order to overcome such issues, an Emergency Evacuation Service is proposed for BAS, where requirements of such central management model are analyzed and model content and subservice definitions are prepared. A crucial scenario, which could be a necessity for future BAS, is defined and an approach for evacuation of people in the buildings at emergency situations is proposed. For real-life scenarios, the Evacuation Service is implemented by using a low-cost design, which is appropriate for Internet of Things (IoT) based BAS applications. As demonstrated, the proposed service model can provide effective performance in real-life deployments.

1. Introduction

In accordance with the development of sensor technologies that has been recently surging, smart system deployments to the buildings increase. Smart systems that are deployed in buildings increase user comfort and management of building resources becomes more efficient. These systems are referred to as building automation systems (BAS). Automated management of functions like heating, ventilation, lighting, security, and energy management is provided with BAS by using hardware and software based techniques. Specifically, utilization of BAS in schools, hospitals, factories, offices, and homes brings certain quality improvements [1]. Furthermore, BAS can provide significant cost advantages. According to a research conducted by Navigant Research, BAS industry is expected to reach 91.9 billion dollars in 2023 which is quite high compared to its size, 58 billion dollars, in 2013 [2].

Management of buildings, especially those which have high commercial value, is a challenging task due to complexity and size of the included control mechanisms, systems, and functions. On the other hand, advancing sensor technologies create an expectation on the improvement in smart content of buildings. However, BAS contains several deployment difficulties because of facts like increasing number of users and diversity of expected services and utilized hardware. Integration of BAS with information and communications technology (ICT) and other related technologies is a certain requirement in order to provide full smart building functionalities. At this point, modeling of properties and functions of a building plays a crucial role and eases the management of the building in accordance with smart building approaches. In parallel with the need for integrated management of different control systems, European Union funded BaaS project aims to meet comprehensive, open cross-domain management and control services requirements of buildings [3]. A generic service platform for commercial buildings is developed where integration of BAS with ICT infrastructures is provided.

In this study, an Emergency Evacuation Service model is proposed as part of the BaaS project and details of this model are explained. At emergency situations, especially in densely populated buildings, evacuation of people to safe places is a very challenging task because of complexity of the building floor plans. An emergency service is targeted in this study in order to solve this issue. Requirements and suitable hardware selection are analyzed in order to render the service applicable to variety of scenarios with various hardware configurations and systems. Evacuation service model and subservice definitions are prepared accordingly. The system design is then implemented and demonstrated.

Internet of Things (IoT) is a global-scale network that covers usage of virtual objects or virtual things with attributes, auto-IDs, and self-configuration, receptivity [4]. IoT notion mostly involves low power devices with diverse set of characteristics. As demonstrated in [4], integration of IoT and BAS can provide various benefits. In this paper, similar facts are considered and, in order to provide suitability to real-life IoT based solutions, hardware and software components are determined with regard to IoT requirements. Applicability of the service is investigated with a real-time implementation. Details of this implementation are also explained.

This paper is outlined as follows. In Section 2, related studies are summarized. In Section 3, design requirements of the target service and suitable hardware selection for a real-life implementation are detailed. Content of Emergency Evacuation Service model is explained in Section 4 and subservice definitions are given in Section 5. Implementation details are explained in Section 6 and the paper is concluded in Section 7.

2. Related Works

In [5], the importance of the utilized communication system in the building is highlighted due to necessity of joint control and management of mechanisms targeting diverse characteristics, through BAS applications' perspectives. Thus, standards such as LonWorks and BACnet are analyzed and detailed literature review is given. It can be concluded that, because of components with various differences, an efficient and practical BAS model is hard to be proposed, however; such an effort provides many benefits. Similarly, in [6], possible benefits of BAS utilization on daily life are mentioned and a communication system deployment is analyzed. As part of these systems, BACnet and LonWorks are evaluated, and the related principals are detailed. After highlighting the importance of increasing energy costs in the recent term, an intelligent energy consumption model within the scope of BAS is proposed in [7]. According to the model, system consumption is tracked by analyzing the usage profile of the building user, and the alarm is generated when usage exceeds the determined level. In [8], usage of BAS with computer-integrated facility management (CIFM) systems is evaluated with the aim of decreasing limitations of combined usage of BAS with different technologies. Accordingly, possible usage models are proposed. Usage of wireless communication technologies in BAS solutions is detailed and corresponding advantages as well as disadvantages are explained in [9]. Similar to this study, commercial wireless communication technologies that are utilized in the BAS solutions are analyzed from distinct perspectives such as implementation costs,

reliability, and flexibility that allow suitable joint usage with other systems. Moreover, benefits and limitations of corresponding systems are detailed.

In [10], in order to increase usage efficiency of BAS, communication networks are evaluated and wireless communication based approaches are highlighted. Due to insufficient ontologies that target only limited use-cases, a solution that models BAS to be used with different use-cases and provides modularity is proposed in [11]. The proposed solution is called BASont and has suitable usage for various use-cases. Moreover, BASont integrates building information modeling (BIM) that is used for data collection of the building and BAS models by supporting retrieval operations, data access, and synchronization with the previously deployed system. The proposed ontology is implemented with a Web service in order to provide efficient usage with self-commissioning and data access, and, as demonstrated with these use-cases, the solution has suitable functionalities for such deployments. It is highlighted in [12] that recent developments about ambient intelligent paradigm lead to a growing interest on autonomous home and building automation (HBA) solutions. However, most of the corresponding solutions do not include dynamic functionalities. To this end, a flexible multiagent approach that contains semantic-based resource discovery and orchestration functions is proposed in [12]. Semantic annotation of user profiles and device capabilities is supported within the proposed solution. Accordingly, environment is monitored by devices in the building, and data from users or devices are collected by a component called home mediator. This process is managed with one-to-one negotiations between home and device agents. By characterization of usage profiles of components in the building, semantic model is used to manage corresponding scenario efficiently. With real-time experiments, performance measurements for agents such as mediator, KNX device, and user agents are done and functionality of the solution is demonstrated.

In [13], a service-oriented architecture- (SOA-) based BAS model is proposed, where Web technologies are included. As the most important aspect of this study, BAS is integrated with a Web service, SOA, and semantic Web, where dynamic management of devices/services is provided within changing contexts. Such integration brings two crucial difficulties; it is hard to serve diverse and complex requirements of different services, and dynamic context changes are difficult to be tracked. These issues can be solved by composing services based on predefining policies and defining user requirements with composite service plans by using Composition Plan Description Language (CPDL) [13]. These functionalities are combined in the proposed solution. Performance of the model is quantified with experiments and two key results that show the effectiveness of the solution are obtained. The composition time is kept low even in critical conditions, and the service cache provides a significant improvement in service execution process. As mentioned in [14], the well-known BAS types such as KNX, BACnet, or ZigBee have suitable properties to local control scenarios by using non-IP communications. However, for large-scale BAS design and deployment, such technologies may not be sufficient due to the need for heterogeneous system interaction. In order to overcome this problem, an integration approach for BAS is proposed in [14], where an IPv6-based service-oriented architecture is considered. The most important property of this solution is the suitability to the smart city cases. Implementation of this approach is given in detail and its applicability is shown.

Cybersecurity concerns in BAS are critical and any security leakage could cause serious problems. This is detailed in [15] and the lack of proper solutions that integrate cyber-security and BAS effectively is mentioned as a serious threat for the future of BAS applications. Furthermore, importance of the security is explained with comprehensive examples. Possible solution points and approaches that could be effective for real-life deployments are highlighted. It is almost impossible not to care about security threats because of commercial value of BAS. Thus, it is suggested that compatibility between software-hardware and traditional-new deployed systems is a must in order to overcome security challenges. Moreover, the best option is to prepare a plan for the worst case while not totally obeying assertions suggested by software and hardware providers.

3. Design Requirements and Hardware Selection

3.1. Design Requirements. As stated earlier, BAS solutions are limited with implementation related obstacles and these limitations need to be overcome if an increase of the BAS usage is targeted. A flexible solution is a must for user comfort, which can only be provided with coordinated management of different hardware and software configurations. Thus, generated solution should be compatible with the previously deployed BAS solutions in the building and with other solutions that have probability of being deployed. This is a huge advantage because of certain cost and engineering benefits that are provided. Such compatibility can be provided with a modular approach and when required, new services can be deployed easily without harming other processes. One other significant issue is the security of the information. BAS solutions are based on information exchange within system components and a reliable communication is a must. This creates an inevitable concern about possible information leakages, since such buildings usually have users that produce valuable data. Moreover, privacy of the personal data must be protected according to legal procedures and any leakage may cause serious problems. Therefore, security of the data transmission must be provided in the BAS solution. A secure BAS solution should include security components demonstrated as follows:

Mutual authentication protocols

Cryptographic primitives for confidentiality

Privacy preserving listing and searching a database

Privacy preserving localization protocols

Implementation of localization protocols by using radiofrequency identification (RFID), related security issues

Implementation of localization protocols by using ultrasonic sensors, related security issues

Implementation of counting algorithms by using stationary passive infrared (PIR) sensors, related security issues

A database is required with the assumption that most of the solutions store some data and hence contain a database or a similar component. Moreover, since we specifically target emergency evacuation scenario in BAS, localization of person is a necessity for a comprehensive service and related facts that are ordered above. Possible hardware that can be used within Localization Service is mentioned in the previous list. One other important issue is the suitability of service definitions to the real-life hardware usage. Hardware that can be used in BAS applications usually has common technical capabilities and software features. Services that are defined as part of a BAS solution should be defined according to a comprehensive hardware analysis. Such services can be different from each other in most cases, but there are certain common points from the implementation perspective. As mentioned earlier, the used hardware for each service can be different, but technical definitions include similarities. Hardware requirements of the implementation of a service should be thoroughly analyzed and definitions should match technical capabilities of such hardware; that is, type of the analog-to-digital converter (ADC) that is used and operating frequency of radiofrequency identification (RFID) can be suitable design points. Efficiency of the system operation and management of the tasks also need to be considered when a BAS solution is designed. Tasks that are assigned to the hardware must be planned well in order to protect technical efficiency and life cycle of the hardware. Hardware that is used in such applications usually consumes a low amount of energy. However, the system could consist of a central computer unit that has various tasks to implement and energy consumption during implementation of these tasks could be very high. In order to keep these values low, tasks should be divided well and data obtained by hardware should be managed efficiently on the software side. Any recursive task could create certain energy inefficiency especially in large-scale buildings. Currently, green building is an important and beneficial concept that is aimed at being deployed in almost all countries. For realization of this notion, the mentioned energy management must be considered.

3.2. Utilized Hardware. To provide modularity in the proposed Emergency Evacuation Service model, different hardware modules were chosen to realize the system. Each different module is used to perform a particular task. Aside from central computer used for decision making and further evacuation maintenance, there are four modules used that are Arduino Uno microcontroller-based board, RFM23B radiofrequency module, HC-05 Bluetooth module, and LM35 temperature sensor.

3.2.1. Arduino Uno. Arduino Uno is a microcontroller-based board with an ATmega328 microcontroller. Arduino Uno has every needed component to maintain ATmega328; it can simply be attached via USB cable to a computer or by using an AC-to-DC adapter or a battery to start working.

Specific software called Arduino IDE is available to program any Arduino compatible board with C-like programing language. This software supplies a serial monitor which allows not only reading but also sending data through serial connection. With growing number of product-specific libraries, Arduino offers useful tools for designs related to embedded systems.

Arduino has several technical specifications such as containing ATmega328 microcontroller and having 5 V operating voltage, 14 digital I/O pins, and 6 analog input pins, with 16 MHz clock speed [16].

3.2.2. RFM23B Radiofrequency Module.
HopeRF's RFM22B/23B is an integrated, cost effective, 433/470/868/915 MHz wireless industrial, scientific, and medical (ISM) transceiver module. Extended range and refined connection performance guaranteed by low receive sensitivity (−121 dBm) are coupled with industry leading +20 dBm output power [17].

This module has a proper design to be used directly with a microcontroller, which enables the creation of a very low-cost system. RFM23B also supports digital Received Signal Strength Indicator (RSSI). RFM23B radiofrequency (RF) module is used for RFID active tag and reader hardware configurations. This module is used in various applications such as remote control, sensor networks, industrial control, and home automation.

RFM23B module communicates with microcontroller by SPI communication protocol. To connect microcontroller-based Arduino with RFM23B, connections between SDI and MOSI, SDO and MISO, NSEL and SS, and SCK and SCK must be provided for SPI communication. Communication protocol is used for writing to registers and reading from registers on the module.

RFM23B consumes low power and has data rate capability from 0.123 to 256 kbps [18]. It has a temperature sensor and 8-bit ADC and supports temperature range from −40 to +85°C. It can also provide frequency hopping.

3.2.3. HC-05 Bluetooth Module.
HC-05 Bluetooth module is a well-known Bluetooth serial module. Designed for clear wireless serial connection establishment, HC-05 is an easy-to-employ Bluetooth Serial Port Protocol (SPP) module. Serial port Bluetooth module is a completely competent Bluetooth V2.0 + EDR (Enhanced Data Rate) 3 Mbps modulation with complete 2.4 GHz radio transceiver and baseband [19]. In master mode, HC-05 module can both search and pair with a Bluetooth device automatically.

This module has −80 dBm typical sensitivity, can support RF transmit power up to +4 dBm, and has UART interface with programable baud rate [19]. Bluetooth module can support baud rates 9600, 19200, 38400, 57600, 115200, 230400, and 460800 and 8 data bits with 1 stop bit are included [19].

3.2.4. LM35 Temperature Sensor.
The LM35 is an accuracy temperature integrated-circuit, which has linearly proportional output voltage to the Centigrade temperature. Since the user is not demanded to subtract a large constant voltage from the output to get handy Centigrade scaling, the LM35 device has an advantage over Kelvin-calibrated linear sensors. No outer calibration or trimming is needed to provide typical precision of ±1/4°C at room temperature and ±3/4°C over a full −55°C to 150°C temperature range [20]. The sensor can be calibrated directly in Celsius (Centigrade), and 0.5°C ensured accuracy [20]. It is also suitable for remote applications.

4. Emergency Evacuation Service Model

The proposed emergency evacuation solution for BAS consists of two important structures, the Alarm Server (AS) and the Building Management System (BMS), which play central roles in the evacuation process. The AS has initial responsibilities and mainly deals with alarm generation. Sensor sources constantly send information to the AS and by evaluating certain conditions, data received from sensor sources is analyzed. Depending on the values, an alarm is generated (or not). If an alarm is generated, AS communicates with BMS informing about the alarm. BMS is a BaaS application that manages services and conducts service procedure. Moreover, BMS stores the information about the employee and visitors having entered the building. This information is accessible in a way which keeps personal data private. Stored information within BMS also includes age and disability status of users in a database, capacity and usage status of each room or office in the building. As a significant security component, access to this database is valid only for authorized administrators. Furthermore, the communication between BMS and AS is authenticated by both parties. After receiving alarm information, BMS activates a procedure depend on the scenario.

The block diagram of the Evacuation Service is shown in Figure 1. Main part in the architecture is the EVAC which includes Web&Provisioning, Media and Application, location-based servers (LBS) and Alarm Servers. There is also Database Cluster included where EVAC Management and EVAC Reporting Interface are located. Communication between this Database Cluster and Media and Application and LBS and Alarm Servers is provided with TCP/IP protocol. Moreover, Session Initiation Protocol (SIP) and Integrated Services Digital Network (ISDN) services which are controlled over voice channels by Media and Application server are included in the private automatic branch exchange (PABX) structure of the building. LBS Server has two options to obtain location information: fixed passive infrared (PIR) sensors which are used in dynamic setup and wearable devices (WD) which are used in controlled setup. Evacuation procedure over this architecture is realized as follows:

(i) AS receives an alarm from Fire Alarm System or from BaaS.

(ii) After determination of the alarm, employees or the people in the building are first informed via internal alarm system by voice message or calling them.

(iii) At the same time, an onscreen mask at the reception desk carries out a dedicated evacuation of the individual floors or the entire building complex.

(iv) To carry out the evacuation efficiently and quickly, the language of the client is identified via interface to the

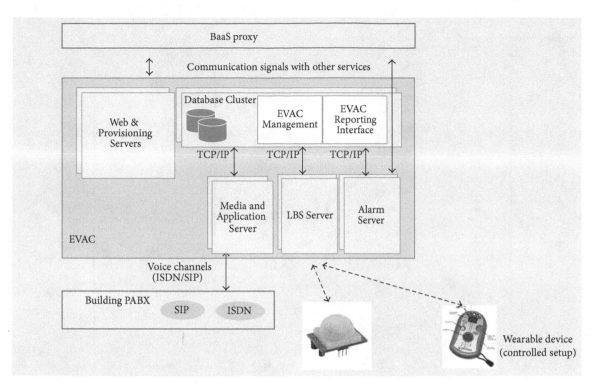

FIGURE 1: The block diagram of the Evacuation Service.

BaaS. The evacuation message is then sent in the user's native language.

(v) Occupancy is controlled by the system by getting results from the WD with controlled setup or from PIR detectors with dynamic setup.

(vi) AS calls the building sections-rooms/people via all available lines. The system collects every reaction in every call status mode, that is, ringing, busy, pick-up, answer, and hang-up.

(vii) If the call is not answered during the ring phase (20 sec.) the system continues and flags this room/guest.

There are two BaaS emergency evacuation scenarios, controlled and dynamic setups. Contents of these two setups are demonstrated in Figures 2 and 3. Common and different requirements of content in these two figures can be given with explanations of steps as follows:

(1) *Alarm.* Corresponding alarm should be triggered and authenticated by AS successfully. If an alarm is valid and type of the emergency situation is found out, emergency evacuation scenario becomes active.

(2) *Info Request.* In this step, AS requests some information about database content from BMS. That request has to be compatible with BaaS components.

(3) *Alarm System Info-Set.* BMS responses request from the AS some information that can contain identity (ID_EU), language, age, disability information of the person, and room/office fullness. Information content

can change according to the emergency type stated with Info Request step. It is important to protect confidentiality of the information set to be sent.

(4) *Match ID_EUs and ID_WDs.* This step is only valid for the controlled setup. Privacy is a must. In order to preserve the privacy of the end users, pseudo ID_P_EUs can be sent rather than actual ID_EUs which are kept at BMS in that case. Access to this matched list must be limited to authenticated users.

(5) *Calls and Actions.* Mutual authentication between AS and SIP Proxy is needed.

(6) *ID_WD/ID_SEN Measurements.* ID of WD or ID of Stationary Sensors (SEN) is shared and confidentiality has to be ensured.

(7) *ID_DCN and ID_WD/ID_SEN Measurements.* Similar to previous one, confidentiality of measurements must be provided.

(8) *Localization/Counter.* Localization/counter measurements have to be analyzed and data for each user has to be produced according to the processed analysis. However, certain security protection must be provided. Obtained matched list should not violate the privacy of the end users. There must be authenticated access to this list.

(9) *Action Feedback.* AS has to send back localization/counter information to the BMS after or during the evacuation. Confidentiality of that localization/counter information has to be ensured.

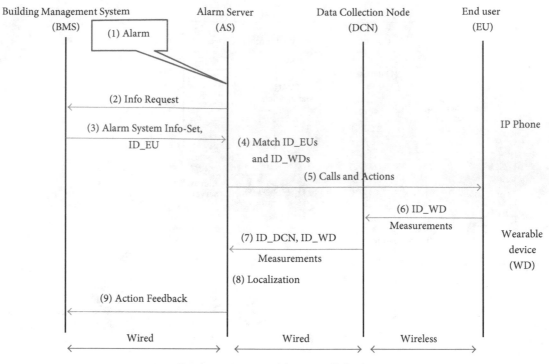

FIGURE 2: Content of the controlled setup.

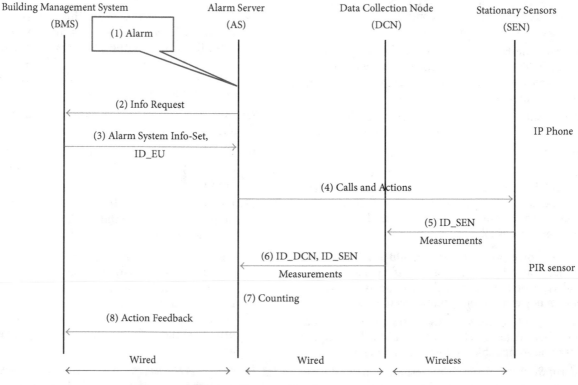

FIGURE 3: Content of the dynamic setup.

For both setups, communication between BMS-AS and AS-Data Collection Node (DCN) is provided with wired based methods. However, wireless communication methodology is valid for the communication between DCN and SEN. As mentioned earlier, one other difference between two setups is usage of PIR sensor in dynamic setup and WD in controlled setup. Few details need to be mentioned about these setups. For localization, passive RFID ultrasound tags will be on certain places on the walls and positions of the tags will be determined according to the floor plan. At real-life deployment stage of these setups, design and implementation of a handheld device that includes RF reader, ultrasonic sensor, and counting protocol by using PIR measurements should be considered. Moreover, wireless channel between DCN and WD or PIR sensors is important. This can be determined according to three types of wireless networks: personal area network (PAN), local area network (LAN), and wide area network (WAN). From our perspective, Bluetooth or ZigBee, Wi-Fi, and 2G/3G/4G can be used for PAN, LAN, and WAN respectively. Usage of Bluetooth RFID reader and tags is decided because of their several benefits. These can be summarized as follows.

4.1. Bluetooth.
Bluetooth technology is a global wireless standard that enables short range wireless data communication. It has been proposed by major companies in the communication industry in order to create an alternative data transmission standard that is not based on cable connections. Bluetooth is widely used because usage cost is not high and it is compatible with almost all devices. It is very suitable to IoT applications with its advantages like being power-efficient and low-cost. 2.4 GHz industrial, scientific, and medical (ISM) radio band is the operating frequency band of the Bluetooth technology. In most countries, 80 MHz band is allocated to this band. Some radio front end features are detailed in [21, 22].

Due to Bluetooth's suitability to IoT applications and its related benefits, we used this technology in our system. Hardware settings and communication configuration are quite easy with Bluetooth technology. The communication quality obtained with this usage is another advantage. One disadvantage would be distance limitation of such usage. Bluetooth does not support long distances. However, building environment usually does not include long distances and if a sufficient number of hardware components are used with suitable distances, distance is no more an issue as in our implementation scenario.

4.2. Radiofrequency Identification.
Nowadays, mobility and thus wireless communication are primary concern in consumer computing. Radiofrequency identification is one of the most widely used wireless technologies for automatic identification and data capture applications. Due to its light weight, low power consumption, cost-effectiveness, and non-line-of-sight readability RFID offers practical technology for context-aware computing like indoor localization systems [23]. An RFID module uses electromagnetic waves and employs a chip and an antenna for two-way transfer of the data. RFID systems can be classified as tag and reader, where reader reads data generated by tag as the names suggest. Currently, various types of applications such as asset tracking, supply chain management, and payment systems (electronic tickets) include RFID systems [24].

The most distinctive property of RFID from earlier barcode technology is that it does not require a line of sight. RFID provides identification from a distance varying according to type of the module employed. Based on their power consumption, RFID tags can be categorized as active tags, passive tags, and semipassive (battery-assisted) tags [24]. Another categorization can be made by frequency range since RFID systems operate at a variety of radiofrequencies from 120 Hz to 10 GHz, which is explained in [25].

4.3. RFID Tags.
For object identification, tags are used in radiofrequency identification systems. Depending on the battery property, tags can be categorized into three types which are passive, active, and semipassive. Two parts are specific main components of RFID tag. These parts are an integrated-circuit and an antenna. Processes like information storage and processing and RF signal modulation and demodulation are controlled with integrated-circuit. Transmission and reception of signals are realized via antennas.

4.4. RFID Readers.
An RFID reader is a device that is used in RFID systems in order to provide connection between tag and system software [26]. Readers connect with tags which are located in the area of readers and start to perform some operations such as classifying tags in terms of meeting a criteria and encoding of tags. Readers also contain antennas for signal transmission with tags. Received data is sent to a computer for processing. Readers can be used in a stationary position or can be used with a microprocessor or mobile unit.

As the most important step of the emergency evacuation solution, subservices (where each one realizes part of the solution process) are defined according to these hardware details. Details of subservices are explained in the next section.

5. Subservice Definitions

According to the evacuation model, data obtained by sensors is processed, alarms are defined in accordance with predetermined criteria, and alarms are activated when corresponding conditions are valid. Moreover, location information of the people in building is monitored by using RFID technology and voice based help is provided to the people based on the Evacuation Service. In order to render model practical and efficient, subservices are defined and service management is organized accordingly. Services and relation between these are shown in Figure 4. Subservices are detailed below.

5.1. Alarm Monitoring Service.
With this service, received data from the sensors is collected and a table that includes that data is created. This service is a key service for the Alarm Generation Service. Sensor IDs, type of the services (fire

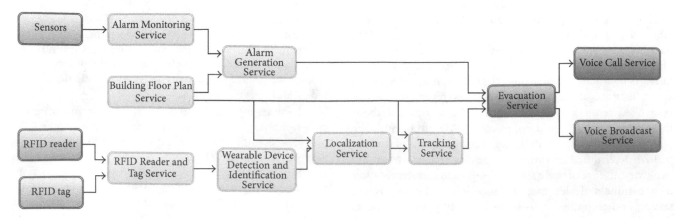

FIGURE 4: Services defined in Emergency Evacuation Service model and input-output relationship.

TABLE 1: Output table of the Alarm Monitoring Service.

Sensor ID (unsigned long)	Sensor type (short)	Measurement (short)
Sensor_ID1	1	5
Sensor_ID2	2	1

TABLE 2: Output table of the Building Floor Plan Service.

Building/Floor/Room ID (integer)	Building/Floor/Room Geometry X, Y, and Z coordinates (float)
Building/Floor/Room_ID1	$X = 5$, $Y = 3$, $Z = 10$
Building/Floor/Room_ID2	$X = 10$, $Y = 4$, $Z = 6$
Building/Floor/Room_ID3	$X = 4$, $Y = 8$, $Z = 12$

or gas), and measurement data that is sent by sensors are received by this service and collected data is sent to the Alarm Generation Service. An exemplary output table is shown in Table 1. Definitions like ID and measurement information are defined in accordance with technical properties of sensors that have wide-usage in the market.

5.2. Building Floor Plan Service. Building Floor Plan Service is a core service for other services. This service does not get any input; it stores some information such as room, floor, building ID, and three-dimensional location information as shown in Table 2. Building Floor Plan Service is crucial, especially for the Evacuation Service.

5.3. Alarm Generation Service. This service makes decision of alarm generation by evaluating the table and location information received from the Alarm Monitoring Service and Building Floor Plan Service, respectively. Depending on the sensor type, measurement result is compared with predetermined threshold and alarm generation decision is made by evaluating these inputs. Alarm generation is a necessity for the Evacuation Service; thus proper operation of Alarm Generation Service is very crucial. As an output of

this service, if an alarm is valid, then location and level of the alarm are sent to corresponding services as shown in Table 3.

5.4. RFID Reader and Tag Service. This service has a crucial role in the process, where evacuation plan is activated and specific plan for each person is presented. Location information is very critical in such plan and RFID Reader and Tag Service generates an important part of the location information. RFID readers obtain ID and RSSI information of tags that are located in the range of readers and give as output a table that is created by readers with obtained ID and RSSI information. RSSI information is used because RSSI level demonstrates the distance between tag and reader. Output table is similar to table shown in Table 4.

5.5. Wearable Device Detection and Identification Service. This service receives the table that is generated by the RFID Reader and Tag Service for a corresponding reader and also receives the table that includes list of the RFID readers located in the building. Firstly, it scans the registered readers IDs in order to find corresponding ID of the reader, and decides whether this reader is in the list or not. Then, if a reader is registered, Wearable Device Detection and Identification Service request RSSI levels from the reader. As a result, a table is created that contains the same content as table of RFID Reader and Tag Service. The difference is that only registered readers are included in this table, rather than all readers.

5.6. Localization Service. Localization Service receives table of registered RFID readers from the Wearable Device Detection and Identification Service and corresponding information from the Building Floor Plan Service. By evaluating the building plan, exact locations of RFID readers in the floor plan are calculated and given as output table as shown in Table 5.

5.7. Tracking Service. Tracking Service takes output table of Localization Service as input and calculates velocity and direction of the corresponding person for tracking. A table that includes these is given as output similar to Table 6.

TABLE 3: Output table of the Alarm Generation Service.

Sensor ID (unsigned long)	Measurement (short)	Alarm level (integers (1 to 5))	Zone ID (unsigned long)	System time
Sensor_ID1	1	1	Zone_ID1	16:24
Sensor_ID2	8	5	Zone_ID2	10:12

TABLE 4: Output table of the RFID Reader and Tag Service.

RFID Reader ID (integer)	RFID Tag ID (string)	RFID RSSI level (float)
Reader_ID1	Tag_ID1	−43
Reader_ID2	Tag_ID1	−57

TABLE 5: Output table of the Localization Service.

RFID Reader ID (integer)	X, Y, and Z coordinates (float)	System time
Reader_ID1	5, 3, 10	11:23
Reader_ID2	10, 8, 3	17:00

TABLE 6: Output table of the Tracking Service.

RFID Reader ID (integer)	Velocity (float)	Direction (integer)	System time
Reader_ID1	3	Direction_1	10:47
Reader_ID2	4	Direction_2	12:26

5.8. Evacuation Service. Evacuation Service is one of the most important services in the service model. A variety of information is taken as input which includes list of people inside the building received from Access Control Management; emergency type, place, and level received from the Alarm Generation Service; output table that includes velocity and direction information, received from the Tracking Service; and corresponding details received from the Building Floor Plan Service. Duty of this service is to combine generated data from previous services and decide whether to start evacuation process. Combined data is given as output and Voice Call or Voice Broadcasting Services are activated. Output consists of these elements: Voice Call ID (integer), Caller ID (integer), User ID (integer), Voice Broadcast ID (integer), and Area (integer).

5.9. Voice Call Service. Voice that is generated by Evacuation Service is taken as input and voice call is directed. Output content is as follows: Voice Call ID (integer), Caller ID (integer), and User ID (integer)

5.10. Voice Broadcast Service. Voice that is generated by Evacuation Service is taken as input and voice is broadcasted. Output content is as follows: Voice Broadcast ID (integer) and Area (integer).

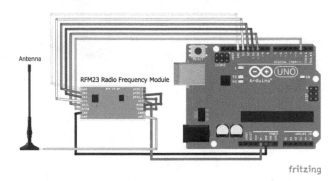

FIGURE 5: Scheme of tag configuration.

6. Implementation Details

6.1. Hardware Configurations. To implement the proposed Emergency Evacuation Service, three configurations are determined by using the previously explained modules. They are tag, reader, and sensor configurations.

6.1.1. Tag Configuration. The RFID tag is planned as an active device which continuously sends a message, supplying RSSI knowledge to a reader. Moreover, in terms of reliability, tag should supply an appropriate ID to the reader. According to the demands explained above, tag configuration is planned as a RFM23B module attached to an Arduino Uno card (Figures 5 and 6). The role of Arduino Uno is to drive RFM23B electrically and make RFM23B module transmit the message, which is a program embedded into Arduino's microcontroller. Hence, in tag configuration, Arduino Uno transfers the message through SPI to RFM23B which sends the message via radiofrequency antenna. It depends on the power supply of Arduino Uno whether tag is stationary or moving.

6.1.2. Reader Configuration. The messages sent by tag configurations should be read and transferred to the central computer by a reader configuration. Therefore, reader configuration has a RFM23B module and an Arduino Uno. Moreover, reader configuration has an HC-05 module (in slave mode) for redirecting tag data to central computer. This way, reader receives messages from tags and redirects it to central computer contemporaneously via HC-05 Bluetooth module over serial port protocol. Configuration is depicted in Figures 7 and 8. It should be mentioned that Arduino Uno has enough power to drive both RFM23B and HC-05 modules simultaneously. Additionally, reader configuration can be mobile or stationary depending on the power source type.

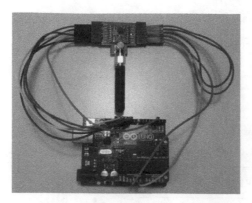

FIGURE 6: Real-time implementation of tag configuration.

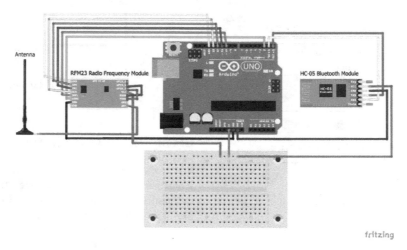

FIGURE 7: Scheme of reader configuration.

FIGURE 8: Real-time implementation of reader configuration.

6.1.3. Sensor Configuration. If a dangerous situation emerges, to create an alarm, sensory data is needed. To provide sensory data, sensor configuration is planned as an Arduino Uno with attached LM35 temperature sensor and HC-05 module (Figures 9 and 10). Thus, while LM35 supplies sensory data through analog input to Arduino Uno, it computes the right temperature and redirects new data to a central computer via HC-05 Bluetooth SPP module in slave mode. Because LM35 sensor's supply voltage can be 5 V and its current drain is very low, Arduino Uno easily drives both LM35 temperature sensor and HC-05 module. Similar to the previous two configurations, sensor configuration can be either immovable or mobile with dependence on the type of the power supply used.

6.2. Hardware Scenario. To implement the proposed Emergency Evacuation Service model, a demo is planned. The aim is to gather central computer with all configurations in a big enough room and to test the proposed Emergency Evacuation Service model. The room is thought to be separated into four areas. Each area is planned to have stationary reader and static sensor configurations. Also, each area is thought to have people with tags inside. The model of the room is depicted in Figure 11 and real-time implementation views of readers and tags used in the demo are shown in Figure 12.

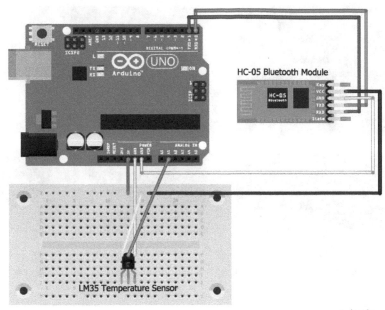

FIGURE 9: Scheme of sensor configuration.

FIGURE 10: Real-time implementation of sensor configuration.

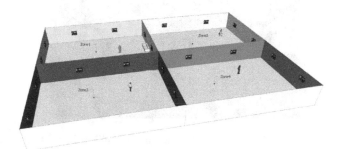

FIGURE 11: Figure of the room plan.

Fixed readers are planned to watch mobile tags on the people. First, each tag configuration sends its ID and message continuously by using RFM32B module. While tags send messages, readers are supposed to get messages and measure their RSSI values via RFM32B modules. Then, readers redirect collected data to the central computer via embedded programs inside Arduino Unos through HC-05 modules. Next, the data received by the central computer via its Bluetooth SPP module is thought to come through as many serial ports as readers and, by using serial Python program, processed and saved in a steady-size file as a table similar to the one shown in Figure 13 which is called the table of tags.

At the same time, stationary sensors are planned to send temperature data, through as many different serial ports as sensors, to the central computer, which decides whether there

is a fire or not. In the first step, because each sensor configuration sends its data through independent serial port (Figure 14 depicts receiving continuous temperature data from one serial port) via HC-05 Bluetooth SPP modules, by using serial Python program, a table of all temperature sensors, similar to the table of RSSI values, is planned to be created as a fixed-size file called the table of temperature sensors. Then, the central computer decides whether there is a fire or not by checking the table of temperature sensors via BaaS application. In the next step, if there is no fire, the central computer continues to collect and monitor data. Otherwise, BaaS application activates Emergency Evacuation Service.

By reading RSSI values from the table of tags, it computes each person's position in the room (localization algorithm), then computes a safe route, and, by using voice signals, guides people to the safe location.

7. Conclusions

In this study, an effective Emergency Evacuation Service for BAS is proposed. Requirements of such services that can be

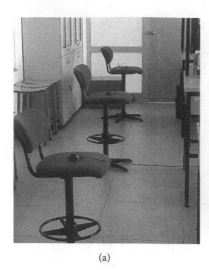
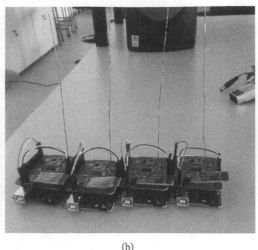

(a)   (b)

FIGURE 12: Implementation of demo scenario, (a) positions of three readers, and (b) tags carried by people.

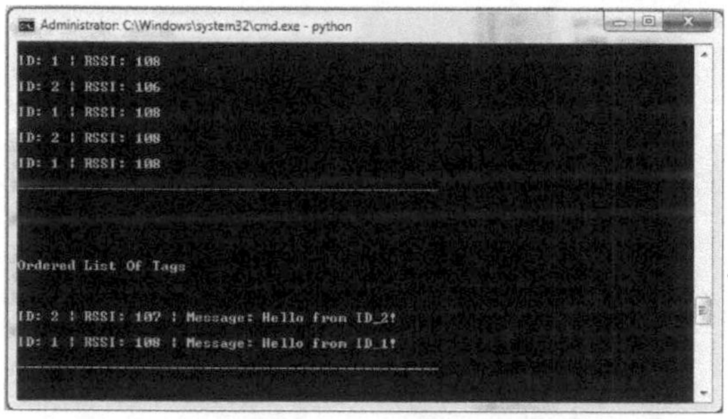

FIGURE 13: An example of the table of data collected from tags.

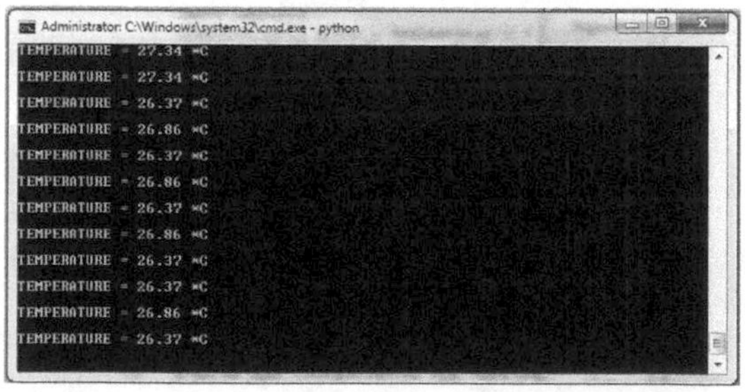

FIGURE 14: An example of a serial connection of a sensor.

implemented with complex and separate functions are analyzed and, in accordance with these, a service model structure is created. This structure consists of several functions and services that are defined with hardware compatibility. Details of these are given. Applicability of this model is observed with real-time implementation and corresponding details are mentioned. As a result, suitability of model to real-life BAS deployments is observed.

Competing Interests

The authors declare that there is no conflict of interests regarding the publication of this paper.

References

[1] F. Shu, M. N. Halgamuge, and W. Chen, "Building automation systems using wireless sensor networks: radio characteristics and energy efficient communication protocols," *Electronic Journal of Structural Engineering*, vol. 9, pp. 66–73, 2009.

[2] N. Research, "Commercial building automation systems market report," October 2015, https://www.navigantresearch.com/research/commercial-buildingautomation-systems.

[3] BaaS, September 2016, http://www.baas-itea2.eu/cms/home-menu-item.

[4] J. Yu, M. Kim, H.-C. Bang, S.-H. Bae, and S.-J. Kim, "IoT as a applications: cloud-based building management systems for the Internet of Things," *Multimedia Tools and Applications*, vol. 75, no. 22, pp. 14583–14596, 2016.

[5] W. Kastner, G. Neugschwandtner, S. Soucek, and H. M. Newman, "Communication systems for building automation and control," *Proceedings of the IEEE*, vol. 93, no. 6, pp. 1178–1203, 2005.

[6] D. Snoonian, "Smart buildings," *IEEE Spectrum*, vol. 40, no. 8, pp. 18–23, 2003.

[7] H. Wicaksono, S. Rogalski, and E. Kusnady, "Knowledge-based intelligent energy management using building automation system," in *Proceedings of the Conference Proceedings (IPEC '10)*, pp. 1140–1145, October 2010.

[8] A. Bozány, "Integration of building automation systems and facility information systems," *Hungarian Electronic Journal of Sciences*, vol. 7108, HU ISSN 1418, 2003.

[9] C. Reinisch, W. Kastner, G. Neugschwandtner, and W. Granzer, "Wireless technologies in home and building automation," in *Proceedings of the 5th IEEE International Conference on Industrial Informatics (INDIN '07)*, pp. 93–98, IEEE, Vienna, Austria, June 2007.

[10] A. Pinto, M. D'Angelo, C. Fischione, E. Scholte, and A. Sangio-vanni-Vincentelli, "Synthesis of embedded networks for building automation and control," in *Proceedings of the American Control Conference (ACC '08)*, pp. 920–925, June 2008.

[11] J. Ploennigs, B. Hensel, H. Dibowski, and K. Kabitzsch, "BAS-ont—a modular, adaptive building automation system ontology," in *Proceedings of the 38th Annual Conference on IEEE Industrial Electronics Society (IECON '12)*, pp. 4827–4833, IEEE, Montreal, Canada, October 2012.

[12] M. Ruta, F. Scioscia, G. Loseto, and E. D. Sciascio, "Semantic-based resource discovery and orchestration in home and building automation: a multi-agent approach," *IEEE Transactions on Industrial Informatics*, vol. 10, no. 1, pp. 730–741, 2014.

[13] S. N. Han, G. M. Lee, and N. Crespi, "Semantic context-aware service composition for building automation system," *IEEE Transactions on Industrial Informatics*, vol. 10, no. 1, pp. 752–761, 2014.

[14] M. Jung, J. Weidinger, W. Kastner, and A. Olivieri, "Building automation and smart cities: an integration approach based on a service-oriented architecture," in *Proceedings of the 27th International Conference on Advanced Information Networking and Applications Workshops (WAINA '13)*, pp. 1361–1367, IEEE, Barcelona, Spain, March 2013.

[15] D. Fisk, "Cyber security, building automation, and the intelligent building," *Intelligent Buildings International*, vol. 4, no. 3, pp. 169–181, 2012.

[16] Arduino UNO, September 2016, http://datasheet.octopart.com/A000066-Arduino-datasheet-38879526.pdf.

[17] Hoperf Electronic, "RFM22B/23B ISM transceiver module," RFM22B/23B Datasheet, 2016.

[18] RF22 Library for Arduino, September 2016, http://www.airspayce.com/mikem/arduino/RF22/.

[19] HC Serial Bluetooth Products User Instructional Manual, September 2016, http://www.tec.reutlingenuniversity.de/uploads/media/DatenblattHC-05_BT-Modul.pdf.

[20] LM35 Temperature Sensor, September 2016, http://www.ti.com/lit/ds/symlink/lm35.pdf.

[21] P. Bhagwat, "Bluetooth: technology for short-range wireless apps," *IEEE Internet Computing*, vol. 5, no. 3, pp. 96–103, 2001.

[22] Bluetooth Radio Architecture, September 2016, https://developer.bluetooth.org/TechnologyOverview/Pages/Radio.aspx.

[23] B. Violino, "RFID business applications," September 2016, http://www.rfidjournal.com/article/view/1334.

[24] S. A. Weis, "RFID (radio frequency identification): principles and applications," *System*, vol. 2, no. 3, 2007.

[25] R. Want, "An introduction to RFID technology," *IEEE Pervasive Computing*, vol. 5, no. 1, pp. 25–33, 2006.

[26] RFID, September 2016, http://www.impinj.com/resources/about-rfid/how-do-rfid-systems-work/.

8

Approaches to Addressing Service Selection Ties in Ad Hoc Mobile Cloud Computing

Ayotuyi Tosin Akinola ⓘ **and Matthew Olusegun Adigun**

Department of Computer Science, Centre of Excellence at University of Zululand, Private Bag X1001, Ongoye, KwaDlangezwa 3886, South Africa

Correspondence should be addressed to Ayotuyi Tosin Akinola; ruthertosin@gmail.com

Academic Editor: Youyun Xu

The ad hoc mobile cloud (AMC) allows mobile devices to connect together through a wireless connection or any other means and send a request for web services from one to another within the mobile cloud. However, one of the major challenges in the AMC is the occurrence of dissatisfaction experienced by the users. This is because there are many services with similar functionalities but varying nonfunctional properties. Moreover, another resultant cause of user dissatisfaction being coupled with runtime redundancy is the attainment of similar quality computations during service selection, often referred to as "service selection ties." In an attempt to address this challenge, service selection mechanisms for the AMC were developed in this work. This includes the use of selected quality of service properties coupled with user feedback data to determine the most suitable service. These mechanisms were evaluated using the experimental method. The evaluation of the mechanisms mainly focused on the metrics that evaluate the satisfaction of users' interest via the quantitative evaluation. The experiments affirmed that the use of the shortest distance can help to break selection ties between potential servicing nodes. Also, a continuous use of updated and unlimited range of users' assessments enhances an optimal service selection.

1. Introduction

Service-oriented computing (SOC) is an emanating interdisciplinary paradigm for realizing a distributed computation, thereby changing the traditional pattern of incurring the cost of access to unwanted software applications, thus depicting a better service delivery on various service request provisioning schemes [1]. The software applications that are made available in the SOC are primarily a product of fundamental resources which are *services*. The services are self-describing and computational resources that enhance an automatic, rapid, and low-cost provisioning of software applications in a distributed environment. Due to the explosive growth of various mobile applications, the Internet serves as a linking medium between the mobile clients and the service providers. Therefore, with the view to achieving agility and flexibility between provider and client interaction, the SOC has been generally adopted. The SOC assumed business functions as modular packages in the form of services that run on any service-oriented architecture (SOA) [2].

Moreover, the cloud computing paradigm is an example of the SOA that serves as an information technology servicing model where computing services are delivered on demand to customers over a network in a self-service fashion, independent of devices and locations [3]. Thus, the resources required to provide the requisite quality of service levels are shared, dynamically scalable, rapidly provisioned, and virtualized with minimal service provider interaction. Users pay for the service as an operating expense without incurring any significant initial capital expenditure, with the cloud services employing a metering system that divides the computing resources into appropriate blocks.

There are three basic processes that are involved in the provisioning of services in any service-oriented platforms which include service discovery, service selection, and service composition [2, 4, 5]. By the discovery of services, we refer to the process of identifying potentially available web services which can carry out a particular task. However, among the available web services, there would certainly be a particular service in the midst of the discovered web services which best satisfies the request of the present service user at the time of request based on the quality of service that was specified. This process is termed "web service selection." The composition of web services involves the integration of two or more web services together to implement interconnected tasks. For example, this interconnected task can be a web service which searches for a flight schedule as well as another that locates a meter taxi or a hotel reservation. This kind of request is being carried out via a composite web service from the provisioning platform.

These three concepts are very important in any service provisioning platform and thus become one of the central focus to research scholars. Therefore, this calls for adequate mechanisms to be deployed to enable these processes to run smoothly in the course of providing optimal services on the aforementioned platforms. Addressing these three concepts poses various challenges in the modern service provisioning platforms today especially the concern with the enormous release of web services that are performing similar functionalities. In the same vein, when mobile devices were connected to the cloud platforms for service usage, it becomes imperative that optimal service selection is addressed to avoid the dissatisfaction with service responses to the intended users. A typical example of such a mobile service consumption scenario is the mobile cloud computing paradigm. This paradigm enables the use of mobile devices to consume resident web services within the cloud computing architecture [6–9]. The dissatisfaction becomes very tasking in a situation where the users eventually become the platform for service provisioning in the case of the AMC system, wherein mobile users are constantly in a move while consuming the web service [10].

Several parastatals such as military and other forms of organizations which are involved in emergency operations have been adopting the AMC technology towards addressing the pressing need for total avoidance of interconnectivity issues, both in less-developed areas as a result of bad infrastructure and even in developed places due to natural disasters, etc. [11]. For example, in an emergency operation which utilizes an AMC setup, the nearest mobile nodes with the required service must be the chosen node for the operation so that the task at hand will be carried out successfully and promptly within the limited allotted time frame. Moreover, the occurrence of service selection ties during the course of selection especially in a range of different service locations within the mobile devices needs to be addressed as this has a lot to speak to the measure of satisfaction that the users experience within such a system [12, 13].

A contemporary project that is currently under development, which looks into most of the aforementioned issues, is GUIISET (GRID-based utility infrastructure-infrastructure less for SMME-enabled technology) from the Centre of Excellence of the University of Zululand in South Africa. It is an advancement on the previous GUISET project through the incorporation of this infrastructure less (ad hoc model) platform into the system [14–17]. The goal of this incorporation is to enable the developed platform to be able to render services to mobile devices especially in the context of m-Health, m-Learning, and m-Commerce.

Several works have been done which ranges from GUISET's implementation [18–20] to its performance evaluation [17, 21, 22] and security [15, 16, 23] as well as the Pricing strategy to be used on the platform [14]. However, little research has been conducted in relation to providing an optimally satisfactory service especially in the newly integrated ad hoc model system. In addition, issues relating to similar computation scores (selection ties) which often inform unsatisfactory service usage have not been fully addressed in most of the articles to the best of our knowledge. Hence, this article contributes to the existing knowledge via providing solutions to "service selection ties" in both mobile nodes and web service provisioning to various patronizing customers via deployable selection mechanisms. Moreover, service response delay is also addressed to reduce the time taken to deliver a selected service to intended users.

The remainder of this article is as organized as follows. Section 2 reviews various service selection approaches in different platforms to bring out the gap that is missing which is very important on the AMC. The section also reviews the earlier attempts to address the issue of service selection in various platforms. Section 3 discusses the QoS property resolution strategy, while Section 4 enumerates the modes of selection occurrence in the AMC. Section 5 addresses the selection ties in AMC mobile nodes using the multidynamic distance-based approach, where a typical surgical emergency service is used as a scenario. Section 6 discusses the feedback-based selection approach for optimal web service selection in an AMC, while Section 7 explains how the performance evaluation was conducted with some discussions. Section 8 explains the conclusion and future work.

2. Literature Review

This section elucidates the methodologies of the service selection process with a view to discussing various methods that can be deployed for selection of services in general from any service-oriented computing platform. Moreover, the selection approaches that are often deployed in an ad hoc environment were also discussed. Hence, we shall be explaining service selection methodologies and service selection approaches in the AMC. In addition, this section also attempts to review other approaches to optimal selection in the AMC.

2.1. Service Selection Methodologies. The selection methodologies are the various methods that are adopted for selection services within a service-oriented architecture platform. The methodologies used in service selection are generally classified into three according to the work of Swarnamugi [24]. These are explained below:

(1) Functional-based method: This method selects the appropriate service based on the retrieval of a functional description of a service from the registries and then certifies that the description and requirement of the interfaces match each other. There is always a need to convert the web service into the semantic web to enhance the easy description of web service functionality. The semantic web service selection was implemented in the work of Klusch and Kapahnke using the hybrid version of the SAWSDL matchmaker called SAWSDL-MX [2, 25]. The drawbacks of the functional service selection approach make the service provider seek for a more informative alternative that could differentiate their products from others in relation to performance. Moreover, considering the AMC environment, the use of the highly logical algorithm and complex ontological data storage generate a challenge for memory-restrained mobile devices; therefore, the approach is considered unsuitable for deployment.

(2) Nonfunctional-based method: It is a common experience in the service provisioning environment for services to provide similar functionalities with different nonfunctional properties. Hence, such services can only be differentiated by considering their nonfunctional attributes which can either be quality of service or context-based [24]. In [26], the author proposed the architecture for a web service selection using the QoS-based approach in a service provisioning environment where the service user searches the service registry (UDDI) for the list of all services that address the concerned request. The service broker here assists in differentiating the various services in the registry. Thus, the service registry becomes a complex task for an AMC-based environment. Xin and others in [27] considered a framework that combines QoS attributes with user preferences of a group of consumers to propose an algorithm and a mobile service selection model to solve the selection challenge. But the selection was based on a group of collective users which is not individually tailored as expected in an AMC environment. The work of Amoretti and others in [28] proposed a reputation-based selection framework which emphasizes on an intra- and inter-SOP (service-oriented peers) module interaction. The framework contains a component called SAFE that ensures that a mobile peer computes the reputation of a provider based on the previous experience. The SAFE component is assigned the task of "voting strategies" to ensure that proper record of the aggregated reputation influences selection decisions. However, this work was silent about the situation where web service attains similar computation aggregates (otherwise called selection ties) thereby

leaving behind gap to fill. Furthermore, the study conducted by Akingbesote and others [18] proposed a quality of service aware Multilevel Ranking Model (MLRANK) for selecting an optimal web service in cloud computing. The study addressed the occurrence of ties within a number of services that are available in the UDDI. The study highlights the challenge of selecting an optimal web service when there are ties with the used criterion where performance alternatives have the same score. The study achieved optimal selection by comparing the service consumer's QoS preference with the web service QoS offerings. The provider offering that best fits the QoS preference is taken as the optimal web service. The study used nondeterministic QoS metrics and concentrated on various information services to test the performance of the proposed model. However, this study serially considers each of the selected qualities one after the other and checks which one is higher than the other to make a selection. This approach is not reliable in the context of the AMC. This is because decisions are expected to be as fast as possible. In addition, the work never considered the possibility of the consumers having relatively equal priority for the specified QoS properties which makes the selection yardstick less efficient. Keidl and Kemper in [29] proposed a context processing framework to influence context-aware web service provisioning. However, the framework uses an insufficient number of context parameters among which are location and client addresses. The location specified by the SOAP message body of the web service is fixed; thus, it is not suitable for a dynamic environment like the AMC system. Since the mobile device keeps changing location, the use of fixed location as one of the parameters will be irrelevant to service selection. Keskes proposed the combination of context and QoS for service selection and considered the effectiveness and consistency of the method in relation to using an increasing number of service parameters more than six [30]. But, the use of the ontological context to decipher the information brings about the issue of ambiguity if deployed to memory-constrained mobile devices for service selection.

(2) User-based selection method: The measure of the trustworthiness of a particular web service is termed "the Reputation." This measure mainly depends on the end users' experience of using the particular service. Various end users may have dissimilar views about the same web service. However, the reputation is expressed as an average ranking that is given to a web service by the end users, thus deriving a range of ranking from these end users. This system determines the QoS of a service provider through calculation of the difference between the published service provider value and the user feedback response. A higher difference value typically shows a lower QoS rating for that particular service provider or web service. The service users are allowed to provide a feedback

through the use of a pair of keys [31]. The users authenticate with the aid of these keys, and they are allowed to update the QoS criteria based on their experience. However, the provider would not always be available to affirm and see to the proper updating of the QoS properties. The high possibility is that both the user and consumer would likely not be available at a similar time, therefore resulting into overloading of the system through unconsumed user requests.

2.2. AMC Service Selection Approaches. The approaches to service selection in the AMC require more criteria to be taken care of because of its inherent nature. This is because in an AMC, there might be the need for the selection of the nearest mobile node to provide a particular service, and at some other times, it could be the web service that is resident within the mobile node that needs to be shared among the AMC mobile devices. Considering the influx of mobile devices within an AMC, there could be a sudden increase in the number of connecting mobile devices which invariably increases the number of service requests; thus, we itemize the following concern with respect to AMC selection approaches: (1) any approach that must be used should cater for sudden increment in service requests [32]. (2) The approach must address the dynamic nature of the mobile environment, and (3). the approach should eradicate the arbitrary selection of mobile nodes and web services during the occurrence of service selection ties which is a major challenge in service provisioning in the AMC environment [18, 33].

According to [34, 35], service selection in the ad hoc mobile environment is carried out using the following approaches: (1) hop-based, (2) QoS-based, and (3) integrated/hybrid-based. The hop count has been used for time-constrained mobile service selection in wireless mesh networks and sensor networks, especially where the response time is very pivotal such as in critical and life-saving situations [36, 37]. This system considers time as a very important issue and therefore looks or searches for the closest node to the requestor. This has the advantages of (i) a lower risk of downlink with the least distances apart; (ii) a lower rate of battery consumption with the reduced distances between the nodes, and (iii) lesser possibilities for the two nodes, to be out of reach of each other [38].

The integrated approach combines the properties from the route/hop count with the QoS approach to arrive at the optimal solution for a particular request. Due to the nature of the request that a service user specified, there might be a need to prefer particular properties more than the other. For example, time constraint might be very imperative for a user in need of urgent medical attention or user who needed to catch up quickly on a flight, whereas for another user that is requesting for an educationally related service might not be as more urgent. Mobile devices enable the use of various services on transit through a wireless connection either to the cloud server or within themselves. Thus, the integrated (hop count, QoS properties, and feedback response) selection approach seeks to address users' satisfaction by ensuring that the optimal service is being selected at every request.

3. QoS Property Resolution Strategy

The impact of quality of service cannot be overemphasized in the process of service selection. It serves as a building foundation upon which other service approaches can be integrated to enhance optimal service selection in any service-oriented provisioning. The selection of service is built by mapping the requests onto a web service among the available ones. The mapping process helps in locating the actual web service. The aggregation of the QoS for service selection is based on the individual preferences with regard to QoS properties. The following two steps assist in ensuring that this process is properly carried out.

3.1. The Scaling Process. This study uses a simple scaling or normalization technique. This concept of scaling ensures even distribution of QoS properties since these properties differ in value from each other with hardly any comparability among them. The range of values derived fully expresses the order and level of competitiveness among the available web services [39]. $\{Ss\}$ = set of ad hoc mobile services of $\{s_1, s_2, s_3, \ldots, s_j\}$ with a set of qualities $\{Q_q\}$ being $\{q_1, q_2, q_3, \ldots, q_m\}$. This implies that when a sample of the AMC web service is selected such as s_i, it will have a corresponding set of qualities such as $\{q_{i1}, q_{i2}, q_{i3}, \ldots, q_{ij}\}$. Now, assume that the value of the minimum and maximum ith QoS properties within all the available services are $Q_j^{\min}$ and $Q_j^{\max}$. For example, the general quality of some QoS properties decreases with an increase in the value of the property such as service cost and response time; thus, by scaling, we try to minimize the property as much as possible using the normalization equation (1) according to [40] as

$$\acute{V}_j = \begin{cases} \dfrac{Q_j^{\max} - Q_{i,j}}{Q_j^{\max} - Q_j^{\min}} & \text{if } Q_j^{\max} - Q_j^{\min} \neq 0 \\ \\ 1 & \text{if } Q_j^{\max} - Q_j^{\min} = 0. \end{cases} \quad (1)$$

In a similar manner, other services whose QoS properties increase with an increasing value of such a property such as availability and reliability are all normalized using the expression in (2) according to [38] as

$$\acute{V}_j = \begin{cases} \dfrac{Q_{i,j} - Q_j^{\min}}{Q_j^{\max} - Q_j^{\min}} & \text{if } Q_j^{\max} - Q_j^{\min} \neq 0 \\ \\ 1 & \text{if } Q_j^{\max} - Q_j^{\min} = 0. \end{cases} \quad (2)$$

An interval of the range of [0, 1] is produced from (1) and (2), where "1" represents the best QoS property, while "0" represents the least QoS property, thereby reflecting any form of changes that occur to the general quality of any of the services whether it decreases or increases. The algorithm for normalization process is as shown in Algorithm 1.

From Algorithm 1, a new matrix V was generated:

$$V = \left(V_{i,j}; 1 \leq i \leq n, 1 \leq j \leq m\right). \quad (3)$$

```
Input:
    A set of qualities of a Web Service S(t) = {s₁, s₂, ….sₘ}
    that each describes a service
Output:
    A matrix of normalized QoS parameters
Step 0: Initialization, create m by 5 matrix P
Thus, having:

for (i = 0; i < m; i + +)do
for (j = 0; j < n; J + +)do
if (qf [j]eq0)
if (diffqos[j]! = 0)
v[i][j]← ((qmax[j] − p[i][j])/diffqos[j]);

else
  v[i][j]
endif
else if (qf [j]eq1)

if (diffqos[j]! = 0)
v[i][j] ← ((p[i][j] − qmin[j])/diffqos[j]);

else
  v[i][j]←1
endif
return
  V = (V_{i,j}; 1 ≤ i ≤ n, 1 ≤ j ≤ m; )
endif
  endif
```

ALGORITHM 1: QoS property normalization algorithm.

3.2. Weighted Summation Assignment.

There is a need to assign weight to the respective normalized value of each of the service users so that the preferences and the importance of a particular quality can be expressed by the user when requesting a service. Therefore, treating the pool of services as a sample space with coordinates that are having origin as a vector, the services can be represented as

$$\vec{S} = \acute{V}_1\widehat{V}_1 + \acute{V}_2\widehat{V}_2 + \acute{V}_3\widehat{V}_3 + \cdots + \acute{V}_m\widehat{V}_m, \tag{4}$$

where the service is represented by $\vec{S}$ and $\acute{V}_1$, $\widehat{V}_j$; both represented normalized QoS properties as well as the unit vector along the axis of the normalized property. Supposing the mean quality of service is given by S_{mean} and if $\acute{V}_{\text{mean}}$ represents the mean value of the ith QoS property, then,

$$\vec{S}_{\text{mean}} = \acute{V}_{1\,\text{mean}}\widehat{V}_1 + \acute{V}_{2\,\text{mean}}\widehat{V}_2 \\ + \acute{V}_{3\,\text{mean}}\widehat{V}_3 + \cdots + \acute{V}_{m\,\text{mean}}\widehat{V}_m. \tag{5}$$

Considering the mean value of the normalized qualities, we have the summation of the means ranging towards 0.5 as $1 \geq \acute{V}_j \geq 0$; hence, we can rewrite the expression to be

$$\widehat{S}_{\text{mean}} = \frac{1}{\sqrt{m}}\left(\widehat{V}_1 + \widehat{V}_2 + \widehat{V}_3 + \cdots + \widehat{V}_j\right). \tag{6}$$

Carrying out the dot product of the ith service of $\vec{S}_i$ as it projects over the mean $\vec{S}_{\text{mean}}$, then we have the expression

$$\vec{S}_i \cdot \vec{S}_{\text{mean}} = \frac{1}{\sqrt{m}}\left(\acute{V}_1 + \acute{V}_2 + \acute{V}_3 + \cdots + \acute{V}_j\right). \tag{7}$$

Hence, the summation of quality of service properties can be expressed as

$$\text{Summation of quality properties} = \frac{1}{\sqrt{m}}\sum_{i=1}^{m}\acute{V}_j. \tag{8}$$

Assuming the user request for a special preference in any of the qualities of service that are highlighted, the summation of the preference in terms of weight assignments could be expressed for the ith QoS property; thus,

$$\text{Weighted summation assignment} = \frac{1}{\sqrt{m}}\sum_{i=1}^{m}\acute{V}_j * W_i. \tag{9}$$

The output generated from this normalization and weighted summation assignment often results in several web services and service nodes with similar aggregate scores [18]. This challenge shows that there is a need for a mechanism that helps to inform optimal service selection through breaking the occurrence of selection ties in the heterogeneous web service provisioning.

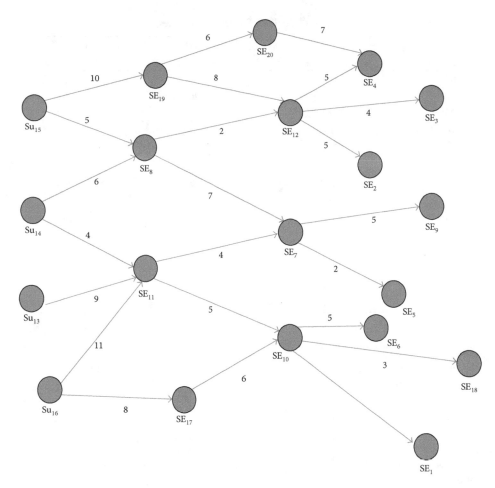

FIGURE 1: m-Health scenario routing traffic from the source to the sink.

4. Modes of Selection Ties in the AMC

Selection ties occur in a situation where there are two or more "*objects*" that qualify to attend to a particular request from a service consumer [11, 18]. In the case of the AMC, a mobile node can be a service provider where it helps to forward a traffic via the shortest route mechanism to the traffic destination. In addition, the resident web services within the mobile nodes in an AMC can attain similar computation scores via the processes discussed in Section 3. The literature currently selects any of the mobile nodes or web services that attain similar computation scores to address the service request which in turn is usually not the optimal option. This invariably results in some level of dissatisfaction on the path of service consumers when at other times, a close friend was able to experience a better service delivery than them due to random selection at "ties" occurrence.

For example, let us consider a case where teachers and students formed an AMC within the school premises, in which they all consume similar educational resources. The experiences of the teachers and the students will virtually be different from one another in situations where there are similar computation scores in the selection process. Therefore, to avoid this kind of situation, this article addresses two major modes of "*selection ties*" occurrence in the AMC:

(A) The mobile node selection ties

(B) The web service selection ties

This article offers substantiated mechanisms with respect to these two modes towards the selection of an optimal service provider to various service requests that are issued in the context of the AMC environment.

5. Multidynamic Distance-Based Approach

The term *multidynamic* distance in this context refers to the use of QoS properties alongside with distances apart among the mobile nodes, otherwise referred to as the shortest route in the course of service provisioning. The approach here is deplorable in an emergency state especially in a typical m-Health situation as shown in Figure 1. The SU_{nodes} is the principal service users.

The traffics are expected to take the shortest route to the destination while bearing in mind that the intended nodes have the capacity to offer the required services. The hypothetical quality of service parameters is as shown in Table 1, containing the prices, response time, reliability, and availability of the mobile nodes. The last column in the table also depicts the summation of route distances apart for the intended traffic. Suppose that a service user (SU_{15}) in Figure 1 is issuing a request for a surgical emergency service (SE_x)

TABLE 1: Quality of service properties.

Services SE services	Price (R)	Response time (ms)	Properties Reliability (%)	Availability (%)	Route (m)
SE_1	82	200	69	75	29
SE_2	70	360.0	20.2	43	12
SE_3	75	330.0	36.5	50	11
SE_4	74	310.10	31.6	41	12
SE_5	81	236.5	35.7	48	14
SE_6	80	210	40.3	60	25
SE_7	82	208	67	72	12
SE_9	82	210	48	78	17
SE_{10}	73	250	35	45	20
SE_{12}	67	233	60	88	7
SE_{17}	55	214.5	55	48	26
SE_{18}	78	305	67	53	23
SE_{19}	76	300	82	64	10
SE_{20}	80	295	45	81	16

```
Set parameters (p, rₜ, r)
Input consumers required QoS
      Call normalization
      Set weights
Calculate score
      if Ss(Score) > 1 then
call DP
Print Ss(Sortestroot)
      else
print Ss(score)
      end if
end.
```

ALGORITHM 2: Multidynamic algorithm.

```
v = vertex and n = node
Input (v, n)
Shortestroot ← 0
Array Shortpernode ← 0
Shortestroot ← 0
Shortrootest ← 0
Repeat
    For i = v − 1 to v
       For j = 1 to n
          For k = 1 to edgeno
          Shortpernode[k] = search min cost {u, v}
             Next k
             Sort Shortpernode[1 − k] in descending
             if
                    shortrootest > Shortpernode [1]
             then
                    shortrootest = Shortpernode [1]
             endif
          Next j
          Shortestroot ← Shortestroot + shortrootest
          v = v − 1
       Next i
Until v = 1
```

ALGORITHM 3: Shortest route DP algorithm.

from any mobile nodes (all SE_x) who can render such a service. We implemented the multidynamic algorithm that was depicted in Algorithm 2. We used the normalization algorithm to analyze the considered qualities of service (price, response time, reliability, and availability), which generated the normalization results that were depicted in Table 2. These outputs are the results that are fed into the weight assignment stage to determine the interest of the service consumer who requests for the service of the mobile nodes.

Algorithm 2 calls for the computation of the normalization and weight assignment and the calculation of aggregate scores. The occurrence of ties further initiates the call to Algorithm 3 which invariably differentiates the services with similar scores. The "*Sortestroot*" uses the dynamic programming algorithm to effect the choice of the shortest route that needs to be calculated in the process. It considers only the mobile nodes with the same computation or aggregate scores as shown in Table 3 and Figure 2. The algorithm selects the mobile nodes among those with similar computation and further selects the one closest to the requesting node for user consumption.

5.1. Selection of Optimal SE Service. The selection of the surgical emergency service (SE) that meets the requested QoS is selected by first providing ranges of weights that depict the amount of priority given to each QoS which ranges from 0 to 1. This weight represents the degree of importance associated with a specific QoS property, and they are fractions whose sum must be equal to 1. For example, if a consumer's topmost priority is on price for surgical emergency service, then the higher weight is given to price. The other properties take lesser fractions, respectively, till the least of them. The service that provides the best utility level based on

TABLE 2: Normalization of SE services.

Services	Properties				
SE services	Price (R)	Response time (ms)	Reliability (%)	Availability (%)	Route (m)
SE_1	0.8181	0.2373	0.6175	0.9290	29
SE_2	0.2727	0.064	0.0802	0.7828	12
SE_3	0.5	0.2523	0.3843	0.6829	11
SE_4	0.4545	0.3763	0.2929	0.8942	12
SE_5	0.7727	1.1064	0.9533	0.5620	14
SE_6	0.7272	1	0.4552	0.7296	25
SE_7	0.8181	0.9688	0.3694	0.3827	12
SE_9	0.8181	1	0.8504	0.9284	17
SE_{10}	0.4328	0.4270	0.3894	0.530	20
SE_{12}	0.45	0.8639	0.8693	0.7829	7
SE_{17}	0.8012	0.4390	0.5728	0.7328	26
SE_{18}	0.6013	1	0.3874	0.4038	23
SE_{19}	0.520	0.2089	0.8429	0.7829	10
SE_{20}	0.3720	0.7823	0.7832	0.5390	16

price becomes the chosen one provided that it is the only one. The weighted summation assignment generates the aggregate score as given in (9).

When the number of ad hoc surgical emergency services that have the maximum score is greater than one, then we consider the route to each of the destination. We then applied the dynamic programming as shown in Algorithm 3. This is done by describing our data elements needed in the form of cities and distances. We then formulate this as an optimization problem, and the minimum route is determined based on the minimum cost tour.

The idea in this section has been used in our previous paper [11], but we considered a larger number of mobile nodes in this experiment; thus, this solution becomes one of the solution approaches under the present article. The detailed comparison among the mobile nodes with aggregate scores was depicted in Figure 2. Other approaches with respect to this particular scenario select any of the mobile nodes among those that attain the request of the service user, but a better utility level is guaranteed with this mechanism in place for mobile service selection.

6. Feedback-Based Approach for Web Services

The user feedback has been an approach that is generally used for improving the performance of a system. This is due to the fact that it gives an updated and continuous information about the performance of an application (web services) with a view to making informed decisions about the behaviour of such an application. In this section, we deployed the use of user feedbacks to enhance better service selection that eradicates the occurrence of web service ties during dynamic service selection. Again, citing the case of teachers and students who team up to form a group as an AMC that exists within a school environment where both participants share educational materials, the challenge that is often experienced is that we want the system to be able to render the optimal web service that guarantees the highest level of

TABLE 3: Shortest route-based selection.

Services	Properties	
SE services	Route (m)	Aggregate scores
SE_1	29	0.7830
SE_2	12	0.7828
SE_{12}	7	**0.7827**
SE_{20}	16	0.7829

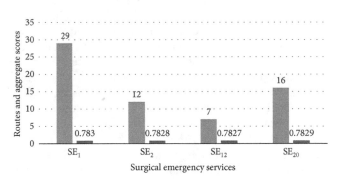

FIGURE 2: Shortest route service selection in critical situations.

satisfaction each time to the service user. Thus, we propose a middleware engine that collects the users' view after consuming web services and use it to range the performance of the resident web services on the system to enhance an optimal selection in future requests. The diagram in Figure 3 shows the interrelated components for effective service selection within an AMC.

The main purpose of introducing the feedback mechanism is to eradicate the possibility of service selection ties within the AMC. The setup mechanism majorly contains the rater, the feedback composer, and the database wherein the

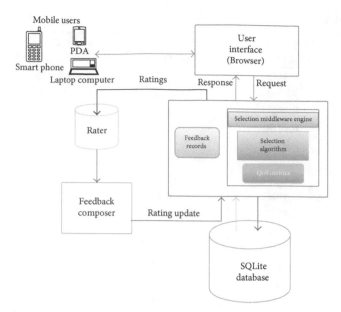

FIGURE 3: Rating mechanism in AMC service selection.

feedback records are kept. Most of the previous steps such as the normalization and the weight assignment are already assumed to have been carried out in this stage. We also assumed that various users provide the system with truthful responses. The rating process follows two major steps which are the collection of the user feedback and the prediction of the appropriate services for the service requestor.

6.1. Collection of User Feedback.

The influx of the AMC with various forms of web services ultimately results in the occurrence of similar ties within the environment. When the similar ties occur, the instruction is to select any out of those ones to carry out the task, and in the absence of such an instruction, the system goes into a temporary redundancy state in which indecision sets in. Eradicating the challenge of similar ties in service selection will enhance prompt response to users through overcoming the possibility of occurrence of redundancy states [41]. The user feedback system uses the credibility level system to collect, process, and rank the responses from the users. Thus, five categories of credibility trust on web services were assigned, namely, the most credible (l_5), more credible (l_4), credible (l_3), less credible (l_2), and the least credible (l_1). The associated strength to each user response can be normalized in

$$\sum_{i=1}^{5} l_i = 1. \tag{10}$$

Using this definition, the researcher assigned the value of 0.2 to express the least credibility value l_1 which shows a lack of trust regarding the selected service. Other values starting from 0.4 to 0.6 are assigned to l_2 and l_3, respectively, where they both typify a low credibility trust. The last sets of values of 0.8 and 1.0 which represent l_4 and l_5 express reliable trust from the service users. Every rating selection made by the user is computed by finding the average or mean of the feedback values selected. This is used to update the system for the latest rating regarding

a particular service. This credibility trust utilized in the proposed system is coupled with a recommendation technique that will assist to make the right decision for the service user [41]. The recommendation technique that is adopted is an item-based collaborative system which is a subset of the collaborative filtering approach. This recommendation system is important in this context for two major reasons:

(1) It identifies the best of the peer of web services among those attaining similar aggregate scores.

(2) It helps to compute final selection based on the services used by the requesting user, provided the user has invoked services in the system before.

The item-based collaborative approach helps addresses these two highlighted points thereby helping to carry out the prediction creation tasks on web services with the similar aggregate scores.

6.2. Prediction Creation.

This section of the service recommendation predicts the best web services based on the previous ratings recorded by the system from earlier service users. The prediction proposed uses the binomial probability density distribution. In this approach, the following variables were used as expressed below:

Let k be the context of service selection such as m-Learning.

X_k is the user's rating for a service in context k.

P_k is a user's preference for a service in context k.

The feedback composer rates each service to select the optimal service for users according to the following density for random variables X_k for which x_k is a typical instance:

$$X_k \sim \frac{1}{n} \text{Binomial}(n, P_k), \tag{11}$$

where n = no. of mobile devices (nodes).

$$E(X_k) = P_k, \tag{12}$$

$$\text{Var}(X_k) = \frac{1}{n} P_k (1 - P_k).$$

We deployed the user rating into the probability prediction for selection. By expressing the ranges over the binomial distribution, the summary was explained in two ways:

(1) When the feedback is very low, the mean of the rating distribution X_k should correspond to a very low value. For example, if the credibility from the user based on quality experienced is l_2, then the feedback composer normalizes the probability to assign $E(X_k) = 0.2$.

(2) Contrariwise, when the feedback is high, $E(X_k)$ is also expected to be high. Thus, the feedback composer chooses $E(X_k) = 1$ when the response is high.

This study implements the following variation on the mean X_k; thus,

$$E(X_k) = \mu_k = P_k + 2 \left(q_k - \frac{1}{2} \right) (q_k - P_k). \quad (13)$$

Every service user draws a rating from the mean X_k for every service that has been rated. These sets of all users' ratings are the inputs to the composer for proper selection to take place. The result of (13) produces series of mean distributions with each of the provided users' ratings, thus aligning the results into a format of a binomial distribution curve. This is because it continually finds the mean of the ratings submitted by the users which always tends to reach the maximum value of ratings as given by a typical binomial distribution diagram curve. The ratings maintain their value if similar values are provided by the new users who make no difference from the earlier value in the feedback record. But whenever the value of the new ratings is more than the previous record, the rating increases. Thus, the feedback rating falls and rises along the binomial distribution curve. The peak of the dome-shaped top of the binomial curve corresponds to the least rating from the users, and such services are not often predicted to users for use because of the low value or rating which shows that the service performs poorly within the specified service functionality. The flattened edge tending towards 1.0 shows the best services to be predicted to the user for use, and the higher it moves from the dome-shaped curve towards the flattened end, the better the web services that are predicted for use in terms of QoS.

6.3. Environmental Specification. To test this proposed approach, this work deploys the use of the Sun Wireless Toolkit 2.5 Beta Version J2ME from the Sun Microsystems packages to test the behaviour of the selection mechanism. The SQLite database is shown outside of the physical connection setup according to Figure 4 to depict the three-layer network model setup (consumer layer, middle layer, and database layer); however, the DB was actually embedded within the server machine. The emulator interface design is developed to run on the J2ME-enabled devices such that it can be easily deployed on real smartphone mobile devices that support communication through the Hypertext Transfer Protocol interconnections.

The implementation of the server is accomplished by the use of J2EE-compliant servers such as Glassfish Application Server 3.1.2. The server-side components are configured to run on any server that conforms to the J2EE specification. The server handles messages from clients through the use of WMA Bridge API, which enhances message interaction during client service invocation from the server. The server contains the web component which runs within the servlet container and also uses the JAXP to communicate with the external data sources. The external data sources originate as information from the XML database, which is a collection of mobile web services.

The whole setup was tested using a mobile laptop running on Windows 7 Professional Edition as an operating system. The laptop had an Intel Core(TM) i7-4500U

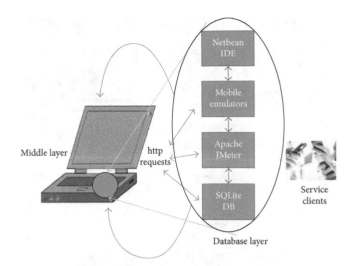

FIGURE 4: Mechanism simulation setup.

processor with a processing speed of 2.40 GHz and 8.00 GB RAM. The application consumed 10.4 MB of the hard drive storage which is favourable to the mobile computing environment due to low memory consumption. Figure 4 also contains the mobile emulators developed from the Netbeans IDE together with the Apache JMeter load generator. The emulator shows the typical interface of the nature of service requests which is similar to requests generated by a typical Apache JMeter for the purpose of testing the performance of the proposed selection model. Figure 5 shows a typical emulator interface for service specification and query interface. The Apache JMeter allows the setting of network parameters like latency and jitters, during the experiments. Therefore, this setup mimics the AMC service provisioning environment for testing the performance of the deployed mechanism.

7. Performance Evaluation

The performance of the selection mechanism on service selection ties was tested with a series of experiments to ensure that the concerned challenge is being addressed. This article first evaluated the selection system using certain parameters such as throughput and service availability to check up that the system is operating normally under a good condition. We later conducted experiments to determine the effect of user feedback on the selection process that involves selection ties and as well use a case of a real-life scenario where service selection ties occur to see how ties' breaking of services might occur before offering the service to the users.

7.1. Service Availability Rates and Throughput Performance. There are many options for quantifying the rate of service availability within interconnected systems. One of the popular options is the use of statistical analyses [42–44]. These approaches are more feasible in a very stable environment where mobility is not occurring too often. Thus, the constant dynamic nature of the AMC will not

FIGURE 5: Service specification and query interface.

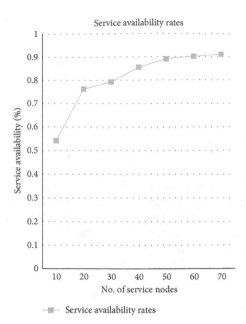

FIGURE 6: Service selection effect on web service availability.

favour these approaches. However, in this experiment, we assigned some weight indicators to certain parameters (fundamental resource availability, i.e., HTTP authorization manager, response assertion, HTTP response default, and Hypertext Markup Language (HTML) link parser) in the Apache load generator which is indicated at runtime by assigning values ranging from 0 through 1 for each of the parameters. Based on these parameters, suppose P_{xy} represents the weight of set parameters S_{xy}, where S_{xy} sums up the indicator values I_{xy}, and given that

$$\sum_{x=1}^{x=a} I_{xy} = 1 , \tag{14}$$

then the service availability of the AMC is therefore calculated using the expression:

$$\text{Ava} = \sum_{x=1}^{a} \sum_{y=1}^{b} P_{xy}S_{xy}. \tag{15}$$

As the number of mobile nodes in the AMC is increased, there is a relative increase in the number of requests and it invariably has the corresponding impact on the percentage number of service availability rates as shown in Figure 6. From the graph shown, it can be deduced that as the number of service provider nodes increases, the service availability climbed steeply at the initial stage but increased more at 20 nodes (i.e., as the nodes doubled). This can be interpreted to mean that all things being equal, the greater the number of service providers, the more the number of services available for consumption within the system. It was noticed that as the number of nodes increases within the AMC, their rate of service availability was not so significant in increment, due to relatively similar web services which also perform similar nonfunctional qualities. This can be assumed to be the result of similar recurring service requests which exist within the cloud. The central server PC is stabilized and the feedback records are properly aligned to enhance

relatively optimal selection without excessive delay of the queries.

In a similar manner, the throughput measures the rate of successful service request delivery over the AMC communication channel. It determines the time it takes to perform a transaction (E) over a number of sessions. The throughput was measured through the JMeter simulator that was integrated via the Netbeans IDE tool. Since the proposed AMC system consists of connecting mobile devices, the experiment is vital to access the performance of the service selection mechanism. To compute the throughput of the system, the following expression is used:

$$\frac{1}{k} \sum_{c=0}^{k} ET, \tag{16}$$

where the variable c represents the request index and k is the number of requests at a particular session. Figure 7 shows the results of the throughput for the load generator.

The number of mobile nodes represented the number of available mobile devices within the system at the time the experiment was conducted, while the number of simultaneously issued service requests showed the number of users that were making an HTTP request during the experiment. The throughput of a system clearly showed the number of completed service deliveries to the requesting service consumer. The results displayed on Figure 7 show that the throughput performance of the web service selection mechanism increases as the number of users increases. The proposed selection mechanism performed well when the test for throughput was conducted. The linear increment in the values of the throughput with the increasing number of node requests performs in a realistic way. Thus, the throughput averagely increases with the increasing number of requests, which

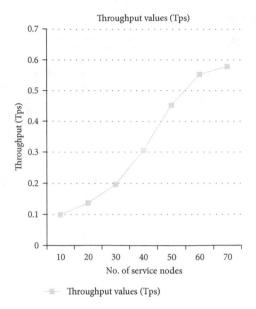

FIGURE 7: Mechanism selection throughputs.

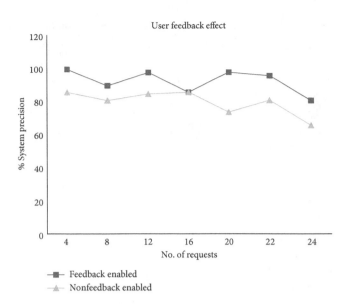

FIGURE 8: Selection precision based on the feedback effect.

confirms a good performance from the system. Therefore, having confirmed the performance of the AMC system with respect to provisioning of service availability as well as the rate of completed service delivery, we have achieved a good platform upon which the effect of feedback can be tested on the system as well as the contribution of the selection mechanism to the body of knowledge when compared with other AMC selection approaches under similar conditions (occurrence of selection ties).

7.2. User Feedback Effect Evaluation. The proof of the concept system here was implemented through deploying the Glassfish Web Server 3.1.2 platform on the central server PC within the AMC. This platform works together with the SQLite database which acquires the WSDL file as well as the QoS information provided by the various mobile service providers. The test deployed a total of 100 web services for this experiment to simulate a real-world selection challenge in terms of user dissatisfaction. To evaluate the feedback-enabled QoS selection, this experiment evaluated the number of service selections that coincide between feedback-enabled and nonfeedback service selections which were adopted from the existing works [45, 46]. The goal of this experiment is to determine how precise the two approaches are at ensuring that the most relevant service is selected.

In the first approach, the service was selected directly without the aid of feedback ratings of the ad hoc mobile selection mechanism (an approach that is already used in cloud computing), while in the other approach, the selection was carried out with the aid of the feedback selection ratings.

The same values of QoS parameters are requested with the increasing number of users. This evaluation revealed the kind of services retrieved after each service request

and recorded the level of satisfaction ranging from a 1-star to a 5-star rating. Starting with the feedback-enabled approach, the expression for percentage precision is given as

$$\text{Precision} = \frac{|\{\text{relevant web services}\} \cap \{\text{retrieved web services}\}|}{|\{\text{retrieved web services}\}|}\%.$$

(17)

This gives the percentage precision through calculating the mean of responses from the number of users at each level of the service request. This precision is expressed to determine the percentage level of satisfaction derived by each of the service users. Figure 8 shows that the feedback indicates highly satisfactory service selection at every incidence of service invocation when compared with selection based on the quality of service alone. At some point during selection ties, the nonfeedback effect can make a selection that coincides with the optimal service at that point, and this accounted for both approaches achieving a similar value only at experiment number four where the number of requests is 16. In addition, the feedback-enabled selection mechanism enhanced the selection of web services and also gave a high tendency to solve the issue of service selection ties, thereby providing an optimal service for users.

The user feedback effect experiment shows that the use of a continuous updated and unlimited range of users' web service assessment only enhances the selection of optimal services for the service users. It should, however, be noted that the greater the number of services that attain the selection ties, the higher the effect of the feedback-enabled system in selecting appropriate and more satisfying services for the user. In a situation where there were few numbers of services, both approaches often, though not always, assumed the same output result. The feedback rating system, however, enhanced the selection of the highly rated service

TABLE 4: QoS metrics for various available e-mail verification web services.

Web services	Response time (ms)	Throughput (b/s)	Availability (%)	Cost (rands)	Reliability (%)	Feedback (%)
XMLLogic	720	6	85	1.2	87	59
XWebservices	1100	1.74	81	1	79	49
StrikeIron Emails	710	12	98	1	96	86
CDYNE	912	11	90	2	91	65
Webservicex	910	4	87	0	83	89
ServiceObjects	1232	9	99	5	99	94
StrikeIron Address	391	10	96	7	94	70
Kickbox	428	5	86	8	60	67
Byteplant	601	8	70	4	75	100
QuickEmail	205	3.5	95	5	89	62
TowerData	504	9	75	1	77	79
Leadspend	832	8	81	3	83	76
Briteverify	911	3	80	5.1	78	26
Mailbox	604	10	89	5	87	69
Emailanswers	505	7	85	6	95	29
BulkEmailVerifier	600	5	90	4	88	96
BulkEmailChecker	195	3.5	85	0	89	55
Emailtor	220	6	87	8	75	28
Verifalia	950	5	90	3	86	38
Xverify	350	8	96	4	94	56

among the selection ties for the user at each point of service invocation where ever it occurs.

7.3. Feedback Mechanism on Real-Life Scenario.
This experiment extracted data samples from the work of Al-Masri and Mahmoud in [45]. This gives us the QoS of seven different web services that were chosen from the same domain. These web services are e-mail web services that share the same functionalities. The data were provided in StrikeIron.com and XMethods.net. A total number of 20 web services were used in this experiment to actually see the effect of the proposed selection mechanism at solving the occurrence of web service ties. However, if more web services are deployed, then the possibility of web service ties increases in the system.

The QoS of the 20 web services is measured by WS-QoSMan. WS-QoSMan is a module that is responsible for collecting and measuring the QoS information of web services. The values of the QoS metrics are normalized and assigned weights accordingly as described in Section 3. The free spider simulator (FSS) tool is also an online tool that helps to get a free report about web service actionable insights. The feedback for over 2 weeks was collected and presented. The last column of Table 4 also specifies the feedback of each of the web services as derived from the FSS. The results of various web services were computed as shown in Table 4. We compare our approach with the two other approaches used in the literature which are the web service ranking function approach [45] and nonfeedback outputs from [47]. The values of the data collected under each approach were expressed in Table 5 which are the

normalized and ranked outputs. More details can be found in [48].

7.4. Discussions.
The results from Table 5 and Figure 9 showed a critical observation that both feedback and nonfeedback techniques achieved the same ordering of web services according to QoS-based selection although different values were obtained and the same ordering was realized. This confirmed that both techniques achieved similar results. However, the WsRF technique only selects at random from the set of services that attain similar QoS scores. The idea discussed in Section 4 helps to solve the challenge by carrying out the prioritization based on the trusted user feedback data that were generated by the AMC web service selection mechanism.

The e-mail validation web services of numbers 6, 9, and 16 ("ServiceObjects," "Byteplant," and "BulkEmailVerifier," resp.) all achieved similar QoS computation. It is understood however that the normalization technique found in [31, 40, 42] ensures that it provides the three best web services amongst those considered. However, this information is not enough to justify the best of the three web services as the feedback rating system shows quite clearly that the web service number 9 (Byteplant) is rated above others of comparable performance. The rating of the Byteplant e-mail validation was seen to be relatively constant over a two-week period and maintained a rating of 100% from different service users. This final choice of the Byteplant over the other two is not only confirmed by the high range of computation selected based on the normalization during QoS computation but

TABLE 5: Results of WsRF, non-FB, and FB QoS metric computation.

ID	Web services	WsRF computation	Rank	Nonfeedback-enabled computation	Feedback-enabled computation	Rank
1	XMLLogic	3.6638	13	4.7648	0.68	13
2	XWebservices	3.2166	15	4.3176	0.64	16
3	StrikeIron Emails	4.6103	4	5.7113	0.87	5
4	CDYNE	3.9246	11	5.0256	0.72	11
5	Webservicex	4.2679	5	5.3689	0.89	4
6	ServiceObjects	4.6700	1	5.7705	0.90	3
7	StrikeIron Address	4.1955	7	5.2965	0.79	8
8	Kickbox	4.0428	10	5.1438	0.74	10
9	Byteplant	4.6700	1	5.7704	0.97	1
10	QuickEmail	3.9205	12	5.0215	0.69	12
11	TowerData	4.2504	6	5.3514	0.83	6
12	Leadspend	4.0832	8	5.1842	0.81	7
13	Briteverify	2.0911	20	3.1921	0.58	20
14	Mailbox	4.0604	9	5.1614	0.75	9
15	Emailanswers	3.0505	18	4.1617	0.62	18
16	BulkEmailVerifier	4.6700	1	5.7706	0.92	2
17	BulkEmailChecker	3.2195	16	4.3205	0.65	15
18	Emailtor	2.3020	19	3.4031	0.60	19
19	Verifalia	3.0950	17	4.1961	0.63	17
20	Xverify	3.5077	14	4.6087	0.66	14

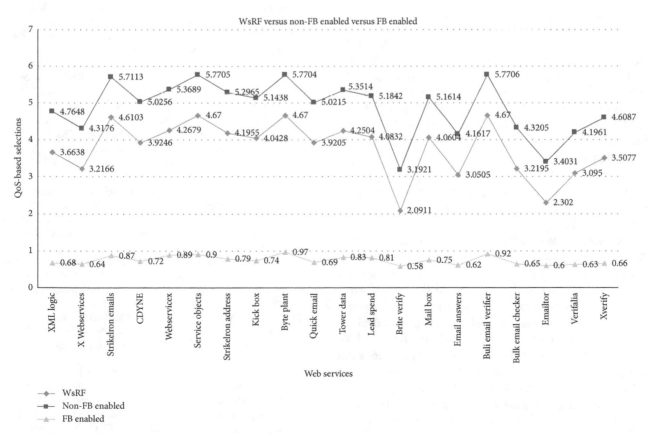

FIGURE 9: The comparison of WsRF, non-FB, and FB-enabled web service selection.

also affirmed by the extensive feedback range of quality maintenance. The binomial probability distribution used by the recommendation system predicts in such a manner that web services are arranged orderly even to the least significant value to bring about the needed differences to differentiate a web service from another one of similar computation. Hence, the whole experiments were focused on improving the user satisfaction in the AMC, as this will promote frequent patronage and regular interest in consumption of services on the GUIISET business platform.

Summarily, multidynamic and feedback mechanisms have contributed to the knowledge base of AMC service selection in the following ways:

(1) Outrightly removal of the possibility of delay/redundancy as a result of selection ties

(2) Breaking of service selection ties whenever they occur

(3) Ensuring that an optimal service is selected in any service requisition

(4) Promotes prompt service delivery via the multi-dynamic distance approach

(5) Increasing the user satisfaction level in the course of service provisioning.

8. Conclusion and Future Work

Many services in the AMC platform are with similar functional qualities which open up the understanding that the effective and efficient use of a various combination of nonfunctional QoS will enhance higher user satisfaction through provision of optimal services. We performed a series of experiments within interconnected mobile network nodes as well as P2P mobile devices. Our experiments proved that distances within mobile networks can be an important QoS tool that will enhance the optimal selection process, which is typically useful in the case of emergency needs, for example, natural disaster, mining process, and health monitoring systems.

Moreover, the user feedback effect on web services can be computed to effect proper ordering of these services within the mobile devices in such a manner that eradicates selection ties. The outcome of the experiments showed that, out of seven selection samples, only one is likely to produce an optimal selection without the feedback mechanism with the calculated probability of 0.13. Thus, we can conclude that the use of the feedback mechanism section of the proposed system enhances better performance in users' satisfaction in comparison with existing works such as WsRF [45] and nonfeedback [47].

Possible future works need to consider the context of the device and mobile environment. Thus, inculcating the environmental context as well as the device context into the selection process is a good note for the furtherance of this work with proper checks in place to avoid complexity issues. Another area for future work includes the implementation of an autoswitching system into the mechanism to switch to the new server during failure.

Acknowledgments

This work is based on the research support in part by the National Research Foundation of South Africa (Grant UID: tp11062500001 (2017-2018)). The authors also acknowledge funds received from the industrial partners Telkom SA Ltd., Huawei Technologies SA (PTY), and Dynatech Information Systems, South Africa, in support of this research.

References

[1] R. Yu, X. Yang, J. Huang, Q. Duan, Y. Ma, and Y. Tanaka, "QoS-aware service selection in virtualization-based cloud computing," in *Proceedings of 14th Asia-Pacific Network Operations and Management Symposium (APNOMS)*, pp. 1–8, Seoul, Republic of Korea, September 2012.

[2] M. Sathya, M. Swarnamugi, P. Dhavachelvan, and G. Sureshkumar, "Evaluation of QoS based web-service selection techniques for service composition," *International Journal of Software Engineering*, vol. 1, no. 5, pp. 73–90, 2012.

[3] S. Marston, Z. Li, S. Bandyopadhyay, J. Zhang, and A. Ghalsasi, "Cloud computing—the business perspective," *Decision Support Systems*, vol. 51, no. 1, pp. 176–189, 2011.

[4] G. Zou, Q. Lu, Y. Chen, R. Huang, Y. Xu, and Y. Xiang, "QoS-aware dynamic composition of web services using numerical temporal planning," *IEEE Transactions on Services Computing*, vol. 5, no. 3, pp. 1–14, 2012.

[5] B. Martini, F. Paganelli, A. A. Mohammed, M. Gharbaoui, A. Sgambelluri, and P. Castoldi, "SDN controller for context-aware data delivery in dynamic service chaining," in *Proceedings of 1st IEEE Conference on Network Softwarization: Software-Defined Infrastructures for Networks, Clouds, IoT and Services, NETSOFT*, pp. 1–5, London, UK, April 2015.

[6] E. E. Marinelli, "Hyrax: cloud computing on mobile devices using MapReduce," vol. 389Pittsburgh, PA, USACarnegie Mellon University, September, 2009 M.S. thesis, Thesis.

[7] F. AlShahwan and M. Faisal, "Mobile cloud computing for providing complex mobile web services," in *Proceedings of 2nd IEEE International Conference on Mobile Cloud Computing, Services, and Engineering*, pp. 77–84, Oxford, UK, April 2014.

[8] N. Kaushik and J. Kumar, "A literature survey on mobile cloud computing: open issues and future directions," *International Journal of Engineering and Computer Science*, vol. 3, no. 5, pp. 6165–6172, 2014.

[9] K. Bahwaireth and L. Tawalbeh, "Cooperative models in cloud and mobile cloud computing," in *Proceedings of 23rd International Conference on Telecommunications, (ICT 2016)*, pp. 1–4, Thessaloniki, Greece, May 2016.

[10] G. Huerta-Canepa and D. Lee, "A virtual cloud computing provider for mobile devices," in *Proceedings of ACM Workshop on Mobile Cloud Computing & Services: Social Networks and Beyond*, pp. 35–39, San Francisco, CA, USA, June 2010.

[11] A. T. Akinola, M. O. Adigun, A. O. Akingbesote, and I. N. Mba, "Optimal service selection in ad-hoc mobile market based on multi-dynamic decision algorithms," in *Proceedings of 2nd World Symposium on Computer Networks and Information Security*, pp. 1–6, Hammamet, Tunisia, 2015.

[12] A. T. Akinola, M. O. Adigun, A. O. Akingbesote, and I. N. Mba, "Optimal route service selection in ad-hoc mobile E-marketplaces with dynamic programming algorithm using TSP approach," in *Proceedings of International Conference on E-Learning Engineering and Computer Softwares*, pp. 74–81, Kualar Lampur, Malaysia, 2015.

[13] J. Cao, K. Hwang, K. Li, and A. Y. Zomaya, "Optimal multiserver configuration for profit maximization in cloud computing," *IEEE Transactions on Parallel and Distributed Systems*, vol. 24, no. 6, pp. 1087–1096, 2013.

[14] M. E. Buthelezi, M. O. Adigun, O. O. Ekabua, and J. S. Iyilade, "Accounting, pricing and charging service models for a GUISET grid-based service provisioning environment," in *Proceedings of the 2008 International Conference on e-Learning, e-Business, Enterprise Information Systems, and e-Government, (EEE 2008)*, pp. 350–355, Las Vegas, NV, USA, July 2008.

[15] O. O. Ekabua and M. O. Adigun, "GUISET LogOn: design and implementation of GUISET-driven authorization," in *Proceedings of First International Conference on Cloud Computing, GRIDs, and Virtualization 2010*, pp. 1–6, Lisbon, Portugal, November 2010.

[16] E. K. Olatunji, M. O. Adigun, E. Jembere, J. Oladosu, and P. Tarwire, "A privacy-as-a-service model for securing data in GUISET environment," in *Proceedings of Southern Africa Telecommunication Networks and Applications Conference (SATNAC'13)*, pp. 143–148, Stellenbosch, South Africa, September 2013.

[17] A. O. Akingbesote, M. O. Adigun, S. Xulu, and E. Jembere, "Performance modeling of proposed GUISET middleware for mobile healthcare services in E-marketplaces," *Journal of Applied Mathematics*, vol. 2014, Article ID 248293, 9 pages, 2014.

[18] A. O. Akingbesote, M. O. Adigun, J. B. Oladosu, and E. Jembere, "A quality of service aware multi-level strategy for selection of optimal web service," in *Proceedings of IEEE International Conference on Adaptive Science and Technology ICAST*, pp. 1–6, Pretoria, South Africa, November 2013.

[19] A. O. Akingbesote, M. O. Adigun, M. A. Othman, and I. R. Ajayi, "Determination of optimal service level in cloud E-marketplaces based on service offering delay," in *Proceedings of 2014 IEEE International Conference on Computer, Communication and Control Technology (I4CT 2014)*, pp. 283–288, Langkwawi, Kedah, Malaysia, September 2014.

[20] T. Shezi, E. Jembere, and M. Adigun, "Towards developing failure tolerant communication framework for GUISET services," in *Proceedings of the Southern Africa Telecommunication Networks and Applications Conference (SATNACT'11), East London International Convection Centre*, East London, South Africa, 2011.

[21] A. O. Akingbesote, M. O. Adigun, E. Jembere, and J. Oladosu, "Modeling the cloud e-marketplaces for cost minimization using queuing mode," *Australian Journal of Basic and Applied Sciences*, vol. 8, no. 4, pp. 59–67, 2014.

[22] A. O. Akingbesote, M. O. Adigun, S. S. Xulu, M. Sanjay, and I. R. Ajayi, "Performance analysis of non-preemptive priority with application to cloud E-marketplaces," in *Proceedings of IEEE International Conference on Adative Technolgy (ICAST)*, pp. 1–6, Paris, France, 2014.

[23] S. Msane, M. O. Adigun, and O. O. Ekabua, "A reputation-based trust management model to enforce trust amongst web services in a GUISET grid environment," in *Proceedings of International conference on Semantic Web abd Web Services (SWWS'08)*, pp. 230–235, Las Vegas, NV, USA, July 2008.

[24] M. Swarnamugi, "Taxonomy of web service selection approaches," *International Journal of Computer Applications*, vol. 2, no. 4, pp. 18–22, 2013.

[25] M. Klusch and P. Kapahnke, "Semantic web service selection with SAWSDL-MX," in *Proceedings of Second International Workshop on Service Matchmaking and Resource Retrieval in the Semantic Web (SMRR 2008)*, pp. 1–15, Karlsruhe, Germany, October 2008.

[26] S. Susila, S. Vadivel, and A. Julka, "Broker architecture for web service selection using SOAPUI," in *Proceedings of International Conference on Cloud Computing Technologies, Applications and Management (ICCCTAM 2012)*, pp. 219–222, Dubai, UAE, December 2012.

[27] M. Xin, M. Lu, and R. Zhang, "A location-based services selection model and algorithm with QoS constraints under mobile internet environment," in *Proceedings of International Conference on Service Sciences*, pp. 124–129, Jiangsu, China, May 2014.

[28] M. Amoretti, M. C. Laghi, A. Carubelli, F. Zanichelli, and G. Conte, "Reputation-based service selection in a peer-to-peer mobile environment," in *Proceedings of IEEE International Symposium on a World of Wireless, Mobile and Multimedia Networks (WOWMOM)*, pp. 1–8, Newport Beach, CA, USA, June 2008.

[29] M. Keidl and A. Kemper, "Towards context-aware adaptable web services," in *Proceedings of the 13th International World Wide Web Conference on Alternate Track Papers & Posters, ACM*, pp. 55–65, New York, NY, USA, May 2004.

[30] N. Keskes, "Context of qos in web service selection," *American Journal of Engineering Research*, vol. 2, no. 4, pp. 120–126, 2013.

[31] Y. Liu, A. H. H. Ngu, and L. Z. Zeng, "QoS computation and policing in dynamic web service selection," in *Proceedings of the 13th International World Wide Web Conference on Alternate Track Papers & Posters, ACM*, pp. 66–73, New York, NY, USA, May 2004.

[32] H. Shah-Hosseini, "Problem solving by intelligent water drops," in *Proceedings of IEEE Congress on Evolutionary Computation*, pp. 3226–3231, Singapore, September 2007.

[33] A. T. Akinola and M. O. Adigun, "Feedback-based service selection in ad-hoc mobile cloud computing," in *Proceedings of 3rd International Conference on Advances in Computing and Communication Engineering (IEEE-ICACCE-16)*, pp. 72–77, Durban, South Africa, November 2016.

[34] Z. Zhang, W. Sun, W. Chen, and B. Peng, "An integrated approach to service selection in mobile ad hoc networks," in *Proceedings of 4th IEEE International Conference on Wireless Communications, Networking and Mobile Computing (WICOM 2008)*, pp. 1–4, Dalian, China, October 2008.

[35] A. T. Akinola, M. O. Adigun, and P. Mudali, "A federated web service selection approach for ad-hoc mobile cloud computing," in *Proceedings of 19th Southern African Telecommunication Networks and Applications Conference (SATNAC)*, pp. 386–373, Frankhurt, South Africa, September 2016.

[36] A. Varshavsky, B. Reid, and E. de Lara, "A cross-layer approach to service discovery and selection in MANETs," in *Proceedings of IEEE International Conference on Mobile Adhoc and Sensor Systems Conference*, pp. 66–73, Washington, DC, USA, November 2005.

[37] R. Lacuesta, J. Lloret, S. Sendra, and L. Peñalver, "Spontaneous ad hoc mobile cloud computing network," *Scientific World Journal*, vol. 14, no. 10, pp. 1–19, 2014.

[38] K. Yang, A. Galis, and H.-H. Chen, "QoS-aware service selection algorithms for pervasive service composition in mobile

wireless environments," *Mobile Networks and Applications*, vol. 15, no. 4, pp. 488–501, 2010.

[39] E. Cavalcante, T. Batista, F. Lopes et al., "Optimizing services selection in a cloud multiplatform scenario," in *Proceedings of the IEEE Latin America Conference on Cloud Computing and Communications, LatinCloud*, pp. 31–36, Porto Alegre, Brazil, November 2012.

[40] M. Makhlughian, S. M. Hashemi, Y. Rastegari, and E. Pejman, "Web service selection based on ranking of QoS using associative classification," *International Journal on Web Service Computing*, vol. 3, no. 1, pp. 1–14, 2012.

[41] J. Zhu, Y. Kang, Z. Zheng, and M. R. Lyu, "A clustering-based QoS prediction approach for web service recommendation," in *Proceedings of 15th IEEE International Symposium on Object/Component/Service-Oriented Real-Time Distributed Computing Workshops*, pp. 93–98, Shenzhen, China, April 2012.

[42] L. Zeng, B. Benatallah, A. Ngu, M. Dumas, J. Kalagnanam, and H. Chang, "QoS-aware middleware for web services composition," *IEEE Transactions on Software Engineering*, vol. 30, no. 5, pp. 311–327, 2004.

[43] N. Kokash and V. D'Andrea, "Evaluating quality of web services: a risk-driven approach," in *Proceedings of Business Information System Conference*, pp. 180–194, Poznan, Poland, April 2007.

[44] O. Kondratyeva, N. Kushik, A. Cavalli, and N. Yevtushenko, "Evaluating quality of web services: a short survey," in *Proceedings of IEEE 20th International Conference on Web Services*, pp. 587–594, Santa Clara, CA, USA, June 2013.

[45] E. Al-Masri and Q. H. Mahmoud, "QoS-based discovery and ranking of web services," in *Proceedings of 16th International Conference on Computer Communications and Networks*, pp. 529–534, Honolulu, HI, USA, August 2007.

[46] R. P. Singh and K. K. Pattanaik, "An approach to composite QoS parameter based web service selection," *Procedia Computer Science*, vol. 19, no. 2, pp. 470–477, 2013.

[47] S. Reiff-Marganiec, H. Q. Yu, and M. Tilly, "Service selection based on non-functional properties," *Service-Oriented Computing-ICSOC 2007 Workshops*, pp. 128–138, Springer, Berlin, Germany, 2009.

[48] A. Akinola, "QoS-based web service selection mechanism for ad-hoc mobile cloud computing," University of Zululand, KwaDlangezwa, South AfricaUniversity of Zululand, 2017 M.Sc. dissertation, Thesis.

9

Energy Efficient Clustering based Network Protocol Stack for 3D Airborne Monitoring System

Abhishek Joshi, Sarang Dhongdi, Rishabh Sethunathan, Pritish Nahar, and K. R. Anupama

BITS Pilani, K K Birla Goa Campus, Goa, India

Correspondence should be addressed to Abhishek Joshi; abhijoshi2008@gmail.com

Academic Editor: Arun K. Sangaiah

Wireless Sensor Network consists of large number of nodes densely deployed in ad hoc manner. Usually, most of the application areas of WSNs require two-dimensional (2D) topology. Various emerging application areas such as airborne networks and underwater wireless sensor networks are usually deployed using three-dimensional (3D) network topology. In this paper, a static 3D cluster-based network topology has been proposed for airborne networks. A network protocol stack consisting of various protocols such as TDMA MAC and dynamic routing along with services such as time synchronization, Cluster Head rotation, and power level management has been proposed for this airborne network. The proposed protocol stack has been implemented on the hardware platform consisting of number of TelosB nodes. This 3D airborne network architecture can be used to measure Air Quality Index (AQI) in an area. Various parameters of network such as energy consumption, Cluster Head rotation, time synchronization, and Packet Delivery Ratio (PDR) have been analyzed. Detailed description of the implementation of the protocol stack along with results of implementation has been provided in this paper.

1. Introduction

Wireless Sensor Network (WSN) is an ad hoc network consisting of large number of nodes distributed in the area of interest in predefined or random manner. WSNs are tightly constrained in terms of computing power, communication range, and energy which also makes unique differentiating factor in the way of operation of the network from rest of the conventional ad hoc networks [1]. A node in WSN consists of computing unit, communication unit, and sensing unit coupled with power supply [2]. Nodes in WSNs are largely dependent on batteries as the primary source of energy.

WSNs can be characterized into different categories depending on their application areas such as military applications [3], environmental applications [4], and home and industrial applications [5]. WSNs play vital part in military applications where they are used for monitoring friendly forces, equipment, ammunition, and surveillance of the battlefield. WSNs are also integral part of environmental applications where they are used for wildlife monitoring, environmental condition monitoring, precision agriculture, forest fire detection, flood detection, air pollution monitoring, and

so on. Home and commercial industries use WSNs in home automation, structure monitoring, inventory management, factory process control, theft detection, vehicle tracking, and so on.

Typically, most of the application areas covered by WSNs take into account only 2D topology of the network which includes x and y planes in the network. But there are crucial emerging areas such as airborne networks [6] and underwater networks [7] which take into account the depth or height (z) parameter of the network as well. Characteristics of airborne networks are high mobility, high bit error rate, and intermittent connectivity [8]. Underwater networks encounter large and variable propagation delay, severe Doppler phenomenon, and multipath effects [9]. Since the depth or height parameter has to be included in 3D WSN, conventional protocols of 2D WSN cannot fulfill the requirements of these application areas. Hence, there is a need for developing protocol stack for 3D WSNs which addresses unique features and challenges of these networks. Air quality monitoring is an application of 3D WSN. In this application, a 3D airborne network has to be deployed to monitor the quality of the air. Particulate Matter (PM), ground level ozone, carbon monoxide, nitrogen oxide, sulfur oxide, and lead are primary sources of air pollutants. They are also called criteria pollutants. These pollutants are required to be monitored for calculating Air Quality Index (AQI) [10]. AQI for an area tells us how healthy the air is to breathe.

Recently authors have proposed network protocol stack for 3D WSN in [11]. This protocol stack has been implemented using Cooja simulation platform. In our work, protocol stack proposed in [11] has been implemented on static 3D airborne wireless sensor network using hardware platform. This platform consists of number of TelosB nodes deployed at various heights in the form of clusters. These clusters consist of a Cluster Head (CH) node and number of Cluster Nodes (CN). Along with this, a single node deployed on the ground has been used as Base Station. Nodes in the network communicate with Base Station (BS) via their respective CH nodes in multihop manner. A complete protocol stack consisting of TDMA MAC and dynamic routing along with services such as time synchronization, power level management, and Cluster Head rotation has been deployed on this 3D airborne network. This hardware implementation of complete protocol stack along with its results and analysis has been discussed in this paper.

The rest of this paper is organized as follows. In Section 2, literature review of various protocols of WSNs such as time synchronization and medium access control has been discussed. A lightweight energy efficient time synchronization protocol proposed by authors Tian et al. in [12] has also been discussed in detail in this section. Proposed 3D cluster-based network architecture of airborne network has been discussed in Section 3. In Section 4, operation of the proposed protocol stack on 3D network has been described in detail. In Section 5 results of this implementation along with analysis of this result have been provided. Conclusions have been provided in Section 6.

2. Literature Survey

In this section, survey of various protocols such as time synchronization and medium access protocols has been discussed. In Section 2.1, description of time synchronization protocols has been provided and in Section 2.2, description of MAC protocols has been provided.

2.1. Time Synchronization Protocols. Time synchronization is a process of achieving a common clock among network nodes [13]. The clock at each node consists of timer circuitry, which is based on crystal oscillators giving a local time to every node. The time in a node's clock is basically a counter that gets incremented with crystal oscillators. The interrupt handler must increment the clock by one unit each time an interrupt occurs. Clock $C(t)$ can be realized with the help of the following equation:

$$C(t) = \alpha t + \beta, \tag{1}$$

where α is a skew and β is an offset of the clock.

Clock skew is defined as the rate of deviation of a clock from the true time and clock offset is defined as the difference between the time reported by a clock and the real time. For the perfect clock, $\alpha = 1$ and $\beta = 0$.

To achieve the common clock, nodes in the network synchronize their local clocks with each other and also with the reference clock. Time synchronization is an important service for various WSN applications such as event detection [14], environment monitoring [15], and target tracking [16]. It is also required for medium access control, coordinated sensing, and multinode cooperative communication. It plays a vital role in saving energy in WSN since it provides the possibility of utilizing sleep-wake cycle in the network [17].

Traditional methods of time synchronization in ordinary networks are not applicable in the sensor network since they are complex in nature and consume more power. Network Time Protocol (NTP) is preferred clock synchronization technique used by time servers operating in the Internet [18]. It provides coordinated universal time (UTC). NTP uses levels of clock servers for the purpose of synchronization but it is not suitable in wireless sensor networks, since it consumes higher amount of energy. In addition, it uses GPS which is an expensive hardware for a low-cost device. GPS may not be available everywhere such as inside buildings or under water. Commonly used time synchronization protocols in WSN include Reference-Broadcast Synchronization (RBS), Timing-sync Protocol for Sensor Networks (TPSN), and Flooding Time Synchronization Protocol (FTSP).

RBS is a broadcast protocol which makes use of receiver to receiver synchronization scheme [19]. The designated root node broadcasts a beacon. Multiple nodes receive this beacon in concurrent manner. Nodes find out their local time at the time of reception of beacon message and then they compare their local time with adjacent nodes. This comparison leads to calculation of phase offset. Main advantage of RBS is that this protocol removes the nondeterminism from the sender. One of the major disadvantages is that it is not suitable for large multihop networks.

TPSN is a sender to receiver synchronization [20]. Working of this protocol is divided into two phases. First phase is called the level discovery phase. Second phase is the synchronization phase. In the level discovery phase, a level is assigned to each node. Root node is considered to be at level zero. In the synchronization phase, nodes from level one initiate the two-way messaging with the root node. This process iterates throughout the network. Root node is the originator of both phases. TPSN provides improvement of precision over RBS protocol. The major disadvantage is that it does not allow dynamic topology changes.

FTSP is another sender to receiver synchronization protocol [21]. FTSP broadcasts timing information to all nodes that are able to receive the message. Those nodes which receive the information message from the root node calculate their offset from the global time. These nodes also calculate their clock skew using linear regression. FTSP is robust in compensating node and link failures. It also allows for a dynamic topology but FTSP is not suitable for large multihop networks.

All of the above-discussed protocols exchange large number of messages during the synchronization phase. For achieving long lifetime of deployed network, minimizing the energy footprint is the primary goal in designing WSN. Time

TABLE 1: Message exchange comparison for time synchronization protocols.

Protocol	Number of message exchanges	
	Nodes = 50	Nodes = 250
TPSN	1000	5000
RBS	1250	30000
FTSP	500	2500

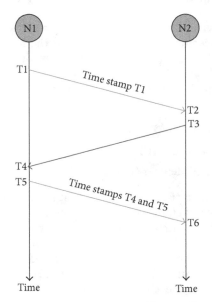

FIGURE 1: Tri-Message time synchronization.

synchronization protocols for WSN cannot be excluded from this constraint. Authors Noh et al. have conducted simulation of above-discussed time synchronization protocols on the basis of number of message exchanges for various numbers of nodes [22]. These results for TPSN, RBS, and FTSP have been tabulated in Table 1.

Recently, a time synchronization protocol has been proposed for underwater acoustic sensor networks. This protocol termed as Tri-Message synchronization protocol is suitable for high latency and resource constrained underwater networks. A brief description of Tri-Message protocol has been provided in following subsection.

2.1.1. Tri-Message Time Synchronization Protocol.
In Tri-Message synchronization there are two nodes, Node N1 and Node N2. N1 is considered to be the originator of Tri-Message synchronization and assumed to have synchronization with the global clock. Figure 1 represents Tri-Message time synchronization process.

In the Tri-Message synchronization phase, N1 transmits first message to N2 at time T1. This message includes the time stamp T1. N2 receives this message at time T2. Later, N2 sends the message back to N1 at time T3, which is received by N1 at time T4. Finally, N1 transmits the third message at time T5. In this message, N1 includes the time stamps T4 and T5. N2 receives this message from N1 at time T6, which completes the Tri-Message synchronization process. After the completion

of this process, N2 has all six time stamps available with it. Time gap between T2 and T3 is considered to be processing time for N2. Similarly, equal duration gap between T4 and T5 is the processing time for N1. Clock skew (α) and offset (β) in the Tri-Message synchronization protocol can be calculated with following equations:

$$\alpha = \frac{T6 - T2}{T5 - T1},$$
$$\beta = \frac{T2 + T3}{2} - \alpha \frac{T4 + T5}{2}. \tag{2}$$

In this way, the Tri-Message time synchronization protocol requires only three message exchanges to achieve time synchronization between two nodes. Hence for time synchronization of 50 nodes, it will require 150 message exchanges whereas for 250 nodes, 750 messages will be exchanged. Thus compared to TPSN, RBS, FTSP, and other linear regression based time synchronization protocols, Tri-Message protocol is a lightweight time synchronization protocol. Depending on advantage of energy efficiency, a Tri-Message time synchronization protocol has been utilized in this work. An extension of this protocol has been proposed for multihop topology and has been implemented on 3D airborne network. For achieving higher accuracy in time synchronization, Tri-Message protocol can be replaced with fine grained time synchronization protocols.

In the next subsection, we provide review of medium access protocols.

2.2. Medium Access Control Protocols.
MAC (Medium Access Control) layer plays important role in WSN protocol to provide the reliability and efficiency. MAC protocols are responsible for channel access policies, scheduling, buffer management, and error control [23]. The medium access control protocols for the wireless sensor networks can be classified broadly into two categories [24]:

(1) Contention based MAC protocols.

(2) Schedule based MAC protocols.

In contention based MAC protocols successful transmission cannot be assured. In these protocols as per requirement, all nodes in the network make use of a single common channel. This method differs from the schedule based MAC protocols in which the channel is further divided and preallocated for all the nodes in the network. In contention based MAC protocols, whenever the node wants to transmit its data, contention mechanism decides whether the node has the privilege to access the common channel [25]. These protocols are advantageous over schedule based MAC protocols in terms of network scalability and traffic in the network. Also they are not largely affected by topology changes in the network. The major drawback of contention based MAC protocols is that they utilize the energy of the network in ineffective manner [26].

Schedule based MAC protocols help in avoiding overhearing, idle listening, and collisions by scheduling transmit and listen periods. Time synchronization is basic requirement for schedule based MAC protocols [27]. These protocols demand stringent time synchronization requirements. The categories of schedule based protocols are as follows:

(1) Time Division Multiple Access (TDMA).

(2) Frequency Division Multiple Access (FDMA).

(3) Code Division Multiple Access (CDMA).

In TDMA protocol, a common channel is utilized by all the nodes in the network which is divided into time slots [28]. The advantage of TDMA protocol is that network has no data collision. Since the time slots are predefined, nodes turn on and off their radios at predefined time which further saves energy in the network. A major drawback of TDMA protocol is the stringent requirement of time synchronization in the network [26]. In FDMA protocol all the nodes in the network use same time slot but they operate at different carrier frequencies. This scheme also avoids data collision in the network but at the cost of additional hardware [29]. CDMA protocol makes use of spread-spectrum technique along with the coding scheme. This allows multiple users to be multiplexed over the same physical channel. This scheme also avoids data collision in the network but requires additional computing requirement resulting into increased energy consumption which is contradictory with the basic requirement for WSNs [30].

Among various schedule based protocols such as FDMA, CDMA, and TDMA based protocols, TDMA based MAC protocols can exploit advantages in terms of simplicity, fairness, and energy efficiency. Collisions, idle listening, and overhearing can be avoided in this protocol. Hidden node problem is easily solved without using an extra message overhead because neighboring nodes transmit at different time slots. Channel utilization can be significantly improved if parallelism in communication is allowed. These concurrent transmission schemes can be exploited using proper channel reuse concept already available in cellular mobile networks. Slots can be reserved for future expansion and can be allocated on dynamic basis to address the scalability issue. If we assume structured deployment and deterministic scheduling scheme with known traffic patterns, then any simple or energy efficient time synchronization can suffice in TDMA MAC protocol.

Authors Handy et al. proposed Low Energy Adaptive Clustering Hierarchy (LEACH) protocol [31]. This protocol is based on TDMA based MAC protocol. Operation of protocol is divided in two phases. In first phase, clusters are organized. During second phase, data from all the nodes in the network gets transferred to the Base Station node. Originally LEACH protocol was developed for 2D WSNs. Authors Baghouri et al. translated existing LEACH protocol for 3D WSNs while retaining its original features [32].

In this work, a new variant of TDMA based MAC protocol has been proposed for 3D airborne networks. This protocol has been implemented as a part of protocol stack on hardware platform of 3D airborne network. In Section 3, architecture of 3D airborne network has to be described in detail.

3. Network Architecture of 3D Airborne Wireless Sensor Network

In this work, a static and structured 3D network architecture has been proposed. This network has been divided into L levels with each level separated by the vertical distance of y m. At every level, a cluster of n nodes has been deployed. This cluster consists of a Cluster Head node and number of Cluster Member Nodes. The nodes of cluster have been deployed within the diameter of x m. These clusters have been deployed vertically above each other. At ground level, a single node has been deployed which serves as the Base Station in the network. In Figure 2, the proposed network architecture has been illustrated.

Nodes in the network are preliminary divided into three categories:

(1) Base Station (BS) node.

(2) Cluster Head (CH) node.

(3) Cluster Member (CN) node.

Base Station (BS) node deployed at ground level is used to send control information to the nodes in the network. Similarly, data sensed from the nodes can be collected at the BS. Initially, the BS node sends the control information to the CH node situated one level above it. After receiving the control information from BS node, this CH node transmits information to the CH node in the level above it. Once the control information has been received by all the CH nodes, these CH nodes send this control information to their respective CN nodes. CN nodes can then transmit the sensed data information to their respective CH nodes. Every CH node aggregates the collected data information and forwards it in hop by hop manner to the BS.

Node addressing scheme has also been illustrated in Figure 2. A node is represented as the address NLxx where L stands for the level number and nn stands for the node number. For example, BS node at level 0 is represented as N000. At level 1, nodes are represented as N100 to N1xx wherein N100 is initially deployed as CH node. Similarly at level 2 nodes are addressed from N200 to N2xx, wherein N200 is initially deployed CH node.

This 3D network architecture has been tested using hardware platform. Hardware implementation of the network has been carried out on TelosB nodes. TelosB node is based on 8 MHz TI MSP430 microcontroller with 10 kB of RAM. It has 250 kbps 2.4 GHz IEEE 802.15.4 wireless transceiver. ADC, DAC, supply voltage supervisor, and DMA controller are integrated into the node. Also, the node has integrated humidity, temperature, and light sensors. TelosB supports ultra-low mode current consumption and it has support for variable transmission power which suits the network requirement in which the packet has to be transmitted at different distances. In this work, for implementation of network architecture on hardware platform, total 3 levels have been deployed. At ground level, BS node has been deployed. At other two levels, 5 nodes each have been deployed. Vertical distance between clusters has been taken as 6 m whereas the diameter of cluster at each level has been taken as 4 m.

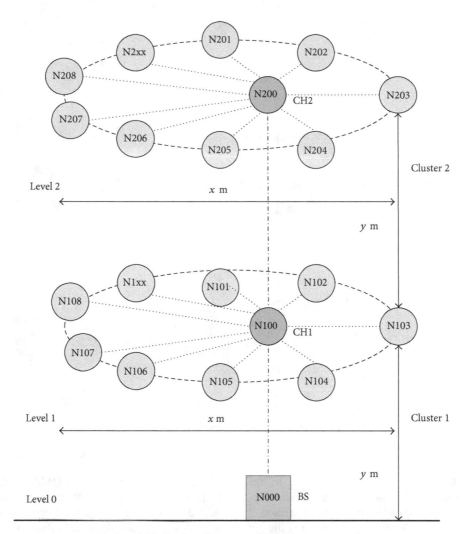

FIGURE 2: Network architecture of 3D airborne network.

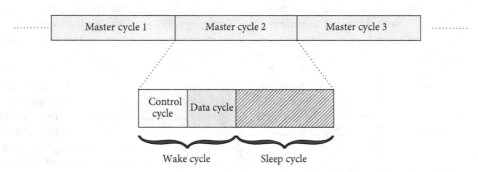

FIGURE 3: Composition of master cycle.

4. Working of the Proposed Protocol Stack

In this work, a variant of TDMA based MAC protocol termed as Dynamic Cluster-Based TDMA MAC (DCB-TDMA MAC) protocol has been proposed and implemented on 3D airborne network. In this protocol, network operation is divided into periodic cycles. These periodic cycles have been termed as master cycles. Every master cycle is divided into sleep and wake cycle. Wake cycle is further subdivided into control and data cycle.

Figure 3 represents composition of master cycle.

Wake cycle begins with control cycle. Time synchronization takes place during control cycle. In control cycle, a multihop version of Tri-Message time synchronization has been used. Description of proposed multihop version has been given in the following subsection.

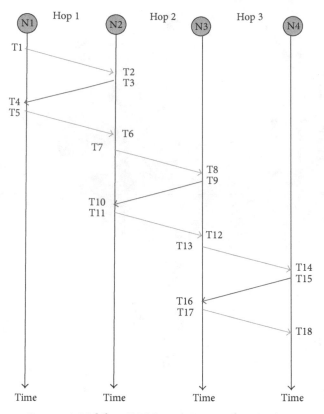

FIGURE 4: Multihop Tri-Message time synchronization.

4.1. Multihop Tri-Message Time Synchronization. In this work, a multihop version of Tri-Message time synchronization protocol has been proposed which is illustrated in Figure 4. Node N1 acts as a reference clock source in the network. Node N2 in hop 1 synchronizes its clock with reference to Node N1 after three messages exchange. At the end of time instance T6, clock of Node N2 gets synchronized with respect to Node N1. At time instant T7, Node N2 initiates time synchronization process with Node N3 on hop 2. Three messages are exchanged between Node N2 and Node N3. At the end of time instance T12, Node N3 gets synchronized with Node N2. Same process is repeated until all the nodes in the network are time synchronized with respect to the reference clock in the network. Considering three-hop structure of the network, the corrected clock at Node N3 can be calculated as follows:

For hop 1

$$C_1(t) = \alpha_1 t + \beta_1. \qquad (3)$$

For hop 2

$$C_2(t) = \alpha_2 t + \beta_2. \qquad (4)$$

For hop 3

$$C_3(t) = \alpha_3 t + \beta_3. \qquad (5)$$

Using (3), (4), and (5) clock of Node N3 can be calculated as

$$t = \frac{C_3(t) - \beta_3 - \alpha_2 \alpha_3 \beta_1 - \alpha_3 \beta_2}{\alpha_1 \alpha_2 \alpha_3}. \qquad (6)$$

4.2. Dynamic Cluster-Based TDMA MAC. During hardware implementation of the protocol, a fourth message has been added in the Tri-Message time synchronization protocol. In this message, clock skew and offset values have been broadcasted by the synchronized node. This message has been used to validate the values of skew (α) and offset (β) for the node. Thus, Tri-Message time synchronization requires exchange of 4 messages between two nodes. Considering one time slot for every message, in every control cycle, 4 time slots have been utilized for time synchronization of two nodes.

In our hardware implementation of 3D airborne network, multihop Tri-Message time synchronization has been used in the following manner. Base Station node (N000) initiates time synchronization in the network. Initially, N000 synchronizes CH node in cluster 1 (N100). After getting synchronized with N000, N100 synchronizes CH node of cluster 2 (N200). This completes synchronization of all the CH nodes in the network in hop by hop manner through vertical communication link. When all the CH nodes in the network are time synchronized with BS, CH nodes begin the process of time synchronization in their respective clusters. The time synchronization between CH nodes and their respective CN nodes takes place over horizontal communication link. In the network, dynamic power levels have been used for the transmission. For example, in hardware implementation, two different levels have been utilized for horizontal and vertical communication links. While communicating over a vertical link of 6 m distance, CH nodes use higher power level of transmission. On the other hand, to communicate over the horizontal

TS1 to TS4	TS5 to TS8	TS9 to TS12	TS13 to TS16	TS17 to TS20	TS21 to TS24	TS25–TS44	
BS (N000) to CH1 (N100)	CH1 (N100) to CH2 (N200)	CH1 (N100) to CN1 (N101)	CH1 (N100) to CN2 (N102)	CH1 (N100) to CN3 (N103)	CH1 (N100) to CN4 (N104)	Future expansion of 5 nodes	
		CH2 (N200) to CN1 (N201)	CH2 (N200) to CN2 (N202)	CH2 (N200) to CN3 (N203)	CH2 (N200) to CN4 (N204)	Future expansion of 5 nodes	

FIGURE 5: Control cycle structure.

TS45	TS46	TS47	TS48	TS49–TS53	TS54	TS55
CN1 (N101) to CH1 (N100)	CN2 (N102) to CH1 (N100)	CN3 (N103) to CH1 (N100)	CN4 (N104) to CH1 (N100)	Future expansion of 5 nodes	CH2 (N200) to CH1 (N100)	CH1 (N100) to BS (N000)
CN1 (N201) to CH2 (N200)	CN2 (N202) to CH2 (N200)	CN3 (N203) to CH2 (N200)	CN4 (N204) to CH2 (N200)	Future expansion of 5 nodes		

FIGURE 6: Data cycle structure.

distance of 2 m, nodes use lower power level of transmission. Use of different power levels in the network helps in achieving parallel communication among the horizontal communication links in the network. CH at different levels communicate with their CN nodes from their respective clusters in same time slots. Parallel communication of CH nodes with their respective CN nodes helps in optimizing the time slot (TS) requirement of the network. Figure 5 represents the structure of the control cycle phase of network operation.

Multihop Tri-Message time synchronization protocol has been used in our network which requires 4 time slots for synchronizing two nodes in the network. In first four time slots TS1–TS4, N100 synchronizes with N000. In TS5–TS8, N200 gets synchronized with N100. By the end of TS8, CH nodes in the network are time synchronized with BS. From TS9 onwards, CH nodes start synchronizing CN nodes of their respective clusters. There are 5 nodes in every level with one among these nodes acting as a CH at any given point of time. There are 4 CN nodes in every cluster. Time synchronization of different CN nodes from different levels with their respective CH nodes takes place in concurrent manner. Total 16 time slots are utilized for synchronizing N101–N104 with N100 in level 1 and N201–N204 with N200 in level 2. Time synchronization of all the nodes is achieved by the end of TS24. In proposed network protocol stack, we have made the provision of dynamically adding 5 nodes in each level to scale the network. Extra 20 time slots are reserved for dynamic addition of nodes in the network. At TS45, control cycle is complete and from subsequent time slot onwards,

the data cycle starts. If no new nodes are added, duration of TS25–TS44 is used as sleep period.

During data cycle, CN nodes transmit their sensed data to their respective CH nodes in preallotted time slot over horizontal communication link. For communication over horizontal link, lower power level of transmission is utilized by CN nodes. These lower power levels permit the parallel intracluster communication. When CN nodes of cluster 2 transmit their data to the CH node of cluster 2, the CN nodes of cluster 1 parallel transmit the data to the CH node of cluster 1. When CH nodes receive the data, it is aggregated at respective CH nodes. After this aggregation, the forwarding of data is initiated over vertical communication link. CH node of cluster 2 forwards the aggregated data to the CH node of cluster 1. Further CH node of cluster 1 appends his own data and forwards it to the BS.

Figure 6 represents the structure of the data cycle phase. In Figure 6, N101 transmits its sensed data to N100 in TS46. Because of utilization of dynamic power levels, N201 also transmits its sensed data to N200 in the same TS. Similarly, N102–N104 transmit their sensed data to N100 in TS46–TS48. N202–N204 also transmit their sensed data to N200 in the same time slts. Extra 5 slots, TS49–TS53, have been reserved for adding extra 5 nodes in each level. In TS54, N200 transmits its aggregated data to N100 over a vertical communication link and finally in TS55, N100 transmits its aggregated data along with data received from N200 to N000. By the end of TS55, the network operation for one wake cycle is complete. After wake cycle nodes in the network sleep which has the same duration of wake cycle, the combined sleep and wake cycle constitute a master cycle. These master cycles repeat in periodic manner throughout the network lifetime.

As discussed earlier in this section, provision of dynamic addition of nodes has been made during control cycle as well as data cycle. Up to 5 nodes can be added in each level at any point of time. The dynamic node addition is controlled by BS. Certain parameters have to be communicated with BS such as number of nodes which have to be added, the levels in which they have to be added, and the master cycle number during which they have to be added. After this information has been externally fed to the BS, it includes this information in control cycle to communicate with respective CH nodes. After receiving the control information about the node addition, CH nodes communicate with the newly added nodes in the predefined master cycle. During control cycle, CH nodes share their timing information for synchronization of the clocks of the newly added nodes and during data cycles, CH nodes collect the sensed data from these newly added nodes which make these nodes as a part of the network.

We have also introduced Cluster Head rotation policy in our network to balance the energy in the network. CH nodes at each level communicate with other CH nodes above and below their level over vertical communication link utilizing higher power level of transmission. Also CH nodes communicate with CN nodes in their respective clusters over horizontal communication link utilizing lower power level of transmission. Because of all these communications, CH nodes consume higher amount of energy compared to CN nodes. If the node acts as a CH node for prolonged duration of time, higher amount of energy would be depleted from this CH node leading to complete drainage of battery. This might result into dead node which would hamper the operation of the network. To avoid the network failure and to balance energy in the network, a CH rotation policy has been implemented which takes into account the depleted energy as the criteria for electing new CH. During hardware implementation of the network, at every fifth master cycle, CN nodes transmit their depleted energy levels along with sensed data to their respective CH nodes. CH nodes locally elect the next CH for its level and transmit the information to the subsequent CH node until this information is available with BS. During sixth master cycle, CH nodes percolate the information about newly elected CH within their respective clusters during control cycle phase. From seventh master cycle onward, the newly elected CH takes effect. This process of Cluster Head election iterates periodically throughout the span of the network.

In LEACH clustering protocol for 2D as well as 3D WSNs, CH nodes communicate with BS node in single hop manner. This results into increased energy consumption of CH nodes since every CH node has to communicate with BS node in direct manner. This technique requires increased amount of energy for communication compared to our 3D airborne protocol stack where CH nodes communicate with BS node in multihop manner. This reduced energy consumption is helpful in prolonging lifetime of the network.

TABLE 2: Design parameters of deployed 3D airborne network.

Network parameter	Value
L	3
y	6 m
x	4 m
n	5

Authors Attarzadeh and Mehrani proposed a new three-dimensional clustering method for WSN [33]. In their protocol, the network is considered static and CH nodes are fixed. Cluster Head rotation policy has not been discussed in their protocol. It leads to reduced lifespan of the network compared to our 3D airborne protocol stack since energy for CH nodes is usually depleted at higher rate compared to rest of the nodes in the network. If no Cluster Head rotation policy is included in the protocol, chances of complete depletion of energy for CH node increase which results into nonfunctioning of node resulting into reduced lifespan of the network.

Network parameters of the 3D airborne network have been described in the following subsection.

4.3. Network Parameters of Deployed 3D Airborne Network. Design parameters of deployed 3D airborne network have been tabulated in Table 2.

Packet Delivery Time is composed of Transmission Time (TT) and Propagation Delay (PD) in the network.

Transmission Time (TT) is defined as ratio of Packet Size (PS) to Bit Rate (BR)

$$TT = \frac{PS}{BR}. \tag{7}$$

Propagation Delay (PD) is ratio of Distance to Speed

$$PD = \frac{Distance}{Speed}. \tag{8}$$

Hence

$$\text{Packet Delivery Time (PDT)}$$
$$= \text{Transmission Time (TT)} \tag{9}$$
$$+ \text{Propagation Delay (PD)}.$$

Time slot for transmission and reception of the node can be calculated from PDT. In our implementation, we have taken time slot values larger than the PDT value considering an application involving data collection at regular intervals. Delay in this network can be reduced significantly by taking time slot values of duration equal to PDT, which can be the optimum values for time slot duration.

As discussed in Section 4, we have made use of dynamic power levels for transmissions. On vertical communication link, higher power level of transmission has been used. A transmission circuitry consumes $I_{TX_{PH}}$ during higher power level of transmission. On horizontal communication link, lower power level of transmission has been used. Transmission circuitry for horizontal link consumes $I_{TX_{PL}}$ during lower power level of transmission.

TABLE 3: Various types of packets used in the network.

Packet type	Link type	Size
Time sync	Vertical	27 bytes
Time sync	Horizontal	29 bytes
Data	Vertical	23 bytes
Data	Horizontal	23 bytes
Data + energy	Vertical	24 bytes
Data + energy	Horizontal	27 bytes

Therefore, energy consumed during transmission of packet at higher power level is given as follows:

$$E_{TX_{PH}} = TT \times V \times I_{TX_{PH}}. \tag{10}$$

Energy consumed during transmission of packet at lower power level is given as follows:

$$E_{TX_{PL}} = TT \times V \times I_{TX_{PL}}. \tag{11}$$

Energy consumption during reception of packet is uniform across all the nodes in the network. Current requirement for reception is given as I_{RX}.

Hence, energy consumption during reception of packet is as follows:

$$E_{RX} = TT \times V \times I_{RX}. \tag{12}$$

5. Results and Discussion

During the hardware deployment of 3D airborne network, we have considered various data packets of different sizes. Table 3 gives detailed information about types and sizes for both horizontal and vertical links.

Bit rate of the nodes is set as 20 kbps. Time slot duration value is kept 20 ms. Also sleep cycle of 60 s has been defined during the operation of the network. A new node has been added in level 1 in master cycle 8 and another new node has been included in level 2 in master cycle 9 to represent dynamic node addition feature of our 3D airborne network. Network has been analyzed for multiple master cycles. Multihop Tri-Message time synchronization results have been discussed in Section 5.1. In Section 5.2, energy consumption analysis of network has been provided. Cluster Head rotation policy has been discussed in Section 5.3. In Section 5.4, Packet Delivery Ratio (PDR) for the hardware implementation of the network has been provided.

5.1. Results of Multihop Tri-Message Time Synchronization Protocol. Multihop Tri-Message time synchronization takes place during control cycle. Skew and offset are important parameters in our time synchronization protocol. With the help of equation (6), we can correct the local clock of a node in the network with respect to global clock in the network. Considering the network parameters discussed in Section 4.3, results obtained by implementing multihop Tri-Message time synchronization protocol in hardware platform have been presented in Tables 4, 5, and 6.

TABLE 4: Skew and offset values during cycles 1 and 2.

Node pair		Cycle 1	Cycle 2
000-100	Skew	0.9999	0.9999
	Offset	12008 ms	83 ms
100-101	Skew	0.9999	0.9999
	Offset	2089 ms	78 ms
100-102	Skew	0.9998	0.9999
	Offset	2061 ms	87 ms
100-103	Skew	0.9998	1.0010
	Offset	2171 ms	92 ms
100-200	Skew	1.0010	1.0010
	Offset	1613 ms	97 ms
200-201	Skew	1.0000	1.0000
	Offset	1678 ms	94 ms
200-202	Skew	1.0000	0.9999
	Offset	1762 ms	79 ms
200-203	Skew	1.0030	1.0030
	Offset	1794 ms	86 ms

TABLE 5: Skew and offset values during cycles 8 and 9.

Node pair		Cycle 8	Cycle 9
000-101	Skew	0.9999	0.9999
	Offset	143 ms	145 ms
101-100	Skew	0.9999	0.9999
	Offset	103 ms	118 ms
101-102	Skew	0.9999	0.9999
	Offset	129 ms	124 ms
101-103	Skew	1.0010	1.0010
	Offset	96 ms	101 ms
101-104	Skew	0.9999	0.9999
	Offset	2076 ms	69 ms
101-201	Skew	1.0010	1.0010
	Offset	113 ms	110 ms
201-200	Skew	1.0000	1.0000
	Offset	143 ms	144 ms
201-202	Skew	0.9999	0.9999
	Offset	123 ms	128 ms
201-203	Skew	1.0030	1.0030
	Offset	129 ms	138 ms
201-204	Skew	—	1.0020
	Offset	—	3174 ms

In Table 4, skew and offset values obtained during hardware implementation of multihop Tri-Message time synchronization protocol in cycle 1 and cycle 2 have been tabulated. N000 is considered to have reference clock for the network. During cycle 1, all the nodes in the network calculate their respective values of skew and offset with help of (2) by comparing their local clocks against the reference clock in the network. Clock correction scheme has been included during the implementation of our network on hardware platform. From cycle 2 onwards the clock correction takes over to correct the

TABLE 6: Skew and offset (ms) values during cycle 13.

Node pair		Cycle 13
0-104	Skew	0.9999
	Offset	148 ms
104-100	Skew	0.9999
	Offset	136 ms
104-101	Skew	0.9999
	Offset	153 ms
104-102	Skew	1.0010
	Offset	123 ms
104-103	Skew	0.9999
	Offset	175 ms
104-204	Skew	1.0010
	Offset	136 ms
204-200	Skew	1.0000
	Offset	134 ms
204-201	Skew	0.9999
	Offset	163 ms
204-202	Skew	1.0030
	Offset	184 ms
204-203	Skew	1.0020
	Offset	108 ms

TABLE 7: Depleted energy during cycles 1, 2, and 5.

Node	Depleted energy (mJ)		
	Cycle 1	Cycle 2	Cycle 5
100	12.8	12.85	12.7
101	2.26	2.3	2.18
102	2.2	2.22	2.24
103	2.1	2.34	2.28
200	10	10.1	10
201	2.20	2.34	2.26
202	2.42	2.26	2.32
203	2.22	2.18	2.26

TABLE 8: Depleted energy during cycles 8, 9, and 11.

Node	Depleted energy (mJ)		
	Cycle 8	Cycle 9	Cycle 11
100	2.40	2.26	2.38
101	15.4	15.43	15.42
102	2.40	2.26	2.38
103	2.30	2.26	2.38
104	2.38	2.20	2.34
200	2.20	2.34	2.26
201	12.8	15.4	15.43
202	2.26	2.3	2.18
203	2.20	2.34	2.26
204	—	2.34	2.28

TABLE 9: Depleted energy during cycle 13.

Node	Depleted energy (mJ)		
	Cycle 13	Cycle 15	Cycle 17
100	2.40	2.30	2.38
101	2.38	2.38	2.34
102	2.3	2.34	2.34
103	2.34	2.26	2.18
104	15.3	15.4	15.44
200	2.20	2.42	2.22
201	2.18	2.26	2.28
202	2.3	2.22	2.34
203	2.26	2.2	2.1
204	15.42	15.4	15.4

local clocks of all the nodes in the network to synchronize them with respect to the reference clock. Results of corrected clocks with respect to reference clock for all the nodes in the network at the end of cycle 2 have been tabulated in columns 4 and 8 for levela 1 and 2 in the network, respectively, in Table 4.

As discussed in Section 4, new CH is elected every 5th cycle and takes effect as new CH two cycles after it has been elected. When network starts, initial CH nodes have been elected during 5th cycle and these nodes take effect as new CH nodes in the network during 7th cycle on network operation. In Table 5, we have represented skew and offset parameters obtained from cycles 8 and 9 in columns 3-4 and 7-8 for levels 1 and 2, respectively. Analysis of skew and offset parameters shows that clock synchronization works robustly even after CH rotation.

New nodes are dynamically added during hardware implementation of 3D airborne network during cycles 8 and 9 at levels 1 and 2, respectively. These newly added CN nodes take effect as CH nodes of their respective cluster during cycle 13 which is based on Cluster Head rotation policy. Hence, to reflect the effect of dynamic addition of nodes in the network, we have taken into account the values of skew and offset parameters obtained at the end of cycle 13 in Table 6. Analyzing columns 3 and 6 from Table 6 and comparing the values obtained for skew and offset parameters at cycle 13 with cycle 2 when initial clock correction technique was applied, we can conclude that dynamic node addition at different levels in the network has no effect on skew and offset parameters of multihop Tri-Message time synchronization protocol.

5.2. Energy Consumption Analysis of the Network. When network starts, N100 and N200 are selected as Cluster Head nodes for the clusters formed at levels 1 and 2, respectively. Initially there are 4 nodes in each cluster which includes one Cluster Head node and 3 Cluster Nodes. Sample calculations for energy depletion during first cycle are shown below which can be verified from depleted energy values obtained during hardware implementation of the network in Table 7.

Tables 7, 8, and 9 represent depleted energy levels of all the nodes in the network.

Using (10), (11), and (12) and taking into account the different types of packets mentioned in Table 3 depleted energy for N100 during cycle 1 can be calculated easily.

The values of $I_{TX_{PH}}$, $I_{TX_{PL}}$, and I_{RX} have been taken from [34]. These values correspond to current consumption at transmission power levels 7 and 23, respectively

$$E_{N100} = E_{TX_{N100}} + E_{RX_{N100}},$$

$$E_{TX_{N100}} = 4.0193 \, \text{mJ}, \tag{13}$$

$$E_{RX_{N100}} = 8.8410 \, \text{mJ}.$$

Hence,

$$E_{N100} = E_{TX_{N100}} + E_{RX_{N100}} = 12.86 \, \text{mJ}. \tag{14}$$

Similarly depleted energy for N200 can be calculated as

$$E_{N200} = 3.0390 \, \text{mJ} + 7.0207 \, \text{mJ} = 10.0597 \, \text{mJ}. \tag{15}$$

Depleted energy of any Cluster Node in the network can be calculated as

$$E_{CN} = 0.8939 \, \text{mJ} + 1.371 \, \text{mJ} = 2.265 \, \text{mJ}. \tag{16}$$

In fifth cycle, Nodes N101 and N201 are elected as CH nodes in level 1 and level 2, respectively. They take effect as new CH nodes in their respective levels during seventh cycle. In Table 8 depleted energies of nodes during cycle 8, 9, and 11 have been tabulated.

New nodes have been added during 8th and 9th cycle in level 1 and level 2, respectively. In cycle 11, these newly added nodes have been elected as new CH nodes for their respective levels. These nodes take effect from cycle 13 onward. The depleted energies of these nodes can be verified from Table 9.

5.3. Cluster Head Rotation. As discussed in Section 4.2, Cluster Head rotation policy has been utilized during hardware implementation of 3D airborne network. Every fifth cycle, CN nodes send their depleted energy values to their respective CH nodes along with the sensed data. CH nodes elect new CH for their levels based upon the node which has depleted minimum energy from their respective clusters. If two or more nodes are found to have depleted same amount of energy, node with lower node id is elected. Figure 7 shows graph of depleted energies of N100, N101, and N102 from level 1 over first 10 cycles of network operation.

During first five cycles of network operation, N100 acts as CH for level 1. From Section 5.2, it depletes 12.86 mJ energy in every cycle. In this graph, we have also included depleted energy values for Nodes N101 and N102. Since both of them act as CN nodes during first five cycles, they consume 2.265 mJ energy in every cycle. N101 and N102 consume the same amount of energy and when new CH has to be elected during fifth cycle; N101 has been given precedence over N102 because of its lower node id. In cycle 7, N101 becomes new CH for level 1 and it depletes 12.86 mJ energy during rest of the cycles until next CH has been elected.

5.4. Packet Delivery Ratio (PDR). In the hardware platform, repetitive master cycles of DCB-TDMA MAC have been implemented. In the control cycle phase of these master cycle,

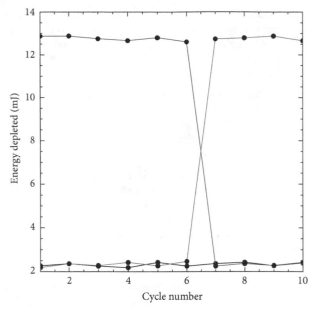

FIGURE 7: Cluster Head rotation policy.

time synchronization has been conducted whereas in the data cycle phase, sensed data has been collected on the ground based Base Station node. After collection of data at BS, sleep cycle (of equal duration of wake cycle) has been scheduled. During the repetition of master cycles it has been observed that all packets have been delivered successfully to intended receiver node, giving the PDR as 100%.

In Section 6, conclusions of this paper have been provided.

6. Conclusions

In this paper, network architecture of 3D airborne network has been proposed. This network architecture is cluster-based hierarchical network consisting of static nodes deployed at varying heights above ground level. For this network architecture, a protocol stack consisting of TDMA based MAC protocol, dynamic routing, time synchronization, Cluster Head rotation, and power level management has been proposed. This complete stack has been deployed on the 3D network using TelosB nodes. This 3D airborne network architecture can be used to monitor quality of the air. Air pollutants are monitored to derive AQI for an area. It has been demonstrated in the paper that this proposed framework is energy efficient and hence suitable for longevity of the deployed network. Energy efficient network operation has been showcased using following features:

(1) The network nodes follow a sleep-wake cycle of 50%. Along with this, since a TDMA based MAC protocol has been utilized, nodes sleep for duration other than preallotted time slots conserving energy.

(2) Energy balancing among network nodes is possible because of Cluster Head rotation, which is performed in regular intervals. It also prevents the network from complete failure in backbone link.

(3) Multihop communication between CH nodes and BS node consumes less power compared to LEACH clustering protocol translated for 3D WSNs. Also Cluster Head rotation policy helps in increasing the network lifespan compared to clustering protocol proposed in [33].

(4) An energy efficient (lightweight) time synchronization protocol has been utilized on the network. This time synchronization protocol requires least amount of message exchanges to achieve time synchronization and hence consumes lesser power, memory, and time in a process.

(5) For communication at various ranges, optimum power levels of transmission have been utilized. Nodes dynamically switch the power levels based on the range of communication optimizing the battery usage.

Competing Interests

The authors declare that there is no conflict of interests regarding the publication of this paper.

References

[1] J. Yick, B. Mukherjee, and D. Ghosal, "Wireless sensor network survey," *Computer Networks*, vol. 52, no. 12, pp. 2292–2330, 2008.

[2] J. A. Stankovic, "Wireless sensor networks," *Computer*, vol. 41, no. 10, pp. 92–95, 2008.

[3] M. P. Đurišić, Z. Tafa, G. Dimić, and V. Milutinović, "A survey of military applications of wireless sensor networks," in *Proceedings of the 1st Mediterranean Conference on Embedded Computing (MECO '12)*, pp. 196–199, IEEE, Bar, Montenegro, June 2012.

[4] A. Mainwaring, D. Culler, J. Polastre, R. Szewczyk, and J. Anderson, "Wireless sensor networks for habitat monitoring," in *Proceedings of the 1st ACM International Workshop on Wireless Sensor Networks and Applications*, pp. 88–97, Atlanta, Ga, USA, September 2002.

[5] X. Shen, Z. Wang, and Y. Sun, "Wireless sensor networks for industrial applications," in *Proceedings of the Fifth World Congress on Intelligent Control and Automation (WCICA '04)*, pp. 3636–3640, June 2004.

[6] J. Allred, A. B. Hasan, S. Panichsakul et al., "SensorFlock: an airborne wireless sensor network of micro-air vehicles," in *Proceedings of the 5th ACM International Conference on Embedded Networked Sensor Systems (SenSys '07)*, pp. 117–129, ACM, Sydney, Australia, November 2007.

[7] M. Erol-Kantarci, H. T. Mouftah, and S. Oktug, "A survey of architectures and localization techniques for underwater acoustic sensor networks," *IEEE Communications Surveys & Tutorials*, vol. 13, no. 3, pp. 487–502, 2011.

[8] E. Kulla, S. Sakamoto, M. Ikeda, and L. Barolli, "MANET approaches for airborne networks: a survey," in *Proceedings of the 16th International Conference on Network-Based Information Systems (NBiS '13)*, pp. 66–70, Gwangju, South Korea, September 2013.

[9] I. F. Akyildiz, D. Pompili, and T. Melodia, "Underwater acoustic sensor networks: research challenges," *Ad Hoc Networks*, vol. 3, no. 3, pp. 257–279, 2005.

[10] World Health Organization, *Air Quality Guidelines: Global Update 2005: Particulate Matter, Ozone, Nitrogen Dioxide, and Sulfur Dioxide*, World Health Organization, 2006.

[11] A. Joshi, S. Dhongdi, K. Anupama, P. Nahar, and R. Sethunathan, "Implementation of protocol stack for three-dimensional wireless sensor network," *Procedia Computer Science*, vol. 89, pp. 193–202, 2016.

[12] C. Tian, H. Jiang, X. Liu, X. Wang, W. Liu, and Y. Wang, "Tri-message: a lightweight time synchronization protocol for high latency and resource-constrained networks," in *Proceedings of the IEEE International Conference on Communications (ICC '09)*, pp. 1–5, IEEE, Dresden, Germany, June 2009.

[13] Y.-C. Wu, Q. Chaudhari, and E. Serpedin, "Clock synchronization of wireless sensor networks," *IEEE Signal Processing Magazine*, vol. 28, no. 1, pp. 124–138, 2011.

[14] A. Nasridinov, S.-Y. Ihm, Y.-S. Jeong, and Y.-H. Park, "Event detection in wireless sensor networks: survey and challenges," in *Mobile, Ubiquitous, and Intelligent Computing*, vol. 274 of *Lecture Notes in Electrical Engineering*, pp. 585–590, Springer, Berlin, Germany, 2014.

[15] M. T. Lazarescu, "Design of a WSN platform for long-term environmental monitoring for IoT applications," *IEEE Journal on Emerging and Selected Topics in Circuits and Systems*, vol. 3, no. 1, pp. 45–54, 2013.

[16] É. L. Souza, E. F. Nakamura, and R. W. Pazzi, "Target tracking for sensor networks: a survey," *ACM Computing Surveys (CSUR)*, vol. 49, no. 2, article 30, 2016.

[17] G. Lu, N. Sadagopan, B. Krishnamachari, and A. Goel, "Delay efficient sleep scheduling in wireless sensor networks," in *Proceedings of the 24th Annual Joint Conference of the IEEE Computer and Communications Societies.*, pp. 2470–2481, Miami, Fla, USA.

[18] D. L. Mills, "Internet time synchronization: the network time protocol," *IEEE Transactions on Communications*, vol. 39, no. 10, pp. 1482–1493, 1991.

[19] J. Elson and K. Römer, "Wireless sensor networks: a new regime for time synchronization," *ACM SIGCOMM Computer Communication Review*, vol. 33, no. 1, pp. 149–154, 2003.

[20] S. Ganeriwal, R. Kumar, and M. B. Srivastava, "Timing-sync protocol for sensor networks," in *Proceedings of the 1st International Conference on Embedded Networked Sensor Systems*, pp. 138–149, ACM, 2003.

[21] M. Maróti, B. Kusy, G. Simon, and Á. Lédeczi, "The flooding time synchronization protocol," in *Proceedings of the 2nd International Conference on Embedded Networked Sensor Systems*, pp. 39–49, ACM, 2004.

[22] K.-L. Noh, Y.-C. Wu, K. Qaraqe, and B. W. Suter, "Extension of pairwise broadcast clock synchronization for multicluster sensor networks," *Eurasip Journal on Advances in Signal Processing*, vol. 2008, Article ID 286168, 2008.

[23] P. Suriyachai, U. Roedig, and A. Scott, "A survey of MAC protocols for mission-critical applications in wireless sensor networks," *IEEE Communications Surveys & Tutorials*, vol. 14, no. 2, pp. 240–264, 2012.

[24] W. Ye, J. Heidemann, and D. Estrin, "An energy-efficient mac protocol for wireless sensor networks," in *Proceedings of*

the 21st Annual Joint Conference of the IEEE Computer and Communications Societies (INFOCOM '02), vol. 3, pp. 1567–1576, IEEE, 2002.

[25] M. I. Brownfield, K. Mehrjoo, A. S. Fayez, and N. J. Davis, "Wireless sensor network energy-adaptive mac protocol," in Proceedings of the 3rd IEEE Consumer Communications and Networking Conference (CCNC '06), January 2006.

[26] U. A. Patil, S. V. Modi, and B. J. Suma, "A survey: MAC layer protocol for wireless sensor networks," International Journal of Emerging Technology and Advanced Engineering, vol. 3, no. 9, pp. 203–211, 2013.

[27] V. Rajendran, K. Obraczka, and J. J. Garcia-Luna-Aceves, "Energy-efficient, collision-free medium access control for wireless sensor networks," Wireless Networks, vol. 12, no. 1, pp. 63–78, 2006.

[28] L. F. W. Van Hoesel, T. Nieberg, H. J. Kip, and P. J. M. Havinga, "Advantages of a TDMA based, energy-efficient, self-organizing MAC protocol for WSNs," in Proceedings of the IEEE 59th Vehicular Technology Conference (VTC '04-Spring): Towards a Global Wireless World, vol. 3, pp. 1598–1602, IEEE, Milan, Italy, May 2004.

[29] M. Salajegheh, H. Soroush, and A. Kalis, "HYMAC: hybrid TDMA/FDMA medium access control protocol for wireless sensor networks," in Proceedings of the IEEE 18th International Symposium on Personal, Indoor and Mobile Radio Communications (PIMRC '07), pp. 1–5, IEEE, Athens, Greece, September 2007.

[30] K. Benkic, "Proposed use of a CDMA technique in wireless sensor networks," in Proceedings of the 6th EURASIP Conference Focused on Speech and Image Processing, Multimedia Communications and Services, 14th International Workshop on Systems, Signals and Image Processing, pp. 343–348, IEEE, 2007.

[31] M. J. Handy, M. Haase, and D. Timmermann, "Low energy adaptive clustering hierarchy with deterministic cluster-head selection," in Proceedings of the 4th International Workshop on Mobile and Wireless Communications Network (MWCN '02), pp. 368–372, IEEE, Stockholm, Sweden, September 2002.

[32] M. Baghouri, A. Hajraoui, and S. Chakkor, "Low energy adaptive clustering hierarchy for three-dimensional wireless sensor network," in Recent Advances in Communications, pp. 214–218, 2015.

[33] N. Attarzadeh and M. Mehrani, "A new three dimensional clustering method for wireless sensor networks," Global Journal of Computer Science and Technology, vol. 11, no. 6, pp. 54–60, 2011.

[34] J. Lee and K. Chung, "An efficient transmission power control scheme for temperature variation in wireless sensor networks," Sensors, vol. 11, no. 3, pp. 3078–3093, 2011.

10

A New Prime Code for Synchronous Optical Code Division Multiple-Access Networks

Huda Saleh Abbasⓘ**, Mark A. Gregory, and Michael W. Austin**

RMIT University, Melbourne, Australia

Correspondence should be addressed to Huda Saleh Abbas; s3225132@student.rmit.edu.au

Academic Editor: Youyun Xu

A new spreading code based on a prime code for synchronous optical code-division multiple-access networks that can be used in monitoring applications has been proposed. The new code is referred to as "extended grouped new modified prime code." This new code has the ability to support more terminal devices than other prime codes. In addition, it patches subsequences with "0s" leading to lower power consumption. The proposed code has an improved cross-correlation resulting in enhanced BER performance. The code construction and parameters are provided. The operating performance, using incoherent on-off keying modulation and incoherent pulse position modulation systems, has been analyzed. The performance of the code was compared with other prime codes. The results demonstrate an improved performance, and a BER floor of 10^{-9} was achieved.

1. Introduction

With the rapid increase in demand for bandwidth, a network technology that provides reliable, low latency, and high-speed data transfer is required, and advances in optical fiber networking make it a promising solution for access networks [1, 2]. Various enabling techniques have been extensively investigated, including time division multiplexing (TDM), wavelength division multiplexing (WDM), and optical code division multiplexing (OCDM). While TDM allows user traffic to share the medium in different time slots, WDM allows user traffic to share the medium over different wavelengths. In contrast, the OCDM technique enables user traffic to share the medium in both time and wavelength domains. Furthermore, OCDM offers unique features, such as high security transmission, dynamic bandwidth allocation, and asymmetric bandwidth capability for both downstream and upstream transmissions, in addition to its capability to accommodate a large number of user connections [3].

The general structure of an OCDM access (OCDMA) network consists of five main parts: a transmitter that includes the laser source and modulation unit; an encoder that

generates a unique optical code that is used to distinguish users one from the other; a star coupler that combines or splits signals; a decoder that extracts the intended user signal; and, finally, a receiver that includes the optical detector and demodulator. At the transmitter, the information source produces a data bit for the laser at every T seconds. The encoder then multiplies the data bit by its code word. The code word can be formed by using either a one-dimensional (1D) encoding scheme in the time or wavelength domain or a two-dimensional (2D) encoding scheme that is a combination of both domains. In time-based encoding, the bit time is divided into smaller chips that are equal in number to the code length, whereas in wavelength-based encoding, the code is formed by dividing the transmitted bits into a number of unique subsets of wavelengths [4].

The spreading codes are characterized based on two correlation functions: the autocorrelation and the cross-correlation functions. The cross-correlation function of a signal is the function in which each signal is distinguished from other users' signals, as well as from their time-shifted version. The autocorrelation function is the cross-correlation of the signal with itself [5]. Multiple access

TABLE 1: PC families and parameters.

PC	Code length	Code weight	Cardinality	Correlation
Basic PC [19]*	P^2	P	P	$C_n \cdot C_m = \begin{cases} p & m = n; \text{ autocorrelation} \\ 1 & m \neq n; \text{ cross-correlation} \end{cases}$
E PC [20]*	$P(2P-1)$	P	P	$C_n \cdot C_m = \begin{cases} p-1 & m = n; \text{ autocorrelation} \\ 1 & m \neq n; \text{ cross-correlation} \end{cases}$
MPC [9]	P^2	P	P^2	$C_n \cdot C_m = \begin{cases} p & m = n \\ 0 & m \neq n; m \text{ and } n \text{ in the same group} \\ 1 & m \neq n; m \text{ and } n \text{ in a different group} \end{cases}$
nMPC [21]	$P^2 + P$	$P+1$	P^2	$C_n \cdot C_m = \begin{cases} p+1 & m = n \\ 0 & m \neq n; m \text{ and } n \text{ in the same group} \\ \leq 2 & m \neq n; m \text{ and } n \text{ in a different group} \end{cases}$
PMPC [9, 22]	$P^2 + P$	$P+1$	P^2	$C_n \cdot C_m = \begin{cases} p+1 & m = n; \text{ autocorrelation} \\ 1 & m \neq n; \text{ cross-correlation} \end{cases}$
DPMPC [2]	$P^2 + 2P$	$P+2$	P^2	$C_n \cdot C_m = \begin{cases} p+2 & m = n \\ 0 & m \neq n; m \text{ and } n \text{ in the same group} \\ \leq 2 & m \neq n; m \text{ and } n \text{ in a different group} \end{cases}$
T-MPC [8]	P^2	P	$2P^2$	$C_n \cdot C_m = \begin{cases} 2p & m = n \\ 1 & m \neq n; m \text{ and } n \text{ in the same group} \\ \leq p & m \neq n; m \text{ and } n \text{ in a different group} \end{cases}$
T-SPMPC [7]	P^2	$(P+1)/2$	$2P^2$	$C_n \cdot C_m = \begin{cases} 0, & \dfrac{3p^3 - p^2 - 3p + 1}{4p^3 - 2p} \text{ probability} \\ 1, & \dfrac{p^3 + p^2 + p - 1}{4p^3 - 2p} \text{ probability} \end{cases}$

*PC and EPC are not synchronous codes.

interference (MAI) is a critical issue in a network with high cross-correlation. The cross-correlation proportionally increases with the number of simultaneous users in the network, inevitably resulting in performance degradation [6]. The correlation properties will improve by increasing the code length and the code weight (number of 1s in the code) [7]. However, this increase leads to an increase in the processing time, hardware complexity, and power consumption [8].

Various address codes that are based on prime code family have been introduced such as basic PCs, extended PC (EPC), modified PCs (MPCs), new MPC (nMPC), padded MPC (PMPC), double-padded MPC (DPMPC), transposed MPC (T-MPC), and transposed sparse-padded MPC (T-SPMPC). The codes and their corresponding parameters including length, weight, cardinality (the number of available code-words), and correlation probabilities are shown in Table 1. As shown in Table 1, some of the codes, including MPC, nMPC, PMPC, and GPMPC, support P^2 users (9 users when $P = 3$) with different lengths and weights. Other codes such as T-MPC and T-SPMPC support up to $2P^2$ users (18 users when $P = 3$). This research paper, however, proposes a new code that aims to increase the number of simultaneous users up to $4P^2$ (36 users when $P = 3$). The new code is referred to as "extended grouped new modified prime code" (EG-nMPC).

On-off keying (OOK) and pulse position modulation (PPM) are the most popular modulation schemes used in OCDMA systems [9]. The PPM-OCDMA scheme has been considered as an energy efficient scheme because, for a given bit error rate (BER), PPM-OCDMA can increase the number of users by increasing the pulse-position multiplicity (M) for the same average power, whereas an OOK-OCDMA scheme cannot increase the number of the users at a given BER [10]. On the other hand, however, the OOK-OCDMA scheme has a simple and improved signaling format when compared to PPM-OCDMA, as the chip duration in the former is longer. In addition, the hardware used for the PPM modulation format has a more complex structure [11].

Optical CDMA systems require optical code acquisition and synchronization methods to improve the system's performance and eliminate the MAI [6]. The main purpose of the synchronization process is to recover data by aligning the time between the transmitted signal and the decoder at the receiver side [12]. Most studies regarding OCDMA systems have assumed perfect synchronization. Limited research on synchronization methods for OCDMA systems has been reported in the literature [12]. The most common methods are serial search and parallel search [13]. In [14], a serial-search synchronization system has been introduced and evaluated with an OOC code in OOK-OCDMA and PPM-OCDMA systems. In addition, the same authors introduced a parallel-search synchronization system based on a dual-threshold sequential method in [12] for an OOC code. In [15], a synchronization method has been introduced for noncoherent OCDMA. The paper emphasizes the significance of synchronization between the transmitter and the receiver in improving the system performance. In [16], an analysis of a serial-search algorithm for an OCDMA system applying an OOC code has been presented. The analysis is based on photon counting, considering the effect of MAI, dark current, and shot noise. In [17], a new algorithm referred to as the multiple-shift (MS) algorithm for code acquisition in OCDMA systems was proposed. The performance of the MS algorithm has been evaluated using an OOC code, and the paper highlights that the proposed algorithm helps to reduce the mean synchronization time. A recent work presented in [18] introduced an improved MS (IMS) algorithm. The proposed algorithm is similar to the conventional one in terms of process, but with an improved performance.

OCDM has been used as a monitoring technique for passive optical networks (PONs) due to its simplicity [23]. Monitoring PON-based OCDM techniques are referred to as optical coding (OC) techniques. PON is a point-to-multipoint (P2MP) connector that is formed by deploying a passive optical splitter and a combiner at a remote node (RN), to connect an optical line terminal (OLT), located at the central office (CO), to multiple optical network units (ONUs) at the customer premises. The OC functions as a transmitter that transmits the monitoring signal from the network management system (NMS) to the RN. This monitoring signal is split into a number of subsignals that are equal to the number of ONUs. Each of the ONUs receives a subsignal, encodes it, and then sends it back to the NMS. The NMS has the capability to identify faulty ONUs by examining the veracity of the received codes [24]. The OC technique utilizes the spreading codes that have been used in OCDMA systems, such as optical orthogonal code (OOC) and PC [23]. The literature shows that OOC is the dominant coding technique implemented for time-domain coding in PON monitoring. A 1D OOC code has improved performance in terms of correlation; however, its construction mechanism is relatively complex. In addition, its cardinality is bound by its length and weight [9]. On the other hand, 1D PC is characterized by a simple construction mechanism, its cardinality does not have an upper bound, and there is an absence of a mathematical limitation on how it is used other than to match the optical transmission system capabilities [6, 9]. The correlation probabilities of OOC are higher than those of PC; however, this feature has become less important in PON due to the use of the time division multiple access (TDMA) technique, and the ranging process is performed by the OLT and ONU to avoid upstream burst collision. The selection of the spreading code implemented in OC techniques is determined by the cardinality of the spreading code chosen [23]. Hence, the main objective is to provide the number of code-words that are compatible with PON splitting ratios (32, 64, and 128). The proposed code can be implemented in OC techniques as it provides compatible cardinality with lower unused code-words when compared to other PCs, thereby leading to an increase in the code utilization factor that is defined as the number of active users at a given BER to the code cardinality.

The rest of the paper is organized as follows: Section 2 explains the code construction and its properties. Section 3 evaluates the performance of the proposed code with an OOK modulation system. Section 4 assesses the performance of the proposed code with an incoherent PPM system. Section 5 discusses the results. The conclusion is provided in Section 6.

2. Proposed Code

A system that uses an incoherent OCDMA is based on the binary 1 and 0, where 1 represents the presence of light and hence the encoding process executes and generates a waveform $s(n)$. The code sequence represents the destination address $f(n)$ [7]. On the other hand, 0 represents the absence of light which means the encoding process will not be executed. After the encoding process and transmission to the user, the receiver correlates the received signal with the destination address. This correlation function is denoted by $r(n)$ and expressed as [7]

$$r(n) = \sum_{i=1}^{N} s(i) f(i-n), \tag{1}$$

where N is the number of users. If the signal arrives correctly, then the received signal is equal to the destination address with $s(n) = f(n)$ and (1) signifies an autocorrelation function. Otherwise, (1) signifies a cross-correlation function [7].

2.1. Construction of EG-nMPC.
The construction of the EG-nMPC is described in the following seven steps:

Step 1. Choose the prime number, for example, $P = 3$.

Step 2. Generate the prime sequence based on a Galois Field GF(P) [6].

$$S_i = \left(S_{i,0}, S_{i,1}, \ldots, S_{i,j}, \ldots, S_{i,(P-1)}\right), \quad i = 0, 1, \ldots, P-1 \tag{2}$$

where the element of the sequence is

$$S_{i,j} = \{i \cdot j\} (\bmod P), \tag{3}$$

where i and j are elements over GF(P) = {0, 1, 2, ..., $P-1$}.

Step 3. Map S_i into a binary sequence C_i as follows [6]:

$$C_i = \left(C_{i,0}, C_{i,1}, \ldots, C_{i,k}, \ldots, C_{i,(n-1)}\right), \quad i = 0, 1, \ldots, P-1, n = P^2, \tag{4}$$

where

$$C_{i,k} = \begin{cases} 1, & \text{if } k = S_{i,j} + j \times P, \text{for } j = \{0, 1, \ldots, P-1\} \\ 0, & \text{elsewhere.} \end{cases} \tag{5}$$

Step 4. Extend the prime code by patching each subsequence by P of 0s.

Step 5. For each code sequence, apply the time-shifting method described in MPC [6]. Table 2 shows the resulting code-words with $P = 3$.

Step 6. Apply the method used in nMPC which is based on repeating the last sequence stream of the earlier code word and rotating it in the group [9]. Table 3 shows the result of this step. In the table, the padded sequence stream of the first code and the last sequence stream of the earlier code are presented in bold.

TABLE 2: Time shifting of extended prime code, $P = 3$.

Group		Binary code C_i		
0	C_{00}	100000	100000	100000
	C_{01}	010000	010000	010000
	C_{02}	001000	001000	001000
	C_{03}	000100	000100	000100
	C_{04}	000010	000010	000010
	C_{05}	000001	000001	000001
1	C_{10}	100000	010000	001000
	C_{11}	010000	001000	000100
	C_{12}	001000	000100	000010
	C_{13}	000100	000010	000001
	C_{14}	000010	000001	100000
	C_{15}	000001	100000	010000
2	C_{20}	100000	001000	010000
	C_{21}	010000	000100	001000
	C_{22}	001000	000010	000100
	C_{23}	000100	000001	000010
	C_{24}	000010	100000	000001
	C_{25}	000001	010000	100000

TABLE 3: Binary sequence of extended new modified prime code, $P = 3$.

Group		Binary code C_i			Padded sequence
0	C_{00}	100000	100000	100000	**000001**
	C_{01}	010000	010000	010000	100000
	C_{02}	001000	001000	001000	010000
	C_{03}	000100	000100	000100	001000
	C_{04}	000010	000010	000010	000100
	C_{05}	000001	000001	**000001**	000010
1	C_{10}	100000	010000	001000	010000
	C_{11}	010000	001000	000100	001000
	C_{12}	001000	000100	000010	000100
	C_{13}	000100	000010	000001	000010
	C_{14}	000010	000001	100000	000001
	C_{15}	000001	100000	010000	100000
2	C_{20}	100000	001000	010000	100000
	C_{21}	010000	000100	001000	010000
	C_{22}	001000	000010	000100	001000
	C_{23}	000100	000001	000010	000100
	C_{24}	000010	100000	000001	000010
	C_{25}	000001	010000	100000	000001

TABLE 4: Binary sequence of extended grouped new modified prime code, $P = 3$.

Group			Binary code C_i			
0	1	C_{010}	000000	100000	000000	000001
		C_{011}	000000	010000	000000	100000
		C_{012}	000000	001000	000000	010000
		C_{013}	000000	000100	000000	001000
		C_{014}	000000	000010	000000	000100
		C_{025}	000000	000001	000000	000010
	2	C_{020}	100000	000000	100000	000000
		C_{021}	010000	000000	010000	000000
		C_{022}	001000	000000	001000	000000
		C_{023}	000100	000000	000100	000000
		C_{024}	000010	000000	000010	000000
		C_{025}	000001	000000	000001	000000
1	1	C_{110}	000000	010000	000000	010000
		C_{111}	000000	001000	000000	001000
		C_{112}	000000	000100	000000	000100
		C_{113}	000000	000010	000000	000010
		C_{114}	000000	000001	000000	000001
		C_{115}	000000	100000	000000	100000
	2	C_{120}	100000	000000	001000	000000
		C_{121}	010000	000000	000100	000000
		C_{122}	001000	000000	000010	000000
		C_{123}	000100	000000	000001	000000
		C_{124}	000010	000000	100000	000000
		C_{125}	000001	000000	010000	000000
2	1	C_{210}	000000	001000	000000	100000
		C_{211}	000000	000100	000000	010000
		C_{212}	000000	000010	000000	001000
		C_{213}	000000	000001	000000	000100
		C_{214}	000000	100000	000000	000010
		C_{215}	000000	010000	000000	000001
	2	C_{220}	100000	000000	010000	000000
		C_{221}	010000	000000	001000	000000
		C_{222}	001000	000000	000100	000000
		C_{223}	000100	000000	000010	000000
		C_{224}	000010	000000	000001	000000
		C_{225}	000001	000000	100000	000000

Step 7. From each group, generate two groups:

(i) Group 1 consists of the $S_{i,j}$, where $i = 0, \ldots, P-1$ and j can take the values of zero or any even number. Other subsequences are patched with blocks of zeros.

(ii) Group 2 consists of the $S_{i,j}$, where $i = 0, \ldots, P-1$ and j is an odd number. Other subsequences are patched with blocks of zeros.

The final code-words are presented in Table 4. The code is represented by C_{xyz}, where x denotes the group (0 to $P-1$), y denotes the subgroup (1 or 2), and z denotes the code sequence (0 to $2P-1$).

2.2. Code Parameters. The code length L, code weight w, code cardinality $|C|$, autocorrelation λ_{xyz}, and cross-correlation $\lambda_{x_1 y_1 z_1, x_2 y_2 z_2}$ of EG-nMPC are given by

$$L = 2P^2 + 2P, \tag{6}$$

$$w = \frac{(P+1)}{2}, \tag{7}$$

$$|C| = 4P^2, \tag{8}$$

$$\lambda_{xyz} = w, \tag{9}$$

$$\lambda_{x_1 y_1 z_1, x_2 y_2 z_2} = \begin{cases} 0, & \dfrac{P^2 - 1}{8P^2 - 2}\ \text{probability} \\[2ex] 1, & \dfrac{7P^2 - 1}{8P^2 - 2}\ \text{probability.} \end{cases} \tag{10}$$

Equation (10) is obtained as follows: each code weight (w) in the code causes a cross-correlation of "1" with only one code from other groups ($P-1$ group), which are $w(P-1)$ cross-correlation pairs. For example, the code C_{010} will not cause cross-correlation with any code in the same group either in the same or another subgroup. In addition, the code will not cause cross-correlation with any code in a different group or in a different subgroup, as a consequence of Step 7 in the code construction. However, the code will have a cross-correlation with one code from other groups and in the same subgroup, for example, C_{114}, C_{115}, C_{214}, and C_{215}.

Thus, from (7), the cross-correlation value of "1" for one user and all users can be formed as

$$\lambda_{1\,(\text{one user})} = \frac{P^2 - 1}{2}, \tag{11}$$

$$\lambda_{1\,(\text{all users})} = 2P^4 - 2P^2. \tag{12}$$

The probability of a cross-correlation value of "1" can be defined as the number of pairs causing a cross-correlation value of 1 divided by the total number of cross-correlation pairs [7] and can be expressed as

$$\lambda_{\text{corr-pairs}} = |C| \cdot |C| - 1. \tag{13}$$

The total number of correlation pairs of EG-nMPC is given by

$$\lambda_{\text{corr-pairs}} = 16P^4 - 4P^2. \tag{14}$$

Thus, the probability of a cross-correlation value of "1" and "0" can be obtained as in (15) and (16), respectively. The probability of a cross-correlation value of 1 is given by

$$\text{Pb}_{\lambda 1} = \frac{\lambda_{1\,(\text{all users})}}{\lambda_{\text{corr-pairs}}} = \frac{P^2 - 1}{8P^2 - 2}. \tag{15}$$

The probability of a cross-correlation value of 0 is given by

$$\text{Pb}_{\lambda 0} = 1 - \text{Pb}_{\lambda 1} = \frac{7P^2 - 1}{8P^2 - 2}. \tag{16}$$

In a synchronous OCDMA system, time synchronization (T) is performed at the end of each bit duration, where $T = L$. chip duration [7]. For a "1 1 0 1" data stream and synchronization time T, the correlation values of alternate codes are presented in Figures 1–6. Figure 1 shows the autocorrelation value of C_{010} at each time interval T, and it is equal to w (2 in Figure 1). Figures 2 and 3 show the cross-correlation value between two codes in a different group but the same subgroup. Figure 2 shows the case when the cross-correlation value is 1, while Figure 3 shows the case when the cross-correlation value is 0. Figures 4–6 present the cross-correlation values of two codes from the same group and same subgroup, same group and different subgroup, and different group and different subgroup, respectively. As shown in these figures, the value of the cross-correlation at time T is 0.

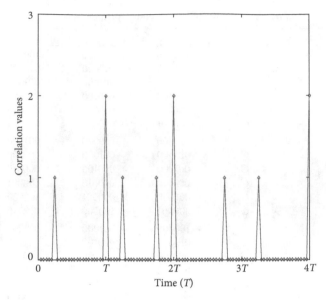

FIGURE 1: Autocorrelation of EG-nMPC of C_{010}, at synchronization time T.

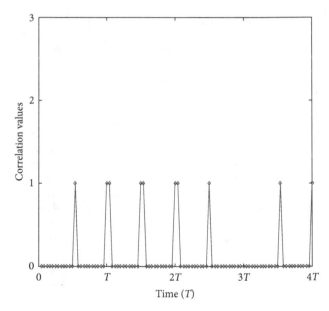

FIGURE 2: Cross-correlation of EG-nMPC of C_{014} and C_{112}, at synchronization time T.

3. Performance Analysis of OOK-OCDMA System

The bit error rate (BER) of the one-dimensional time-spreading code using incoherent OOK modulation system relies on three main factors: the binary stream, the threshold range, and the probability of "hits" between "1s" within different code-words [8]. The BER can be defined as

$$\text{BER} = \frac{1}{2} \sum_{i=0}^{w} (-1)^i \binom{w}{i} \left(1 - \frac{iq}{w}\right)^{N-1}. \tag{17}$$

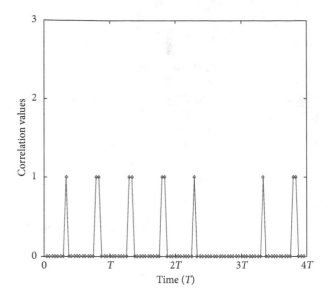

FIGURE 3: Cross-correlation of EG-nMPC of C_{022} and C_{125}, at synchronization time T.

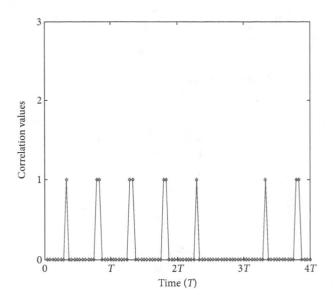

FIGURE 5: Cross-correlation of EG-nMPC of C_{024} and C_{013}, at synchronization time T.

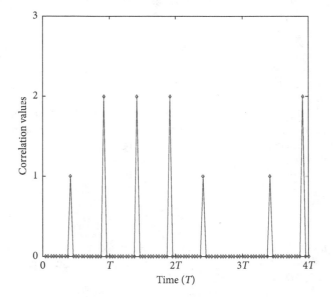

FIGURE 4: Cross-correlation of EG-nMPC of C_{110} and C_{112}, at synchronization time T.

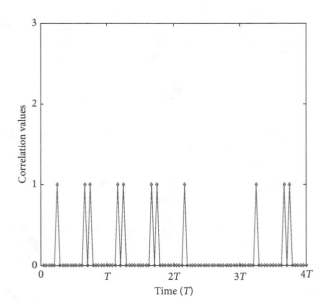

FIGURE 6: Cross-correlation of EG-nMPC of C_{020} and C_{210}, at synchronization time T.

In (17), w is the code weight, N is the number of active users, and q is the hit possibility of 1s between a particular user and the intended user. Equation (17) is for an asynchronous OCDMA system applying an OOC code. The difference between an asynchronous and synchronous system is found in the value of q. In (17), "q" is given by

$$q = \frac{w^2}{2L}, \qquad (18)$$

where the factor (1/2) refers to the possibility that the interfering user sends "1". However, the q for a synchronized OCDMA system depends on the cross-correlation expectation (probability of cross-correlation value of "1") between two codes, which can be expressed as [7]

$$E_\lambda = \frac{\sum \lambda_{x_1 y_1, x_2 y_2}}{|C| \cdot (|C| - 1)}. \qquad (19)$$

By multiplying the above equation with the factor (1/2), the q for a synchronous OCDMA system can be expressed as

$$q = \frac{E_\lambda}{2}. \qquad (20)$$

Thus, the BER probability of EG-nMPC can be formulated as

$$\text{BER} = \frac{1}{2} \sum_{i=0}^{w} (-1)^i \binom{w}{i} \left(1 - \frac{i}{2w} \cdot \frac{P^2 - 1}{8P^2 - 2} \right)^{N-1}. \qquad (21)$$

The BER of MPC and T-SPMPC can be obtained from [7].

4. Performance Analysis of PPM-OCDMA System

EG-nMPC provides $4P^2$ code sequences; thus, the number of users is $4P^2$. By assuming N is the number of active users, $4P^2 - N$ is the number of idle users. Υ_n is defined as a random variable where

$$\Upsilon_n, n \in \left\{1, 2, \ldots, 4P^2\right\}, \tag{22}$$

$$\Upsilon_n = \begin{cases} 1, & \text{if user } n \text{ is active} \\ 0, & \text{if user } n \text{ is idle.} \end{cases} \tag{23}$$

Thus,

$$N = \sum_{n=1}^{4P^2} \Upsilon_n. \tag{24}$$

If user 1 is the desired user, the random variable T and the number of active users who are not causing cross-correlation with user 1 could be defined as in (11):

$$T \stackrel{\text{def}}{=} \sum_{n=1}^{(7P^2+1)/2} \Upsilon_n. \tag{25}$$

If t is the realization of T, the probability distribution of the random variable T can be obtained as

$$P_T(t) = \frac{\binom{(P^2-1)/2}{N-t} \cdot \binom{(7P^2-1)/2}{t-1}}{\binom{4P^2-1}{N-1}}, \tag{26}$$

where $t \in \{t_{\min}, \ldots, t_{\max}\}$,

$$t_{\min} = \max\left(\frac{2N-P^2+1}{2}, 1\right), \tag{27}$$

$$t_{\max} = \min\left(N, \frac{7P^2+1}{2}\right). \tag{28}$$

Let the photon count collection be denoted by the vector Y_n for user n, where $Y_n = (Y_{n,0}, Y_{n,1}, \ldots, Y_{n,M-1})$, the interference be denoted by the random vector k, where $k = (k_0, k_1, \ldots, k_{m-1})^T$, and the vector u is the realization of k, where $u = (u_0, u_1, \ldots, u_{M-1})^T$. By then assuming $T = t$, k can be defined as a multinomial random vector with the following probability [2]:

$$P_{k|T}(u_0, u_1, \ldots, u_{M-1}|t) = \frac{1}{M^{N-t}} \cdot \frac{(N-t)!}{u_0!, u_1!, \ldots, u_{M-1}!}, \tag{29}$$

where

$$\sum_{i=0}^{M-1} u_i = N - t. \tag{30}$$

Then, the BER can be defined by [2]

$$P_b = \frac{M}{2(M-1)} \sum_{t=t_{\min}}^{t_{\max}} P_E \cdot P_t(t), \tag{31}$$

where M denotes the multiplicity and P_E denotes the error probability [2].

Similar to (9) in [2], the lower bounded BER can be obtained in (34) by modifying (5) in [10] based on EG-nMPC properties. By taking $Q \rightarrow \infty$, where Q defined as

$$Q = \frac{\mu \cdot (\ln M)}{w}. \tag{32}$$

μ in (32) is the average photon count per pulse (photons/nat), and nat can be expressed as follows [25, 26]:

$$1 \text{nat} = \log_2 e \text{ bits}, \tag{33}$$

$$P_E \geq \sum_{u_1=((P+1)/2)+1}^{N-t} \binom{N-t}{u_1} \frac{1}{M^{u_1}} \cdot \left(1-\frac{1}{M}\right)^{N-t-u_1} \cdot \sum_{u_0=0}^{\min\left(u_1-(((P+1)/2)1), N-t-u_1\right)} \binom{N-t-u_1}{u_0} \cdot \frac{1}{(M-1)^{u_0}} \cdot \left(1-\frac{1}{M-1}\right)^{N-t-u_0-u_1}$$

$$+ 0.5 \sum_{u_1=(P+1)/2}^{N-t+((P+1)/2)/2} \binom{N-t}{u_1} \frac{1}{M^{u_1}} \cdot \left(1-\frac{1}{M}\right)^{N-t-u_1} \cdot \binom{N-t-u_1}{u_1-\left(\frac{P+3}{2}\right)} \cdot \frac{1}{(M-1)^{u_1-((P+1)/2)}} \cdot \left(1-\frac{1}{M-1}\right)^{N-t-2u_0+((P+1)/2)}. \tag{34}$$

5. Discussion

A comparison of the results obtained from both EG-nMPC and MPC, which is the base for many standard codes reported in the literature, highlights the performance superiority of EG-nMPC. When EG-nMPC is compared with T-SPMPC, a recently developed code that supports a large number of users with a low code weight as in EG-nMPC, the result shows that EG-nMPC provides an improvement.

In Figure 7, the correlation expectation of the MPC, T-SPMPC, and EG-nMPC is presented and, as shown in the figure, the correlation expectation of MPC is the highest. With $P = 5$, the correlation expectation is 0.83. As P increases to 23, this figure reaches 0.96. In comparison, T-SPMPC exhibits lower values of correlation expectation. With $P = 5$, the correlation expectation is 0.32; this figure drops to 0.29 as P increases to 23. EG-nMPC exhibits the smallest values of correlation expectation as compared to the other codes. With $P = 5$, the correlation expectation of EG-nMPC is 0.1212; this figure increases slightly to reach 0.1248 as P increases to 23.

Figure 8 presents the BER performance versus the number of active users of OOK-OCDMA system. It compares the performance of the three codes with $P = 11$ and $P = 13$. The figure shows that at the BER of 10^{-9}, the performances of the three codes are similar with a slight improvement of MPC, followed by EG-nMPC and then T-SPMPC. However, with increasing the number of the users, the performance of the EG-nMPC has improved, and at a point, its performance with $P = 11$ is superior than the performance of the other codes with $P = 13$. In addition, this improvement can be noticed clearly in Figure 9 with $P = 23$ and $P = 37$. Figure 9 shows that EG-nMPC has achieved the required BER with more users.

Figure 10 illustrates the BER performance versus the number of active users of PPM-OCDMA system. The figure compares performances of MPC and EG-nMPC, with, $\mu = 150$, $M = 16$, $P = 11$, and $P = 13$. It is important to note that the comparison is made between EG-nMPC and MPC only. This is so due to the absence of mathematical expressions to evaluate BER of T-SPMPC, in the case of PPM-OCDMA system without interference cancellation. The figure shows that at the BER value of 10^{-9}, both codes support almost the same number of users. However, as the number of users increases, the BER of EG-nMPC acquires smaller values, pointing to a better performance. The smaller values of BER are attributed to the higher capability of EG-nMPC to accommodate a larger number of users. The higher capability of EG-nMPC to accommodate more users with the same average photons/nat is also evident from Figure 10, an outcome that points to the code being energy efficient.

It is important to note the significant role played by the multiplicity, M, in improving the system performance, as shown in Figure 11. Figure 11 shows the performance of BER versus the number of active users, with $M = 16$, $M = 8$, $P = 11$, and $\mu = 150$. As shown in the figure, although an increase in the value of M results in an improvement in system performance, larger values of M lead to an increase in system cost and complexity.

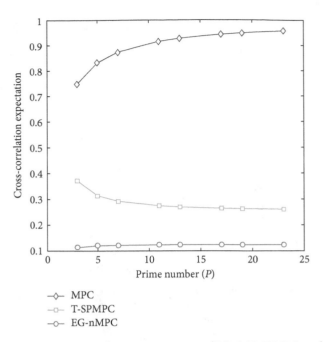

FIGURE 7: Cross-correlation expectations of MPC, T-SPMPC, and EG-nMPC.

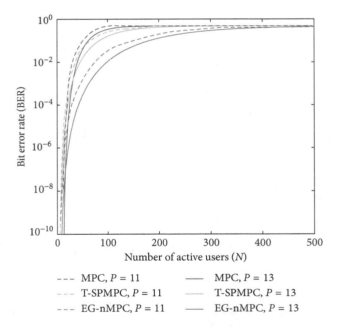

FIGURE 8: BER of MPC, T-SPMPC, and EG-nMPC versus the number of active users of OOK-OCDMA system.

EG-nMPC increases the cardinality of the code and supports more users with a smaller value of P, as shown in Figure 12. Implementing EG-nMPC as a spreading code for OC to monitor PON networks that support splitting ratios of 32, 64, and 128 could be seen to be an optimal solution. Table 5 shows a comparison of the code parameters for the different splitting ratios of PON. For a splitting ratio of 32, EG-nMPC has been shown to have the lowest weight, length, and unused codes, that is, 2, 24, and 4, respectively.

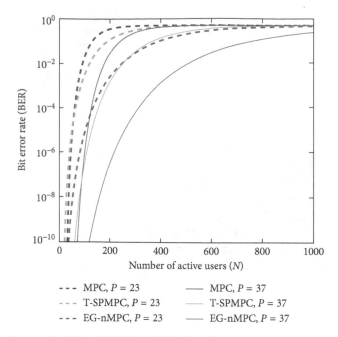

FIGURE 9: BER of MPC, T-SPMPC, and EG-nMPC versus the number of active users, $P = 23$ and $P = 37$.

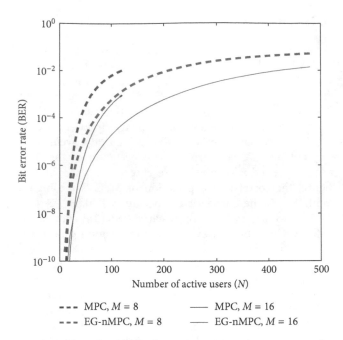

FIGURE 11: The role of multiplicity M in PPM-OCDMA system for MPC and EG-nMPC, with $P = 11$.

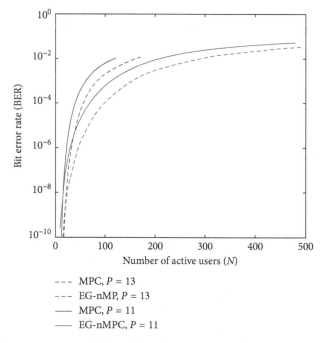

FIGURE 10: BER of T-SPMPC and EG-nMPC versus the number of active users of PPM-OCDMA system for $M = 8$ and $\mu = 100$.

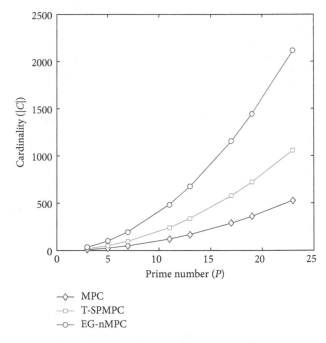

FIGURE 12: Cardinality of MPC, T-SPMPC, and EG-nMPC.

This renders EG-nMPC a superior code for supporting a splitting ratio of 32, as compared to other codes. T-SPMPC ranks second in superiority, with MPC being the least desirable code among the three. The very slight increase in the number of unused codes exhibited by T-SPMPC as compared to MPC does not carry any significant weight on this superiority ranking. The inferiority of MPC, for a splitting ratio of 32, is evidenced by the values

of its weight, its length, and the number of unused codes, that is, 7, 49, and 17, respectively.

For a splitting ratio of 64, MPC shows the least desirable option with largest values for weight, length, and unused codes, that is, 11, 121, and 57, respectively. When it comes to code length and the number of unused code, T-SPMPC is shown to be a better option when compared to EG-nMPC, with a code length of 49, as compared to 60, and the number of unused codes being 34 as compared to 36. However,

TABLE 5: Code parameter comparison.

PC	P	32 Cardinality (unused codes)	Length	Weight	P	64 Cardinality (unused codes)	Length	Weight	P	128 Cardinality (unused codes)	Length	Weight
MPC	7	49 (17)	49	7	11	121 (57)	121	11	13	169 (41)	169	13
T-SPMPC	5	50 (18)	25	3	7	98 (34)	49	4	11	242 (114)	121	6
EG-nMPC	3	36 (4)	24	2	5	100 (36)	60	3	7	196 (68)	112	4

EG-nMPC possesses a lower code weight when compared to T-SPMPC, that is, 3 and 4, respectively. For a splitting ratio of 128, although MPC has the lowest number of unused codes, its code weight is far larger and the code length is far longer than in other codes. EG-nMPC exhibits lower code weight, code length, and a smaller number of unused codes as compared to T-SPMPC. Consequently, it could be concluded that EG-nMPC possesses optimal numerical values for code weight, code length, and the number of unused codes.

6. Conclusion

In this research paper, a new code for a synchronous OCDMA network monitoring that is based on a prime code has been proposed. The paper presents details with respect to code construction and its parameters. The proposed code is based on dividing each code into two groups and patching some subsequences with 0s in order to increase cardinality, reduce probability of cross-correlation values, and reduce energy consumption. The performance of the proposed code has been evaluated using incoherent OOK-OCDMA system, and then compared to both MPC and T-SPMPC. In incoherent PPM-OCDMA systems, however, performance of the proposed code was evaluated and compared to MPC only. In addition, it has been shown that the use of EG-nMPC as a spreading code for a PON monitoring-based OC technique possesses superior characteristics when compared to the other two codes, based on code weight, code length, and the number of unused codes.

References

[1] M. Swadesh and M. S. Islam, "A new modified prime codes for higher user capacity in smart synchronous OCDMA network," in *Proceedings of the 2014 International Conference on Electrical Engineering and Information & Communication Technology (ICEEICT)*, pp. 1–5, Dhaka, Bangladesh, April 2014.

[2] M. M. Karbassian and H. Ghafouri-Shiraz, "Fresh prime codes evaluation for synchronous PPM and OPPM signaling for optical CDMA networks," *Journal of Lightwave Technology*, vol. 25, no. 6, pp. 1422–1430, 2007.

[3] H. Yin and W. Liang, "Transmission approaches for services of variable bit-rate and differentiated QoS using OCDMA," in *Proceedings of the Summer Topical Meeting, 2009, LEOSST'09, IEEE/LEOS*, pp. 11-12, Piscataway, NJ, USA, July 2009.

[4] K. Fouli and M. Maier, "OCDMA and optical coding: principles, applications, and challenges [topics in optical communications]," *IEEE Communications Magazine*, vol. 45, no. 8, pp. 27–34, 2007.

[5] S. Jindal and N. Gupta, "OCDMA: study and future aspects," in *Recent Development in Wireless Sensor and Ad-hoc Networks*, Springer, Berlin, 2015.

[6] H. Yin and D. J. Richardson, *Optical Code Division Multiple Access Communication Networks: Theory and Applications*, Springer, Berlin, 1st edition, 2009.

[7] Q. Jin, M. M. Karbassian, and H. Ghafouri-Shiraz, "Energy-efficient high-capacity optical CDMA networks by low-weight large code-set MPC," *Journal of Lightwave Technology*, vol. 30, pp. 2876–2883, 2012.

[8] M. M. Karbassian and F. Küppers, "Enhancing spectral efficiency and capacity in synchronous OCDMA by transposed-MPC," *Optical Switching and Networking*, vol. 9, no. 2, pp. 130–137, 2012.

[9] H. Ghafouri-Shiraz and M. M. Karbassian, *Optical CDMA Networks: Principles, Analysis and Applications*, vol. 38, John Wiley & Sons, Hoboken, NJ, USA, 2012.

[10] H. M. Shalaby, "Cochannel interference reduction in optical PPM-CDMA systems," *IEEE Transactions on Communications*, vol. 46, no. 6, pp. 799–805, 1998.

[11] J. F. A. Rida, A. Bhardwaj, and A. Jaiswal, "Design optimization of optical communication systems using carbon nanotubes (CNTs) based on optical code division multiple access (OCDMA)," *International Journal of Computer Science and Network Security (IJCSNS)*, vol. 14, p. 102, 2014.

[12] M. M. Mustapha and R. F. Ormondroyd, "Dual-threshold sequential detection code synchronization for an optical CDMA network in the presence of multi-user interference," *Journal of Lightwave Technology*, vol. 18, no. 12, pp. 1742–1748, 2000.

[13] A. Iwata, K. Kamakura, and I. Sasase, "A synchronization method deselecting candidate positions with chip level detection for optical CDMA," *Electronics and Communications in Japan (Part I: Communications)*, vol. 88, no. 3, pp. 21–32, 2005.

[14] M. Mustapha and R. Ormondroy, "Performance of a serial-search synchronizer for fiber-based optical CDMA systems in the presence of multi-user interference," in *Proceedings of the International Symposium on Photonics and Applications*, Singapore, November 1999.

[15] G. C. Yang, "Performance analysis for synchronization and system on CDMA optical fiber networks," *IEICE Transactions on Communications*, vol. E77-B, no. 10, pp. 1238–1248, 1994.

[16] A. Keshavarzian and J. A. Salehi, "Optical orthogonal code acquisition in fiber-optic CDMA systems via the simple serial-search method," *IEEE Transactions on Communication*, vol. 50, no. 3, pp. 473–483, 2002.

[17] A. Keshavarzian and J. A. Salehi, "Multiple-shift code acquisition of optical orthogonal codes in optical CDMA systems," *IEEE Transactions on Communications*, vol. 53, no. 4, pp. 687–697, 2005.

[18] K. Chae and S. Yoon, "A rapid code acquisition scheme in OOC-based CDMA systems," *International Journal of Electronics and Communication Engineering*, vol. 9, no. 4, 2015.

[19] W. C. Kwong, P. A. Perrier, and P. R. Prucnal, "Performance comparison of asynchronous and synchronous code-division multiple-access techniques for fiber-optic local area networks," *IEEE Transactions on Communications*, vol. 39, no. 11, pp. 1625–1634, 1991.

[20] G.-C. Yang and W. C. Kwong, "Performance analysis of optical CDMA with prime codes," *Electronics Letters*, vol. 31, no. 7, pp. 569-570, 1995.

[21] F. Liu, M. Karbassian, and H. Ghafouri-Shiraz, "Novel family of prime codes for synchronous optical CDMA," *Optical and Quantum Electronics*, vol. 39, no. 1, pp. 79–90, 2007.

[22] M. Y. Liu and H. W. Tsao, "Cochannel interference cancellation via employing a reference correlator for synchronous optical CDMA systems," *Microwave and Optical Technology Letters*, vol. 25, no. 6, pp. 390–392, 2000.

[23] M. M. Rad, H. A. Fathallah, and L. A. Rusch, "Fiber fault PON monitoring using optical coding: effects of customer geographic distribution," *IEEE Transactions on Communications*, vol. 58, no. 4, pp. 1172–1181, 2010.

[24] H. Fathallah and M. Esmail, "Performance evaluation of special optical coding techniques appropriate for physical layer monitoring of access and metro optical networks," *Photonic Network Communications*, vol. 30, no. 2, pp. 223–233, 2015.

[25] I. Garrett, "Towards the fundamental limits of optical-fiber communications," *Journal of Lightwave Technology*, vol. 1, no. 1, pp. 131–138, 1983.

[26] I. Kaminow and T. Koch, *Optical Fiber Telecommunications III*, Academic Press Incorporated, Cambridge, MA, USA, 1997.

11

A Novel Audio Cryptosystem using Chaotic Maps and DNA Encoding

S. J. Sheela,[1] K. V. Suresh,[1] and Deepaknath Tandur[2]

[1]Department of E and C, Siddaganga Institute of Technology, Visvesvaraya Technological University, Tumakuru, India
[2]Corporate Research India, ABB, Bengaluru, India

Correspondence should be addressed to S. J. Sheela; sheeladinu@sit.ac.in

Academic Editor: Nasrollah Pakniat

Chaotic maps have good potential in security applications due to their inherent characteristics relevant to cryptography. This paper introduces a new audio cryptosystem based on chaotic maps, hybrid chaotic shift transform (HCST), and deoxyribonucleic acid (DNA) encoding rules. The scheme uses chaotic maps such as two-dimensional modified Henon map (2D-MHM) and standard map. The 2D-MHM which has sophisticated chaotic behavior for an extensive range of control parameters is used to perform HCST. DNA encoding technology is used as an auxiliary tool which enhances the security of the cryptosystem. The performance of the algorithm is evaluated for various speech signals using different encryption/decryption quality metrics. The simulation and comparison results show that the algorithm can achieve good encryption results and is able to resist several cryptographic attacks. The various types of analysis revealed that the algorithm is suitable for narrow band radio communication and real-time speech encryption applications.

1. Introduction

Secured speech communication plays a significant role in military, voice over Internet protocols, confidential voice conferences, and corporate sectors. This necessitates the development of a reliable, fast, and robust security system to provide data confidentiality, integrity, and authentication. In this regard, researchers have developed many cryptographic algorithms to suite the evolvement in wireless communication technologies. The traditional symmetric cryptographic schemes such as advanced encryption standard (AES) and data encryption standard (DES) can attain high level of security. But they have small key space which in turn suffers from brute force attack. These cryptographic algorithms cannot be utilized in real-time speech encryption due to high degree of redundancy among the samples, bandwidth expansion of the encrypted signal, and reduction of signal to noise ratio performance. Because of complex permutation process, these algorithms require more computational time and high computing power. Further, asymmetric encryption algorithms are not suitable for encryption owing to slow speed and complexity [1–3]. Hence, it is necessary to explore the simple speech encryption techniques that can provide high level of security and high speed while attaining excellent audio quality of the decrypted speech signal.

In this contest, many researchers have identified the possibility of applying dynamic and disordered behavior of chaotic system in cryptography. These chaotic systems have outstanding features such as high sensitivity to initial conditions/system parameters, erratic behavior, high security, and simplicity. These subtle nonlinear properties make them a novel and efficient way of providing secured speech communication with low complexity. However, there are some challenges that need to be faced when using chaos theory in the field of cryptography [4]. There exists a data redundancy and all the chaotic maps are not random. Some of them utilize various one-dimensional (1D) chaotic maps in the development of speech security systems [5]. 1D chaotic maps result in single simple predictable chaotic orbits. As a result, the attacker can obtain the initial states and/or system parameters of the chaotic map easily. Further, one-dimensional chaotic map suffers from small key space and weak security.

On the other hand, security can be enhanced by increasing the dimension which in turn increases the nonlinearity. The higher dimensional (HD) chaotic maps are widely used in multimedia encryption owing to tough prediction of a time series and more numbers of positive Lyapunov exponents [6]. Hence, in this paper, two-dimensional modified Henon map is introduced. The 2D-MHM is obtained by using Henon map (HM) as seed map. The dynamic analysis in [7] has shown that the map has broad chaotic regime over an extensive range of system parameters, maximum Lyapunov exponent, and better chaotic performance when compared to seed map. Hence, the speech encryption algorithm using MHM is proposed in [8]. Further, it has been proved that the encryption schemes using only chaos are less secure which necessitates the introduction of new mechanism to enhance the security of the cryptosystem [9–11].

In order to make chaos based cryptosystem more secure, DNA technology has been infiltrated due to its exclusive characteristics such as huge parallelism, enormous information storage, and ultralow power consumption [12, 13]. DNA cryptography uses biomolecular concepts which give hope in the design of unbreakable algorithms. Hence, a new speech encryption scheme based on chaotic maps and DNA encoding is proposed in this paper. The position of speech samples is shuffled by using the sequences generated from 2D-MHM thereby achieving the confusion. Further, DNA encoding and the sequences generated from standard map change the value of the speech samples. The scheme uses dynamic DNA encoding instead of fixed coding which in turn increases the security [14]. The encryption capability of the speech encryption algorithm is assessed through security analysis for various speech signals.

The organization of the paper is as follows. Section 2 introduces the chaotic maps along with their dynamical behavior. The design of speech encryption scheme based on HCST and DNA encoding is discussed in Section 3. The results of security analysis are provided in Section 4. The final section concludes the paper.

2. Preliminary Theory of the Algorithm

This section reviews the chaotic maps used for speech encryption such as MHM and standard map (SM) along with their dynamical behavior. The comparison of dynamical behaviors of MHM and HM through bifurcation diagram is also considered. Further, the basics of DNA encoding along with algebraic operations is presented.

2.1. Modified Henon Map. The modified Henon map [7] is given by

$$H\left(x_k, y_k\right) = \begin{pmatrix} x_{k+1} \\ y_{k+1} \end{pmatrix} = \begin{pmatrix} 1 - b_1 \cos\left(x_k\right) - b_2 y_k \\ -x_k \end{pmatrix}, \quad (1)$$

where b_1 and b_2 are control parameters and (x_k, y_k) represents the two-dimensional state of the system. In the seed map [15], x_k^2 term is replaced by the nonlinear term $\cos(x_k)$ and $b_2 \neq 0$ thereby increasing the chaotic region. For modified Henon map, the bounded solutions will be obtained for all values

of b_1 and $|b_2| < 1$. A wide chaotic range can be obtained by selecting one of the system parameters $b_2 = 0.3$. The chaotic range of MHM is compared with seed map which is evidenced through bifurcation diagram. Bifurcation diagram plots output sequences of a chaotic map along with the change of its system parameter(s). Figure 1 shows the comparison of Henon map and MHM with respect to bifurcation diagram. From the bifurcation diagram, it is clear that Henon map is chaotic for the range of $b_1 \in [1.06, 1.22] \cup [1.27, 1.29] \cup [1.31, 1.4]$ whereas modified Henon map is chaotic for the range of $b_1 \in [2.19, 2.5] \cup [>2.54]$ in the interval $0 \leq b_1 \leq 5$. Thus, the simulation results show an improvement in the chaotic range ratio of 7% to 56% in this interval [7]. The MHM has at least three advantages when compared to seed map which are as follows: (1) The map has broad array chaotic regime over an extensive range of system parameters. (2) MHM is more dynamic as the Lyapunov exponents are greater than those of Henon map. (3) The map is highly sensitive to their initial conditions and system parameters as the correlation between the chaotic sequences is less. Hence, MHM is more suitable to provide secured communication.

2.2. Standard Map. The 2D standard map is the simplest conservative system which originates from the field of particle physics [16, 17]. It is defined by

$$\begin{pmatrix} Z_{n+1} \\ W_{n+1} \end{pmatrix} = \begin{pmatrix} \left(Z_n + W_n\right) \bmod 2\pi \\ Z_n + r \sin\left(Z_n + W_n\right) \bmod 2\pi \end{pmatrix}, \quad (2)$$

where $Z_n, W_n \in [0, 2\pi)$. The nonlinearity of the map is directly proportional to the system parameter. The SM can be discretized from $[0, 2\pi) \times [0, 2\pi)$ to $S \times S$ by substituting $z = ZS/2\pi$, $w = WS/2\pi$, and $R = rS/2\pi$ in (2). The resulting discretized map is given by

$$\begin{pmatrix} z_{n+1} \\ w_{n+1} \end{pmatrix} = \begin{pmatrix} \left(z_n + w_n\right) \bmod S \\ z_n + R \sin\left(\dfrac{z_{n+1} S}{2\pi}\right) \bmod S \end{pmatrix}, \quad (3)$$

where R can take any real value and S is any integer value. The discretized standard map properties may not be as good as the original one, but integer domain implementation is possible which in turn reduces the computational efforts [18]. Further, SM is commonly used in the design of block symmetric cipher because its structure resembles Fiestel network [19]. Hence, SM is more appropriate for real-time information security.

2.3. DNA Encoding. A single DNA sequence is composed of four nucleic bases, namely, adenine (A), cytosine (C), guanine (G), and thymine (T). According to DNA rules, A pairs with T and C pairs with G, where A and T are complementary and C and G are complementary [20]. This complementary rule resembles the binary system. Because 0 and 1 are complementary in binary system, 00 and 11 are complementary and 01 and 10 are also complementary. Thus, there are 24 types of coding combinations. According to Watson-Crick complement rule, only 8 code combinations

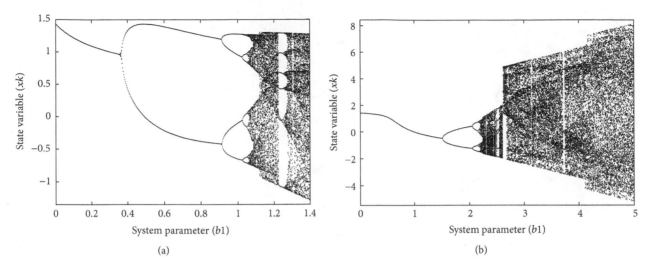

FIGURE 1: (a) Bifurcation diagram of Henon map for the system parameter ($b_2 = 0.3$). (b) Bifurcation diagram of MHM for the system parameter ($b_2 = 0.3$).

TABLE 1: DNA encoding and decoding rules.

	A	T	C	G
Rule 1	00	11	10	01
Rule 2	00	11	01	10
Rule 3	11	00	10	01
Rule 4	11	00	01	10
Rule 5	10	01	00	11
Rule 6	01	10	00	11
Rule 7	10	01	11	00
Rule 8	01	10	11	00

TABLE 2: DNA XOR operation.

	A	T	C	G
A	A	T	C	G
T	T	A	G	C
C	C	G	A	T
G	G	C	T	A

can be used out of 24 coding combinations [21] which are listed in Table 1. With the rapid development in DNA cryptography, researchers have introduced several biological and algebraic operations such as exclusive OR (XOR), addition, and subtraction [22, 23]. In this paper, DNA XOR operation is used to encrypt and decrypt the speech samples. Table 2 shows the DNA XOR operation which is reflexive.

3. HCST and DNA Based Speech Cryptosystem

In this section, the detailed architecture HCST and DNA encoding mechanism adopted for speech encryption is presented. The algorithm uses chaotic maps and DNA encoding to perform primitive operations of cryptography such as confusion and diffusion. These two chaotic maps generate

the secret key for the proposed algorithm. The secret key contains the information of initial conditions and control parameters of these maps. Hence, the key set used for encryption/decryption is (x_0, y_0, b_1, b_2, z_0, w_0, R, S). Two chaotic maps are used to increase the key space and security performance of the algorithm. Confusion and diffusion are applied to shuffle speech sample positions randomly and to change the value of the speech samples, respectively. The complete architecture of the encryption scheme is shown in Figure 2.

3.1. Hybrid Chaotic Shift Transform. In this section, hybrid chaotic shift transform [24] is proposed to shuffle the positions of the speech samples thereby reducing the correlation between the samples. The inherent features of the chaotic map such as random nature and sensitivity to initial conditions/system parameters make them a good candidate to perform confusion operation.

3.1.1. Definition of HCST. Firstly, generate $2N$ chaotic values ($x_1, x_2, \ldots, x_N$), ($y_1, y_2, \ldots, y_N$) from the MHM using (1). Sort the chaotic sequence x_k in descending order and get the column shift matrix from the positions of the sorted sequence which is given by $B = [b_1, b_2, \ldots, b_N]$. Similarly, get the row shift matrix by sorting the chaotic sequence y_k in ascending order which is given by $C = [c_1, c_2, \ldots, c_N]$, where b_i and c_i represent the step size cyclic up/down shift in column i and cyclic right/left shift in row i, respectively.

Let I be an original speech signal which is processed frame by frame with the frame size and frame shift of M with the frame length of 15–30 ms and T be the corresponding shuffled speech signal. Then hybrid chaotic shift transform is defined as

$$T_1 = F(I, B)$$
$$T = F(T_1, C), \tag{4}$$

where T represents the row shifted speech block. The hybrid CST function F is described in Algorithm 1. Therefore,

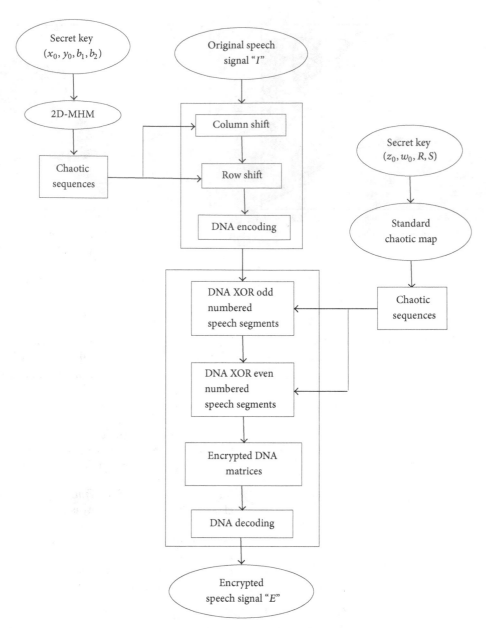

FIGURE 2: Proposed encryption scheme flow diagram.

HCST shuffles the positions of the speech samples efficiently thereby reducing the correlation among samples. Further, without the knowledge of initial conditions and system parameters of MHM it is not possible to predict the results of HCST.

3.2. Dynamic DNA Encoding. In this section, the dynamic DNA encoding mechanism is presented to change the value of the speech samples thereby spreading the effect of plaintext across the ciphertext. In order to enhance the security, the dynamic DNA coding is used instead of fixed coding. The values in the confused speech block are converted to their equivalent decimal values by using 16-bit quantization. The detailed operation of DNA encoding scheme is described and shown in Algorithm 2 and Figure 3.

4. Security Analysis

An efficient encryption algorithm should satisfy mainly two objectives: (1) The algorithm should offer resistance against all kinds of known attacks. (2) It should possess both confusion and diffusion property [25]. The confusion property corresponding to a tiny change in the key should produce entirely different ciphertext, whereas diffusion property refers to spreading the effect of slight change in the plaintext over the corresponding ciphertext. Further, a good cipher should be robust under noisy environment. Hence, the security of the proposed algorithm is evaluated and compared with other existing schemes in this section [5, 8]. Many metrics have been used in the literature to verify the quality of the decrypted signal and residual intelligibility of the encrypted

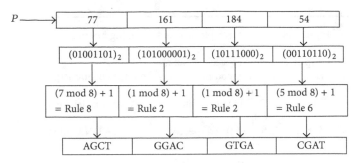

Similarly, encode the matrix "Q" by using the same procedure.

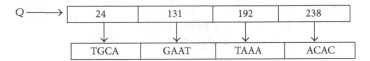

FIGURE 3: An example of DNA encoding process.

Input: The original speech signal I and chaotic series
      matrices B and C
Output: The column and row shuffled speech block T
(1) Generate the column and row shift matrices by sorting x_k
     and y_k chaotic sequence
(2) **for** $i = 1$ to N **do**
(3)   **if** $\mod(b_i, 2) = 0$ **then**
      Cyclic shift the speech segment in column i of I to
      down with the step size of b_i;
(4)   **else**
      Cyclic shift the speech segment in column i of I to
      up with the step size of b_i;
(5)   **end if**
(6) **end for**
(7) Denote the column shifted speech block as T_1.
(8) **for** $i = 1$ to N **do**
(9)   **if** $\mod(c_i, 2) = 0$ **then**
      Cyclic shift the speech segment in row i of T_1 to right
      with the step size of c_i;
(10)   **else**
      Cyclic shift the speech segment in row i of T_1 to left
      with the step size of c_i;
(11)   **end if**
(12) **end for**
(13) Denote the row shifted speech block as T.

ALGORITHM 1: The hybrid chaotic shift transform algorithm.

signal. The metrics also determine the immunity of the encryption scheme to cryptanalysis attacks.

4.1. Residual Intelligibility of Encrypted Signal. In order to evaluate the encryption capability of the proposed algorithm, different American English speech signals with sampling rate of 8 KHz and 16 KHz are encrypted. The original, encrypted, and decrypted speech signal are shown in Figure 4. From the figure, it is clear that the encrypted signal is similar to white noise without any original intonations. This indicates the absence of residual intelligibility in the encrypted signal.

4.2. Statistical Analysis. It has been revealed in the literature that statistical analysis effectively evaluates the cryptosystem [17, 25]. Statistical analysis has been performed to demonstrate the confusion and diffusion property of the cryptosystem which in turn offers resistance against statistical attacks. This has been illustrated by using histogram analysis, correlation analysis, and percent residual deviation (PRD).

4.2.1. Histogram Analysis. Histogram analysis evaluates the cryptosystem to determine its ability to resist against statistical attacks. Figure 5 shows the histogram of clean and

Input: Confused speech block T and encoding matrices P and Q

Output: Encrypted speech signal E

(1) Generate the encoding matrices from the chaotic sequence generated from SM.

(2) Encode P and Q using different DNA rules as depicted in Figure 3.

(3) Encode the confused speech block T using DNA rule 1.

(4) **for** $i = 1$ to M **do**

(5)   **if** $\mathrm{mod}(T(:, i), 2) = 0$ **then**

      $E(:, i) = P(:, i)$ XOR $T(:, i)$

      Rotate P right by one byte

(6)   **else**

      $E(:, i) = Q(:, i)$ XOR $T(:, i)$

      Rotate Q right by one byte

(7)   **end if**

(8) **end for**

(9) Decode the encrypted DNA matrix using DNA rule 3.

ALGORITHM 2: Dynamic DNA encoding.

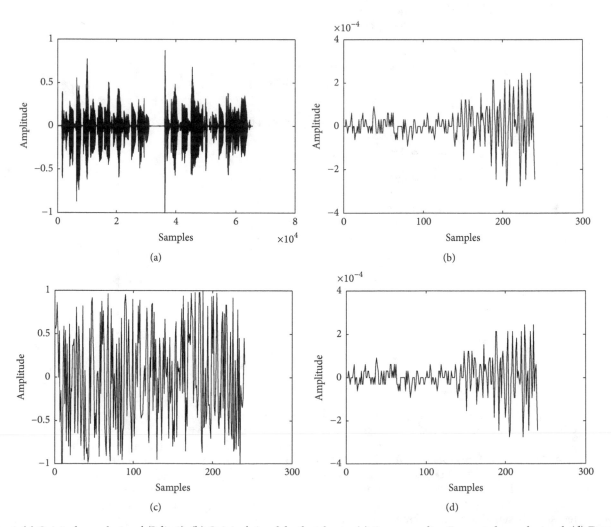

(a) (b) (c) (d)

FIGURE 4: (a) Original speech signal (Julia 8). (b) Original signal for first frame. (c) Corresponding Encrypted speech signal. (d) Decrypted speech signal.

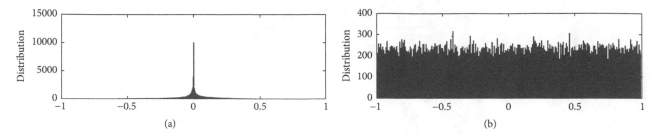

FIGURE 5: Histogram of (a) clean speech signal (Mel 8) and (b) encrypted speech signal.

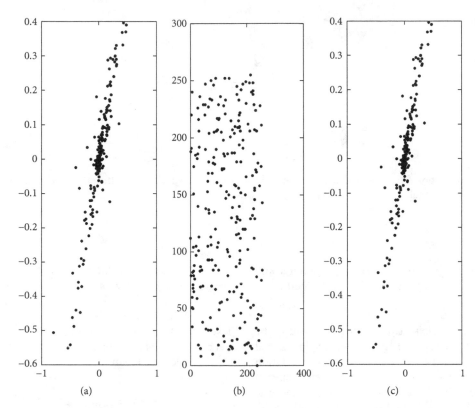

FIGURE 6: Correlation between the samples in (a) original speech signal (Rich 8), (b) encrypted speech signal, and (c) decrypted speech signal.

encrypted speech signals. It is clear that the histogram of the ciphered signal is fairly uniform indicating the best encryption results. Hence, the algorithm does not provide any original information and possesses good confusion property.

4.2.2. Correlation Coefficient Analysis. Correlation coefficient (CC) is one of the statistical measures which determine the encryption quality of the cryptosystem. This analysis measures the correlation between the two speech samples whose value lies between −1 and +1. The correlation coefficient being near zero indicates the weakest relationship between the two samples and it is not possible to predict the secret key by the attackers [1]. The correlation coefficient values between original and encrypted speech signals and their comparison with other algorithms are tabulated in Table 3. Figure 6 shows the correlation coefficient distribution of original and encrypted speech signal. It has been observed that the correlation values are closer to zero which indicates the good encryption quality. The correlation coefficient of this

method is less when compared with the existing methods [5, 8] in almost all the trails, shown in Figure 7. The correlation coefficient r_{xy} is calculated [1] using

$$E(x) = \frac{1}{T_s} \sum_{i=1}^{i=T_s} x_i$$

$$D(x) = \frac{1}{T_s} \sum_{i=1}^{i=T_s} (x_i - E(x_i))^2$$

$$\text{cov}(x, y) = \frac{1}{T} \sum_{i=1}^{i=T_s} (x_i - E(x_i))(y_i - E(y_i))$$

$$r_{xy} = \frac{\text{cov}(x, y)}{\sqrt{D(x)D(y)}},$$

(5)

where x and y are the audio values of the two adjacent audio levels in the speech signal, $E(x)$ is the mean value, $D(x)$ is

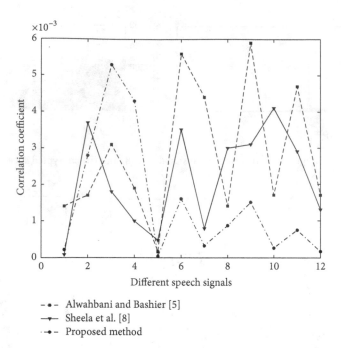

- ‑•‑   Alwahbani and Bashier [5]
- ‑▼‑   Sheela et al. [8]
- ‑•‑   Proposed method

FIGURE 7: Comparison of proposed method with existing method with respect to correlation coefficient between samples of original speech signal and encrypted speech signal.

the variance, and cov(x, y) is the covariance between x and y. The number of samples used in calculations is denoted by T_s.

4.3. Percent Residual Deviation.

This parameter measures the deviation of the encrypted speech signal from original signal [26]. The calculated values of the percent residual deviation for original and encrypted speech signal for different speech signals are given in Table 3. It has been observed that the encrypted signal is highly deviated from its original signal. For the given original signal $I(i)$ and obtained encrypted speech signal $E(i)$, the PRD is defined as

$$\varphi = 100 \times \sqrt{\frac{\sum_{i=1}^{n}\left[I(i) - E(i)^2\right]}{\sum_{i=1}^{n} I^2(i)}}. \tag{6}$$

4.4. Quality of the Decrypted Signal.

It is necessary to measure and compare the quality of the decrypted signal with that of the original signal in order to prove the efficiency of the cryptosystem. The two approaches, namely, objective and subjective metrics, have been adopted in the literature to verify the quality of the decrypted signal. In objective metrics, the quality is measured using physical parameters and computational models. The subjective speech quality metrics require a panel of trained listeners which itself is a very tedious process. In real-time applications, the objective metrics are desirable because they give more consistent results in a shorter period [27]. Signal to noise ratio (SNR), Perceptual Evaluation of Speech Quality (PESQ), and so on are some of the speech quality metrics used to validate the algorithm.

4.4.1. Signal to Noise Ratio (SNR).

SNR is used to measure residual intelligibility of the encrypted signal and quality of the decrypted signal. Generally, the encrypted signal is characterized by low SNR value indicating the higher noise level than the original speech signal whereas the good quality decrypted signal is characterized by high SNR value. The SNR [1, 2] is calculated using

$$\text{SNR} = 10 \log_{10} \frac{\sum_{i=1}^{T_s} I^2(i)}{\sum_{i=1}^{T_s} (I(i) - D(i))^2}, \tag{7}$$

where $D(i)$ is the decrypted speech signal. The SNR values for different speech signals are tabulated in Table 4. Further, the results are compared with existing algorithms [5, 8] which is shown in Figure 8. The comparison results show that the proposed algorithm yields good quality decrypted signal.

4.4.2. Perceptual Evaluation of Speech Quality.

PESQ is one of the widely used and reliable methods used to measure the quality of the decrypted signal. Higher value of the PESQ indicates the better quality of the recovered speech signal. The PESQ score ranges from 1.0 to 4.5 [28, 29]. The PESQ scores for different speech signals are tabulated in Table 4 resulting with average score of 3.7738. Further, the effect of slightly altered key on PESQ is illustrated in Table 6. From the table, it is clear that PESQ value is sensitive to key.

4.5. Key Space.

The key space of the encryption algorithm should be larger than 2^{100} to make the brute force attack infeasible [4, 30]. System parameters and initial conditions of the chaotic map determine the key space. The key set used

TABLE 3: Encrypted signal quality metrics.

Name	Correlation between original and encrypted signal	Alwahbani and Bashier [5]	Sheela et al. [8]	PRD
Claire 8	−0.00021724	−0.0014	0.00001855	2.4379×10^7
Julia 8	−0.0028	0.0017	−0.0037	2.6233×10^7
Lauren 8	0.0053	−0.0031	−0.0018	2.2872×10^7
Mel 8	0.0043	0.0019	−0.0010	2.2492×10^7
Ray 8	0.000038157	−0.00016	0.0001474	2.2362×10^7
Rich 8	−0.0016	−0.0056	−0.0035	2.0496×10^7
Claire 16	−0.00032371	−0.0044	0.0007885	1.3880×10^8
Julia 16	−0.00086778	0.0014	−0.0030	1.5012×10^8
Lauren 16	−0.0015	0.0059	0.0031	1.2983×10^8
Mel 16	−0.000266126	0.0017	−0.0041	1.2752×10^8
Ray 16	0.00074651	−0.0047	−0.0029	1.2721×10^8
Rich 16	−0.00016772	−0.0017	−0.0013	1.1656×10^8

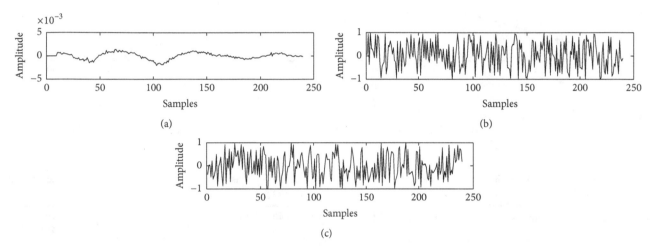

FIGURE 8: Key sensitivity test on encryption process: (a) original speech signal for first frame (Lauren 8); (b) encrypted speech signal for original key; (c) encrypted signal for Key A.

by cryptosystem contains eight parameters: seven floating point numbers and one integer, where $z_0, w_0 \in (0, 2\pi)$. R can take any real value which is greater than 18.0 and S takes any integer value greater than 100. The total number of possible values which can be used as a part of the key space from the MHM is 10^{56}, for the precision of 10^{-14}. Similarly, the total number of possible values which can be used as a part of the key space for z_0 and w_0 is $(6.28)^2 \times 10^{28}$. In the proposed cryptosystem, R has infinite number of possible values which can take part of the key space. But in a particular interval of 2π, R can take 6.28×10^{14} different possible values. Actually, the possible values that the parameter S can take are infinite. The total number of possible values that can be used as a part of the key space is 10^3, if S is ranging from 100 to 1100. So, the complete key space of the proposed algorithm is $(6.28)^3 \times 10^{101}$ which is large enough to resist brute force attack. Further, the key space is very large when compared to existing chaos based and traditional algorithms [5, 19].

4.6. Secret Key Sensitivity Analysis. A secure cryptosystem should be extremely sensitive to its secret key in order to resist exhaustive attack. The effect of key sensitivity on encryption process is verified by using slightly different keys to encrypt the same plaintext. A test speech signal "Lauren 8" is encrypted using the secret key ($x_0 = 0.1, y_0 = 0.6675, b_1 = 5.85, b_2 = 0.3, z_0 = 3.98, w_0 = 0.35, R = 26.4, S = 110$) which is shown in Figure 8(b). The encrypted signal which is obtained by applying a tiny change on x_0 with the variation of 10^{-10} is shown in Figure 8(c). The simulation results show that a tiny change in the key will result in completely different encrypted signal. The difference between two encrypted signals is about 94.4938%. Further, the algorithm is quantified by measuring the correlation between two encrypted signals which are tabulated in Table 5. It has been observed that the two encrypted signals have the least correlation.

The decryption process is analyzed through key sensitivity test by decrypting the encrypted signal with slightly modified key. Figure 9 shows the decryption of the test signal "Claire 8" for the slightly modified key (Key B). From the figure, it is clear that the correct decryption is not at all possible even for the slight change in secret key thereby providing secure communication over noisy wireless channel.

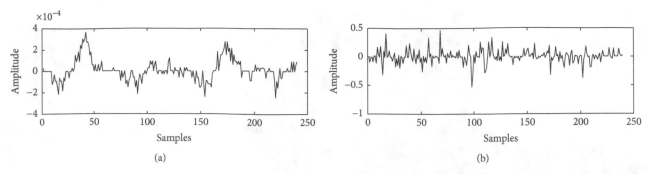

FIGURE 9: Key sensitivity test on decryption process: (a) original speech signal for the first frame (Claire 8); (b) decrypted speech signal for Key B.

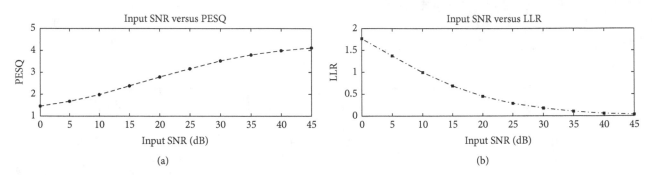

FIGURE 10: Speech quality metrics for the decrypted signal in the presence of AWGN noise: (a) PESQ; (b) LLR.

TABLE 4: Decrypted signal quality metrics.

Name	SNR in dB	Alwahbani and Bashier [5]	Sheela et al. [8]	PESQ
Claire 8	193.6586	30.2338	31.7008	3.34962
Julia 8	192.7466	29.5594	24.9047	3.28308
Lauren 8	194.1332	30.6980	19.1031	3.43439
Mel 8	193.9288	30.9975	22.4523	4.50000
Ray 8	194.6899	30.8710	25.2435	4.50000
Rich 8	194.9421	31.6812	21.7338	3.67965
Claire 16	190.6556	32.2487	25.0827	3.29362
Julia 16	189.6684	32.5668	17.3681	3.23237
Lauren 16	191.1387	33.7090	28.6808	3.37061
Mel 16	190.9293	33.8067	10.7542	4.50000
Ray 16	191.6308	32.8276	31.3426	4.50000
Rich 16	191.8984	34.6931	19.6978	3.64210

TABLE 5: Key sensitivity results for encryption process test signal as "Lauren 8."

Parameter changed with variation of 10^{-10}	Key obtained	CC between two encrypted signals
x_0	Key A	0.0025
y_0	Key B	0.0050
b_1	Key C	−0.0056
b_2	Key D	−0.0035

TABLE 6: Key sensitivity results for decryption process test signal as "Claire 8."

Key used	CC between original and decrypted signal	PESQ
Key A	−0.0099	1.3352
Key B	−0.0030	0.6341
Key C	0.0021	1.0854
Key D	0.0075	1.7541

The decrypted signal for slightly modified key is noise-like encrypted signal. In order to validate the algorithm, the correlation between original and decrypted signals obtained from slightly modified keys compared to the encrypted keys is calculated. The correlation and PESQ values are tabulated in Table 6. PESQ of about 2.5 is required for good speech quality [28]. From the results, it is clear that the correlation and PESQ are very small. Hence, the algorithm gratifies the sensitivity property of the cryptosystem.

4.7. Effect of Noise. The effect of noise needs to be considered in order to evaluate the efficiency of the cryptosystem. Hence, the performance of the cryptosystem is evaluated in the presence of noise for the test speech signal "Ray 8." In order to evaluate the performance of the cryptosystem, the white Gaussian noise varying from 0 to 45 dB is added to the original signal. The effects of noise on objective metrics such as PESQ and log likelihood ratio (LLR) [26–28] are calculated for decrypted signal. The variation of PESQ and LLR with respect to different noise levels is shown in Figure 10. From

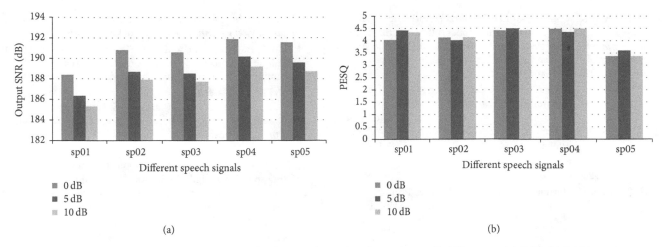

FIGURE 11: Speech quality metrics for the decrypted signal in the presence of babble noise: (a) SNR; (b) PESQ.

the speech quality and noise perception point of view, PESQ score above 2.5 and LLR close to zero are desirable [28, 29]. It has been observed that the decryption quality metrics are better at high SNR values which can withstand noise with low power.

Further, in order to evaluate the algorithm the clean speech sentences which are corrupted by babble noise varying from 0 to 10 dB are considered. These signals are taken from NOIZEUS database for experimentation [31]. The objective metrics such as SNR and PESQ are calculated which is shown in Figure 11. From the results it is clear that the proposed algorithm works satisfactorily. Hence, the algorithm can be used for real-time speech encryption applications.

4.8. Timing Analysis. The time required to encrypt/decrypt the plaintext depends on various factors such as configuration of the system, programming language, and operating system. The environment used for experimental findings is MATLAB 2009 on 1.88 GHz Intel CPU with 2.99 GB RAM in Windows XP Professional operating system. The average encryption and decryption time taken by the cryptosystem for a speech signal with sampling rate of 8 KHz are 59.65358 s and 27.19384 s, respectively. The cryptosystem uses dynamic DNA coding mechanism in order to increase the security which in turn impacts the speed to some extent. The existing algorithm in [5] is faster when compared to the proposed cryptosystem. However, the run time operation can be further improved with hardware as well as software optimization in order to meet the practical requirements. A suitable trade-off between the speed and the required security needs to be considered.

5. Conclusion

In this paper, a new speech encryption scheme based on chaotic maps and DNA encoding is proposed. The algorithm uses chaotic maps such as 2D-MHM and SM along with HCST. The modified Henon map has broad chaotic range over an extensive range of system parameters when compared to seed map. Further, in order to increase the security of the cryptosystem DNA encoding technology is integrated. The

performance of the cryptosystem is evaluated and compared with existing algorithms. Extensive simulation results show that the proposed algorithm can encrypt different types of speech signals with a high security level and resist several attacks. The algorithm offers more security when compared with the existing algorithm. Further, the algorithm can tolerate different types of noise with high SNR. Therefore, the proposed algorithm can be used in real-time speech encryption applications, secured telephone, and narrow band radio communication.

References

[1] E. Mosa, N. W. Messiha, O. Zahran, and F. E. Abd El-Samie, "Chaotic encryption of speech signals," *International Journal of Speech Technology*, vol. 14, no. 4, pp. 285–296, 2011.

[2] F. J. Farsana and K. Gopakumar, "A novel approach for speech encryption: Zaslavsky map as pseudo random number generator," in *Proceedings of the 6th International Conference On Advances In Computing and Communications, ICACC 2016*, pp. 816–823, September 2016.

[3] S. B. Sadkhan and R. S. Mohammed, "Proposed random unified chaotic map as PRBG for voice encryption in wireless communication," in *Proceedings of the International Conference on Communications, Management, and Information Technology, ICCMIT 2015*, pp. 314–323, April 2015.

[4] G. Alvarez and S. Li, "Some basic cryptographic requirements for chaos-based cryptosystems," *International Journal of Bifurcation and Chaos in Applied Sciences and Engineering*, vol. 16, no. 8, pp. 2129–2151, 2006.

[5] S. M. H. Alwahbani and E. B. M. Bashier, "Speech scrambling based on chaotic maps and one time pad," in *Proceedings of the 2013 1st IEEE International Conference on Computing, Electrical and Electronics Engineering, ICCEEE 2013*, pp. 128–133, August 2013.

[6] L. Xu, Z. Li, J. Li, and W. Hua, "A novel bit-level image encryption algorithm based on chaotic maps," *Optics and Lasers in Engineering*, vol. 78, pp. 17–25, 2016.

[7] S. J. Sheela, K. V. Suresh, and D. Tandur, "Performance evaluation of modified henon map in image encryption," *Lecture Notes in Computer Science (including subseries Lecture Notes in Artificial Intelligence and Lecture Notes in Bioinformatics)*, vol. 10063, pp. 225–240, 2016.

[8] S. J. Sheela, K. V. Suresh, and D. Tandur, "Chaos based speech encryption using modified Henon map," in *Proceedings of the IEEE International Conference on Electrical, Computer and Communication Technologies*, pp. 522–529, 2017.

[9] C. Cokal and E. Solak, "Cryptanalysis of a chaos-based image encryption algorithm," *Physics Letters A*, vol. 373, no. 15, pp. 1357–1360, 2009.

[10] R. Bechikh, H. Hermassi, A. A. Abd El-Latif, R. Rhouma, and S. Belghith, "Breaking an image encryption scheme based on a spatiotemporal chaotic system," *Signal Processing: Image Communication*, vol. 39, pp. 151–158, 2015.

[11] E. Y. Xie, C. Li, S. Yu, and J. Lu, "On the cryptanalysis of Fridrichs chaotic image encryption scheme," *Signal Processing*, vol. 132, pp. 150–154, 2016.

[12] T. Head, G. Rozenberg, R. S. Bladergroen, C. K. D. Breek, P. H. M. Lommerse, and H. P. Spaink, "Computing with DNA by operating on plasmids," *BioSystems*, vol. 57, no. 2, pp. 87–93, 2000.

[13] X. Zheng, J. Xu, and W. Li, "Parallel DNA arithmetic operation based on n-moduli set," *Applied Mathematics and Computation*, vol. 212, no. 1, pp. 177–184, 2009.

[14] J. Zhang, D. Hou, and H. Ren, "Image encryption algorithm based on dynamic DNA coding and Chen's hyperchaotic system," *Mathematical Problems in Engineering*, vol. 2016, Article ID 6408741, 11 pages, 2016.

[15] M. Henon, "A two-dimensional mapping with a strange attractor," *Communications in Mathematical Physics*, vol. 50, no. 1, pp. 69–77, 1976.

[16] K.-W. Wong, "Image encryption using chaotic maps," in *Intelligent Computing Based on Chaos*, vol. 184 of *Stud. Comput. Intell.*, pp. 333–354, Springer, Berlin, 2009.

[17] J. Fridrich, "Symmetric ciphers based on two-dimensional chaotic maps," *International Journal of Bifurcation and Chaos in Applied Sciences and Engineering*, vol. 8, no. 6, pp. 1259–1284, 1998.

[18] F. Rannou, "Numerical study of discrete plane area-preserving mapping," *Astronomy and Astrophysics*, vol. 31, pp. 289–301, 1974.

[19] B. Schneier, *Applied Cryptography: Protocols, Algorithms and Source Code in C*, John Wiley & Sons, New York, NY, USA, 1996.

[20] X. Wang and C. Liu, "A novel and effective image encryption algorithm based on chaos and DNA encoding," *Multimedia Tools and Applications*, pp. 1–17, 2016.

[21] X. Wei, L. Guo, Q. Zhang, J. Zhang, and S. Lian, "A novel color image encryption algorithm based on DNA sequence operation and hyper-chaotic system," *Journal of Systems and Software*, vol. 85, no. 2, pp. 290–299, 2012.

[22] Q. Zhang, L. Guo, and X. Wei, "Image encryption using DNA addition combining with chaotic maps," *Mathematical and Computer Modelling*, vol. 52, no. 11-12, pp. 2028–2035, 2010.

[23] O. D. King and P. Gaborit, "Binary templates for comma-free DNA codes," *Discrete Applied Mathematics*, vol. 155, no. 6-7, pp. 831–839, 2007.

[24] W. Liu, K. Sun, and C. Zhu, "A fast image encryption algorithm based on chaotic map," *Optics and Lasers in Engineering*, vol. 84, pp. 26–36, 2016.

[25] C. E. Shannon, "Communication theory of secrecy systems," *The Bell System Technical Journal*, vol. 28, pp. 656–715, 1949.

[26] F. Sufi, F. Han, I. Khalil, and J. Hu, "A chaos-based encryption technique to protect ECG packets for time critical telecardiology applications," *Security and Communication Networks*, vol. 4, no. 5, pp. 515–524, 2011.

[27] E. M. Elshamy, E.-S. M. El-Rabaie, O. S. Faragallah et al., "Efficient audio cryptosystem based on chaotic maps and double random phase encoding," *International Journal of Speech Technology*, vol. 18, no. 4, pp. 619–631, 2015.

[28] J. Ma, Y. Hu, and P. C. Loizou, "Objective measures for predicting speech intelligibility in noisy conditions based on new band-importance functions," *Journal of the Acoustical Society of America*, vol. 125, no. 5, pp. 3387–3405, 2009.

[29] J. F. De Andrade Jr., M. L. R. De Campos, and J. A. Apolinário Jr., "Speech privacy for modern mobile communication systems," in *Proceedings of the IEEE International Conference on Acoustics, Speech and Signal Processing, ICASSP*, pp. 1777–1780, April 2008.

[30] V. Patidar, N. K. Pareek, and K. K. Sud, "A new substitution-diffusion based image cipher using chaotic standard and logistic maps," *Communications in Nonlinear Science and Numerical Simulation*, vol. 14, no. 7, pp. 3056–3075, 2009.

[31] Y. Hu and P. C. Loizou, "Subjective comparison and evaluation of speech enhancement algorithms," *Speech Communication*, vol. 49, no. 7-8, pp. 588–601, 2007.

12

BER Performance of Stratified ACO-OFDM for Optical Wireless Communications over Multipath Channel

Zelalem Hailu Gebeyehu (ID),[1] **Philip Kibet Langat,**[2] **and Ciira Wa Maina**[3]

[1]*Institute of Science, Technology and Innovation, Pan African University, Nairobi, Kenya*
[2]*Jomo Kenyatta University of Agriculture and Technology, Nairobi, Kenya*
[3]*Dedan Kimathi University of Technology, Nyeri, Kenya*

Correspondence should be addressed to Zelalem Hailu Gebeyehu; zelalembet@yahoo.com

Academic Editor: Gianluigi Ferrari

In intensity modulation/direct detection- (IM/DD-) based optical OFDM systems, the requirement of the input signal to be real and positive unipolar imposes a reduction of system performances. Among previously proposed unipolar optical OFDM schemes for optical wireless communications (OWC), asymmetrically clipped optical OFDM (ACO-OFDM) and direct current biased optical OFDM (DCO-OFDM) are the most accepted ones. But those proposed schemes experience either spectral efficiency loss or energy efficiency loss which is a big challenge to realize high speed OWC. To improve the spectral and energy efficiencies, we previously proposed a multistratum-based stratified asymmetrically clipped optical OFDM (STACO-OFDM), and its performance was analyzed for AWGN channel. STACO-OFDM utilizes even subcarriers on the first stratum and odd subcarriers on the rest of strata to transmit multiple ACO-OFDM frames simultaneously. STACO-OFDM provides equal spectral efficiency as DCO-OFDM and better spectral efficiency compared to ACO-OFDM. In this paper, we analyze the BER performance of STACO-OFDM under the effect of multipath fading. The theoretical bit error rate (BER) bound is derived and compared with the simulation results, and good agreement is achieved. Moreover, STACO-OFDM shows better BER performance compared to ACO-OFDM and DCO-OFDM.

1. Introduction

Optical wireless communication is receiving more and more attentions from many researchers in recent years. Due to the high demand of wireless technologies, wireless data traffic in telecom network is tremendously increasing, and over-utilization of the conventional RF spectrum is becoming a big challenge. To tackle the challenge of this RF spectrum crunch, utilizing the optical spectrum for wireless communication is popularly considered to be a potential remedy. The optical spectrum intended for this application can offer wide un-regulated bandwidth compared to the conventional RF spectrum. Moreover, optical wireless communication (OWC) is not easily affected by electromagnetic interference and has excellent security features [1]. The advancement of cost-effective solid state lighting technologies creates a huge motivation towards visible light communication along with illumination purpose at the same time [2]. Intensity modulation and direct detection

(IM/DD) technique is the best candidate for developing low-cost OWC using the shelf transmitters and receivers.

Due to its potential of combating intersymbol interference (ISI), orthogonal frequency division multiplexing (OFDM) is confirmed as the best candidate for high speed OWC [3, 4]. The conventional complex bipolar OFDM scheme cannot be used directly for IM/DD-based OWC. Therefore, the conventional OFDM signal should be changed in to real and positive unipolar OFDM signal to make it suitable for the IM/DD system [4–9]. DCO-OFDM and ACO-OFDM are widely accepted unipolar OFDM schemes proposed for OWC on literatures [4–8]. Because of the imposed Hermitian symmetry in signal generation stage, both schemes waste 50% of the available bandwidth.

DCO-OFDM [4–6] uses additional DC bias to obtain a positive unipolar signal. But, adding a DC bias on the information signal reduces energy efficiency of the system; hence, DCO-OFDM is an energy inefficient modulation

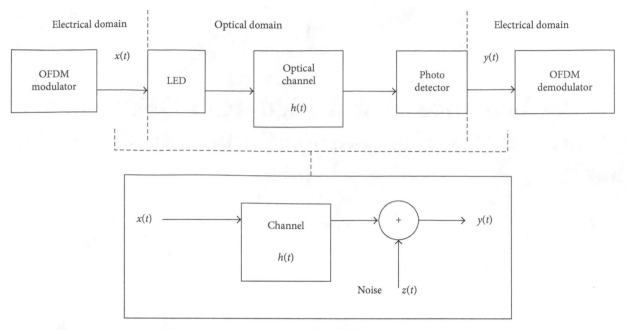

FIGURE 1: IM/DD system and its baseband representation.

scheme. On the contrary, ACO-OFDM [6–8] avoids a DC bias and generates a positive unipolar signal by utilizing only odd subcarriers. Since all of the even subcarriers and half of the odd subcarriers are wasted on the process, ACO-OFDM provides poor spectral efficiency compared to DCO-OFDM. In [10], we proposed STACO-OFDM to increase the data transmission rate along with the power efficiency of the OWC system. STACO-OFDM is intended to transmit multiple OFDM frames on both even and odd subcarriers simultaneously. It adopts a layered structure to use even subcarriers on the first stratum and several odd subcarriers on multiple strata. The indoor optical wireless channel has a low pass nature; therefore, utilizing both odd and even subcarriers becomes important to have more available subcarriers for data transmission in the low frequency region. STACO-OFDM has also an advantage of minimizing communication latency compared to eU-OFDM [11] which also uses a layered approach. In [10], the performance of STACO-OFDM has been analyzed and compared with the performance of ACO/DCO-OFDM in purely AWGN channel environment. The result presented on [10] reveals that STACO-OFDM can provide better BER performance compared to both ACO/DCO-OFDM on purely AWGN channel. In real world scenario, the information signal experiences multipath fading while propagating through optical wireless channel. Multipath fading is known for its challenge on the BER performance of wireless communication system during high speed communication. Due to the frequency selectivity property of the optical wireless channel, the BER performance of the overall system is degraded due to subcarriers having low channel gain. On this paper, the BER performance of STACO-OFDM is analyzed under the influence of multipath fading which is not done before. A diffused optical wireless channel configuration is considered, and ceiling bounce model is used to generate the channel impulse response (CIR).

2. System Model Descriptions

2.1. IM/DD System. Figure 1 shows IM/DD-based indoor OWC system with its equivalent baseband model. Let $x(t)$, $h(t)$, $z(t)$, and $y(t)$ represent transmitted electrical signal, the channel impulse response, the zero mean additive Gaussian noise, and the received electrical signal, respectively, and the relationship between the transmitted and the received signal can be written as follows [12]:

$$y(t) = x(t) \times h(t) + z(t). \tag{1}$$

It is noted that the IM/DD system needs $x(t)$ to be real and positive unipolar.

2.2. Diffused OWC Channel Model. In this paper, ceiling bounce model [1, 9, 13] is used to model the CIR of optical wireless channel. For diffused optical link configuration, ceiling bounce model uses a unit step function to model the CIR as follows:

$$h(t) = H(0) \frac{6a^6}{(t+a)^7} u(t), \tag{2}$$

where $a = 12(\sqrt{11/13})D_{\text{rms}}$ and D_{rms} and $H(0)$ are the channel delay spread and the DC optical gain of the channel, respectively.

2.3. DCO-OFDM. DCO-OFDM [4–6] utilizes both even and odd subcarriers for data transmission. It wastes half of the available subcarriers due to the involvement of Hermitian symmetry during the generation of real bipolar OFDM signal. For the system having N available subcarriers, the spectral efficiency Se_{DCO} of DCO-OFDM can be written as follows:

$$\text{Se}_{\text{DCO}} = \frac{\log_2 M (N-2)}{2(N+N_{\text{CP}})}, \tag{3}$$

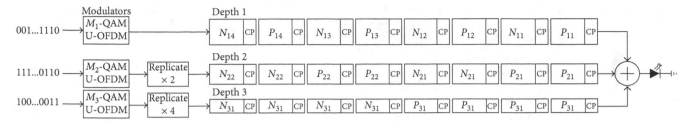

FIGURE 2: Frame design of eU-OFDM.

where M and N_{CP} on (3) represent the level of QAM modulation used at each subcarriers and the number of cyclic prefix, respectively. In DCO-OFDM, DC bias is added on the bipolar signal to generate a positive unipolar OFDM signal. For k amount of added DC bias, the electrical power dissipation of DCO-OFDM is increased by B_{DC} dB compared to the conventional bipolar OFDM [7]:

$$B_{DC} = 10 \log_{10}\left(k^2 + 1\right). \qquad (4)$$

2.4. ACO-OFDM. The conventional ACO-OFDM [6–8] utilizes only odd subcarriers for data transmission. But it is also possible to utilize only even subcarriers by leaving odd subcarriers vacant; hence, ACO-OFDM wastes either even- or odd-indexed subcarriers. The wastage of either odd or even subcarriers makes ACO-OFDM spectrally inefficient scheme compared to DCO-OFDM. For conventional M-QAM, ACO-OFDM having N subcarriers and N_{CP} cyclic prefix, the spectral efficiency is equal to

$$Se_{ACO}^{odd} = \frac{\log_2 M\left(N\right)}{4\left(N + N_{CP}\right)}. \qquad (5)$$

The above equation is only for the case of odd subcarriers that are utilized for information transmission. If only even subcarriers are utilized instead of odd subcarriers, the spectral efficiency becomes

$$Se_{ACO}^{even} = \frac{\log_2 M\left(N - 4\right)}{4\left(N + N_{CP}\right)}. \qquad (6)$$

2.5. eU-OFDM. The modulation concept of eU-OFDM can be considered as the modification of unipolar OFDM (U-OFDM) [11]. In eU-OFDM scheme, multiple U-OFDM frames are superimposed together to form single time domain OFDM frame as shown in Figure 2.

Successive demodulation technique is used to recover the signal carried by all layers. The demodulation process starts from the 1st layer and then continues towards the last layer. In eU-OFDM, the signal transmission is started after enough numbers of bits are received at the transmitter for the generation of one complete eU-OFDM frame. This introduces a significant latency for real time communication which is one practicality issue of eU-OFDM. The latency introduced at the transmitter increases with the available number of layer in the system. If S is the total number of available layers in eU-OFDM, the latency of eU-OFDM at the transmitter is greater than the latency of DCO-OFDM by a factor of $2^S - 1$ for the same M-QAM modulations used on

both systems. Moreover, some latency is also experienced at the receiver of eU-OFDM during successive demodulation. To demodulate the information carried by lth layer, 2^l frames should be received at the receiver. Hence, the latency is worse on higher level layers of eU-OFDM system. For enough number of available layers, the spectral efficiency, Se_{eU}, offered by eU-OFDM is equivalent to the spectral efficiency of DCO-OFDM. For the eU-OFDM system having N subcarriers and S total layers, Se_{eU} can be given by

$$Se_{eU} = \sum_{l=1}^{S} \frac{\log_2\left(M_l\right)\left(N - 2\right)}{2^{l+1}\left(N + N_{CP}\right)}, \qquad (7)$$

where M_l and N_{CP} are the level of QAM modulation at lth layer and the number of cyclic prefix, respectively.

2.6. STACO-OFDM Signal Model. STACO-OFDM [10] utilizes both even and odd subcarriers in stratified or layered architecture. At each stratum, ACO-OFDM modulators are used, and the time domain signals from each stratum are summed up for simultaneous transmission [10]. Only even subcarriers are utilized on the first stratum while odd subcarriers are used on the rest of the strata. Due to the low pass nature of optical wireless channel, subcarriers in the low frequency region are less attenuated and affected by the multipath effect of the channel. While utilizing both even and odd subcarriers, relatively good numbers of subcarriers can be available in the low frequency region for transmission of information bits. For theoretical analysis, we consider a system having a total of S strata on which even subcarriers are used on the 1st stratum while odd subcarriers are utilized on the rest of $S - 1$ strata. As given on (5) and (6), utilizing odd subcarriers on multiple strata has an advantage of maximizing the spectral efficiency since the conventional ACO-OFDM offers one additional information carrying subcarrier per stratum in comparison to even subcarrier-based ACO-OFDM. It is also noted that approximately equivalent spectral efficiency to the STACO-OFDM scheme can be achieved by utilizing only odd subcarriers on all strata. But, utilizing even subcarriers on the 1st stratum of the STACO-OFDM scheme may add further advantage and flexibility for STACO-OFDM during cellular OWC. According to [14], a significant limitation on the performance of optical attocell OWC comes from cochannel interference coming from the nearby cells using the same optical wavelength. In communication scenarios which require deployment of variable bit rate system for different cells in optical attocell, a hybrid system which uses ACO-OFDM for low/medium data rate cells and STAC-OFDM for high data rate cells can be deployed since ACO-OFDM scheme is more economical and cost-effective for low/medium speed communications. If many superimposed symbols are loaded on odd subcarriers of STACO-OFDM in such hybrid optical attocell communication scenarios, the electrical power of those odd subcarriers will be high and will introduce a significant interference on odd subcarriers of the nearby ACO-OFDM based cells which use the same optical wavelength. Therefore, to reduce the power of each individual odd subcarriers of STACO-OFDM, significant numbers of symbols are loaded on even subcarriers at the 1st stratum to distribute the available electrical power over significantly large number of subcarriers. Hence, the interference on individual odd subcarriers of low/medium bit rate cells due to odd subcarriers of high bit rate cells will be significantly reduced. In the proposed STACO-OFDM, the length of OFDM signal is set to be $N_l = N/2^{l-1}$ at lth stratum; hence, N_l-points IFFT/FFT module is used on that specific stratum. To equalize the length of OFDM frames to N, 2^{l-1} copies of the original OFDM signal are regenerated, and two subframes with length of $N/2$ samples are constructed at the lth stratum. To transmit the complete information carried by all strata, the superposition of signal from each stratum is performed based on subframes. On this paper, when we say the 1st and 2nd subframe, we are referring to $N/2$ samples on the 1st and 2nd half of the time domain OFDM signal, respectively. After adding cyclic prefix on each subframe, the 1st subframe from each stratum is combined together and transmitted in the first transmission session. Similarly, the 2nd subframes from each stratum will be combined together and transmitted in the second transmission session. The OFDM signal generation on all strata except the 1st stratum is based on conventional ACO-OFDM while flipping of the 2nd subframe is performed at the 1st stratum. On the first stratum, even subcarriers are loaded with the M-QAM symbol while odd subcarriers are loaded with zero. The vector of M-QAM symbols, X^{s1}, loaded on the subcarriers of the 1st stratum is given as follows (Figure 3):

$$X^{s1} = \left[0, 0, X_2^{s1}, 0, X_4^{s1}, 0, \ldots, 0, X_{N_1-2}^{s1}, 0 \right], \qquad (8)$$

where $N_1 = N$.

The Hermitian symmetry is imposed on subcarriers to generate real OFDM signal by imposing the following relation on the loaded QAM symbols [9]:

$$X_k^{s1} = \left(X_{N-k}^{s1} \right)^*, \quad 0 < k < \frac{N}{2}. \qquad (9)$$

After IFFT operation is done on loaded QAM symbols on subcarriers, the output time domain OFDM signal can be obtained. Throughout this paper, unitary IFFT/FFT operations are used to conserve equal signal power both on time and frequency domain. Therefore, the output discrete time domain OFDM signal $x^{s1}[n]$ and the frequency domain QAM symbols at the 1st stratum are related as follows [15]:

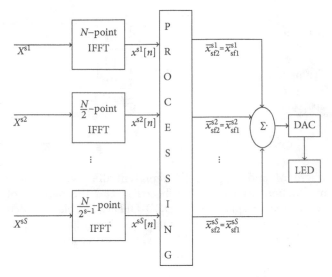

FIGURE 3: STACO-OFDM system model.

$$x^{s1}[n] = \frac{1}{\sqrt{N}} \sum_{k=0}^{N_1-1} X_k^{s1} \exp\left(\frac{2\pi kn}{N} \right), \quad n = 0, 1, 2, \ldots, N-1,$$

$$X_k^{s1} = \frac{1}{\sqrt{N}} \sum_{n=0}^{N-1} x^{s1}[n] \exp\left(\frac{-2\pi kn}{N} \right), \quad l = 1, 2, 3, 4, \ldots, S.$$

$$\hspace{12cm} (10)$$

The sample values in the above equation are related with each other as follows:

$$x^{s1}[n] = x^{s1}\left[n + \frac{N}{2} \right], \quad 0 \leq n \leq \frac{N}{2} - 1. \qquad (11)$$

To ease the interframe interference cancelation at the receiver, the entire frame of the 1st stratum is divided into two subframes with the length of $N/2$ samples each, and flipping of samples is performed on the 2nd subframe before clipping of negative samples is performed. Therefore, the two subframes $x_{sf1}^{s1}[n]$ and $x_{sf2}^{s1}[n]$ can be written as follows [10]:

$$x_{sf1}^{s1}[n] = x^{s1}[n], \quad n = 0, 1, 2, \ldots, \frac{N}{2} - 1,$$

$$x_{sf2}^{s1}[n] = -x^{s1}\left[n + \frac{N}{2} \right], \quad n = 0, 1, 2, \ldots, \frac{N}{2} - 1.$$

$$\hspace{12cm} (12)$$

Then, after clipping the negative samples from both subframes will have clipped signals $\bar{x}_{sf1}^{s1}[n]$ and $\bar{x}_{sf2}^{s1}[n]$ as follows:

$$\bar{x}_{sf1}^{s1}[n] = \begin{cases} 0, & \text{for } x_{sf1}^{s1}[n] \leq 0, \ n = 0, 1, 2, \ldots, \frac{N}{2} - 1 \\ x_{sf1}^{s1}[n], & \text{for } x_{sf1}^{s1}[n] > 0, \ n = 0, 1, 2, \ldots, \frac{N}{2} - 1, \end{cases}$$

$$\bar{x}_{sf2}^{s1}[n] = \begin{cases} 0, & \text{for } x_{sf2}^{s1}[n] \leq 0, \ n = 0, 1, 2, \ldots, \frac{N}{2} - 1 \\ x_{sf2}^{s1}[n], & \text{for } x_{sf2}^{s1}[n] > 0, \ n = 0, 1, 2, \ldots, \frac{N}{2} - 1. \end{cases}$$

$$\hspace{12cm} (13)$$

Now after adding cyclic prefix on each subframe, the two subframes of 1st stratum are ready to be combined with subframes from higher strata. In the rest of strata, only odd subcarriers are loaded with M-QAM symbols while even subcarriers are loaded with zero QAM symbols.

For example, let us consider X^{sl} is the frequency domain QAM symbols loaded on subcarriers at lth stratum where $l \neq 1$ (the superscripts sl stand for stratum $- l$ or lth stratum). Then, X^{sl} which is the vector of QAM symbols loaded on the lth stratum is given as follows:

$$X^{sl} = \left[0, X_1^{s2}, 0, X_3^{s2}, 0, \ldots, 0, X_{N_l-1}^{s2}\right], \qquad (14)$$

where $N_l = N/2^{l-1}$, $l = 2, 3, 4, \ldots, S$.

From the above equation, it is noted that the even subcarriers are left empty while the odd subcarriers are loaded with QAM symbols. The Hermitian symmetry is introduced by imposing the following relations on the loaded QAM symbols for enabling the generation of real bipolar signal [9]:

$$X_k^{sl} = \left(X_{N_l-k}^{sl}\right)^*, \quad 0 < k < \frac{N_l}{2}. \qquad (15)$$

After taking IFFT, the time domain OFDM signal $x^{sl}[n]$ is obtained at the lth stratum as follows:

$$x^{sl}[n] = \frac{1}{\sqrt{N_l}} \sum_{k=0}^{N_l-1} X_k^{sl} \exp\left(\frac{2\pi kn}{N_l}\right), \quad l = 2, 3, 4, \ldots, S. \qquad (16)$$

To equalize the length of time domain signal at each stratum to N, $x^{sl}[n]$ is replicated to generate 2^{l-1} exact copies at the lth stratum. To conserve equal frame energy before and after the replication process, the original frame at the lth stratum should be scaled by a factor of $1/\sqrt{2^{l-1}}$. The 2^{l-2} copies are then merged together to form $x_{sf1}^{sl}[n]$ and $x_{sf2}^{sl}[n]$ which are the 1st and 2nd subframes of the lth stratum, respectively. Clipping of negative samples and adding of cyclic prefixes are then done on the 1st and the 2nd subframes of all strata. Clipping of negative samples can be performed using the following operation:

$$\overline{x}_{sf1}^{sl}[n] = \begin{cases} 0, & \text{for } x_{sf1}^{sl}[n] \leq 0, \quad n = 0, 1, 2, \ldots, \dfrac{N}{2}-1, \quad l = 2, 3, 4, \ldots, S \\[2mm] x_{sf1}^{sl}[n], & \text{for } x_{sf1}^{sl} > 0, \quad n = 0, 1, 2, \ldots, \dfrac{N}{2}-1, \quad l = 2, 3, 4, \ldots, S, \end{cases}$$

$$\overline{x}_{sf2}^{sl}[n] = \begin{cases} 0, & \text{for } x_{sf2}^{sl}[n] \leq 0, \quad n = 0, 1, 2, \ldots, \dfrac{N}{2}-1, \quad l = 2, 3, 4, \ldots, S \\[2mm] x_{sf2}^{sl}[n], & \text{for } x_{sf2}^{sl} > 0, \quad n = 0, 1, 2, \ldots, \dfrac{N}{2}-1, \quad l = 2, 3, 4, \ldots, S, \end{cases} \qquad (17)$$

where $\overline{x}_{sf1}^{sl}[n]$ and $\overline{x}_{sf2}^{sl}[n]$ are the 1st and the 2nd subframes, respectively, at the lth stratum after clipping of negative samples. The entire frame of STACO-OFDM is transmitted in two successive transmission sessions. The 1st subframes from each stratum are combined together to form $x_{t1}[n]$ to be transmitted in the 1st transmission session, and $x_{t1}[n]$ can be written as

$$x_{t1}[n] = \sum_{l=1}^{S} \overline{x}_{sf1}^{sl}[n]. \qquad (18)$$

Similarly, for the second transmission session, $x_{t2}[n]$ is formed by summing the 2nd subframes of all strata as

$$x_{t2}[n] = \sum_{l=1}^{S} \overline{x}_{sf2}^{sl}[n]. \qquad (19)$$

At the receiver of STAC-OFDM, there are two received signals, $x_{r1}[n]$ and $x_{r2}[n]$, from two consecutive transmission sessions as follows [12]:

$$\begin{aligned} x_{r1}[n] &= x_{t1}[n] \times h[n] + z_1[n], \\ x_{r2}[n] &= x_{t2}[n] \times h[n] + z_2[n], \end{aligned} \qquad (20)$$

where $h[n]$ and $z_1[n]$ and $z_2[n]$ are the channel impulse response and the AWGN signal added on the 1st and the 2nd subframes, respectively. The demodulation process is performed by adopting successive demodulation technique stratum by stratum [11, 16]. The 1st stratum information recovery is begun by subtracting $x_{r2}[n]$ from $x_{r1}[n]$. After doing the subtraction, the output signal $x_r^{s1}[n]$ becomes

$$\begin{aligned} x_r^{s1}[n] &= x_{r1}[n] - x_{r2}[n] \\ &= (x_{t1}[n] - x_{t2}[n]) \times h[n] + (z_1[n] - z_2[n]) \\ &= \left(x_{sf1}^{s1}[n] - x_{sf2}^{s1}[n]\right) \times h[n] + z[n] \\ &= x^{diff}[n] \times h[n] + z[n]. \end{aligned} \qquad (21)$$

On the above equation, $z[n]$ is the AWGN noise with single-sided noise spectral density N_0 which is added in one complete OFDM frame, and $x^{diff}[n]$ is the bipolar signal which is exactly equal to the 1st half of $x^{s1}[n]$. In addition, the length of $x^{diff}[n]$ is equal to $(N/2) + N_{CP}$, and the length of $h[n]$ is equal to L, where $N_{CP} \geq L$, $h[n]$ is equal to zero for $n > L$. Therefore, the channel impulse response $h(l)$ can be written in vector form as

$$h(l) = \underbrace{[h[0]\,h[1]\,h[2]\cdots h[L-1]\,0\,0\,0\cdots 0]}_{(N/2)\text{ samples}}. \qquad (22)$$

But we can write (21) by using summation as [17]

$$x_r^{s1}[n] = \sum_{l=0}^{L-1} h[l]x^{diff}[n-l] + z[n], \quad n = 0,1,2,\ldots,\frac{N}{2}+N_{CP}. \qquad (23)$$

The matrix representation for the above (23) becomes [17, 18]

$$\left[x_r^{s1}\right] = [h]\left[x^{diff}\right] + [z], \qquad (24)$$

where $[x_r^{s1}]$, $[x^{diff}]$, and $[z]$ are $((N/2)+N_{CP})\times 1$ matrices while $[h]$ is $((N/2)+N_{CP})\times((N/2)+N_{CP})$ matrix. To recover the information carried by the 1st stratum, $[x_r^{s1}]$ is given to N-point FFT module after removing the first N_{CP} long samples from $[x_r^{s1}]$. But it is also noted that the N-point FFT module will pad $N/2$ zeros by default at the end of $[x_r^{s1}]$. After the default zero padding, $[x_r^{s1}]$, $[x^{diff}]$, and $[z]$ become $N\times 1$ matrices and their last $N/2$ rows are zero valued. Similarly, $[h]$ becomes an $N\times N$ matrix. But $[x^{diff}]$ is exactly similar to $[x^{s1}] = x^{s1}[n]^T$ in which its last $N/2$ samples are clipped to zero. According to [8], the clipped signal can be given by

$$\left[x^{diff}\right] = R\left[x^{s1}\right] + [d], \qquad (25)$$

where R is a constant which is equal to 0.5, and $[d]$ is the clipping noise which is $N\times 1$ matrix, but we can write $[x^{s1}]$ in terms of IFFT matrix F^{-1} and the frequency domain QAM symbol vector $[X^{s1}]$ as follows [18]:

$$\left[x^{diff}\right] = RF^{-1}\left[X^{s1}\right] + [d]. \qquad (26)$$

Substituting (26) into (24), the result becomes

$$\left[x_r^{s1}\right] = RF^{-1}[h]\left[X^{s1}\right] + [d] + [z]. \qquad (27)$$

Taking FFT operation on the above signal by using FFT matrix F [18],

$$\begin{aligned} F\left[x_r^{s1}\right] &= RF^{-1}[h]F\left[X^{s1}\right] + F[d] + F[z] \\ &= R[C]\left[X^{s1}\right] + F[d] + F[z], \end{aligned} \qquad (28)$$

where $[C] = F^{-1}[h]F$ is a diagonal matrix whose diagonal is equal to the Fourier transform of the channel impulse response $h[n]$ as

$$H_k = F\{h[n]\}, \quad k,n = 0,1,2,\ldots,N-1. \qquad (29)$$

The received frequency domain signal at each subcarriers on the 1st stratum becomes

$$Y_k^{s1} = RH_kX_k^{s1} + D_k + Z_k, \quad k = 0,1,2,\ldots,N-1. \qquad (30)$$

Introducing zero forcing equalization for reducing the channel effect [12, 19],

$$\frac{Y_k^{s1}}{RH_k} = X_k^{s1} + \frac{D_k}{RH_k} + \frac{Z_k}{RH_k}, \quad k = 0,1,\ldots,N-1. \qquad (31)$$

On the above equation, it is also noted that the clipping noise only affects the odd subcarriers [8, 10]. Since the even subcarriers are not affected by the clipping noise, we can write the received symbols on the even subcarriers at the 1st stratum as

$$\frac{Y_k^{s1}}{RH_k} = X_k^{s1} + \frac{Z_k}{RH_k}, \quad k = 2,4,6,\ldots,N-2. \qquad (32)$$

The information bits carried by the 1st stratum can be recovered by demodulating the above symbols received on even subcarriers. To recover the information carried by the 2nd stratum, the recovered bits at the 1st stratum should be remodulated again and processed in the same way as it was done at the transmitter. The remodulated time domain subframes are then affected by the CIR of the channel and subtracted from $x_{r1}[n]$ and $x_{r2}[n]$ to remove the contribution of the 1st stratum. By following similar mathematical analysis as it was done for the 1st stratum, the equalized QAM symbols received on odd subcarriers of the 2nd stratum will be in the following form:

$$\frac{Y_k^{s2}}{RH_k} = X_k^{s2} + \frac{Z_k}{RH_k}, \quad k = 1,3,5,\ldots,\frac{N}{2}-1. \qquad (33)$$

Then, by demodulating the above resulted symbols after subtraction by conventional ACO-OFDM demodulator, it is possible to recover the information signal from odd subcarriers. Similarly, by remodulating the bits recovered at the 2nd stratum and subtracting it from the received signal, the equalized QAM symbols received on the 3rd stratum can be written as

$$\frac{Y_k^{s3}}{RH_k} = X_k^{s3} + \frac{Z_k}{RH_k}, \quad k = 1,3,\ldots,\frac{N}{4}-1. \qquad (34)$$

Then, the bits stream carried by the 3rd stratum can be recovered by demodulating the above symbols using the QAM demodulator. The bits carried by the other strata can also be recovered by using the same strategy stratum by stratum.

Due to its efficient signal generation and demodulation strategies, STACO-OFDM has lower system latency compared to eU-OFDM. For same M-QAM modulation used on all of the available S strata of both eU-OFDM and STACO-OFDM schemes, the latency introduced at the transmitter of STACO-OFDM scheme is approximately less than the latency experienced at the transmitter of eU-OFDM by a factor of $2^S - 1$. For example, if we consider $S = 3$ for both schemes, $7(\log_2 M)(N/2-1)$ bits should be received at the transmitter of eU-OFDM before transmission while $(\log_2 M)(7N/16 - 1)$ bits are enough for the case of STACO-OFDM. Furthermore, the latency introduced at the receiver of STACO-OFDM is also lower compared to eU-OFDM since the frame length of STACO-OFDM scheme is less than the frame length of eU-OFDM by a factor of 2^S as shown in Figures 2 and 4. Therefore, STACO-OFDM scheme has better advantage over eU-OFDM for latency sensitive real-time communications.

Furthermore, implementing one tap frequency domain channel equalization is easier in STACO-OFDM than in eU-OFDM. To perform frequency domain channel equalization on the lth layer of eU-OFDM, the CIR of the channel

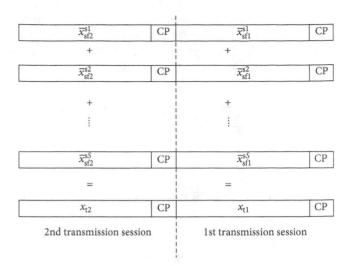

FIGURE 4: STACO-OFDM frame design.

should be constant throughout 8 frames duration. On contrary, the channel effect can be equalized successfully in STACO-OFDM as long as the channel is invariant over one frame duration. Therefore, STACO-OFDM can be used on applications involving fast channel dynamics scenario.

3. Spectral Efficiency of STACO-OFDM

The spectral efficiency of STACO-OFDM can be calculated as the summation of the spectral efficiencies delivered by all available strata. The spectral efficiency Se_l offered by the lth stratum is given by [10]

$$Se_l = \begin{cases} \dfrac{(\log_2 M_l)(N-4)}{4(N+N_{CP})}, & l = 1 \\[4mm] \dfrac{(\log_2 M_1)(N)}{2^{l+1}(N+N_{CP})}, & l \neq 1. \end{cases} \tag{35}$$

Then, the total spectral efficiency Se of STACO-OFDM can be calculated as follows:

$$Se = \sum_{l=1}^{S} Se_l. \tag{36}$$

STACO-OFDM has equivalent spectral efficiency with eU-OFDM and DCO-OFDM schemes, and it can offer better spectral efficiency compared to ACO OFDM.

4. Theoretical BER Bound of STACO-OFDM

4.1. BER Interms of Electrical SNR.
It is known that the real bipolar time domain OFDM signal at each stratum has a Gaussian distribution for enough number of available subcarriers [20]. The average electrical power of the OFDM signal at the lth stratum is equal to σ_l^2 which is the variance of the signal samples distribution. Therefore, the average

transmitted electrical power P_l of the bipolar signal at the lth stratum is given by

$$P_l = \sigma_l^2 = \int_{-\infty}^{\infty} m^2 f_l(m)\, dm, \tag{37}$$

where $f_l(m)$ is the probability density function (PDF) of the signal at the lth stratum and given by [20]

$$f_l(m) = \frac{1}{\sqrt{2\pi}\sigma_l} e^{-m^2/2\sigma_l^2}, \quad l = 1, 2, 3, \ldots, S. \tag{38}$$

Let $x_l[n]$ is the complete frame signal at lth stratum after clipping and scaling of the signal for conserving the symbol energy, so $x_l[n]$ can be written by merging the two sub-frames as

$$x_l[n] = \left[\overline{x}_{sf1}^{sl}\ \overline{x}_{sf2}^{sl}\right], \quad l = 1, 2, 3, \ldots, S. \tag{39}$$

The clipping of negative samples reduces the average electrical power by a factor of 1/2 compared to the bipolar signal. The average electrical power P_l' of the time domain signal $x_l[n]$ at the lth stratum becomes:

$$P_l' = E\left[x_l^2[n]\right] = \frac{1}{2}\left(\frac{P_l}{2^{l-1}}\right) = \frac{\sigma_l^2}{2^l}, \quad l = 1, 2, \ldots, S. \tag{40}$$

In (40), the factors 1/2 and $1/2^{l-1}$ come from the clipping of negative samples and the scaling of signal, respectively. Considering $x_T[n]$ is the aggregate OFDM signal after combining the OFDM signals from all strata as

$$x_T[n] = \sum_{l=1}^{S} x_l[n]. \tag{41}$$

The average electrical power P_{el}^{avg} of the combined OFDM signal $x_T[n]$ becomes [11, 20, 21]

$$\begin{aligned} P_{el}^{avg} &= E\left[x_T^2[n]\right] = E\left[\left(\sum_{l=1}^{S} x_l[n]\right)^2\right] \\ &= \sum_{l=1}^{S} E\left[x_l^2[n]\right] + \sum_{l_1=1}^{S}\sum_{\substack{l_2=1 \\ l_1 \neq l_2}}^{S} E\left[x_{l_1}[n]\right]E\left[x_{l_2}[n]\right] \\ &= \sum_{l=1}^{S} \frac{\sigma_l^2}{2^l} + \sum_{l_1=1}^{S}\sum_{\substack{l_2=1 \\ l_1 \neq l_2}}^{S} \left(\frac{\sigma_{l_1}}{\sqrt{2^{l_1}\pi}}\right)\left(\frac{\sigma_{l_2}}{\sqrt{2^{l_2}\pi}}\right) \\ &= \sum_{l=1}^{S} \frac{\sigma_l^2}{2^l} + \frac{1}{\pi}\sum_{l_1=1}^{S}\sum_{\substack{l_2=1 \\ l_1 \neq l_2}}^{S} \frac{\sigma_{l_1}\sigma_{l_2}}{\sqrt{2^{l_1+l_2}}}. \end{aligned} \tag{42}$$

The average achieved SNR per bit at the kth subcarrier of the entire combined system is given by [11, 16]

$$\gamma_k = \frac{|H_k|^2 P_{el}^{avg}}{BN_0(Se)}. \tag{43}$$

But the SNR per bit at the kth subcarrier has different values at different strata; the SNR per bit at the kth subcarrier of the lth stratum can be given by

$$\gamma_{l,k} = \frac{|H_k|^2 P_l'}{BN_0(Se_l)},\qquad(44)$$

where P_l' is the electrical power of the clipped signal at the lth stratum which is equal to $\sigma_l^2/2$. The theoretical BER at the kth subcarrier of the lth stratum can be given by the BER formula of M-QAM modulation as follows [22]:

$$BER_{l,k} = \frac{4}{\log_2 M_l}\left(1 - \frac{1}{\sqrt{M_l}}\right)\sum_{i=1}^{\sqrt{M_l}/2} Q\left((2i-1)\sqrt{\frac{3\log_2 M_l\gamma_{l,k}}{M_l-1}}\right).\qquad(45)$$

From the above equation, the overall BER at the lth stratum can be calculated as

$$BER_l = \frac{1}{N_l^{\text{info}}}\sum_{k=1}^{(N_l/2)-1} BER_{l,k},\quad l = 1,2,3,\ldots,S,\qquad(46)$$

where N_l^{info} is the number of information-carrying subcarriers at the lth stratum. For the 1st stratum (i.e., $l = 1$), k is even as $k = 2,4,6,\ldots,(N/2)-2$ since only even subcarriers

are carrying information. For the rest of the strata, k is odd as $k = 1,3,5,\ldots,(N_l/2)-1$.

The theoretical BER bound of STACO-OFDM on multipath channel can be derived from the theoretical BER bound achieved at the available strata. Let S and N_l^{bits} stand for the total number of used strata and the total number of bits transmitted at the lth stratum in one complete OFDM frame transmission, respectively, the BER of the overall STACO-OFDM system is then given by [10]

$$BER_{\text{tot}} = \frac{\text{total number of erroneous bits per STACO-OFDM frame}}{\text{total number of transmitted bits per STACO-OFDM frame}}$$

$$(47)$$

$$= \frac{\sum_{l=1}^{S}\left(BER_l\, N_l^{\text{bits}}\right)}{\sum_{s=1}^{S} N_l^{\text{bits}}}.$$

4.2. BER Interms of Optical Power of Transmitted Signal.
Percival's theorem can be applied at each stratum since unitary IFFT/FFT is used on each stratum [15]. Therefore, at any lth stratum, the electrical power is equal in time and frequency domain as

$$E\left[\sum_{k=0}^{N-1}|X_k^{sl}|^2\right] = E\left[\sum_{n=0}^{N-1}|x^{sl}[n]|^2\right] = \sum_{n=0}^{N-1} E\left[|x^{sl}[n]|^2\right].\qquad(48)$$

According to the above equation, the average electrical power of the bipolar signal at the lth stratum can be calculated as

$$P_l = \frac{1}{N_l}\sum_{n=0}^{N_l-1} E\left[|x^{sl}[n]|^2\right]$$

$$= \frac{2^{l-1}}{N}\sum_{n=0}^{(N/2^{l-1})-1} E\left[|x^{sl}[n]|^2\right]\qquad(49)$$

$$= \sigma_l^2,$$

where $l = 1,2,3,\ldots,S$.

But from (48) and (49), we have

$$\frac{2^{l-1}}{N}\sum_{n=0}^{(N/2^{l-1})-1} E\left[|x^{sl}[n]|^2\right] = \frac{2^{l-1}}{N}E\left[\sum_{k=0}^{(N/2^{l-1})-1}|X_k^{sl}|^2\right]\qquad(50)$$

$$= \sigma_l^2,$$

where $l = 1,2,3,\ldots,S$.

Then, after clipping the negative samples of the signal, the average electrical power P_l' of the unipolar signal at the lth stratum will equal to the average symbol power of the clipped symbol $\overline{X}_k^l$ as

$$P_l' = \frac{2^{l-1}}{N}E\left[\sum_{k=0}^{(N/2^{l-1})-1}|\overline{X}_k^{sl}|^2\right]\qquad(51)$$

$$= \frac{\sigma_l^2}{2},$$

where $l = 1,2,\ldots,S$.

Similarly, the average optical power of the transmitted signal on the lth stratum can be calculated as mean of truncated random variables [11, 21]:

$$P_l^o = E[x_l[n]] = \frac{\sigma_l}{\sqrt{\pi 2^l}},\quad l = 1,2,3,\ldots,S.\qquad(52)$$

But using (51) and (52), we can write P_l' as

$$P_l' = \pi\left(2^{l-1}\right)\left(P_l^o\right)^2,\quad l = 1,2,3,\ldots,S.\qquad(53)$$

Then, it is possible to write P_l' as

$$P_l' = \frac{2^{l-1}}{N}E\left[\sum_{k=0}^{(N/2^{l-1})-1}|\overline{X}_k^{sl}|^2\right]\qquad(54)$$

$$= \pi\left(2^{l-1}\right)\left(P_l^o\right)^2,$$

where $l = 1,2,3,\ldots,S$.

If we assume all the clipped version of QAM symbols on subcarriers at the lth stratum have equal average electrical power, we will have

$$E\left[\left|\overline{X}_k^{sl}\right|^2\right] = \pi\left(2^{l-1}\right)\left(P_l^o\right)^2. \tag{55}$$

Then, at the receiver, the transmitted clipped QAM symbol at the kth subcarrier of lth stratum is further attenuated by the channel gain $|H_k|$; hence, the received QAM symbol Y_k^{sl} at the kth subcarrier of the lth stratum will have average electrical power of

$$E\left[\left|Y_k^{sl}\right|^2\right] = |H_k|^2 E\left[\left|\overline{X}_k^{sl}\right|^2\right] = \pi\left(2^{l-1}\right)\left(P_l^o\right)^2|H_k|^2. \tag{56}$$

To calculate the effective SNR of the QAM symbol received at the kth subcarrier, the AWGN noise power at kth the subcarrier should be known. Let N_0 be the single-sided noise spectral density; the noise variance σ_z^2 at each subcarriers is given by [15]

$$\sigma_z^2 = E\left[\left|Z_k\right|^2\right] = \left(\frac{N_0 B_{sc}}{2}\right)\left(\frac{N}{2^{l-1}}\right), \quad l = 1, 2, \ldots, S, \tag{57}$$

where B_{sc} is the bandwidth of subcarrier, and $N/2^{l-1}$ term comes from the definition of the unitary IFFT/FFT algorithm. The SNR of the symbol received at the kth subcarrier is then given by [7, 15]

$$\mathrm{SNR}_k = \frac{E\left[\left|Y_k^{sl}\right|^2\right]}{\sigma_z^2} = \frac{2^{2l-1}\pi\left(P_l^o\right)^2|H_k|^2}{N_0 B_{sc} N}, \quad l = 1, 2, \ldots, S. \tag{58}$$

But for more simplicity, writing SNR_k in terms of the total average optical power of the combined signal is vital. The average optical power P_o^{avg} of the combined signal $x_T(t)$ can be given by [11, 21]

$$P_o^{\mathrm{avg}} = E[x_T[n]] = E\left[\sum_{l=1}^{S} x_l[n]\right] = \sum_{l=1}^{S} \frac{\sigma_l}{\sqrt{\pi 2^l}}. \tag{59}$$

The optical power penalty of the combined system with respect to the optical power at the lth stratum can be written as follows:

$$\alpha_l^o = \frac{\left(P_o^{\mathrm{avg}}\right)^2}{\left(P_l^o\right)^2}, \quad l = 1, 2, \ldots, S. \tag{60}$$

Therefore, SNR_k can be written in terms of the overall transmitted optical power of STACO-OFDM system as follows:

$$\mathrm{SNR}_k = \frac{2^{2l-1}\pi\left(P_o^{\mathrm{avg}}\right)^2|H_k|^2}{N_0 B_{sc} N \alpha_l^o}, \quad l = 1, 2, \ldots, S. \tag{61}$$

The SNR per bit $\gamma_{l,k}$ can also be calculated as

$$\gamma_{l,k} = \frac{\mathrm{SNR}_{l,k}}{\log_2 M_l} = \frac{2^{2l-1}\pi\left(P_o^{\mathrm{avg}}\right)^2|H_k|^2}{N_0 B_{sc} N \alpha_l^o\left(\log_2 M_l\right)}, \quad l = 1, 2, \ldots, S. \tag{62}$$

Then, the BER at the kth subcarrier of the lth stratum becomes [22]

$$\mathrm{BER}_{l,k} = \frac{4}{\log_2 M_l}\left(1 - \frac{1}{\sqrt{M_l}}\right)\sum_{i=1}^{\sqrt{M_l}/2} Q\left((2i-1)\sqrt{\frac{3\left(2^{2l-1}\right)\pi\left(P_o^{\mathrm{avg}}\right)^2|H_k|^2}{\left(M_l - 1\right)\left(B_{sc} N_0 N \alpha_l^o\right)}}\right). \tag{63}$$

The total theoretical BER bound of the lth stratum is then calculated by using the same formula as (46):

$$\mathrm{BER}_l = \frac{1}{N_l^{\mathrm{info}}}\sum_{k=1}^{(N_l/2)-1} \mathrm{BER}_{l,k}, \quad l = 1, 2, 3, \ldots, S. \tag{64}$$

The overall theoretical BER bound of STACO-ODM can be calculated by using similar formula defined on (47).

5. Simulation Results

The performance of the developed stratified ACO-OFDM (STACO-OFDM) is analyzed and compared with the performance of ACO-OFDM, DCO-OFDM, and eU-OFDM schemes for nonflat dispersive diffused optical wireless channel. Zero-forcing equalizer is used in all cases. The performance comparison is based on energy efficiency and BER performance over channels having different amount of delay spread and normalized channel impulse response (CIR). The simulation models used for comparisons (ACO/DCO-OFDM)

are verified by simulation results presented in [12, 23] for the same parameters. The major simulation parameters are listed out in Table 1.

In the proposed STACO-OFDM and eU-OFDM schemes, the length of the cyclic prefix is set to be 32 for each subframes which are transmitted into two consecutive sessions. To achieve similar spectral efficiency for the three schemes and for fair comparison, 64 samples long cyclic prefix is used for ACO-OFDM and DCO-OFDM.

5.1. Channel Impulse Response (CIR). Figure 5 shows the discrete time simulation result of normalized time domain CIR of the diffused optical channel h_n for channel delay spread of 10 ns and 20 ns. The time duration between two discrete points is used to generate the channel samples with consideration of no blocking object which blocks the reflected light from arriving at the receiver. The result in Figure 5 confirms that 32 samples long cyclic prefix is enough to avoid ISI since the magnitude of h_n is almost zero for samples beyond the 12th sample. Figure 6 shows the plot of

TABLE 1: Major simulation parameters.

OFDM parameters			
IFFT/FFT size	2048		
Cyclic prefix length	64		
Sampling frequency (f_s)	100 MHz		
Channel delay spread (D_{rms})	10 ns, 20 ns		
Modulation techniques			
	Stratum-1	Stratum-2	Stratum-3
STACO-OFDM/	16-QAM	8-QAM	4-QAM
eU-OFDM	32-QAM	16-QAM	16-QAM
	64-QAM	64-QAM	16-QAM
ACO-OFDM	64, 256, 1024-QAM		
DCO-OFDM	8, 16, 32-QAM		
Spectral efficiency	≈1.5, 2, and 2.5 bits/s/Hz		
Bit rate	145 Mbs, 194 Mbs, 242 Mbs		

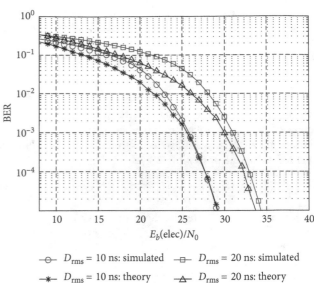

FIGURE 7: Theoretical and simulated BER of STACO-OFDM for spectral efficiency of 2 bits/s/Hz.

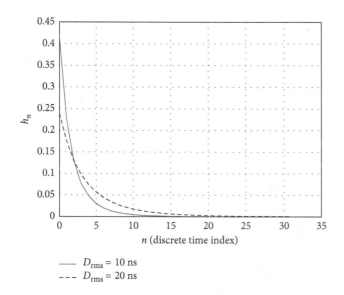

FIGURE 5: The normalized time domain CIR from ceiling bounce model for $D_{rms} = 10, 20$ ns.

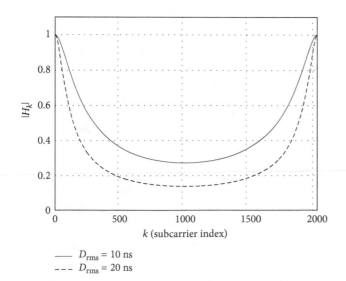

FIGURE 6: Frequency domain subcarrier gain for CIR with $D_{rms} = 10, 20$ ns.

frequency domain subcarrier gain of the optical wireless channel for the normalized CIR with D_{rms} of (10 ns, 20 ns). As presented in Figure 5, the optical wireless channel has low pass nature and is becoming more frequency selective when the quantity of D_{rms} is increased. The subcarriers near to the zero frequency are relatively in better condition to achieve relatively better SNR since they have relatively higher channel gain. Moreover, while the channel delay spread is increasing, the channel gains of the subcarriers are decreasing; hence, it is difficult to achieve enough SNR for better BER performance while the quantity of the channel delay becomes large.

5.2. BER versus Electrical SNR per Bit. To compare the electrical energy efficiencies of the four schemes, the BER performances versus electrical E_b/N_0 are analyzed for all modulation schemes having similar spectral efficiencies and bit rates. As shown in Figure 7, the simulation result and the theoretical BER bound have shown good agreement apart from the inclusion of the residual error introduced by the successive demodulation on the simulated BER. The result in Figure 8 presented the comparison of the four schemes in terms of electrical energy efficiency for the system providing 1.5 bits/s/Hz and bit rate of 145 Mb/s over diffused optical channel. As the simulation result shows, to achieve a BER of 10^{-5} over multipath channel having delay spread of 10 and 20 ns, respectively, the proposed STACO-OFDM delivers electrical energy savings of about 1.7 and 1.6 dB compared to ACO-OFDM, about 4.8 and 5.5 dB electrical energy savings compared to DCO-OFDM, and about 1.2 and 1.6 dB electrical energy savings compared to eU-OFDM.

In Figure 9, the BER performance with respect to electrical SNR is presented for the four schemes providing spectral efficiency of 2 bits/s/Hz and a bit rate of 194 Mb/s. As the simulation result confirms, the performance of proposed STACO-OFDM scheme outsmarts the performances of ACO-OFDM, DCO-OFDM, and eU-OFDM for

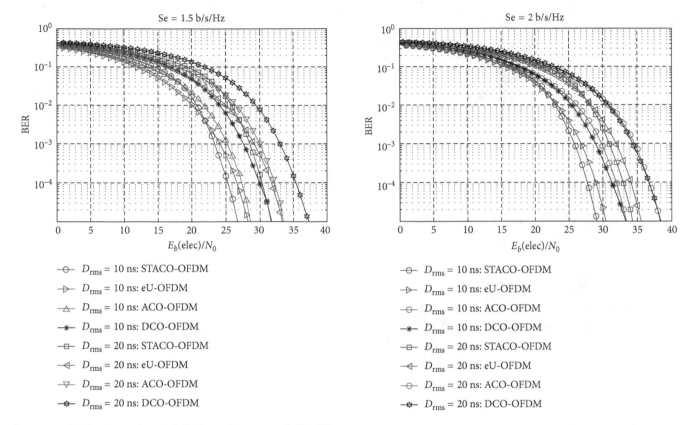

FIGURE 8: BER versus electrical SNR performance of STACO-OFDM, ACO-OFDM, and DCO-OFDM with spectral efficiency of 1.5 bits/s/Hz over multipath channel with $D_{rms} = 10, 20$ ns.

FIGURE 9: BER versus electrical SNR performance of STACO-OFDM, ACO-OFDM, and DCO-OFDM with spectral efficiency of 2 bits/s/Hz over multipath channel with $D_{rms} = 10, 20$ ns.

nonflat multipath channel with the given channel delay spreads. To achieve a BER of 10^{-5} over multipath channel having D_{rms} of 10 ns, STACO-OFDM provides electrical energy savings of about 4.3, 1.3, and 4.3 dB, respectively, compared to ACO-OFDM, eU-OFDM, and DCO-OFDM. To achieve the same BER (10^{-5}) on channel with D_{rms} of 20 ns, STACO-OFDM offers 4.1, 1.6, and 4.1 dB electrical energy savings compared to ACO-OFDM, eU-OFDM, and DCO-OFDM, respectively. The BER performances of the four schemes over multipath channel for system having spectral efficiency of 2.5 bits/s/Hz and bit rate of 242 Mb/s are presented in Figure 10. For the channel with D_{rms} of 10 ns, STACO-OFDM achieves BER of 10^{-5} with 6.1, 5, and 3.1 dB lower electrical energy consumption compared to ACO-OFDM, DCO-OFDM, and eU-OFDM, respectively. Similarly, for the second channel scenario ($D_{rms} = 20$ ns), the energy consumption of STACO-OFDM is lower by 5.9, 5.7, and 3.7 dB compared to ACO-OFDM, DCO-OFDM, and eU-OFDM, respectively.

The overall presented simulation results also show that when the spectral efficiency increases the SNR penalty of ACO-OFDM in comparison to STACO-OFDM is increased since higher order QAM modulations are used in ACO-OFDM to fill the spectral efficiency gap.

It is noted that higher order QAM modulation are not energy efficient. To achieve a better BER over multipath channel having relatively larger channel delay spread, the electrical power of the transmitted signal should be high to achieve enough SNR. But while increasing the electrical power of the transmitted signal, the peak of the negative samples also increase in the negative region, and this will introduce large clipping noise for the case of DCO-OFDM since most peaks are left in the negative region even after adding a DC bias. Thus, the presented simulation results show that DCO-OFDM is more affected by multipath fading due to the presence of unavoidable clipping noise. The presented results also revealed that the residual noise propagating from stratum to stratum during successive demodulation affects the energy efficiencies of STACO-OFDM and eU-OFDM for large channel delay spreads.

According to the results given on previous literatures [10, 16], both STACO-OFDM and eU-OFDM schemes have shown equivalent BER performances as a function of electrical SNR for a linear AWGN channel. Nevertheless, the results presented on this paper have shown that STACO-OFDM can offer somehow better BER performance compared to eU-OFDM on frequency selective multipath channel. As given in Figure 6, the optical wireless channel has low pass nature and the subcarriers on the high frequency region are more attenuated by the effect of the channel. eU-OFDM utilizes those subcarriers in the low and high frequency region at each layer for transmission of information bits. On the other hand, STACO-OFDM avoids utilizing those high frequency subcarriers on higher depth strata. Therefore, the usages of high frequency

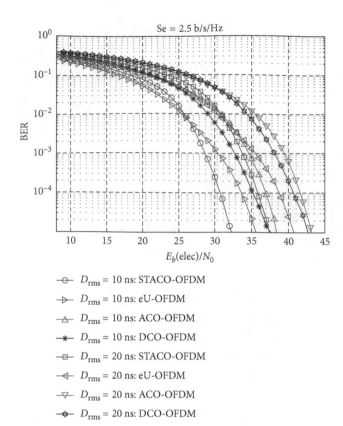

FIGURE 10: BER versus electrical SNR performance of STACO-OFDM, ACO-OFDM, and DCO-OFDM with spectral efficiency of 2.5 bits/s/Hz over multipath channel with $D_{rms} = 10, 20$ ns.

TABLE 2: Simulation parameters for BER versus optical power.

Simulation parameters	
DC channel gain (H_0)	10^{-6}
Noise spectral density (N_0)	3.05×10^{-23}
Transmitted optical power (P_0)	$25-40$ dBm

region subcarriers on all layers reduce the BER performance of eU-OFDM.

5.3. BER versus Optical Power. To evaluate the BER performance of STACO-OFDM scheme in terms of transmitted optical power, the parameters listed in Table 2 are used in addition to the main parameters listed in Table 1.

The channel parameters (D_{rms}, H_0, and N_0) in Table 2 for simulation are consistent with channel parameters presented on literature [1]. The results from numerical simulation and the theoretical BER bound given at (64) and (47) have shown good agreement as shown in Figure 11.

The BER versus P_0 (transmitted optical power) performances of the three optical OFDM schemes over multipath channel having a delay spread of 10 ns are presented in Figures 12–14 for spectral efficiencies of 1.5, 2, and 2.5 bits/s/Hz, respectively. For a system delivering spectral efficiency of 1.5 bits/s/Hz, STACO-OFDM shows better performance with around 0.6 dB and 2.6 dB optical energy savings to achieve a BER of 10^{-5} compared to ACO-OFDM

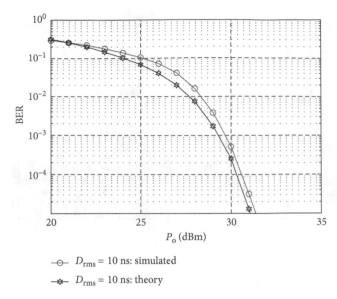

FIGURE 11: Theoretical and simulated BER of STACO-OFDM in terms of transmitted optical power for a system with spectral efficiency of 1.5 bits/s/Hz over multipath channel with D_{rms} of 10 ns.

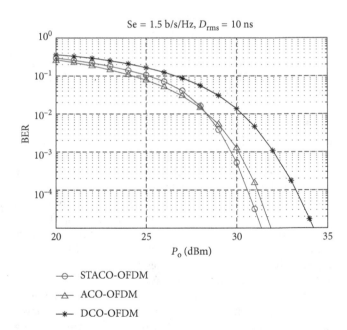

FIGURE 12: BER versus optical power performance of STACO-OFDM, ACO-OFDM, and DCO-OFDM with spectral efficiency of 1.5 bits/s/Hz over multipath channel with $D_{rms} = 10$ ns.

and DCO-OFDM, respectively, as shown in Figure 12. The simulation results in Figure 13 revealed that STACO-OFDM saves about 1.5 dB optical energy compared to ACO-OFDM and 2.5 dB optical energy compared to DCO-OFDM for the system offering spectral efficiency of 2 bits/s/Hz with a BER of 10^{-5}. The optical power penalty of ACO-OFDM with respect to STACO-OFDM is increased because of higher level QAM (256-QAM) usage to equalize the spectral efficiency of ACO-OFDM to 2 bits/s/Hz. Due to the energy inefficient properties of higher level QAM modulations, the

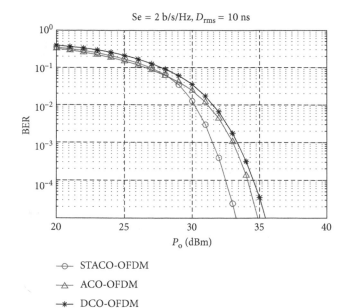

FIGURE 13: BER versus optical power performance of STACO-OFDM, ACO-OFDM, and DCO-OFDM with spectral efficiency of 2 bits/s/Hz over multipath channel with D_{rms} = 10 ns.

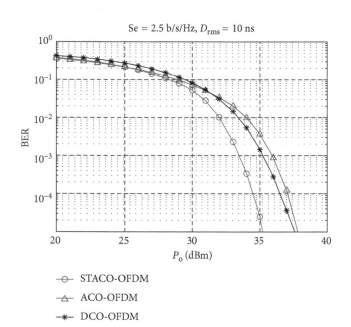

FIGURE 14: BER versus optical power performance of STACO-OFDM, ACO-OFDM, and DCO-OFDM with spectral efficiency of 2.5 bits/s/Hz over multipath channel with D_{rms} = 10 ns.

power penalty of ACO-OFDM has become large. Similarly, as the results in Figure 14 confirmed, the performance of STACO-OFDM outsmarts the performance of both ACO-OFDM and DCO-OFDM for the system providing a spectral efficiency of 2.5 bits/s/Hz.

To achieve a BER of 10^{-5}, STACO-OFDM requires 35.3 dBm optical power while DCO-OFDM and ACO-OFDM schemes require optical power of 37.6 dBm and 37.8 dBm, respectively. Therefore, compared to ACO/DCO-OFDM

schemes, the overall presented results have shown that STACO-OFDM provides better optical power efficiency which has huge significance for solving drawbacks of optical power constraints to meet eye and skin safety regulations in indoor optical wireless communications.

6. Conclusions

The BER performance of the proposed STACO-OFDM is evaluated under the influence of multipath fading. Performance comparisons based on BER have been also made with ACO-OFDM, DCO-OFDM, and eU-OFDM. For systems providing similar bit rates, the results from simulation have confirmed that STACO-OFDM provides better energy efficiency and BER performances compared to ACO-OFDM, DCO-OFDM, and eU-OFDM over multipath channel. Moreover, STACO-OFDM has reduced communication latency compared to eU-OFDM scheme. The future research will focus on improving the performance of STACO-OFDM on frequency selective optical wireless channel by incorporating bit and power loading adaptive capabilities.

References

[1] J. M. Kahn and J. R. Barry, "Wireless infrared communications," *Proceedings of the IEEE*, vol. 85, no. 2, pp. 265–298, 1997.

[2] Y. Tanaka, T. Komine, S. Haruyama, and M. Nakagawa, "Indoor visible communication utilizing plural white LEDs as lighting," in *Proceedings of the 12th IEEE International Symposium on Personal, Indoor and Mobile Radio Communications (PIMRC 2001)*, vol. 2, pp. F-81–F-85, San Diego, CA, USA, September 2001.

[3] R. V. Nee and R. Prasad, *OFDM for Wireless Multimedia Communications*, Artech House, Norwood, MA, USA, 2000.

[4] T. Ohtsuki, "Multiple-subcarrier modulation in optical wireless communications," *IEEE Communications Magazine*, vol. 41, pp. 74–79, 2003.

[5] O. Gonzalez, R. Perez-Jimenez, S. Rodriguez, J. Rabadan, and A. Ayala, "OFDM over indoor wireless optical channel," *IEE Proceedings–Optoelectronics*, vol. 152, no. 4, pp. 199–204, 2005.

[6] J. Armstrong and B. Schmidt, "Comparison of asymmetrically clipped optical OFDM and DC-biased optical OFDM in AWGN," *IEEE Communications Letters*, vol. 12, no. 5, pp. 343–345, 2008.

[7] J. Armstrong, "OFDM for optical communications," *Journal of Light Wave Technology*, vol. 27, no. 3, pp. 189–204, 2009.

[8] J. Armstrong and A. Lowery, "Power efficient optical OFDM," *Electronics Letters*, vol. 42, no. 6, pp. 370–372, 2006.

[9] N. Fernando, H. Yi, and E. Viterbo, "Flip-OFDM for unipolar communication systems," *IEEE Transactions on Communications*, vol. 60, no. 12, pp. 3726–3733, 2012.

[10] Z. Hailu, K. Langat, and C. Maina, "Stratified ACO-OFDM modulation for simultaneous transmission of multiple frames both on even and odd subcarriers," *Journal of Communications*, vol. 12, no. 5, pp. 261–270, 2017.

[11] D. Tsonev, S. Videv, and H. Haas, "Unlocking spectral efficiency in intensity modulation and direct detection systems,"

IEEE Journal on Selected Areas in Communications, vol. 33, no. 9, pp. 1758–1770, 2015.

[12] J. Panta, P. Saengudomlert, and K. Sripimanwat, "Performance improvement of ACO-OFDM indoor optical wireless transmissions using partial pre-equalization," *ECTI Transactions on Electrical Engineering, Electronics, and Communications*, vol. 14, no. 1, pp. 1–11, 2015.

[13] S. K. Wilson and J. Armstrong, "Transmitter and receiver methods for improving asymmetrically clipped optical OFDM," *IEEE Transactions on Wireless Communications*, vol. 8, no. 9, pp. 4561–4567, 2009.

[14] S. Dimitrov, H. Haas, M. Cappitelli, and M. Olbert, "On the throughput of an OFDM-based cellular optical wireless system for an aircraft cabin," in *Proceedings of the 5th European Conference on Antennas and Propagation (EuCAP 2011)*, Rome, Italy, April 2011.

[15] X. Li, J. Vucic, V. Jungnickel, and J. Armstrong, "On the capacity of intensity-modulated direct-detection systems and the information rate of ACO-OFDM for indoor optical wireless applications," *IEEE Transactions on Communications*, vol. 60, no. 3, pp. 799–809, 2012.

[16] M. Islim, D. Tsonev, and H. Haas, "A generalized solution to the spectral efficiency loss in unipolar optical OFDM-based systems," in *Proceedings of the IEEE International Conference on Communications*, pp. 5126–5131, London, UK, 2015.

[17] L. Rugini, P. Banelli, and G. Leus, "OFDM Communications over time-varying channels," in *Wireless Communications over Rapidly Time-Varying Channels*, pp. 285–297, Academic Press, Oxford, UK, 1st edition, 2011.

[18] B. Muquet, Z. Wang, G. B. Giannakis, M. de Courville, and P. Duhamel, "Cyclic prefixing or zero padding for wireless multicarrier transmissions?," *IEEE Transactions on Communications*, vol. 50, no. 12, pp. 2136–2148, 2002.

[19] P. Saengudomlert, "On the benefits of pre-equalization for ACO-OFDM and flip-OFDM indoor wireless optical transmissions over dispersive channels," *Journal of Lightwave Technology*, vol. 32, no. 1, pp. 70–80, 2014.

[20] X. Li, R. Mardling, and J. Armstrong, "Channel capacity of IM/DD optical communication systems and of ACO-OFDM," in *Proceedings of the IEEE International Conference on Communications*, Glasgow, UK, June 2007.

[21] J. Burkardt, *The Truncated Normal Distribution*, in press.

[22] F. Xiong, *Digital Modulation Techniques*, chapter 9, Artech House, Norwood, MA, USA, 2nd edition, 2006.

[23] T. Kozu and K. Ohuchi, "BER performance of Superposed ACO-OFDM in multi-path fading channel," in *Proceedings of the IEEE International Symposium on Signal Processing and Information Technology (ISSPIT)*, Limassol, Cyprus, December 2016.

13

An SDN-Based Approach to Ward Off LAN Attacks

René Rietz,[1] **Radoslaw Cwalinski◉,**[1] **Hartmut König◉,**[1] **and Andreas Brinner◉**[2]

[1]*Brandenburg University of Technology, Department of Computer Science, Group Computer Networks, PF 101344, Cottbus, Germany*
[2]*Genua GmbH, Domagkstraße 7, 85551 Kirchheim Near Munich, Germany*

Correspondence should be addressed to Hartmut König; hartmut.koenig@b-tu.de

Guest Editor: Ting Wang

The detection of attacks on large administrative network domains is nowadays generally accomplished centrally by analyzing the data traffic on the uplink to the Internet. The first phase of an infection is usually difficult to observe. Often attackers use e-mail attachments or external media, such as USB sticks, hardware with preinstalled malware, or contaminated mobile devices to infect target systems. In such scenarios, the initial infection cannot be blocked at the network level. The lateral movement of attack programs (exploits) through internal networks and the exfiltration of data, however, which are the main purpose of targeted attacks, run always over the network. Security measures against such internal network attacks require a comprehensive monitoring concept that spans the entire network to its edge. Especially for preventive measures, this means providing a security concept for local area networks (LANs). In this paper, we propose based on an analysis of typical LAN-based attacks an approach for preventing these attacks for both IPv4 and IPv6 networks. It applies the software-defined networking (SDN) paradigm for centralizing the related network decisions in a central authority—the SDN controller—that manages all network connections and hence the associated data flows.

1. Motivation

Capturing traffic to detect attacks on larger administrative network domains, e.g., an enterprise network composed of multiple local area networks (LANs), is nowadays typically centralized by picking up and analyzing traffic on the uplink to the Internet. This approach allows one to identify attacks from the Internet, but it has though a couple of important disadvantages. Insider attacks are not detected regardless of whether they are initiated deliberately or triggered by compromised devices. External attacks are equally difficult to detect because the initial compromise often takes place via mail by means of unknown vulnerabilities in file attachments or by simple social engineering, which tricks the recipient to run the executable code from mail attachments. In addition, threats, such as references to external web-based content as they are used for phishing and attacks using web-based content, are not recognized by existing preventive and reactive security measures.

The problems that current monitoring technologies have in detecting such attacks is that these attacks consist of different phases. The first phase of an infection (*phase of initial compromise*) is often carried out by an e-mail attachment or a contaminated USB stick on a PC in one of the local subnets. As these activities take place only locally on this PC, they are outside the viewing range of network-based monitoring systems. In order to attack servers in other subnets, an escalation of privileges has to be performed to bridge the intermediate system between two network segments. This can be done, for instance, using a domain-controller-based login on a PC in the subnet of interest with locally captured login information from the first infected PC—a step that is difficult to detect because the login may be legal. Next, the attack program needs information about the respective network segment. For this, scans of the link layer are often deployed to collect information about other systems (*internal reconnaissance*). Existing monitoring methods, e.g., the flow analysis, use primarily accounting information of the network and transport layer [1] and are thus unable to detect actions at the data link layer. Therefore, an attacker can use any link layer attack to propagate into the target segment (*lateral movement*) to collect more data from all servers and to move the data within the network domain. Moreover, these attacks are not limited to the data link layer. Due to the only slowly growing deployment of the next Internet protocol (IP) standard, IPv6-based attacks are often overlooked by current monitoring systems. In a last step, the collected data must be moved out of the network (*exfiltration of data*). According to analyses of targeted attacks, such as the Regin framework [2], this step can also be performed quite stealthily, e.g., by means of the server message block (SMB) protocol for intermediate stations (data-link-layer variant) and a Transport Layer Security (TLS) socket for the final move out of the network.

In order to solve these monitoring issues, additional security measures have to be introduced into such corporate/private networks. This leads to new challenges. However, preventive security measures for the Internet uplink, e.g., packet filtering, proxies, or an application level gateway (ALG), are easy to implement because there is only one data path, and a monitoring concept has to be developed that ensures an equivalent security level for a domain network consisting of several local networks connected by switches with multiple ports and data paths. In this paper, we present an approach to prevent layers 2 and 3 (L2/3) attacks on local area networks which are directed against the switching elements and the synchronization at these layers and which often are deployed to circumvent higher-level monitoring measures. We apply software-defined networking (SDN) [3, 4] as a vehicle for centralizing information on related network activities in a central controller authority. SDN provides the ability to separate the control and the data plane in a switch. As a result, the switch logic can be outsourced to a separate controller. Thus, decisions regarding packet forwarding are no longer made autonomously in the switch but can be passed to the central controller [5]. The approach requires no changes to the host systems and allows one to effectively prevent attacks at layers 2 and 3. The SDN paradigm has accelerated the discussion about new efficient methods for controlling and managing computer networks, for making them "programmable" [6]. It has attracted much attention. Regarding security, SDN possesses two facets. It offers a lot of advantages to make networks more secure, but it also enables new vulnerabilities and attacks, as discussed only recently [7]. Possible attack vectors exploit vulnerabilities across controller, switches, and their communication channel [8]. On the contrary, with its holistic control of the network devices and a standardized interface to interact with them, SDN enables new, cross-platform security mechanisms to prevent, detect, and react to network attacks [9]. Our approach considers the usage of SDN for improving network security. The reminder of the paper is organized as follows. In Section 2, we exemplarily introduce some typical attacks on local area networks. Existing approaches to ward off these attacks are discussed in Section 3. Thereafter, in Section 4, we introduce the principle of our approach for preventing L2/3 attacks on local area networks using the software-defined networking paradigm. In the subsequent Section 5, we introduce several security services that can be included in the SDN controller to disable the attacks described in Section 2. Some final remarks conclude the paper.

2. Threats to Local Area Networks

In local area networks, there are plenty of vulnerabilities that allow a traffic redirection with the possibility of reading and overwriting content [10]. Related attacks focus on layers 1 and 2 of the TCP/IP stack. One indication of the actual use of these attacks is the application of appropriate techniques in the Archimedes framework (https://wikileaks.org/vault7/#Archimedes). In this section, we present some examples of these attacks in the context of both the traditional IPv4 and the more modern IPv6 networks.

2.1. IPv4-Based Attacks. Typical examples for these attacks are ARP scan, ARP spoofing [11], port stealing, DHCPv4 starvation [12], and DHCPv4 spoofing. As representative examples, we describe in more detail ARP scan and port stealing here.

2.1.1. ARP Scan. In a first attack step, an attacker or an attack program has to explore the local network. The attacker can already obtain first information from existing hosts or even compromised hosts. The current IP address, the subnet mask, and/or the default gateway address may reveal the maximum size of the network because gateway addresses are usually reserved to the upper end of the network range. Then, the attacker can scan the network range based on the previously acquired information. The main scan variant used is the Address Resolution Protocol (ARP) scan (Figure 1).

The purpose of the ARP scan is to look for active devices in the subnet. For this, the attacker (e.g., station A) usually generates a list of all possible host addresses and checks them using ARP requests (*ares_op$REQUEST*) (Step 1–4). The addresses are shuffled (*ar$tpa*) to request them in a random order. (Step 5) If there is a host that matches an address, it responds with an ARP reply (*ares_op$REPLY*), containing its MAC address (*ar$sha* = MAC(< Host >)). To perform this scan, the attacker requires a large number of requests (#Requests ≫ #Hosts). After determining potential targets of interest, e.g., routers or servers, the attacker is capable of kidnapping individual or even all links in the network in a further step. In this respect, one has to distinguish between attacks with half- and full-duplex capabilities. Half-duplex attacks kidnap only one direction of the communication (e.g., to the Internet), e.g., by spoofing the hardware address of the gateway. Data that are routed from the client through the gateway to the Internet may be intercepted and manipulated by the attacker. The responses in the reverse direction, however, are sent directly to the client. Full-duplex attacks can manipulate communications in both directions.

2.1.2. Port Stealing. The purpose of port stealing is to "steal" traffic that is directed to another port of a LAN switch (Figure 2). If an attacker A wants to directly take over packets addressed to another host C1 from the switch he/she

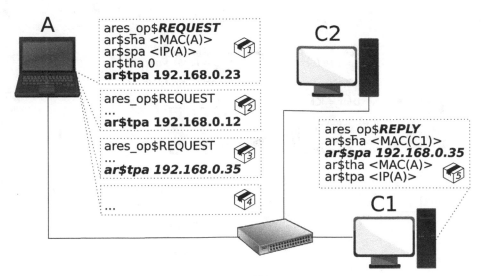

FIGURE 1: ARP scan.

first must delete the port registration of C1. This can be achieved by repeatedly sending ARP request frames to the switch in which the source MAC address is the one of C1 and the destination address is the MAC address of A (Step 1–3). The switch assigns the MAC address of C1 to the port of A, but it does not forward the ARP frames because A has addressed itself, i.e., the attack is stealthy. If the attacker receives a packet with destination C1 (in the example from C2) (Step 4), he/she sends an ARP request via broadcast to C1 and asks for its IP address (Step 5). After receiving the ARP reply (Step 6), the attacker knows that the switch has registered the MAC address of C1 again to the original port and can forward the intercepted (and possibly manipulated) packet to C1.

2.2. IPv6-Based Attacks.

Due to the slow spreading of IPv6, a situation has arisen in which each installed network device (router, host) is IPv6-capable, while the protocol is often not used actively. Because of the intended transition from IPv4 to IPv6, the latter has automatically priority in the case of a simultaneous configuration of IPv4 and IPv6 parameters. Attackers can use this fact to examine the network using IPv6 methods and hijack individual connections. Existing monitoring methods are often not able to analyze the IPv6 protocol—a situation that makes IPv6 attacks particularly attractive. Typical examples for IPv6-related attacks are IPv6 multicast alive scan, ICMPv6 neighbor discovery spoofing, ICMPv6 router advertisement spoofing, and firewall circumvention with IPv6 fragment headers. As representative examples, we describe the multicast alive scan and the router advertisement spoofing here.

2.2.1. IPv6 Multicast Alive Scan.

IPv6 does not use ARP anymore to find the MAC address for a given IP address. In IPv6, active addresses can be determined through a network discovery using multicast alive scans (Figure 3). The attacker sends only a single ICMPv6 EchoRequest packet with an invalid IPv6 destination option to the all-nodes multicast address (FF02 : 1) (Step 1). If the attacker is only interested in local routers, he/she can choose the all-routers multicast

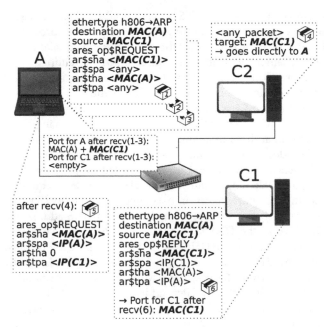

FIGURE 2: Port stealing.

address (FF02 : 2). All nodes in the network reply with an error message (the ICMPv6 parameter problem) that contains their address in the header because of the incorrect option (Steps 2-3). A similar network scan is possible by using a multicast listener general query [13] to address FF02 : 1. In this case, the hosts respond with a multicast listener report for each network interface. An advantage of the second approach is that the packet rate of the responding hosts to the multicast queries decreases due to random delays of the response which enables an evasion of possible anomaly detection systems.

2.2.2. ICMPv6 Router Advertisement Spoofing.

The basic idea behind ICMPv6 router advertisement spoofing [14] is the same as for DHCP and DNS spoofing in traditional IPv4

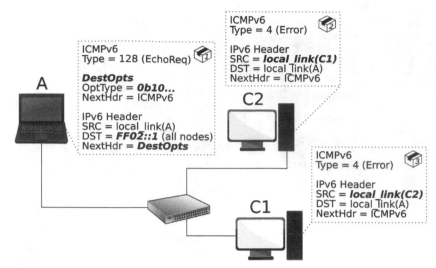

FIGURE 3: IPv6 multicast alive scan.

networks to assign a DNS server to all local hosts that is under control of the attacker. Figure 4 depicts the procedure for the IPv6 variant. First, the attacker sends a fake router advertisement with its own source link layer address (slla) and a randomly selected local network prefix (unique local address–ULA) which prompts the clients to start auto-configuration ($A = 1$) with the option to obtain other parameters ($O = 1$) via DHCP (Steps 1–3). The receiving client selects an address that contains the ULA prefix and its own MAC address or a random 64-bit postfix (Step 4). The client validates the uniqueness of the selected address via IPv6 neighbor solicitation and sends a DHCPv6 solicit request to obtain other parameters, in particular DNS servers (Step 5). In response, the attacker provides its own IPv6 address via DHCPv6 as the DNS server (Step 6). The DHCPv6 part is similar to that of the DHCPv4 attack, but there are detailed differences in the following step. Since the attacker is usually the only IPv6 router on the network, he/she can respond to DNS queries with any IPv6 address (Step 7–8). The subsequent IPv6 traffic is then routed through the attacking computer.

3. Approaches to Ward Off LAN Attacks

There are various approaches to protect physical networks, at least partially, against these attacks. In this section, we present some of these approaches.

In order to secure classical physical systems, the networks are often divided into smaller segments. This can be done on a logical level by configuring IP subnets, but this is only a very weak division or physically by an appropriate Ethernet wiring of the systems. At the transition points, e.g., routers or switches, data can then be analyzed by packet filters. Packet filters are the basis of traditional network- and host-based security measures, but they are inconvenient to manage in large network infrastructures—a weakness that distributed firewalls [15] do not have due to a centralized policy design and distributed policy enforcement. Distributed firewalls demand, however, implementations for each

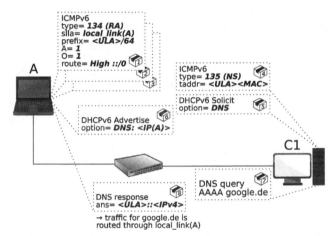

FIGURE 4: ICMPv6 router advertisement spoofing.

operating system and are themselves an attractive attack target.

Virtual LANs (VLANs) represent another possible security measure. They can be used for separating clients, so that only the systems that are associated with the same VLAN can communicate with each other. However, there are also attacks that aim at the so-called VLAN hopping (http://www.ciscopress.com/articles/article.asp?p=1681033&seqNum=3). Moreover, the use of VLANs is quite inflexible because a client is either assigned to a particular VLAN or to none at all.

Another security measure is the use of intelligent switches that provide some protection against rogue DHCP servers and ARP attacks. Smarter L3 switches use, for instance, DHCP snooping against DHCP attacks to enforce a fixed mapping between IP, MAC, and switch addresses/ports. ARP spoofing is prevented in this context by discarding nonapproved source addresses. On some switches, this security measure can be circumvented by another attack which uses the spanning tree protocol (STP) to redirect traffic to an attacker. Such attacks can be avoided by limiting STP to ports which are explicitly used for switch coupling. Currently, no security measures are known that reliably protect against similar IPv6-based attacks. In addition, there are problems with port-stealing attacks that override the internal cache of the switches with fake MAC/port pairs.

With the advent of software-defined networking (SDN), projects like SANE [16] and Ethane [17] tried to concentrate complex functions, such as routing, naming, and firewall policing, in a central controller. The main focus of these projects was on access control and enforcement of communication relations rather than on preventing layer 2/3 attacks. In particular, the Ethane approach [17] for local area networks focused on improving security. It couples flow-based Ethernet switches with a centralized controller that knows the global network topology and grants access by explicitly enabling permitted flows within the network switches along a centrally computed route. The controller enforces a strong binding between a packet and its source by restricting the port access to a switch on the IP addresses assigned via DHCP. One of the biggest problems that were reported in this implementation is the handling of broadcast traffic. Most broadcast traffic is caused by address resolution protocols, e.g., ARP, which generate a huge load on the controller. Other address resolutions, such as the IPv6 neighbor discovery, were apparently not implemented resulting in further shortcomings with regard to the spoofing of Ethernet/IP addresses. Accordingly, there is still a need for research on a method that simultaneously limits broadcast traffic and implements the address assignment and resolution in a secure manner for all major protocols (IPv4 and IPv6 including auxiliary protocols).

Beside these approaches for attack prevention, some approaches for anomaly detection with SDN capabilities were proposed. Mehdi et al. suggest several anomaly detection algorithms [18] that were implemented on the NOX controller (https://github.com/noxrepo/nox). Zhang published an adaptive flow counting method to detect additional anomalies in SDN-based networks [19]. The projects FRESCO [20] and OrchSec [21] provide beyond anomaly detection additional signature-based analysis methods that can detect ARP cache poisoning, DDoS attacks, and DNS amplification attacks. Due to the central management of the controller, port-stealing attacks cannot run in a software-defined network. Methods that are able to cope with IPv6-based attacks have not been reported, yet.

4. An SDN-Based Approach to Protect Switched LANs

We now present an approach to protect switched LANs against attacks at layers 2 and 3 using the software-defined networking (SDN) paradigm. It does not require any changes in the stations/host systems.

Software-defined networking provides the ability to separate the control and the data plane in a switch. As a result, the switch logic can be outsourced to a separate controller with the aim to control network flows from this centralized control application, running on a server or

virtual machine. Decisions regarding packet forwarding are no longer be made autonomously in switches or routers but are passed to the central controller. In a certain way, they become "slaves" of this controller. The controller can contain various applications, among them dedicated security services, which define the rules how to handle and route network traffic, data packets, and frames in the network. Admins can readily write/rewrite them. Thus, SDN-enabled switches can support user requirements for a wide range of applications (service level agreements, quality of service management, policy enforcements, etc.). A further key advantage is the ability to define routing choices at a much finer granularity level, i.e., per application flow, than at the usual IP level.

Since SDN is not limited to network devices of a certain vendor, it can be applied to devices from various vendors if the same protocol is used. Most SDN solutions rely on the widely-used OpenFlow (OF) protocol (for current specification, see https://www.opennetworking.org) [22] for the communication between the controller and the switches. OpenFlow is a vendor-independent standard that allows for interoperability between heterogeneous devices. Version 1.5 of the protocol supports 44 different types of header fields to match a packet against, to choose the flow it belongs to, and, thus, to determine the route it should follow. The protocol is also applied here.

4.1. SDN-Based Secure Switching. In order to prevent the above-introduced attacks on switched LANs, the interactions (or a part thereof) of the mentioned protocols (ARP, DHCP, etc.) have to be forwarded to a security unit that proves the meaningfulness and correctness of the interactions. Such a redirection can easily and efficiently be implemented by the software-defined networking paradigm using OpenFlow as the capture protocol, for instance. Figure 5 shows the principle of the approach. It uses an OpenFlow-enabled switch as the data forwarding component. The data plane switch is connected via the OpenFlow protocol with the control plane, in which various applications to control the data flows may be installed, and among them security services enforce a correct protocol behavior. By shifting the switch logic into this separate controller, packet forwarding decisions are made in a policy-based software switch inside this controller and not in the data plane switch. Thus, the software switch gains complete control over the network and the data routing.

One of the big problems in local area networks is that address configuration and resolution protocols, such as ARP and DHCP, broadcast packets on the network, and thus, each station can listen in and also respond. Therefore, it makes sense to proactively set rules in the OpenFlow switches that ensure that all ARP and DHCP packets are routed to the controller and no longer distributed. To be able to answer legitimate inquiries, an appropriate ARP and DHCP server should be integrated as application into the OF-controller. Most of the vulnerabilities can be resolved with these simple measures alone. ARP spoofing and poisoning are prevented by no longer broadcasting (malicious)

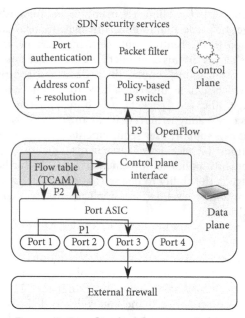

FIGURE 5: Openflow-based secure switching.

ARP packets in the network, but instead being answered or rejected by the OF-controller only. The same applies to DHCP packets to block rogue DHCP servers. An attacker does not even see the DHCP requests of other systems necessary to send a malicious reply at the right moment.

This approach also allows us to address the target systems with IP instead of MAC addresses. Many of the mentioned vulnerabilities are based on the fact that two different levels are responsible for addressing a system (layers 2 and 3), which must be adjusted. For example, ARP is used to obtain the MAC address associated with an IP address. At this point, an attacker can begin to bring the system into an inconsistent state and to intercept or block connections. To avoid this, the ARP server should be implemented in the OF-controller, so that it can answer all the ARP requests of the clients with a virtual, nonexistent MAC address. When sending Ethernet frames, clients use these MAC addresses together with the IP addresses of the target computer. The OF switches forward this information to the controller which uses the IP address to determine a suitable route and to create corresponding match entries in the switches. The last switch on this route is given the task of rewriting the MAC addresses in such a way that they are valid for the target system. Due to the use of virtual MAC addresses, each client knows only its own MAC and the IP addresses of the other systems. The MAC addresses of the other systems and the actual network topology remains hidden from them. Thus, each system knows only the information which is essential for a successful communication. The corresponding concept is referred to as IP switching. In Section 5, we describe such a security service more in detail.

4.2. Authentication at Switch Ports. Port authentication is an important problem of this approach for uniquely identifying hosts that are accessing the switch and thus the network. We

implemented it as a service in the OF-controller using the extensible authentication protocol (EAP) [23], which is often applied in wireless networks and point-to-point communications. The existing authentication infrastructure of most corporate networks in the form of RADIUS servers and LDAP [24] directory services can directly be used for a compatible SDN-based authentication service based on EAP. The EAP standard is a port-based access restriction for switch ports that only unlocks after a successful authentication. The switch acts as an intermediary between the host (supplicant) and the authentication server—usually a RADIUS server—that optionally queries a directory service (Figure 6). The problem to be solved is the integration of two different authentication formats in a SDN-based network. Although all parties, i.e., the hosts, the switch, and the RADIUS server, communicate with each other via EAP, the EAP packets are encapsulated differently, e.g., in Ethernet frames (EAP over LAN (EAPoL)) or UDP packets (RADIUS over UDP). The solution is that only the EAPoL packets are allowed at a nonauthenticated switch port (ether type = 0x888E, address = 01:80:C2:00:00:03 multicast). These packets are identified by the OF switch and redirected to the OF-controller. The OF-controller sends the EAP messages as RADIUS packets to an authentication server. If authentication succeeds, the controller transfers appropriate rules to the OF switch allowing the host to participate in the communication. Hostapd (http://w1.fi/hostapd/) is used as the authentication server. It is a daemon running in the user mode with software WLAN access point functionality. In addition, it provides an EAP authenticator as well as a RADIUS client and server. The EAP standard supports various authentication methods. For a prototype of this approach, the EAP-MD5 protocol was selected which does not use a protected communication channel. In practical use, more secure alternatives, such as EAP-TLS, EAP-TTLS, or EAP-PEAP, should be deployed. In the SDN-controlled network, however, the broadcast traffic is blocked and the communication partners communicate in a circuit-switched manner. Clients are unable to analyze or modify packets that are not addressed to them (even in the promiscuous mode). Thus, EAP vulnerabilities that primarily relate to networks that use a shared medium, such as the IEEE 802.11 wireless networks or the classic Ethernet, cannot be exploited.

4.3. Further Services. In addition to these security services, further security functionality, e.g., packet filters, deep packet inspection, or application-level gateways, can be integrated into the controller. Here, however, the following problem occurs. The OpenFlow data plane works internally flow- and not packet-oriented, i.e., each incoming packet for which there is no flow rule in the flow tables of the data plane switch is redirected to the OF-controller (path P3 in Figure 5) which causes a high overhead. Only after the controller has stored an appropriate flow rule in the flow tables of the affected OpenFlow-enabled switch, subsequent packets can be forwarded to the respective ports (see paths P2 and P1 in Figure 5). For a packet filter, the high overhead for the first packet of a flow is not critical. A deep packet inspection, in

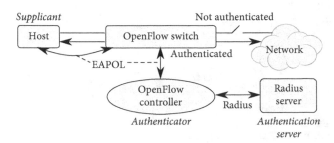

FIGURE 6: EAP/RADIUS authentication using SDN/Openflow.

TABLE 1: IPv4 address resolution service rules.

Rule	eth_type	ip_proto	udp_src	udp_dst	out_port
DHCP4c	0x0800 (IPv4)	17 (UDP)	68 (client)	67 (server)	Controller
ARP	0x0806 (ARP)				Controller

contrast, must examine each packet or a sequence of consecutive packets of a flow. To avoid the expensive sending of packets to the controller, a specific rule can be stored in the flow table of the data plane switch that directs security-critical packets to a separate external analysis unit.

5. SDN-Based Security Services

The attacks presented in Section 2 are basically caused by the decentralized management of network services in LANs. In the following, we outline several security services that can be installed in the centralized OF-controller and describe their implementation by indicating the respective flow rules.

5.1. Spoofing and Scan Resistance.

As argued above, many of the LAN security issues result from the fact that two different addressing schemes are used in layers 2 and 3 that have to be reconciled. To obtain the corresponding MAC address of a system with an IP (v4/v6) address, ARP and ICMPv6 Neighbor Discovery (ND) are deployed, respectively. One of the major problems is that address configuration and address resolution frames are broadcasted within the networks. These frames can be monitored from any host and responded. This enables an attacker to bring the system into an inconsistent state, to eavesdrop on running network connections, or to suppress further communication. The following address configuration and address resolution schemes implement the necessary functionality to prevent various aspects of these attacks.

5.1.1. IPv4 Address Configuration Service.

Countermeasures against spoofing can mainly be avoided by means of address configuration services. The IPv4 address configuration service proposed here is based on a controller-internal DHCPv4 service that redirects all DHCP client packets according to the following flow rule to the OF-controller (see rule DHCP4c in Table 1).

The contents of the rule can be interpreted as shown in Figure 7. The rule header corresponds to the matching and action data structures defined in the OpenFlow standard that are initially transferred to the controller (lower left part of the figure). The prefixes OFPXMT_OFB and OFP_ACTION have been omitted in the rule; the suffixes *eth_type, ip_proto, udp_src*, and *udp_dst* correspond to the grey-marked fields of the protocol stack shown in the upper part of the figure. The internal representation of the matching data structures

in the flow tables is not defined in the standard. In physical switches, it is typically converted into a sort of bit mask for a TCAM (Ternary Content Addressable Memory) (see lower middle part of the figure). If a packet matches this mask, it is sent to the specified *out_port* defined in the rule. The internal DHCPv4 service of the controller assigns IP addresses or renews leases for the connected systems. Allocated address entries are kept in the configuration of the controller for the address resolution services which are discussed below. This measure prevents attacks from rogue DHCPv4 servers because a spoofing is not possible without knowledge of the 32 bit DHCP transaction ID and the exact time of the client requests. An attacker does not even see the DHCP requests of the other systems required to send the malignant answer in the right moment.

5.1.2. IPv4 Address Resolution Service.

Countermeasures against network scans and further antispoofing measures can be implemented in the IPv4 address resolution service which is based on the knowledge of the DHCPv4 address configuration service. The ARP service part installs rules in all switches that redirect Ethernet frames with the *eth_type* 0x0806 (ARP) to the controller (see rule ARP in Table 1). Thus, no ARP frames are forwarded in the switches. The OF-controller sends accordingly ARP responses based on the knowledge of the DHCPv4 service. In addition, ARP requests that are not related to the gateway address in the appropriate subnet of the requesting client are ignored. These measures effectively prevent attacks, such as ARP scans, ARP spoofing, and ARP flooding.

5.1.3. IPv6 Address Configuration Services.

IPv6 address configuration is provided by an internal ICMPv6 router advertisement (RA) service and a DHCPv6 service linked to the internal DHCPv4 server. The former enforces configuration of IPv6 addresses using DHCPv6. This is done through regular flooding on all switch ports using router advertisements with the managed address configuration flag set. Initially, the DHCPv6 service works similar to the DHCPv4 service by redirecting DHCPv6 messages to the controller (Table 2). DHCPv6 requests are answered exclusively using the IPv4-mapped IPv6 address of the requesting client based on the knowledge from the DHCPv4 service [25]. The IPv4 address 192.168.120.63, for instance, is mapped to IPv6 address: FFFF:192.168.120.63. DHCPv6 spoofing is therefore even more limited as in DHCPv4 because in addition to the lack of the transaction ID and request time, there is also no possibility to exhaust the address pool. Another advantage is that the communication can be processed by existing firewall logic derived from IPv4

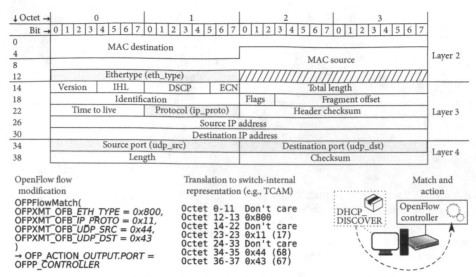

FIGURE 7: Matching packet header fields for rule DHCP4c of Table 1.

TABLE 2: IPv6 address configuration rule.

Rule	eth_type	ip_proto	udp_src	udp_dst	out_port
DHCP6c	0x8DD (IPv6)	17 (UDP)	546 (client)	547 (server)	Controller

firewall rules. The disadvantage of nonroutable IP addresses associated with the mapping may be compensated by a very simple form of NAT which applies a direct (IPv6) address to (IPv6) address translation (static one-to-one address assignment without protocol/port translation) at the edge of the network.

TABLE 3: IPv6 address resolution rules.

Rule	eth_type	ip_proto	icmpv6_type	out_port
ICMPv6nds	0x8DD (IPv6)	58 (ICMPv6)	135 (solicit)	Controller
ICMPv6nda	0x8DD (IPv6)	58 (ICMPv6)	136 (advertise)	Controller

5.1.4. IPv6 Address Resolution Service. ICMPv6 neighbor discovery is based on the same idea as ARP for IPv4. It installs two flow rules on all switches to redirect ICMPv6 neighbor discovery solicitations and advertisements to the controller (Table 3). All solicitation requests except those to the gateway's IPv4-mapped address in the subnet of the requesting client are ignored. This prevents standard IPv6 scans as discussed in Section 2.

5.2. IP Switching with Topology Hiding and Routing Enforcement. The security services introduced above provide a secure initialization of the network configuration but no secure message routing. They prevent that data connections are kidnapped by means of ARP spoofing or corresponding IPv6 attacks, but packets can still be hijacked if a false identity (MAC address) is adopted by a host and only a simple MAC-learning switch is applied in connection with the OF-controller. In addition, broadcasts like in ARP are a major problem as already mentioned in the Ethane approach [17] because they flood the controller too much. Moreover, broadcasts and ARP can be used to explore the network topology at the link. Therefore, a service is required that (1) binds the identity of a system to a switch port, (2) limits the number of possible requests for other systems, and

(3) implements the route of the data connection between two systems in a secure way.

Historically, broadcasts have always been limited by separation of networks. The binding of a system to a switch port is also a special case of network separation in some way. Therefore, objectives (1) and (2) can be achieved by network separation with address configuration. For this purpose, the address configuration service assigns a private/30 subnet to each host using DHCPv4. This addressing scheme allows one to hold four IP addresses for each subnet. The lowest address is the network address. The next two addresses are assigned to the host and to a virtual gateway that references the OF-controller. The upper address remains for further use, e.g., as the IPv4 broadcast address. The hosts in the subnets are forced by this addressing scheme to use routes via the virtual gateway instead of direct communication to reach the target systems. The only possible broadcast request—an ARP request for the virtual gateway address—is intercepted by the OF-controller and not flooded.

Figure 8 exemplifies this address configuration. The address resolution service in the controller assigns host C1 to the network X.Y.Z.0/30. The resulting address configuration (IP(C1) = X.Y.Z.1, GW(C1) = X.Y.Z.2) is deposited together with the host's MAC address in a database of the controller. The next available subnet (X.Y.Z.4/30) is assigned to host C2,

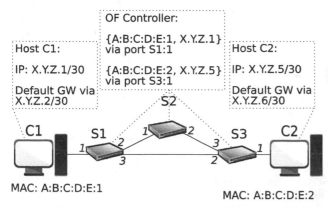

FIGURE 8: IP switch configuration with virtual gateway addresses.

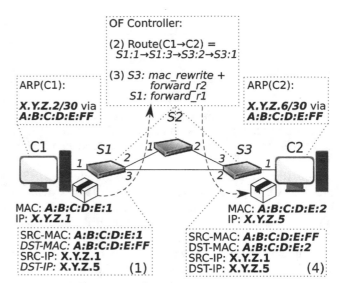

FIGURE 9: IP switching (a.k.a. routing) with virtual MAC addresses.

and its configuration is also stored in the database. The hosts know only their own IP address and the respective virtual gateway, thus limiting their ability to scan for other hosts with layer-2 protocols. Only the IP addresses are known of the other systems, and even the actual network topology remains hidden.

Based on the information of the (subnet) address configuration service, a secure routing service uses reactive flow instantiation to bind the identity of the participating systems for the duration of a connection to their source and destination switch ports to prevent data kidnapping. The routing process is exemplified in Figure 9 (based on the address configuration of Figure 8). The virtual gateway address is the only address that is resolved via ARP or ICMPv6-ND (MAC address A:B:C:D:E:FF in the ARP caches ARP(C1) and ARP(C2) of the figure). (1) When sending IP packets, the hosts use this address as the destination MAC address (DST-MAC) together with the IP address (DST-IP) of the target computer. The OpenFlow-enabled switches forward the first packet of a connection to the OF-controller. (2) The controller determines a suitable route based on the source and target IP addresses (switch 1, port 1 (S1:1) via switch 1, port 3 (S1:3), via switch 3, port 2 (S3:2) to switch 3, port 1 (S3:1)). (3) Appropriate match entries are created in the switches (Table 4, nw_src = SRC-IP, nw_dst = DST-IP).

The rules are installed in the reverse transport direction of the packet (first *mac_rewrite + forward_r2* on switch S3, then *forward_r1* on switch S1) to avoid multiple redirects of the same packet by the subsequent switches to the controller. The last switch on the route is given the task to rewrite the MAC addresses (*set_field* part of the *mac_rewrite + forward_r2* rule), so that they are valid for the target system. (4) The queued packet is released (by forwarding to switch 1, port 3–S1:3) and reaches the target in accordance with the defined rules. A glance at the chain created in this way in Table 4 illustrates the binding of each packet to its source and destination. In switch S1 the source IP address X.Y.Z.1 is bound by the rule *forward_r1* for the exemplary data flow to input port (*in*) 1. The rule *mac_rewrite + forward_r2* for switch S2 rewrites the virtual destination MAC address to the MAC address of host C2 and binds the data flow and the destination IP

address to output (*out*) port 1. Thus, a spoofing of IP addresses is prevented.

5.3. In-Network Firewalling and Robustness against Firewall Bypassing.
Physical switches often implement simple firewall logic in the form of access control lists–a concept that is also feasible with SDN. Firewalls can be implemented as a combination of SDN-based rules on the switches and controller-based firewall logic. Simple packet filtering can be implemented directly by respective rules on the switches. In addition, firewalls with stateful connection management can be implemented on the switches with some help of the controller and the dynamic creation of rules. IP switching is basically a flow-based switching with packet filtering functionality. For each new connection, a request is sent to the OF-controller which then decides whether this connection should be permitted or not. Then, a specific rule is stored in the switches ensuring that the other packets of this connection no longer needs to be treated by the controller. Thus, there is no additional overhead for the subsequent communication. All these security rules can individually be stored in the OF-controller for each client and are enforced independently of the switch port to which the client is connected to. Thus, each port on each SDN-enabled switch becomes a firewall.

Important security measures that should be contained in every firewall are static firewall rules which are directed against the circumvention of the firewall logic. The concept described above, for instance, allows a filtering on packet basis, but fundamental problems that affect pure packet-based firewall logic, e.g., the processing of fragmented oversized packets, as supported by IPv4 and IPv6, cannot be solved. Past experience has shown that it is not possible to implement packet fragmentation in a secure manner. For this reason, the presented approach installs rules on all switches to discard IPv4 and IPv6 packets with fragmentation options/headers (see rule fragment in Table 5). Another IPv6 issue to bypass the OF-controller is the

TABLE 4: Routing rules for Figure 9.

Rule	In	eth_type	nw_src	nw_dst	set_field	Out
forward_r1	1	0x800 (IP)	X.Y.Z.1	X.Y.Z.5		Port 3
mac_rewrite + forward_r2	2	0x800 (IP)	X.Y.Z.1	X.Y.Z.5	eth_dst = A : B : C : D : E : 2	Port 1

problematic IPv6 extension headers. The following headers should be redirected through rules on the switches to the controller (to log attack attempts) or discarded: *hop-by-hop options, routing header, destination options*, and *mobility header* (the mobility header supports Mobile IPv6) (Table 5). Although these are almost all IPv6 extension headers, these rules are in line with recent observations in transit networks (https://tools.ietf.org/html/draft-ietf-v6ops-ipv6-ehs-in-real-world-02) which discard packets with the same headers. They represent special use cases that are often not supported or configured but are, however, used within the IPv6 attack suites as an evasion method for IPv6 security measures. Another packet type that should be blocked is ICMPv6 redirects (Table 5). This packet type allows another attack in which a client can be redirected to a fake gateway address.

5.4. Evaluation. As part of the research for the described concept, an OF-controller that realizes the described functionality was implemented with the help of the Ryu framework (http://osrg.github.io/ryu/). During the development phase, the controller was tested extensively with Mininet [26]. The proposed defensive measures against ARP scans, ARP spoofing, port-stealing, and DHCPv4 spoofing with DNS spoofing worked as expected. There were, however, mixed results for IPv6. Scans of the IPv6 test network, neighbor discovery spoofing, router advertisement spoofing, and DHCPv6 with DNS spoofing were blocked successfully. The defensive capabilities against malformed IPv6 packets, however, depend on the used IPv6 stack, e.g., the Linux IPv6 stack discussed below.

In order to test the defenses against malformed IPv6 packets, two virtual clients were evaluated with the penetration test suite from the THC IPv6 toolkit (https://github.com/vanhauser-thc/thc-ipv6). One of the clients was acting as a test server to check which packets have passed through the firewall, and the other client was used to send manipulated packets. The test suite consisted of 56 test cases that were first executed without the SDN-enabled switch to test the Linux IPv6 stack and then with it including the OF-controller prototype with all services presented above. The purpose of this comparison was to evaluate the additional benefit of the SDN-based architecture compared to the default stack with decentralized packet management. The test purpose of the penetration test suite was to prove whether the firewall can be bypassed (pass) or whether the packets are blocked (fail). 38 tests failed (were successfully blocked) with the standard Linux stack and also with the Linux-based SDN-enabled switch. Among the tests that failed in both approaches were also those with overlapping fragment headers. The structure of the test suite is interesting in itself. Approximately half of the circumvention test cases

TABLE 5: Static rules against firewall bypass.

Rule	eth_ Type	ipv6_ exthdr	ip_ Proto	icmpv6_ Type	Output
Fragment	0x8DD	44			Controller
hop_by_hop	0x8DD	0			Controller
Routing	0x8DD	43			Controller
Destination	0x8DD	60			Controller
Mobility	0x8DD	135			Controller
icmpv6_redirect	0x8DD		58	137	Controller

started with a single extension header type and increased the number of types up to three. As expected, all standard test cases with *hop-by-hop, destination options*, and *source routing options* passed the Linux stack (i.e., they were forwarded without complaints) and failed with the controller prototype (i.e., they were successfully blocked). However, there were test cases with multiple destination option headers in a packet. They passed the firewall policy of the controller for unknown reasons. Three more test cases passed through the firewall because they were not covered by a policy and were also not efficient to implement: ICMPv6 echo requests (ping6) with bad checksum, zero checksum, and with hop count 0. All other test cases failed in the controller. A direct neighbor solicitation test was successful on the standard stack but failed in the prototype because of the defenses against network scans.

To sum up, the default stack successfully blocked 38 attacks (67.86% of the malicious traffic), while the SDN-based approach blocked 53 attacks (94.64%). Thus, the SDN security architecture blocks about 39% more attack cases. The remaining 3 cases still require further research. One probable reason is that the SDN-enabled switch (Open vSwitch) does not correctly analyze nested IPv6 extension headers because these extensions should be blocked by our static rule set.

6. Conclusions

In this paper, we have considered security measures against attacks on switched LANs in the context of IPv4 and IPv6 networks which are often deployed to circumvent monitoring measures in domain networks. A significant similarity of these attacks is the spreading of the malicious code in the internal networks and the extraction of data from compromised subnets and hosts. As part of a potential mitigation strategy against these attacks, software-defined networking (SDN) has been proposed as a vehicle for centralizing information about all network activities in a central authority—the SDN controller—that manages all network connections and hence the associated data flows. The SDN technology allows us to provide networks with security services that perform basic tasks, such as address configuration, address resolution, and firewalling within the network, much more efficient than on scattered individual systems. The resulting secure networks are based on switched routing which uses auxiliary information from the address configuration services to enforce a strong binding between a packet and its origin as well as its target that disables these attacks. Our approach can also be integrated into existing policy-based security frameworks, such as OpenSec [27].

We are currently extending the approach to secure the data exchange between virtual machines that represent blind spots in network monitoring. Conventional firewall systems cannot protect virtual machines because communication between virtual machines runs only within the virtualization server/host. The network interfaces to wireless local area networks (WLAN) represent an additional blind spot for network monitoring [28]. Often, the WLAN access points are not part of the monitoring and security infrastructure but represent only the last hop to the devices. As a consequence, sensitive information of the communication between access point and device gets lost. A software-defined networking approach, in which the access point passes authentication and monitoring information to the SDN-based security services to analyze incoming data streams, seems more reasonable [29].

Acknowledgments

This research was supported by the Bundesministerium für Bildung und Forschung (Grant 01BY1204A).

References

[1] B. Claise and B. Trammell, *Information Model for IP Flow Information Export (IPFIX)*, RFC 7012 (Proposed Standard), 2013, http://www.ietf.org/rfc/rfc7012.txt.

[2] R. Symantec, "Top-tier espionage tool enables stealthy surveillance," Technical report, August 2015, http://securityresponse.symantec.com/content/en/us/enterprise/media/security_response/whitepapers/regin-analysis.pdf.

[3] M. Casado, *Architectural Support for Security Management in Enterprise Networks*, Ph.D. thesis, Stanford, CA, USA, 2007.

[4] D. Kreutz, F. M. V. Ramos, P. E. Versssimo, C. E. Rothenberg, S. Azodolmolky, and S. Uhlig, "Software-defined networking: a comprehensive survey," *Proceedings of the IEEE*, vol. 103, no. 1, pp. 14–76, 2015.

[5] J. Xie, D. Guo, Z. Hu, T. Qu, and P. Lv, "Control plane of software defined networks: a survey," *Computer Communications*, vol. 67, pp. 1–10, 2015.

[6] B. A. A. Nunes, M. Mendonca, X. N. Nguyen, K. Obraczka, and T. Turletti, "A survey of software-defined networking: past, present, and future of programmable networks," *IEEE Communications Surveys Tutorials*, vol. 16, no. 3, pp. 1617–1634, 2014.

[7] S. Scott-Hayward, S. Natarajan, and S. Sezer, "A survey of security in software defined networks," *IEEE Communications Surveys and Tutorials*, vol. 18, no. 1, pp. 623–654, 2016.

[8] I. Alsmadi and D. Xu, "Security of software defined networks," *Computers and Security*, vol. 53, pp. 79–108, 2015.

[9] M. C. Dacier, H. König, R. Cwalinski, F. Kargl, and S. Dietrich, "Security challenges and opportunities of software-defined networking," *IEEE Security and Privacy*, vol. 15, no. 2, pp. 96–100, 2017.

[10] T. Kiravuo, M. Sarela, and J. Manner, "A survey of ethernet LAN security," *IEEE Communications Surveys Tutorials*, vol. 15, no. 3, pp. 1477–1491, 2013.

[11] N. Hubballi, S. Biswas, S. Roopa, R. Ratti, and S. Nandi, "LAN attack detection using discrete event systems," *ISA Transactions*, vol. 50, no. 1, pp. 119–130, 2011.

[12] H. Mukhtar, K. Salah, and Y. Iraqi, "Mitigation of DHCP starvation attack," *Computers and Electrical Engineering Special Issue on Recent Advances in Security and Privacy in Distributed Communications and Image processing*, vol. 38, no. 5, pp. 1115–1128, 2012.

[13] R. Vida and L. Costa, *Multicast Listener Discovery Version 2 (MLDv2) for IPv6*, RFC 3810 (Proposed Standard), updated by RFC 4604, 2004, http://www.ietf.org/rfc/rfc3810.txt.

[14] T. Chown and S. Venaas, *Rogue IPv6 Router Advertisement Problem Statement*, RFC 6104 (Informational), 2011, http://www.ietf.org/rfc/rfc6104.txt.

[15] S. Ioannidis, A. D. Keromytis, S. M. Bellovin, and J. M. Smith, "Implementing a distributed firewall," in *Proceedings of 7th ACM Conference on Computer and Communications Security CCS 2000*, pp. 190–199, Athens, Greece, November 2000.

[16] M. Casado, T. Garfinkel, A. Akella et al., "A protection architecture for enterprise networks," in *Proceedings of 15th USENIX Security Symposium*, Vancouver, BC, Canada, July-August 2006, https://www.usenix.org/conference/15th-uscnix-security-symposium/sane-protection-architecture-enterprise-networks.

[17] M. Casado, M. J. Freedman, J. Pettit, J. Luo, N. McKeown, and S. Shenker, "Ethane: taking control of the enterprise," in *Proceedings of ACM SIGCOMM Conference on Applications, Technologies, Architectures, and Protocols for Computer Communications*, pp. 1–12, Kyoto, Japan, August 2007.

[18] S. A. Mehdi, J. Khalid, and S. A. Khayam, "Revisiting traffic anomaly detection using software defined networking," in *Proceedings of Recent Advances in Intrusion Detection-14th International Symposium*, pp. 161–180, RAID 2011, Menlo Park, CA, USA, September 2011.

[19] Y. Zhang, "An adaptive flow counting method for anomaly detection in SDN," in *Proceedings of Conference on emerging Networking Experiments and Technologies*, pp. 25–30, CoNEXT'13, Sydney, Australia, June 2013.

[20] S. Shin, P. A. Porras, V. Yegneswaran, M. W. Fong, G. Gu, and M. Tyson, "FRESCO: modular composable security services for software-defined networks," in *Proceedings of 20th Annual Network and Distributed System Security Symposium*, NDSS 2013, San Diego, CA, USA, February 2013.

[21] A. Zaalouk, R. Khondoker, R. Marx, and K. M. Bayarou, "OrchSec: an orchestrator-based architecture for enhancing network-security using Network Monitoring and SDN Control functions," in *Proceedings of 2014 IEEE Network Operations and Management Symposium*, pp. 1–9, NOMS 2014, Krakow, Poland, May 2014.

[22] N. McKeown, T. Anderson, H. Balakrishnan et al., "OpenFlow: enabling innovation in campus networks," *Computer Communication Review*, vol. 38, no. 2, pp. 69–74, 2008.

[23] B. Aboba, L. Blunk, J. Vollbrecht, J. Carlson, and

H. Levkowetz, *Extensible Authentication Protocol (eap)*, RFC 3748, Proposed Standard, 2004, http://www.ietf.org/rfc/rfc3748.txt.

[24] K. Zeilenga, *Lightweight Directory Access Protocol (ldap): Technical Specification Road Map*, RFC 4510 Proposed Standard, 2006, http://www.ietf.org/rfc/rfc4510.txt.

[25] R. Hinden and S. Deering, "IP version 6 addressing architecture," RFC 4291 draft standard, updated by RFCs 5952, 6052, 7136, 7346, 7371, 2006, http://www.ietf.org/rfc/rfc4291.txt.

[26] B. Lantz, B. Heller, and N. McKeown, "A network in a laptop: rapid prototyping for software-defined networks," in *Proceedings of 9th ACM Workshop on Hot Topics in Networks*, p. 19, HotNets 2010, Monterey, CA, USA, October 2010.

[27] A. Lara and B. Ramamurthy, "Opensec: policy-based security using software-defined networking," *IEEE Transactions on Network and Service Management*, vol. 13, no. 1, pp. 30–42, 2016.

[28] H.-J. Liao, C.-H. R. Lin, Y.-C. Lin, and K.-Y. Tung, "Intrusion detection system: a comprehensive review," *Journal of Network and Computer Applications*, vol. 36, no. 1, pp. 16–24, 2013.

[29] R. Cwalinski and H. König, "RADIator—an approach for controllable wireless networks," in *Proceedings of IEEE NetSoft Conference and Workshops, NetSoft 2016*, pp. 260–268, Seoul, South Korea, June 2016.

[30] R. Rietz, "Optimization of network intrusion detection processes," Doctoral thesis, Faculty of Mathematics, Computer Science, Physics, Electrical Engineering and Information Technology of the Brandenburg University of Technology, 2018.

14

Joint Channel Assignment and Routing in Multiradio Multichannel Wireless Mesh Networks: Design Considerations and Approaches

Omar M. Zakaria,[1,2] **Aisha-Hassan A. Hashim,**[1] **Wan H. Hassan,**[2] **Othman O. Khalifa,**[1] **M. Azram,**[1] **Lalitha B. Jivanadham,**[2] **Mistura L. Sanni,**[1] **and Mahdi Zareei**[2]

[1]*Department of Electrical and Computer Engineering, International Islamic University Malaysia, 50728 Kuala Lumpur, Malaysia*
[2]*Malaysia-Japan International Institute of Technology (MJIIT), Department of Electronic Systems Engineering,
  Universiti Teknologi Malaysia, 54100 Kuala Lumpur, Jalan Semarak, Malaysia*

Correspondence should be addressed to Omar M. Zakaria; dr.omar.zakaria@ieee.org

Academic Editor: Sabrina Gaito

Multiradio wireless mesh network is a promising architecture that improves the network capacity by exploiting multiple radio channels concurrently. Channel assignment and routing are underlying challenges in multiradio architectures since both determine the traffic distribution over links and channels. The interdependency between channel assignments and routing promotes toward the joint solutions for efficient configurations. This paper presents an in-depth review of the joint approaches of channel assignment and routing in multiradio wireless mesh networks. First, the key design issues, modeling, and approaches are identified and discussed. Second, existing algorithms for joint channel assignment and routing are presented and classified based on the channel assignment types. Furthermore, the set of reconfiguration algorithms to adapt the network traffic dynamics is also discussed. Finally, the paper presents some multiradio practical implementations and test-beds and points out the future research directions.

1. Introduction

Wireless Mesh Network (WMN) is a multihop wireless network characterized by low deployment cost that consists of mesh routers and Internet gateways. It is a special ad hoc network with static topologies where unlike the general ad hoc networks mesh routers have no energy limitations. WMN deployments are found in surveillance [1, 2], building automation, remote healthcare delivery [3, 4], and smart grids [5–7]. Mesh routers are the fundamental part of wireless mesh network, which gives routing support for network traffic of mesh clients. Mesh routers can also be equipped with multiple radios to increase the network capacity and to reduce the interference level over the network. The availability and flexibility of IEEE 802.11 components make it a good candidate for wireless mesh deployment. 802.11-based networks provide a cheap and flexible wireless access capability and are easy to deploy in campuses, airports, and hospitals.

Backhaul links in 802.11-based WMN can be operated on one of the several nonoverlapping channels (i.e., 12 channels for 802.11a and 3 channels for 802.11b). Furthermore, the cost-effectiveness of network interface cards made it possible to use multiple radios and channels to increase the throughput. Multiple radio configurations allow the utilization of the available multiple orthogonal channels (partially overlapped channel also can be considered as in [8, 9]). The network architecture of multiradio wireless mesh networks (MR-WMNs) is illustrated in Figure 1. Multiradio mesh routers are connected through wireless backhaul links over multiple orthogonal channels. Mesh clients are connected to mesh routers through different set of links referred to as network access links. Mesh clients are user entities with no routing functionality. In the rest of this paper, the term link will refer to backhaul link. The gateway is a mesh router that connects the mesh components with external networks.

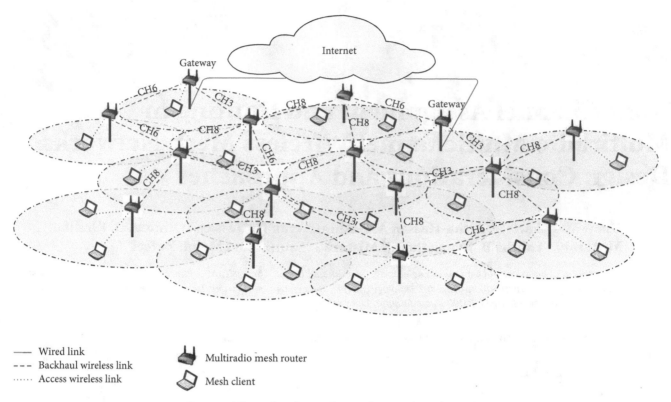

— Wired link
--- Backhaul wireless link
...... Access wireless link

Multiradio mesh router

Mesh client

FIGURE 1: The multiradio wireless mesh networks architecture.

Recently, MR-WMN has attracted numerous numbers of research efforts to utilize the advantages that this network is offering. Several proposed approaches on channel assignment (CA) algorithms, multichannel MAC protocols, multichannel routing metrics, links scheduling (LS), multichannel multicast protocols, power and topology control, and network planning exist in the literature. However, the designs that are considering combinations of these issues have shown more efficient performance such as joint routing and link scheduling [10], joint CA and power control [11], joint QoS multicast routing and CA [12], joint gateway selection, transmission slot assignment, routing and power control [13], joint CA, power control and routing [14], joint CA, power control and rate assignment [15], joint routing and topology control with directional antennas [16], and partially overlapped CA [8, 9].

CA algorithms aim to assign channels to the radio interfaces and links with the objective of minimizing the overall contention and interference over the wireless links. CA can either be solved as a separated problem as in [17, 18] or jointly solved with routing as in [19, 20]. Furthermore, it can be developed as centralized solutions [19, 20] and distributed solutions [21, 22]. The availability of the entire network view makes centralized solution more effective than distributed solutions, which only relayed on local information. Typically, CA algorithms must have knowledge on network load in order to assign channels to links. However, some other algorithms do not require any traffic information, as in [23], where the interference is minimized by conserving a k-connected topology.

Joint design approaches in WMNs are surveyed in many works in the literature such as [24–27]. However, none of the works in the literature have comprehensively investigated the Centralized Joint Channel Assignment and Routing (C-JCAR) approaches. This motivates us to undertake an in-depth review of different C-JCAR proposals in the literature. Figure 2 shows the research direction of this paper. The rest of the paper is organized as follows. Section 2 discusses key design issues, models, and approaches for C-JCAR algorithms. Section 3 presents reviewed works under two subsections of C-JCAR approaches and reconfiguration CA/routing algorithms. Section 4 investigates some practical implantations and test-beds for MR-WMNs. Finally, Section 5 describes the future research directions and concludes the paper.

2. Design Issues, Modeling, and Approaches for C-JCAR

This section identifies the key design issues from link and network layers for C-JCAR approaches to address and clarifies interference model and network model to be used in problem formulation and algorithms. It also presents the mathematical formulation of the problem including optimization objectives, constraints, and fairness. Besides, this section also gives the general classifications to C-JCAR algorithms.

2.1. Key Design Issues

2.1.1. Channel Assignment Schemes. Based on the underling hardware, CA can be implemented in one of three schemes.

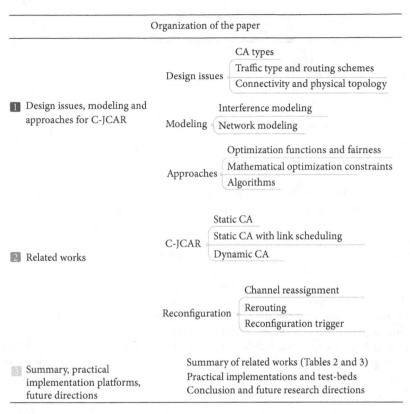

FIGURE 2: Organization of the paper.

If the implemented technology does not support any link-level synchronization then only Static CA (SCA) can be implemented and channels are assigned to radio interfaces for a long term. However, if synchronous coordination is supported at link layer then SCA can be implemented with link scheduling (LS) and the wireless link can be active on specific time slots only; let us refer to this case by SCA-LS. Dynamic CA (DCA) is the general case where radio interfaces are capable of switching their channel in a small time compared with the time slots. Thus, wireless links can operate on different channels at different time slots. To illustrate the difference between the three CA schemes, Figure 3 shows the possible channel allocation on a wireless link. As it is shown in Figure 3, for SCA links are allowed to be active on one channel only at all times. In SCA-LS links are allowed to be active on one channel only and on specific time slots. However, if DCA is adopted links can operate on different channels on different time slots.

2.1.2. Traffic and Routing Issues. As in load-aware algorithms, the aggregated traffic loads over mesh routers are required as an input. This traffic information can either be measured/estimated online as in [28, 29] or assumed based on a historical profile [19]. WMNs can be used to deliver two types of traffic, the Internet traffic and peer-to-peer traffic. Internet traffic is the traffic received or directed to the Internet [20, 30–33]. Either outbound traffic (to the gateway) [20, 30] or inbound traffic (from the gateway) [31] can be considered in finding the network configuration. In [28], specific software

such as IPFIX system [34] is used at the gateway to collect the traffic information. The upper and lower bound of the traffic demand are assumed to be available for each mesh router [33]. A traffic profiler at each mesh router collects the traffic information and sends it to a centralized entity [29, 35] where peer-to-peer traffic is assumed. References [36, 37] assume the traffic load is elastic and only information on source-destination communication pairs are considered.

Routing algorithms in wireless ad hoc networks are categorized as proactive (table-driven), reactive (on-demands), and hybrid algorithms. In proactive algorithms such as [38–40], routing table is built individually through exchanging routing information with other nodes in the network. In reactive algorithms such as [41–43], no routing tables are maintained and instead each node triggers the route discovery process whenever it has traffic to deliver to a destination. Hybrid algorithms [44–47] implement the concepts of proactive and reactive routing protocols. Ad hoc routing protocols are extended to be used in WMNs. The routing decisions in these protocols are decentralized process and each node is responsible to make its routing decision. On the other hand, in centralized routing paradigm routing decision is performed at a centralized entity and nodes build their routing/forwarding table based on the updates received from a centralized entity. In WMNs, if traffic is identified per mesh client then mesh routers must maintain a forwarding entry for each mesh client and layer-2 addresses are used to identify each flow. This is similar to 802.11s standard with Hybrid Wireless Mesh Protocol (HWMP) where path

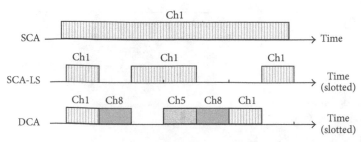

FIGURE 3: CA types on a wireless link.

selection is based on layer two addressing. However, path selection is usually associated with scalability issues. On the other hand, if the traffic is identified per mesh router and flow is defined as aggregated traffic that originated from one mesh router to another mesh router, then layer-3 routing is used. In most cases, centralized routing approaches follow the latter definition of flow. A TCP-level flow path selection is assumed in [28]. However, this introduces more overheads to the routing layer. Centralized routing proposals built routing tables based on source-destination manner, where both source and destination addresses are required in the routing decision. With centralized routing in MR-WMN, modification is required on the routing table structure and the Address Resolution Protocol (ARP). However, a complicated routing scheme is required for dynamic CA especially if no static binding is applied between radio interfaces and neighbors. For better exploitation of the topology structure of MR-WMN, multipath routing is assumed in most related works to achieve load balancing. However, the out-of-order problem and the configuration complexity are the main drawbacks of multipath scheme.

2.1.3. Topology and Connectivity Issues. Several mechanisms have been used in the literature to control the topology formations in WMNs. This includes power control [48–50], the use of directional antennas [16, 51], and routing [23, 52–54]. Furthermore, in multiradio architecture CA is another factor that determines the physically connected topology. An overview of the topology control mechanisms and issues in MR-WMNs is presented in [55]. In centralized algorithms, the full network topology is assumed to be available at the centralized entity. Topology can be obtained using existing routing protocol such as OLSR [28] or the network management protocol as in [32]. In order to define different possible types of topology formation, let us define logical links as the set of potential links that directly connect mesh routers if proper channels are assigned to their radios, and let us define the physical links as the actual wireless links with a designated channels assigned to it. Since inappropriate mapping can lead to disjoint topology, mapping the logical link onto physical link must be carefully determined. Furthermore, assigning channels to all logical links affects the channel diversity on the network. This is due to node-radio constraint (elaborated more in next subsections), more specifically with a small number of radio interfaces. On the other hand, physical links need to be mapped onto the active links, where active links are the set of links carrying traffic and are determined by

routing algorithm. Figure 4 shows two types of physical and logical links mapping. In Figure 4(a), channels are assigned to each logical link as in [19, 29, 37]. In Figure 4(b) channels are assigned to a number of logical links only as in [20, 36, 56, 57]. However, some works allow multiple physical links to exist between adjacent mesh routers [30, 56] which need to be considered in the routing procedure. Meanwhile, connectivity must also be addressed in CA algorithms to prevent isolating parts of mesh routers from receiving the control messages and the configuration updates from the centralized controller. Connectivity is achieved in [19, 29, 37] by assigning a channel to each virtual link or by dedicating a radio on a common channel at each mesh router [58].

2.2. Interference and Network Modeling

2.2.1. Interference Modeling. Interference plays an important role in wireless networks and has a significant impact on the network performance. MR-WMNs are proposed to reduce the contention on the communication channel and to distribute the transmission over several channels. CA algorithms tend to exploit the channel diversity to reduce the interference levels in the network. Several interference models are proposed in the literature to model the interface in the wireless networks. Three different interference models are presented in this section, namely, the interference-range model, the protocol model of interference, and the physical model of interference. In order to explore these interference models let us assume that all radios in the network have fixed transmission power with omnidirectional antennas and the signal propagation model is based only on frequency and distance. Each radio will have a fixed transmission-range (R_T) and two radios can form a wireless link if they are within the transmission-range of each other; see Figure 5(a). The receiver radio at each wireless link can correctly receive and decode the transmission in the absence of any interfering radio.

The interference-range model is the simplest model where each radio has its interference range (R_I) where $R_I = \Delta \cdot R_T$: $\Delta > 1$ (default $\Delta = 2$). A directional transmission on a wireless link is successfully completed if the receiving radio is not within the interference range of another active transmitting radio, as shown in Figure 5(b). Thus, in order to successfully receive the transmitted signal from radio (v) to radio (x) on wireless link (v, x), (1) must be true:

$$|j - x| \geq R_I \quad \forall j \in \text{Radio Interfaces} / \{v\}$$
$$|v - x| \leq R_T. \tag{1}$$

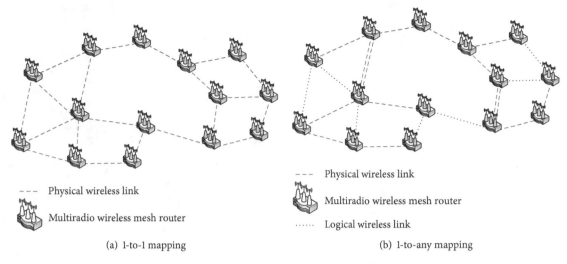

(a) 1-to-1 mapping

(b) 1-to-any mapping

FIGURE 4: Topology formation, logical-to-physical links mapping.

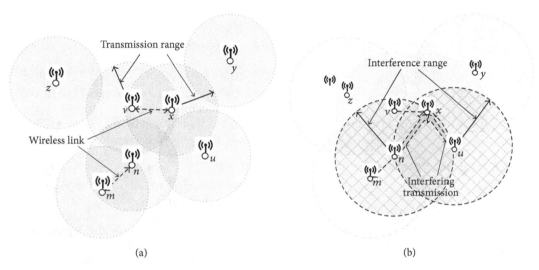

(a)

(b)

FIGURE 5: (a) Transmission-range and (b) interference-range model.

On the other hand, interference in protocol model does not assume a fixed interference range. Instead, the interference is determined based on the Euclidean distance between interference radios, transmitting radio, and receiver radio. Thus, a directional transmission on a wireless link can be successfully completed if the distance between the interfering radio and the receiving radio is larger than the link's length. Thus, in order to successfully receive a signal transmitted from radio v to radio x on wireless link (v, x) in protocol model (see Figure 6(a)), (2) must be true:

$$|j - x| \geq \Delta \cdot |v - x|$$

$$\forall j \in \text{Radio Interfaces}/ \{v\}, \ \Delta > 1 \quad (2)$$

$$|v - x| \leq R_T.$$

In comparison with the previous two models, the physical model is the most realistic model, where concurrent transmissions from multiple interfering radios are accounted in this model. In order to successfully receive the transmitted signal the SINR (signal-to-interference-and-noise ratio) at the receiving radio must be greater than a predefined threshold. Thus, v radio can successfully receive the transmitted signal from radio x on wireless link (v, x) (see Figure 6(b)), if (3) is true:

$$\frac{P_v}{N + \sum_{j \in \text{radios}/\{v\}} P_j} \geq \beta_{vx}, \quad (3)$$

where N is the thermal noise power in the frequency channel, β_{vx} is an SINR-threshold which is determined based on the considered modulation and coding schemes, and P_v is the received power from v at x. SINR-threshold is chosen in a way that the resulting BER is higher than acceptable BER by the modulating technique. SINR-threshold is based on the experimental observation and can be mapped onto a bit error probability [59]. The physical model of interference is extended in [60] to include the shadowing effect of the RF signals. The work of [60] studied the minimum required

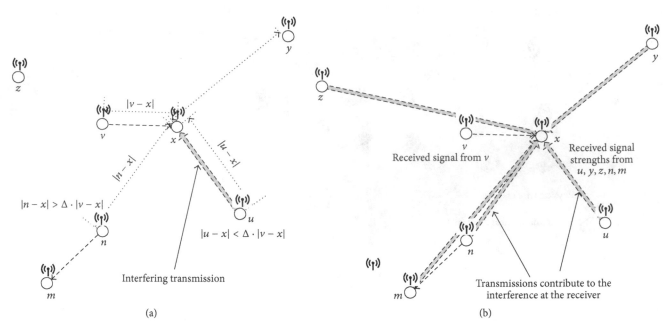

(a)   (b)

FIGURE 6: Interference based on (a) protocol model and (b) physical model.

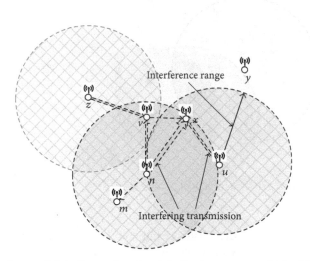

FIGURE 7: Interference based on interference-range model for 802.11.

number of channels to achieve interference-free channel assignments under realistic interference model called SINR model with shadow.

In the conventional 802.11 MAC protocol with Carrier Sense Multiple Access-Collision Avoidance (CSMA/CA), wireless links are bidirectional since the sender still needs to receive acknowledgement messages from the receiver (if RTS-CTS is enabled, it also receives CTS message). Therefore, all transmissions causes that interfere with the sender or the receiver must be avoided for successful transmission. In this model, sending and receiving nodes on a link are potential source of interference to another link transmission. Figure 7 shows the set interfering radios to wireless link (v, x) based on the 802.11 bidirectional model.

2.2.2. Network Modeling. Network in MR-WMN architecture can be modeled using either a router-to-router model [20, 56, 57] or a radio-to-radio model [31, 36, 61]. In router-to-router model, the network is modeled as a directed graph $G(V, E)$, where V represents the set of mesh routers in the networks and E is the set of directed links. A directional link exists between two mesh routers if direct communication is possible between them. In radio-to-radio model, vertices represent the radio interfaces. A link exists between two vertices, if radios can communicate directly and are placed in two adjacent mesh routers. Radio-to-radio model is usually used if the radio interfaces are heterogeneous and support different technologies or if different radios operate on different subsets of channels. Figure 8 illustrates the difference between radio-to-radio and router-to-router model for single channel. For multichannel scenarios, each link between two radios must be replicated into the number of available orthogonal channels supported by the mesh router or radio pairs [31].

2.3. Problem Formulation and Approaches for C-JCAR

2.3.1. Optimization Objective Functions and Fairness. The C-JCAR algorithms have been designed in the literature for different optimization objectives and metrics; below is the set of optimization objective functions and metrics:

   (i) Maximize aggregated network throughput [29, 31, 33, 36, 62].

   (ii) Maximize achievable scaling factor (λ) [20, 30, 31, 56, 61].

   (iii) Maximize the aggregated utility of flows [37].

   (iv) Minimize the maximum interference on all channels [20, 63].

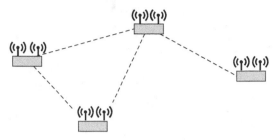

Router-to-router model

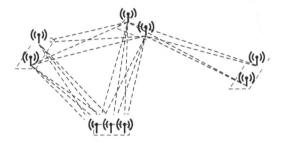

Radio-to-radio model

---   Directional link

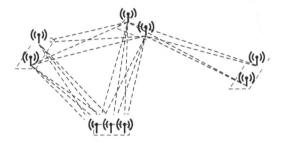 Multiradio wireless mesh router

((ᵰ))   Radio interface

FIGURE 8: Router-to-router versus radio-to-radio models.

(v) Maximize the minimum unutilized capacity on links [57].

(vi) Maximize the cross-section good-put [19].

(vii) Minimize the path length and link contention [32, 64].

Fairness is also another objective to be considered. Fairness ensures a fair resource allocation among network users or traffic. Several fairness constraints are introduced for C-JCAR. To elaborate the fairness constraints let us assume FL is the set of flows in the network and let $\omega_f, \emptyset_f$ be the demanded load and the actual achieved load of flow $f \in$ FL; the four types of fairness constraints in the literature are as follows.

(i) Min-λ Fairness. This constraint is to ensure that each flow achieves at least λ of its demands. The Min-λ fairness constraint is presented in

$$\emptyset_f \geq \lambda * \omega_f \quad \forall f \in \text{FL}. \tag{4}$$

(ii) Max-to-Min Fairness. This constraint is to constrain the deference between the highest and the lowest achieved loads. Then, for a given μ the Max-to-Min fairness constraint is given in

$$\mu \geq \frac{\emptyset_{\max}}{\emptyset_{\min}}, \tag{5}$$

where $\emptyset_{\min}$ is the lowest and $\emptyset_{\max}$ is the highest load.

(iii) Proportional Fairness. This fairness can be used as an optimization objective function and it is given as in

$$\text{maximize} \quad \sum_{f \in \text{FL}} \log\left(\emptyset_f\right). \tag{6}$$

(iv) Bounded Fairness. This fairness configuration bounds each flow with specific upper and lower bound.

Min-λ fairness is considered in [20, 29–31, 56, 61] where flows may have different demands. Other fairness constraints such as Max-to-Min fairness, proportional fairness, and bounded fairness are used in [37, 62] and [33], respectively.

2.3.2. Mathematical Formulation Constraints. The general set of constraints to be considered in the mathematical formulation of the C-JCAR problem can be divided into six sets as follows.

(1) Flow Routing Conservation Constraints. These constraints ensure that for each traffic flow f from source to destination the net amount of traffic out of each mesh router is equal to the flow rate (f_r) if the mesh router is the source of the traffic and $(-f_r)$ if it is the destination and otherwise 0. More constraints can be added to the problem to determine the routing scheme (for multipath or single-path).

(2) Radio Constraints. These constraints ensure that the number of channels assigned to each incident link on a mesh router (at any given time slot for dynamic CA) does not exceed the number of radio interfaces at that node. This integer-value constraint can be relaxed to linear constraints to ensure that the total load on the links on each node is not higher than the number of radios on that node multiplied by the channel capacity.

(3) Interference Constraints (or Capacity Constraints/Schedule-Ability Constraints). These constraints ensure that the amount of data flows on interfered links does not exceed a specific value. This is to constraint the maximum contention level over the collision domains if contention-based MAC is considered or to ensure a feasible interference-free link scheduling if contention-free MAC is used.

(4) Link Capacity Constraints. These constraints ensure that the traffic load on a wireless link is not exceeding the link capacity. This constraint is implicitly considered under the interference constraints if only sufficient condition for schedule-ability is considered.

(5) Fairness Constraints. These constraints ensure fairness in allocating resources to different traffic flow demands.

Apart from the above-mentioned constrained, other constraints on the topology can also be introduced. The remaining part of this section will be discussed with regard to the radio and interference constraints. The Notations depicts a set of notations for mathematical formulation employed in the derivation.

If CA and interference-free scheduling is computed for all links in time slotted system, the allocated capacity of a wireless link l can be obtained by

$$\text{Link capacity } (l) = \frac{t_l}{T} \cdot C_l, \tag{7}$$

where t_l is number of time slots when l is active, T is the total number of time slots, and C_l is the channel capacity at link l. However, in contention-based networks and without supported time slotting, it is not possible to allocate a dedicated bandwidth (capacity) to a link. Instead, virtual link capacity may be estimated for each active link. By considering that the link capacity is equal for all links and all links can utilize the maximum channel capacity (C_O) with the absence of interference transmission, the virtual capacity for each link l can be calculated as

$$\text{VC} (l) = \frac{g (l)}{\sum_{l' \in \{I(l) \cup l\}} g (l')} \cdot C_O : l \in L. \tag{8}$$

In [57] the virtual capacity (effective capacity) of a link is defined as follows:

$$\text{VC} (l) + \sum_{l' \in I(l)} \text{VC} (l') = C_O \quad \forall l' \in L. \tag{9}$$

The link capacity constraints in [19, 57] are given as follows:

$$\frac{g (l)}{\text{VC} (l)} \leq 1 \quad \forall l \in L. \tag{10}$$

To find a virtual link capacity, independent set of edges is considered in [37]; however, this approach is not applicable in multiradio multichannel since radio constraints are not considered in the channel allocation for the independent sets.

Among the interference models mentioned in the previous section, the protocol and interference-range models are binary pairwise models, where the interference between any two links either exists or does not exist. The interference constraints with necessary condition for interference-free scheduling can be presented as

$$\sum_{l' \in \{I(l) \cup l\}} \frac{g (l')}{C_{l'}} \leq \theta \quad \forall l \in L, \tag{11}$$

where θ is the interference constant that depends only on the interference model. For instance, θ in the interference-range model is a function of the ratio between the transmission and interference range (R_T / R_I), where it represents the maximum number of links interfering with a specific link but not a pairwise interfere. Interference constraints can also be considered for sufficient condition only, as follows:

$$\sum_{l' \in \{I(l) \cup l\}} \frac{g (l')}{C_{l'}} \leq 1 \quad \forall l \in L. \tag{12}$$

Thus, for any solution that satisfies the sufficient condition, there is a feasible link scheduling (proof is stated in [20]). The interference constraint with sufficient condition is

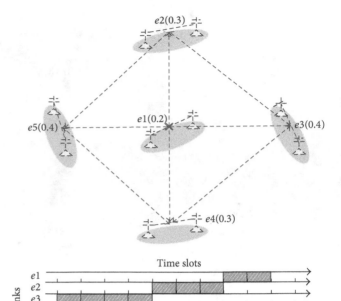

Time slots

FIGURE 9: Example of links scheduling (sufficient condition is not satisfied).

used in [30, 33, 36, 56, 57, 62]. Figure 9 demonstrates that it is possible to have feasible interference-free links scheduling even though only necessary conditions are satisfied. Let us assume that the channel capacity is equal to 1 and the number that associated with each link represents the amount of traffic load carried on each link.

From Figure 9, the link flows do not satisfy the sufficient condition of link scheduling (larger than 1). However, a feasible scheduling exists as obtained in Figure 9. It can be concluded from the previous example that solutions based sufficient conditions will have an optimality gap. Using the notation (see Notations), interference and radio constraints with different CA schemes are presented in Table 1.

Another way to model the interference on wireless mesh network is by using empirical interference measurement. This can be done by taking the advantage of the static nature of WMN, where the required information can be easily measured and recorded beforehand. Empirical interference measurement is presented in [37]. The packet error rate (PER) of a wireless link at a receiver is empirically determined when another link is active. Based on this measurement, the objective of the CA algorithm is to minimize the summation of the PER of one link when another link is actively multiplied with the load on each link. The objective function in [37] is as follows:

$$\text{Minimize} \quad \sum_{l_1} \sum_{l_2 \in I(l_1)} g (l_1) * g (l_2) * \text{PER} (l_1 \mid l_2), \tag{13}$$

TABLE 1: Mathematical formulation (interference & radio constraints).

Operating mode	Network model	Interference (capacity) constraints	Node-radio constraints
SCA	Router-to-router model general	LP: Necessary condition $$\sum_{l' \in \{I(l) \cup l\}} \frac{g(l')}{C_{l'}} \le \theta, \quad \forall l \in L$$ Sufficient condition $$\sum_{l' \in I(l)} \frac{g(l')}{C_{l'}} \le 1, \quad \forall l \in L$$	IP: $$\sum_{i \in C} h_m^i \le K(u), \quad \forall u \in N$$ LP: $$\sum_{\substack{l: \\ h(l)=m \\ \text{or } t(l)=m}} \frac{g(l)}{C_l} \le K(u), \quad \forall u \in N$$
	Router-to-router model [37]	LP: Link virtual capacity (effective capacity) $$\sum_{l' \in \{I(l) \cup l\}} VC(l') \le C_l, \quad \forall l \in L \,\&\, g(l) > 0$$ $$\frac{g(l)}{VC(l)} \le 1, \quad \forall l \in L$$	
DCA/SCA-LS	Router-to-router model general	IP: Necessary & sufficient condition $y^t(l) + y^t(l') \le 1, \quad \forall l \in L \,\&\, l' \in I(l)$ Sufficient condition $$\sum_{l' \in \{I(l) \cup l\}} y^t(l') \le 1, \quad \forall l \in L, t \in T$$ Or LP: relaxation Necessary condition $$\sum_{l' \in \{I(l) \cup l\}} \frac{g(l')}{C_{l'}} \le \theta, \quad \forall l \in L$$ Sufficient condition $$\sum_{l' \in I(l)} \frac{g(l')}{C_{l'}} \le 1, \quad \forall l \in L$$	IP: $$\sum_{\substack{l \in L: \\ t(l)=u \\ \text{or } h(l)=u}} y^t(l) \le K(u), \quad \forall u \in N$$ LP: $$\sum_{\substack{l \in L: \\ t(l)=u \\ \text{or } h(l)=u}} \frac{g(l)}{C_l} \le K(u), \quad \forall u \in N$$
	Router-to-router model [56]	IP: Necessary & sufficient condition If n, m interfere with each other $$\sum_{\substack{l' \in \\ \{E(n) \cup E(m)\}}} y^t(l') \le 1, \quad \forall n, m \in N; t \in T$$ LP: Sufficient condition $$\sum_{l' \in I(l)} \frac{g(l')}{C_{l'}} \le 1, \quad \forall l \in L$$	
	Radio-to-radio model [31]	IP: Necessary & sufficient condition $y^t(\bar{l}) + y^t(\bar{l}') \le 1, \quad \forall \bar{l}' \in I(\bar{l})$ LP: Sufficient condition $$\sum_{\bar{l}' \in I(\bar{l})} \frac{g(\bar{l}')}{C_{\bar{l}'}} \le 1, \quad \forall \bar{l} \in \tilde{L}$$	IP: $$\sum_{\substack{\bar{l} \in L: \\ t(\bar{l})=u \\ \text{or } h(\bar{l})=u}} y^t(\bar{l}) \le K(u), \quad \forall u \in N$$ LP: $$\sum_{\substack{\bar{l} \in \tilde{L}: \\ t(\bar{l})=r \\ \text{or } h(\bar{l})=r}} \frac{g(\bar{l})}{C_{\bar{l}}} \le 1, \quad \forall r \in R$$
	Radio-to-radio model [36]	LP: Sufficient condition (both interference and radio constraints are considered) $$\sum_{\bar{l}' \in \{IR(\bar{l}) \cup \bar{l}\}} \frac{g(\bar{l}')}{C_{\bar{l}'}} \le 1, \quad \forall \bar{l} \in \tilde{L}$$	
	Radio-to-radio model [61]	Each critical maximum independent set (MIS) is a set of links which satisfy interference and radio constraints and only one critical independent set is allowed to be active at any time slot. Therefore, interference and radio constraints are implicitly considered in the LP formulation	

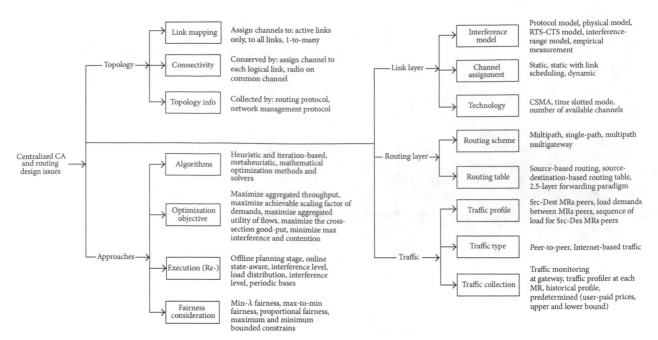

FIGURE 10: C-JCAR: key design issues and approaches.

where $\text{PER}(l_1 \mid l_2)$ is the PER at receiver node of link l_1 when l_2 is active.

To present the interference constraints using the physical model of interference two approaches can be used as presented in [62]. The first approach proposed in [65] is based on length classes that distributed links to different sets based on their lengths. For each length set (j), the area is divided into a set of square grid cells A_j. Let $A \in A_j$, $\Delta(A)$ be the set of links from j with their receiver lying inside A and operate on the same channel. The interference constraints are then presented as

$$\sum_{e \in \Delta(A)} x(l) \le \varphi \quad \forall j, A \in A_j, \tag{14}$$

where φ is a constant number and $x(l)$ is 1 if the link is active and 0 if otherwise.

The second model is weight-based model, where $W_{l_1}^{l_2}$ is the receiving power at l_2 receiver when both links are active on the same channel; thus,

$$W_{l_1}^{l_2} = \beta * \frac{P_v(r)}{P_v(u)}:$$
$$\forall l_1, l_2 \in L \ \& \ l_1 = (r, s, c), \ l_2 = (u, v, c), \tag{15}$$

where $P_x(y)$ is the transmission power received at x when y is transmitting the signal. The interference constraint can be presented as

$$g(l_1) + \sum_{l_2 \in L/\{l_1\} \& \text{Ch}(l_2) = \text{Ch}(l_1)} N\left(W_{l_1}^{l_2}\right) \cdot g(l_2) \le \vartheta(l_1)$$
$$\forall l_1 \in L, \tag{16}$$

where $N(x)$ is the normalized value of x and $\vartheta(l)$ is a constant based on the receiving power at the receiver when l is active.

2.3.3. *Approaches for C-JCAR.* The general formulation of the C-JCAR problem can be presented as Integer Linear Programming (ILP) problem. However, the CA problem which is part of C-JCAR problem is an NP-hard [19], where, with given link loads, finding the CA for a set of radio interfaces such that the link loads are schedulable is NP-hard problem. Moreover, interference-free link scheduling problem for a given link flows is also NP-hard [66]. Therefore, the problem is then transformed into a linear programming problem by relaxing some constraints [20, 31, 36, 56, 62]. The problem can then be considered as multichannel multicommodity flow problem with constraints on radios, interference, and link capacities. The optimal solutions are obtained for feasible problems only [33, 57] or with some fairness considerations [20, 56]. Due to the NP-hardness of the problem, standard methods and solvers are not able to solve the problem for real-life network sizes. A set of heuristic algorithms [19, 29, 37, 58] and metaheuristic algorithms [33, 57] are proposed in the literature [20, 31, 56]. Furthermore, approaches can also be classified based on their execution time into online [29, 37] and offline for planning stage [33]. Figure 10 shows the set of design consideration, classification, and methods in designing a load-aware C-JCAR proposal.

3. Related Works

In this section, related works for CA and routing are presented in two subsections. The related works in the literature to solve C-JCAR are presented in the first subsection. The works are classified based on their CA scheme (SCA, SCA-LS, and DCA) into three categories. This is followed by a comprehensive summary table (Table 2) that compares all approaches based on the design issues presented in previous part of the paper and highlights their assumptions and

TABLE 2: C-JCAR proposals summary.

Work	Link layer and channel assignment			Traffic & routing			Topology		Objective & fairness		Notes/limitations
	CA type:	Interference:	Technology:	Traffic type:	Traffic load:	Routing scheme:	Mapping: (1-to-x): x	Connectivity:	Objective:	Fairness:	
[19]	SCA	B-IRM	802.11	P2P	Yes	SP, MP	1	Yes	Maximize cross-section good-put	No	Optimality is not guaranteed. No accurate link capacity estimation in a heavy traffic load. Less channel diversity due to link mapping
[56]	DCA, SCA-LS	B-IRM	—	P2P	Yes	MP	0,1	Yes	Maximize λ (scaling factor)	Min-λ	Out-of-order problem and configuration complexity on routing. Switching overhead issues
[20]	SCA-LS	B-IRM	—	Internet	Yes	MP	Any	For MRs w/traffic	Maximize λ (scaling factor)	Min-λ	Radio constraints are not considered in the LP. Out-of-order problem due to multipath routing
[36]	DCA	B-IRM	—	P2P	src-des MRs	MP	Any	No	Maximize aggregated throughput	No	Out-of-order problem and configuration complexity on routing. Switching overhead issues. Optimality issue since only sufficient conditions are considered
[57]	SCA	B-IRM	802.11	P2P, Internet	Yes	SP	Any	For MRs w/traffic	Maximize min spare link capacity	Min-λ on link utilization	Using sufficient condition in MILP may not lead to global optimal solution. Single channel initial topology may lead to infeasible solution in heavy traffic load scenarios
[30]	SCA-LS	THM	—	Internet	Yes	MP, predefined	0,1	For MRs w/traffic	Maximize λ (scaling factor)	Min-λ	Considering only necessary condition may lead to infeasible solution. Out-of-order problem due to multipath routing
[70]	SCA	PHM (w/o accumulation)	802.11	Internet	No	MP (M-GW) L2.5 forwarding	≥1	Yes	Minimize max link utilization	No	Radio or interference constraints are not accounted in initial traffic load estimation. Assume same traffic demands in all mesh routers. Out-of-order problem due to multipath routing. Link rate assignment is considered
[31]	DCA	PRM, IRM	—	Internet	Yes	MP (M-GW)	Any	For MRs w/traffic	Maximize aggregated throughput	Min-λ	Out-of-order problem and configuration complexity on routing. Each radio can be operated on a subset of channels. Combination of multiple channels to single channel is possible
[32]	SCA	THM	—	Internet	Yes	SP	Any	Yes	Metric on hop count & interference	No	Solving subproblem with local constraints does not guarantee global optimality. Information on received power at a node when another node is transmitting is assumed available
[62]	DCA	IRM, PRM, PHM	—	P2P	No	SP, MP	Any	No	Maximize aggregated throughput	Max-to-Min	Equal load demand is assumed at mess routers. In single-path routing optimality is not guaranteed since mathematical formulation is for multipath
[61]	DCA	B-IRM	—	P2P	Yes	MP	Any	No	Maximize λ (scaling factor)	Min-λ	The quality of the solution is highly dependent on the performance of critical MIS finding algorithm
[33]	SCA	B-IRM	802.11	Internet	Lower & upper bound	MP (MGW)	Any	For MRs w/traffic	Maximize aggregated throughput	Bounded fairness	Developed for planning stage with different resources constraints. Not practical for large networks since fitness function involves solving entire network LP
[29]	SCA-LS	THM	—	P2P	Yes	MP (predefined)	1	Yes	Maximize aggr. achieved demands	No	Link loads used to the CA are estimated without considering radio or interference constraints. Less channel diversity due to link mapping

TABLE 2: Continued.

Work	Link layer and channel assignment			Traffic & routing			Topology		Objective & fairness		Notes/limitations
	CA type:	Interference:	Technology:	Traffic type:	Traffic load:	Routing scheme:	Mapping; (1-to-x): x	Connectivity:	Objective:	Fairness:	
[37]	SCA	EM		Internet	Number of active flows	MP (SP per follow)	1	Yes	Minimize contention (CA)	No	Link loads estimated without considering radio or interference constraints. Not clearly stated where and how to implement flow rate control
[63]	SCA	B-IRM	802.11	Internet	Yes, sequence of traffic	MP	Any	For MRs w/traffic	Minimize the maximum congestion (of worst case)	No	Number of facets increase exponentially in large-scale networks; this increases the number of constraints in LP problem; however, relaxing the convex hull to box ranges affects the efficiency

Note. SCA: static channel assignment, DCA: dynamic channel assignment, LS: link scheduling, IM: interference model, IRM: interference-range model, PRM: protocol model, PHM: physical model, B-: bidirectional, THM: two-hop model, EM: empirical measurement, P2P: peer-to-peer, SP: single-path, MP: multipath, MGW: multigateway, MR: mesh router, and LL: link layer.

limitations. The second subsection presents the set of CA or routing proposal, which deals with the reconfiguration problem (state-aware proposals). These works consider the current network configuration in finding the next one to reduce the overhead associated with the reconfiguration process. The works are divided into channel reassignment proposals, traffic rerouting proposals, and the reconfiguration policy. The latter one discusses some policies that determine when to trigger the reconfiguration process. This subsection followed by a summary table (Table 3) discusses state-aware works and highlights the approaches and the limitation of each work.

3.1. C-JCAR Proposals

3.1.1. C-JCAR Based on SCA.
In [19] a heuristic algorithm is developed to solve the C-JCAR problem. Given the traffic load information for set of source-destination pairs of nodes, the algorithm finds the routing paths for each flow and assigns channels to virtual links. Multipath and single-path routing schemes are considered. The optimization objective in this work is to maximize the cross-section good-put which is determined by matching the expected load on links with virtual capacity. The virtual capacity of a link is estimated based on the total load of the interfering links. The algorithm iterates over CA and routing steps to improve the overall cross-section good-put. The algorithm retains the network configuration and tries to improve the configuration by rerouting nonconforming flows. When the allocated virtual bandwidth meets the flow demands for each flow or when the maximum number of iterations is reached, the algorithm is terminated.

C-JCAR problem in 802.11-based wireless mesh network is formulated as Mixed-Integer Linear Programming (MILP) in [57]. In this work, the virtual capacities are assigned to logical links. The MILP minimizes the maximum contention on the channel assigned to each link by maximizing the minimum difference between the effective capacity and the traffic load on each link. This leads to the reduction in overall regions interference across the network. For small-scale network, MILP can be solved using commercial software such as CPLEX [67]. However, this is not feasible for large-scale networks. Therefore, metaheuristic algorithm based on Iterated Local Search (ILS) is proposed to solve the MILP problem. This algorithm commences with logical topology consisting of single channel assigned to all logical links. Then, MILP is solved iteratively using relaxed binary routing variable to simplify computation of the cost. In each iteration, a set of variables is considered as a constant, which takes their values from previous iteration till one link is selected randomly based on worse case congestion ranking. The next phase involves finding based on the maximum relaxed routing variable values. However, the algorithm in [57] starts the solution from a single channel assumption with limited network capacity and this can result in an infeasible solution if heavy traffic load is applied. Therefore, in [68] Tabu search with iterated local search algorithm is proposed to overcome the above-mentioned problem in [57]. The Tabu-search based algorithm selects the solution with

minimum number of conflicting links in each iteration and the remaining procedure in the algorithm is similar to [57]. Furthermore, [69] has extended the work of [57] to support directional antenna to reduce the interference in the topology.

The CA is jointly solved with link transmission rate assignment in [70]. A centralized greedy heuristic is designed to assign channels to given schedulable flow rates. The heuristics algorithm starts off with throughput optimization for a precomputed flow rate. The initial traffic rate on links is computed by assuming interference-free links with objective to maximum achievable aggregated throughput on the network and then solves the CA and rate assignment problems. To ensure network connectivity, a designated channel is assigned to a link between every node pair. Then, the links are stored in the queue and extracted one at a time in decreasing order of priority. Channels are assigned to links to minimize the maximum utilization. This involves first assigning the highest available transmission rate to links. However, decreasing the transmission rates on some links may help in improving the network performance. This is because reducing the interference on the network consequently reduces the size of the link's collision domain. This is since increasing the transmission rate on a link leads to a higher SINR-threshold at the receiver, as compared with greater difficulty in decoding of the received signals. This also results in more links interference with the transmission on this link and an increase with collision domain size. The flow rates obtained from precomputed flow are then scaled down to satisfy the sufficient condition of schedule ability, based on the computed CA. A layer-2.5 forwarding scheme is proposed in [70] to forward the Internet traffic to and from gateway nodes. The forwarding scheme does not maintain routing table. Instead, it assigns static flow rate to its links that forms the basis of forwarding criteria and updating of the link cost information locally. Additionally, each mesh router must know the hop vector to all its neighbors where a hop vector contains the minimum hop count to other mesh routers. The source mesh router inserts the maximum allowable hop count to each packet. The forwarding decision is determined based on the utilization of the links and the remaining allowable hop count to reach its destination.

In [32], the C-JCAR problem is decomposed into subproblems wherein the number of subproblems is equal to the number of mesh routers. The subproblem at each node is formulated as an ILP with local constraints and similar to objective function of [57]. The nodes are grouped into subsets defined as network crew that is visited based on some ranking function. For a given network crew and ranking function the nodes at each subset are visited one by one to sequentially solve the subproblem, while the channels and paths assigned in the visited nodes are considered as constants in the next subproblems. Branch-and-cut method is used to solve each subproblem. Then connectivity is tested and ensured using a postprocessing phase, which also checks for unused radio interfaces. A new metric based on contention on links, routes length, and interference is used to select the best solution over all network crew and ranking.

Genetic algorithm is used to model the C-JCAR problem in the network planning stage [33]. For a given CA, a linear

TABLE 3: State-aware channel assignment/routing proposals summary.

Work	State aware		Approach	Notes/limitations
	Channel reassignment	Flow rerouting		
[35]	Cost is based on channel-link reassignment	Not applicable since a fully connected topology and fixed predefined paths are considered	(i) Reorder channel in the new CA to reduce the cost during migration from existing cluster to the new cluster	(i) Out-of-order problem (ii) Assigning channels to all logical links affects the channel diversity (iii) Performance degradation if the traffic load sequences are highly uncorrelated
[85]	Cost is based on channel-link reassignment	Not applicable since a fully connected topology is considered	(i) Previous channels are reassigned to links if they are among the set of channels which best reduce the interference and do not violate radio constrains	(i) Internet traffic information is collected at the gateway (ii) Performance degrades with small number of radios due to ripple effect on channel reassignment (iii) Assigning channels to all logical links affects channel diversity
[29]	Cost is based on channel-link reassignment	Not applicable since a fully connected topology and predefined paths are considered	(i) Effective data for each channel is computed and channel with the highest effective capacity is selected. If the channel is not previously assigned to that link reconfiguration cost is subtracted from the effective data value	(i) Out-of-order problem due to multipath (ii) Assigning channels to all logical links affects channel diversity (iii) The channel assigned to a link will be considered as final assignment; thus, earlier assignments are not aware of later assignments; this may lead to an improper final channel assignment (iv) Due to radio constraint some links will be forced to assign more congested channels and this will result in inefficient channel assignment
[84]	Cost is based on channel-node reassignment	Not addressed	(i) Starts from the existing CA and finds new CA by making some adjustment on the previous one (ii) Number of radio-channel reassignments is constrained to a predefined number	(i) Performance degrades with small number of radios due to ripple effect on channel reassignment (ii) Transmission rate is jointly solved with CA links to optimize the network performance
[37]	Cost is based on channel-link reassignment	Not addressed	(i) Starting from existing channel assignment, a new channel is assigned to a link if it does not violate the radio constraints and reduces the interference (ii) Number of link-channel reassignments is constrained to a predefined number	(i) Performance degrades with small number of radio interfaces and due to that reassignment is restricted to channels that do not violet the radio constraints (ii) Assigning channels to all logical links affects channel diversity (iii) Flow-level routing introduces overhead to the routing procedure and requires a routing entry of each flow in routing tables. This is impractical for high number of flows
[58]	Not addressed	Considered, where rerouting cost is based on the number of flows having different routing path	(i) Heuristic routing based on Dijkstra algorithm (ii) The number of flows which allowed having new routes is constrained to a predefined value	(i) Flow rerouting cost is not accurately defined. For instance, two new flow path assignments may result in different disruption while having both are considered equally in rerouting cost

program model of multichannel routing with an objective of maximizing network capacity and total traffic from/to the Internet is adopted as fitness function. For different hardware resources constraints, three types of optimization problems are formulated in [33]. In the first case, the algorithm optimizes the network by assigning channels to radios while assuming the number of radios at each node is constrained. The second case optimizes the network by assuming that the number of radios can be distributed into mesh router, where only the total number of radios in the network is constrained, while the third formulation further optimizes the network considering the gateway placement problem involving selection of mesh routers to serve as gateways. In the first case, channel assigned to each radio is presented as integer encoding with value equal to the channel assigned to it. In the second and third formulations, binary encoding is used for representing CA. Each mesh router is represented by bit string with a length equal to the total number of channels, with each bit representing the assignment of channel to one of the mesh router's radios. Then, the algorithm starts with generation of an initial population. The selection, crossover, and mutation operation are performed at each evolution cycle. A roulette wheel procedure is used for the selection operation in all formulations.

In [37], routing, channel reassignment, and TCP flows rate allocation are studied for optimization of dynamic flows in MR-WMN. Channel reassignment is recomputed for every change in the network traffic state. The channel reassignment algorithm is used to limit the number of links, which requires reassignment. The routing model allows multiple flows between pair nodes, while packets in a TCP flow follow single path. This problem is formulated as Mixed-Integer Nonlinear Program (MINLP). The objective is to maximize the proportional fairness. Heuristic algorithms are proposed to solve the C-JCAR problem. The proposal starts with finding the flow routes based on greedy heuristics. The algorithm then selects routes iteratively based on maximum path utilization fitness. Interference-free links are assumed in the routing stage and neither radio nor interference constraint is considered. A greedy CA routine is then carried out based on current CA. Finally, flow rate allocation is performed based on consideration of the routes and CA obtained from previous steps. Their later work of [71] further improves their earlier proposal by integrating the link transmission rate allocation with the solution and by determining the active links to control the network topology.

In [63] a concept of oblivious routing is used in solving the C-JCAR with scenarios when traffic is highly dynamic. The oblivious routing optimization aims at finding route configuration that optimizes the worst case network performance over a set of possible traffic demands. Based on historical traffic demands profile with a periodic variation during the day's hours, the solution starts by dividing the time intervals into time slots with each configuration bearing separate time intervals. The partitioning is conducted to optimize the network performance by characterizing the traffic demands at each time slot as a convex region with number of dimensions equal to the number of mesh routers. Initially, the traffic demand is scaled such that the total traffic load from all

mesh routers at any time is constant. A local search heuristic algorithm called Hill climbing algorithm is used to partition the traffic profile into a predefined number of slots with the objective of minimizing the convex hull volume over all partitions. For a given time slot, a traffic demand is constructed as multidimensional convex hull with a number of facets. In case of a large number of mesh routers, the number of facets increases exponentially. Thus, relaxation of such convex hull to box range is constructed for such convex region. Then, robust routing is computed for each time slot. The problem is mathematically formulated as nonlinear problem with the objective of minimizing the maximum congestion over all interference sets on all channels. The problem comprises four sets of constraints, namely, interference, radio, flow conservation, and facet constraints. The formulation is transformed to LP problem by finding the dual formulation of the slave LP problem of the original problem. The flow-link-channel variable is determined by solving the routing problem using LP solver. The same channel is later assigned to all links. Then, the algorithm iteratively selects the most utilized link and assigns the channel obtained from flow-link-channel variable to that flow provided that such assignment will not disconnect the flow. Then, the simulated annealing algorithm is used to improve the solution.

Some other works in the literature tackle the C-JCAR problem based on SCA configuration. A heuristic approach is proposed for C-JCAR for cognitive-radio-based WMN using TV white space in [72]. The C-JCAR is addressed with power control in Liu et al. [73], while [74, 75] solve the C-JCAR problem for multicast traffic using genetic algorithm and genetic algorithm with simulated annealing, respectively.

3.1.2. C-JCAR Based on SCA-LS. In [20], the problem is formulated as an MILP and relaxed to LP with objective to maximize the achievable scaling factor of demands. The obtained routes from solving the LP are serving as input to the CA step. The CA algorithm is performed with the objective of minimizing interference over all channels. The obtained channel-link assignment ends with some infeasible links due to the radio constraints and a postprocessing step is carried out to redistribute the traffic load to links with feasible CA only. Thus, for each logical link, the total traffic load that passed through all channels over that link is redistributed over the common channels between the links mesh routers pairs only. The objective of solving the LP formulation is to minimize the maximum interference by redistributing traffic to the links. Then, the scaling down of traffic demand is performed. This ensures feasible link scheduling for realizing sufficient condition. Eventually, a link scheduling algorithm is also obtained.

Similar to [20], in [30] the original MILP problem is relaxed to LP with a set of four constraints. The optimization objective maximizes the fraction of traffic load demands that can be routed for each node. The LP is solved to obtain link-traffic-load assignments. Then, CA is performed to assign channels to links while the LP is solved again but with addition of constraints to force the links to assign the same channels obtained from the previous CA steps. This is accomplished by giving more weight (cost) to the assignment of different channel to a link than the one that has been previously assigned. Finally the link scheduling is performed.

In [29], CA and link scheduling are formulated as MILP problem with the objective of maximizing throughput in CA and link scheduling. The link load is first estimated by distributing the new load of each flow on all available predefined paths based on hop count without considering any interference or radio constraints. A heuristic algorithm is proposed for handling the CA problem. Channel reassignment cost is considered in this stage by minimizing the amount of current traffic affected by channel reassignment. Then a greedy heuristic algorithm schedules the link to time slots for meeting the expected load on each link. Thus, flow allocation is computed for determining the amount of traffic to be routed on each path with the objective of maximizing the amount of traffic routed for each flow.

3.1.3. C-JCAR Based on DCA.

C-JCAR are formulated as an MILP for different objective functions in [56]. The problem is then relaxed to a LP problem. A prime-dual algorithm based on shortest path routing is used to solve the LP problem by finding the loads on links for the scaled down demands. The link loads are then used as an input to the CA stage. The CA algorithm is developed for two scenarios, the SCA-LS and DCA. In SCA, a greedy algorithm finds link-channel assignment followed by a greedy coloring algorithm for finding a conflict-free scheduling. In the case of DCA, packing based heuristic algorithm is used to find both CA and scheduling simultaneously.

A C-JCAR problem with a given set of elastic flow is formulated as LP problem in [36]. The objective is to maximize the throughput using radio-to-radio model. In this way, radio and interference constraints are replaced with a feasibility of the time fraction vector. The time fraction vector represents a vector of time fraction of all links and the fraction for each link must be large enough to meet the traffic load requirement on that link. The LP problem is solved to obtain the CA and routing. Then, vertex-coloring algorithm is used to obtain a feasible scheduling. More efficient coloring algorithm leads to better throughput by lifting the resulted flows from solving the LP problem.

DCA, multipath routing, and link-channel scheduling are jointly formulated as MILP in [31]. The objective is to maximize the network fairness or throughput. The work assumes that radios can operate on subset of channels. Furthermore, the possibility of combining several consecutive channels into one channel is explored so that network interface card can use the channel with larger range of frequencies. Four different interference models are considered in this work. The sufficient and necessary interference constraints for loads on interfering links to be scheduled for each interference model are obtained. This is by deriving the interference constant (which replaces θ) for each interference model. Then, mixed IP is relaxed to a linear programming by using the sufficient condition of the interference constraint. A greedy link scheduling algorithm is developed to find a feasible link scheduling, given the flow found by the LP. The algorithm is proved within a constant factor of the optimum solution when it optimizes the fairness or the throughput.

A parametric search is applied to improve the overall achieved flows. Instead of using the sufficient condition with the interference constant equal to one, the algorithm in the first instance uses the maximum possible value for the interference constant in the LP. If no feasible solution is obtained after solving the LP problem and applying the scheduling algorithm, then the interference constant is reduced by one. This is repeated until feasible solution is obtained.

In [62], joint DCA and routing are considered for multipath and single-path routing under two interference models. The first model is the pairwise model, where the interference among the wireless links can be modeled as conflict graph. This can be represented by different models such as the interference-range and the protocol models. Meanwhile, the second model is the physical model. The joint problem is formulated as LP and considered as multichannel multicommodity flow problem. The problem considers multipath routing with the objective of maximizing the total throughput of a given set of source-destination pairs, with some fairness constraints. The LP is solved to obtain the traffic load on each link. The resulting flow rates are scaled down with specific factor to obtain a feasible link scheduling. The algorithm provides a constant-approximation solution. A greedy placement approach is then used to construct link scheduling for the scaled down links. The first algorithm uses multipath routing, while single-path routing presents a modified algorithm. The LP problem is first solved to obtain load for each flow routed through multipath that is forced to follow single path that is randomly chosen for each flow. Then, for each flow path, striping is performed using the procedure presented in [76].

A joint scheduling, CA and routing, is formulated as LP multicommodity flow problem in [61], augmented with maximal independent set (MIS) constraints. First, the MR-WMN resources are constructed as multidimensional conflict graph (MDCG). Each vertex in MDCG is a radio-link-channel tuple (RLC-tuple). The problem is transformed to the problem of finding all MIS in conflict graph. This is because in general, some MIS sets have more probability to be selected in the optimal solution. These are critical MIS sets; however, finding all MIS in a graph is NP-complete problem [77]. Therefore, a heuristic algorithm based on scheduling index ordering is developed to identify the critical MIS sets. The scheduling index metric is associated with each link that is based on the network topology and network flow information. The algorithm first finds all possible shortest paths between the source-destination pairs of each flow. Then the SI for each tuple is determined based on the number of shortest paths passing through it and its interfering neighbors. The link is then ordered based on its SI. An iterative algorithm is performed starting with tuples with higher SI first. It is terminated if specific condition is reached. Thus, tuples for links associated with lower SI value will have lower possibility to be selected. The resulting maximum independent sets are used in the link capacity constraint for the multicommodity flow linear problem. The solution to the linear problem is determined by the fraction of time where each MIS will be active. Therefore, only single MIS can be active at a time. Table 2 shows a summary of the C-JCAR proposals.

3.2. Channel/Routing Reconfiguration Proposals. DCA algorithms assume that channel switching is supported with negligible delay overhead [36]. A per-packet switching with neglected overhead is assumed in [78]. However, with current hardware channel switching delay is still considerable [79]. In [80] a hybrid CA is developed and the channel switching cost is obtained by dividing the switching delay of an interface over the number of packets transmitted before the interfaces switch their channel. According to [81], the delay involved in channel switching is approximately 80 microseconds. According to [82] the switching delay in 802.11a is around 328 microseconds which is equal to the time of transmission of 1024 bytes in a rate of 25 Mbps using the same technology. Furthermore, research [83] shows that this latency can rise up to scale of seconds due to the effect of upper layer protocols. Reference [3] presented an experimental study on the interruption associated with channel switching, which is in order of 10 seconds with the use of OLSR protocol. This is due to fast link failure update in channel switching. Thus, the authors have recommended a modification to the existing routing protocol that can reduce the overhead associated with channel switching. This can be concluded as, even in a centralized routing paradigm that involves no link status update, the channel switching overhead due to synchronization issues will still be induced. This is due to the inability of radios on a link to achieve perfectly the same switching time. This will cause the link to be down for specific period of time. In addition to channel switching, traffic rerouting can also disrupt the real-time traffic, thereby causing packet drop. The small overhead and delays caused by channel reassignment or traffic rerouting may be unacceptable for the most of real-time multimedia applications. Therefore, state-aware proposals are proposed to fill this gap. There are several existing works, which deal with channel reassignment or traffic rerouting problems. The aim of these works is to reduce the reconfiguration overhead associated with channel reassignment procedures. These works are categorized as state-aware proposals.

3.2.1. Channel Reassignment Proposals. Reference [79] addresses the problem of recomputing CA after every variation in the traffic pattern. The work proposes heuristic reassignment algorithm that aims to minimize the maximum utilization in the collision domain for a given limited number of channels. The input to the algorithm is the network topology and current CA and link-flow rates serve as input to the heuristic algorithm. The collision domain of a link is defined as a set of links, which interfere with this link. The total utilization of a collision domain is defined as the summation of the flow rate over all links in that collision domain. The algorithm begins with a previous CA to find the new one. The link with the highest total utilization is selected iteratively, while the channel that reduces the total utilization over the effected collision domains is then selected. The radio constraints may lead to inappropriate assignments on some links due to the ripple effect and this can increase the utilization on the affected links. The number of channel reassignments is bounded by a predefined parameter. The work is further extended in [84] to integrate the transmission

rate control. This is by starting with the highest possible transmission rate to links and then decreases iteratively till reaching the optimal configuration.

Work in [85] tackles channel reassignment problem assuming the network traffic as elastic TCP flows. This algorithm does not account for traffic loads of each flow; instead it accounts for the number of active TCP flows. This is since TCP flows tend to utilize the entire available bandwidth and is not restricted to a specific demand. Any fluctuations in the traffic may necessitate a consequent channel reassignment to account for the changes, where a simple greedy algorithm handles this problem. In finding channel for a link, the previous channel on a link is reassigned if it does not violate the radio constraints and produces the minimum interference level on that link. The algorithm traverses each edge once, except for cases when merge operation is required, and it assigns channel to it. A common minimum interference channel is assigned to a link; however, if no common channel is available, then merge operation is invoked to create and assign the common channel required. This requires violating the constraints at the radio interfaces. Such cases evolve in situations where the number of channels is higher than the number of radios on the node.

Similar to [79], the channel reassignment problem is also considered in [37] also, where the number of links that is allowed to reassign their channels is constrained. The CA algorithm assigns a channel, which reduces the interference in the iteration. To do so, the algorithm selects a channel from the set of channels which reduces the interference level and do not violate the radio constraints. If the candidate channel set is empty, then previously assigned channel is reassigned again. If the old channel is among the candidate channels, then it is reassigned again; otherwise one of the candidate channels is assigned and the reassignment counter is incremented by one. The algorithm terminates when the total number of reassignments is reached. Meanwhile, connectivity is maintained by assigning a channel for each logical link. The routing on TCP flow level adds extra overhead, which usually requires complex implementation. In their technical report [28], the routing is inserted in each packet. Thus, packets in each flow carry its route information to/from the gateway, while intermediate mesh routers forward each packet based on the included routing information. However, inserting the full route on each packet excessively increases the overhead.

A state-aware channel reassignment is proposed in [35]. Upon receiving new traffic matrix, the algorithm performs a state-aware migration to minimize the reconfiguration costs. This problem is a well-known assignment problem and it is modeled as maximum weighted bipartite matching problem while the matching is determined for less reassignment traffic disruption.

Another state-aware algorithm is introduced in [29]. In this work, the CA stage calculates the expected load on each interference region by using the expected load on each link, which is then used to sort the links. For each visited link, the expected throughput is calculated for the channel and the channel with higher expected throughput is assigned. The channel switching overhead is introduced in the expected throughput function if the evaluated channel is different than the current channel on a link. At any iteration, unassigned links incident on saturated nodes are forced to assign the last used channels that affects the channel spatial diversity.

The channel switching problem in cognitive network has been studied in [86]. As in cognitive radio networks, secondary users can operate in different licensed bands and primary users' activities may frequently force secondary users to switch their radios to other unoccupied frequency bands, which are unnecessarily continuous. The channel switching problem is formulated as MILP with the objective to reduce the frequency distance between the current and the successive channels. A heuristic approach is proposed to solve it. However, the nature of the problem is different than the channel switching problem in the traditional MR-WMN.

3.2.2. Traffic Rerouting.
The traffic demand dynamics can trigger the reconfiguration of the network. In this process, some flows might need to be rerouted. This disrupts the traffic flows and results in higher packet drop where flying packets cannot find their routes to destinations. Therefore, rerouting cost should be considered in the algorithm designed for environments with high dynamic traffic variation. Many works avoided this problem by assuming the existence of multipaths between senders and receivers, so that the algorithm maintains same paths after reconfiguration [29, 35]. Other works such as in [28] take the advantage of existing links between adjacent mesh routers to use the source routing scheme where full path to the destination is inserted in each packet to overcome rerouting problem.

A heuristic algorithm is proposed in [58] to addresses the flow rerouting problem. The algorithm comprises three steps: a routing discovery for new flows, rerouting of existing flows, and assigning channels to active links. The number of rerouted flows is restricted to a predefined threshold. The algorithm starts with discovery step to find the routes to the newly coming flows. Since channel information is not considered, the traffic load on each link is distributed evenly on all channels. The link cost metric for each link is calculated and inactive links in the previous configuration are assigned with higher cost. The cost for inactive link is obtained by multiplying the normalized utilization by a predefined penalty constant. Dijkstra algorithm is employed to find routes for the new flows based on the link cost. In the second step, only a predefined number of previous flows are allowed to be rerouted. The new routes are selected if they produce less contention to the network. Lastly, the channels are assigned to active links such that maximum traffic load is minimized on each channel.

3.2.3. Reconfiguration Trigger.
In reconfiguration algorithms, the algorithm must decide when to trigger the reconfiguration process. Typically, reconfiguration algorithms trigger the reconfiguration process if some set of conditions are satisfied as in [35, 84, 87]. Reference [84] proposes to use the maximum total utilization over all collision domains as an indicator for channel reassignment trigger. In [87], the triggering is based on traffic load monitored by the gateway on its adjacent links. The new CA is recomputed for when the fraction of the total load on a given channel is less than a certain threshold, while the reconfiguration trigger may also be periodic for specific interval or based on policy for aggregating similar traffic load matrices within a cluster [35].

In [35], a reconfiguration policy based on existing CA is proposed for addressing the problem of optimum utilization and reduction of cost of reconfiguration in MR-WMN. Traffic profilers at mesh nodes collect and observe the traffic information and provide the controller with traffic matrices periodically. Each traffic matrix presents the existing traffic demand between node pairs. The arriving traffic matrices are grouped into clusters where traffic matrices belonging to one cluster apply same CA configuration. Each cluster is represented with a weighted traffic matrix of all traffic matrices within the cluster. For each new matrix, the distance between the new matrix and all existing clusters is found; new traffic will then be added to the clusters if their distances are less than a predefined value from the arriving matrix. Based on the distance, the algorithm determines to add the received traffic matrix to one of the existing clusters or to form a new cluster. Channel reassignment is triggered if the received traffic matrix does not belong to the current cluster. Table 3 shows state-aware schemes with their approaches and limitations.

To disseminate the new configuration to the other part of the network a dedicated radio on each mesh router is used in [58] to exchange control information on a default channel. In [28], a simple distribution protocol is proposed. This is by taking the advantage of having a fully connected topology, where each link is assigned to a channel. A spanning tree rooted at the gateway is used to disseminate the configuration with specific control messages where higher priority is given to those messages, that is, by using 802.11e in 802.11-based WMNs.

As overall summary of the reviewed C-JCAR approaches and issues, there are few points to be highlighted that can guide the network designer to develop efficient C-JCAR solutions:

(i) The hardware capability of the mesh router and the wireless interface determine the type of CA scheme. The SCA-LS and DCA can achieve more efficient and flexible utilization of the radio spectrum resources than SCA. However, DCA require a link layer synchronous coordination that is difficult to be achieved in multihop environment with commodity IEEE 802.11a/b/g hardware. Furthermore, the switching overhead is not neglected factor and can have great impact over real-time traffic in multihop routes. On the other hand, SCA-LS also requires link layer synchronous coordination but can be operated with lower overhead if it compared with DCA. Therefore, we believe that SCA-LS is most suitable one to be implemented.

(ii) Due to scalability reasons, it is not recommended to maintain routing functionalities at layer-2. Multipath routing is recommended to apply since it is able to achieve load balancing and can lead to better exploitation of the topology structure of MR-WMN.

(iii) Topology is one important issue that can affect the performance of the network. Both CA and routing determine the physical topology of the network. 1-to-1 mapping, as has been considered by several works to maintain the network connectivity, affects the channel spatial diversity and results in underutilizing the network resources. Determining the active links is one effective step for any C-JCAR algorithm.

(iv) The unrealism of the current interference models can severely affect the quality of solutions of C-JCAR especially for those applied in multihop networks. Therefore, it is recommended to develop a new interference model based on empirical measurement. This can be easily achievable due to the static deployment of WMNs, where site survey and interference information can be easily measured and recorded beforehand.

(v) Approaches in the literature still lack an accurate modeling to the link capacity (effective capacity or virtual capacity) of wireless link under different level of traffic load, contention, interference, and location in respect to the gateway node. This is essential in order to develop efficient algorithms to optimize the traffic distribution in multichannel multihop architecture.

(vi) The majority of the C-JCAR approaches in the literature are load-aware and most works assume having a stable traffic distribution over the network. Unfortunately, this is not the case in real scenarios where the traffic is more dynamic since the traffic is aggregated from different mesh clients with different mobility degrees. Therefore, in order to reduce the effects of the traffic dynamics the C-JCAR most apply adaptive state-aware solutions and might also be integrated with a traffic prediction model and user association model to further reduce the effect of the traffic variation on the performance.

4. Practical Implementation and Test-Beds for MR-WMNs

In order to validate the optimization models for MR-WMNs, simulations approaches may not lead to realistic results. This is due to the difficulty of having an accurate characterization of the interference in multihop environment. Moreover, in order to support cross-layer solutions current hardware and protocol stack architecture need to be revised, and hence, several practical implementations and real-life test-beds are presented and implemented in the literature [4, 88–95]. Moreover, these efforts provide the researchers with practical frameworks to implement and evaluate their solution in real architectures. Most of these test-beds support multiple interfaces per mesh router and are developed using off-the-shelf 802.11 components or software-defined radios when heterogeneous technologies are implemented [96, 97].

Net-X project [98] is a popular framework developed to provide generic software architecture for MR-WMN. Particularly, it is designed to support hybrid CA configuration with two types of interfaces: (I) interfaces with SCA to receive data from neighbors and (II) switchable interfaces with DCA to transmit data to its neighbors at configurable channel switching intervals. A channel abstraction module is implemented between data link and network layer to support multiradio configuration and to coordinate the functionality of different channels. Packets are inserted to a specific channel queue of the switchable interface to be forwarded to next-hop nodes over different channels, data rates, or transmitting powers. The routing table entry contains destination IP address, next interface channel, and the output interface. A broadcast table is also maintained to select the proper output interfaces and channels to forward the broadcast packets.

MUP (Multiradio Unification Protocol) [99] is another software architecture that supports multiradio implementation using 802.11-based radios. Neighbor table is maintained at link layer that stores the MAC addresses and channel information for each neighbor interface. In [90, 91], a 20-node test-bed called KAUMesh is developed in Karlstad University in Sweden. KAUMesh is implemented based on Net-X and OLSR [38] with a modified Network Interface Controller (NIC). Mesh routers are built by single board platforms and equipped with several radios based on 802.11 with several gateway points. OLSR module is extended to support additional functionalities and its messages modified to enable exchanging the network status between mesh routers and to disseminate the channel configuration and the traffic demands in the network.

WARF [100] is a Linux based framework that designed to develop routing protocols and to perform resource monitoring and autonomous configuration over IPv6 networks. Multiradio nodes are also supported in this architecture, where a set of messages is defined for channel radio resources monitoring and configuration. This is achieved by exchanging control WARF messages piggybacked in the extension headers of IPv6 packets. WARF modules can also support cross-layer operations and different data forwarding and routing paradigm such as multipath routing.

Integrating Software-Defined Networking (SDN) [101] with WMN is researched in several works [93–95]. SDNs is an emerging architecture with a centralized controlling paradigm that enables a global control and configuration of the entire network through a set of configuration commands that are sent from SDN controllers down to the data plane. This feature enables applying global optimization strategies to WMNs. A WMN architecture based on open-flow [102] (standard protocol in SDN) is presented in [95]. The architecture is used to support flow-based routing and to reduce the overhead associated with mesh client's mobility. The architecture is implemented on KAUMesh test-bed and results show better performance than traditional schemes.

5. Conclusion and Future Research Directions

With the recent development of radio technologies nowadays, wireless technologies are expected to replace the existing wired infrastructure in the near future. In this context, WMNs are recognized to play a key role in the next-generation networks. Multiradio architecture based on IEEE 802.11 has been introduced to improve the network capacity to meet these new application requirements. In this paper, an effort is made to provide an insight into the existing approaches proposed for C-JCAR where these two problems are disclosed as vital issues to improve the network performance in multiradio architectures.

The contributions of this paper are summarized as follows. First, the key design issues for C-JCAR approaches are identified. These issues cover the topology aspects, algorithm design aspects, routing and link layer specifications, and traffic types. Second, the problem formulation and mathematical modeling are presented for the joint problem under different CA types and link specifications proposed approaches according to their link specifications and CA types. A set of optimization objectives and fairness constraints are also presented. Finally, based on the above key designed issues, joint configuration proposals and reconfiguration proposals are reviewed and followed by summary tables that highlight the design issues and present limitations and assumptions of each work. The above information can help network operator/planners to decide which approaches to be used based on the deployment scenario, network architecture, hardware capabilities, and traffic dynamics and characteristics.

For the main research direction in MR-WMNs, we argue that more effort needs to be done in the context of joint centralized approaches, because joint approaches in the literature have shown a considerable improvement to the network performance. This promotes toward integrating multiple cross-layer solutions and optimization issues in a unified centralized framework to achieve the highest network performance. In this architecture, the optimal configurations are obtained for all network components by taking the advantage of having the global network view. Several issues can be addressed in this framework such as configuring the parameters for directional antennas, transmission power and rates, mac protocols, channel assignments and spectrum management, routing decisions, network coding and adaptive modulation, users' association, and mobility management. The framework also performs other provisioning, management, and monitoring functions.

Besides the above research direction, there are still some remaining issues that still need further investigation by the C-JCAR approaches. These issues include the design of an efficient channel and route reconfiguration solution with a reconfiguration policy that adapts to the traffic dynamics and the channels status with lower reconfiguration overhead. Evolutionary techniques can be considered for this purpose. Moreover, other issues also need to be addressed in multiradio architecture such as fault-management and traffic profiling. Finally, developing an association mechanism for multiradio wireless mesh networks is also recommended for further research. Thus, mesh clients' association mechanism has to be determined based on the interference and load distribution on backhaul links in addition to the signal strength. The association problem can also be jointly solved with the C-JCAR problem to further optimize the network performance.

Notations

N:	Set of mesh routers
R:	Set of radio interfaces
CH:	Set of orthogonal channels
L:	Set of links where each link $l = (m, n, c) \in L$ connects two mesh routers m and n and operates on a channel c
$\widetilde{L}$:	Set of links where each link $\widetilde{l} = (x, y, c) \in \widetilde{L}$ connects two radios x and y and operates on a channel c
T:	Number of time slots
θ:	Interference constant (based on the interference model)
C_l:	Channel capacity on link l
C_O:	Maximum channel capacity
$I(l)$:	Set of links from L interfering with link l
$g(l)$:	The amount of load carried on link l
$y^t(l)$:	Link activation variable, equaling 1 if link is active in time slot t and 0 otherwise
$IR(\widetilde{l})$:	Set of links from $\widetilde{L}$ interfering with link $\widetilde{l}$ or incident on one of $\widetilde{l}$ radio pairs
$t(l)$:	Transmitter mesh router of link l
$h(l)$:	Receiver mesh router of link l
$E(n)$:	Set of links incident in mesh router (n)
$VC(l)$:	Virtual capacity of link l
$Ch(l)$:	The channel assigned to link l
$K(u)$:	Number of radio interfaces in mesh router (u)
h_m^i:	Channel-node variable equal to 1 if there is any link l incident on mesh router m with channel i and $g(l) > 0$
$PER(l_1 \mid l_2)$:	PER at receiver node of link l_1 when l_2 is active.

Competing Interests

The authors declare that there is no conflict of interests regarding the publication of this paper.

References

[1] V. A. Siris, E. Z. Tragos, and N. E. Petroulakis, "Experiences with a metropolitan multiradio wireless mesh network: design, performance, and application," *IEEE Communications Magazine*, vol. 50, no. 7, pp. 128–136, 2012.

[2] M. Portmann and A. A. Pirzada, "Wireless mesh networks for public safety and crisis management applications," *IEEE Internet Computing*, vol. 12, no. 1, pp. 18–25, 2008.

[3] S. Avallone and G. Di Stasi, "An experimental study of the channel switching cost in multi-radio wireless mesh networks," *IEEE Communications Magazine*, vol. 51, no. 9, pp. 124–134, 2013.

[4] I. F. Akyildiz, X. Wang, and W. Wang, "Wireless mesh networks: a survey," *Computer Networks*, vol. 47, no. 4, pp. 445–487, 2005.

[5] Y. Xu and W. Wang, "Wireless mesh network in smart grid: modeling and analysis for time critical communications," *IEEE Transactions on Wireless Communications*, vol. 12, no. 7, pp. 3360–3371, 2013.

[6] P. H. Huynh and C. E. Chow, "Design and analysis of hybrid wireless mesh networks for smart grids," in *Advances in Intelligent Systems and Applications-Volume 1*, pp. 713–721, Springer, New York, NY, USA, 2013.

[7] H. Son, T. Kang, H. Kim, J.-B. Park, and J. H. Roh, "A fair and secure bandwidth allocation for AMI mesh network in smart grid," *The Computer Journal*, vol. 55, no. 10, pp. 1232–1243, 2012.

[8] Y. Ding, Y. Huang, G. Zeng, and L. Xiao, "Using partially overlapping channels to improve throughput in wireless mesh networks," *IEEE Transactions on Mobile Computing*, vol. 11, no. 11, pp. 1720–1733, 2012.

[9] P. B. F. Duarte, Z. M. Fadlullah, A. V. Vasilakos, and N. Kato, "On the partially overlapped channel assignment on wireless mesh network backbone: a game theoretic approach," *IEEE Journal on Selected Areas in Communications*, vol. 30, no. 1, pp. 119–127, 2012.

[10] P. Cappanera, L. Lenzini, A. Lori, G. Stea, and G. Vaglini, "Optimal joint routing and link scheduling for real-time traffic in TDMA wireless mesh networks," *Computer Networks*, vol. 57, no. 11, pp. 2301–2312, 2013.

[11] M. Yu, X. Ma, W. Su, and L. Tung, "A new joint strategy of radio channel allocation and power control for wireless mesh networks," *Computer Communications*, vol. 35, no. 2, pp. 196–206, 2012.

[12] H. Cheng and S. Yang, "Joint QoS multicast routing and channel assignment in multiradio multichannel wireless mesh networks using intelligent computational methods," *Applied Soft Computing*, vol. 11, no. 2, pp. 1953–1964, 2011.

[13] K. Gokbayrak and E. A. Yıldırım, "Joint gateway selection, transmission slot assignment, routing and power control for wireless mesh networks," *Computers & Operations Research*, vol. 40, no. 7, pp. 1671–1679, 2013.

[14] S. Avallone, "An energy efficient channel assignment and routing algorithm for multi-radio wireless mesh networks," *Ad Hoc Networks*, vol. 10, no. 6, pp. 1043–1057, 2012.

[15] S. Avallone, F. P. D'Elia, and G. Ventre, "A new channel, power and rate assignment algorithm for multi-radio wireless mesh networks," *Telecommunication Systems*, vol. 51, no. 1, pp. 73–80, 2012.

[16] W. Wong, X. Chen, F. Long, and S.-H. G. Chan, "Joint topology control and routing assignment for wireless mesh with directional antennas," in *Proceedings of the IEEE Global Communications Conference (GLOBECOM '12)*, pp. 5699–5704, IEEE, Anaheim, Calif, USA, December 2012.

[17] A. P. Subramanian, H. Gupta, S. R. Das, and J. Cao, "Minimum interference channel assignment in multiradio wireless mesh networks," *IEEE Transactions on Mobile Computing*, vol. 7, no. 12, pp. 1459–1473, 2008.

[18] K. N. Ramachandran, E. M. Belding, K. C. Almeroth, and M. M. Buddhikot, "Interference-aware channel assignment in multi-radio wireless mesh networks," in *Proceedings of the 25th IEEE International Conference on Computer Communications (INFOCOM '06)*, pp. 1–12, IEEE, Barcelona, Spain, April 2006.

[19] A. Raniwala, K. Gopalan, and T.-C. Chiueh, "Centralized channel assignment and routing algorithms for multi-channel wireless mesh networks," *ACM SIGMOBILE Mobile Computing and Communications Review*, vol. 8, pp. 50–65, 2004.

[20] M. Alicherry, R. Bhatia, and L. E. Li, "Joint channel assignment and routing for throughput optimization in multiradio wireless mesh networks," *IEEE Journal on Selected Areas in Communications*, vol. 24, no. 11, pp. 1960–1971, 2006.

[21] B.-J. Ko, V. Misra, J. Padhye, and D. Rubenstein, "Distributed channel assignment in multi-radio 802.11 mesh networks," in *Proceedings of the IEEE Wireless Communications and Networking Conference (WCNC '07)*, pp. 3981–3986, Kowloon, Hong Kong, March 2007.

[22] A. Raniwala and T.-C. Chiueh, "Architecture and algorithms for an IEEE 802.11-based multi-channel wireless mesh network," in *Proceedings of the IEEE 24th Annual Joint Conference of the IEEE Computer and Communications Societies*, vol. 3, pp. 2223–2234, IEEE, March 2005.

[23] J. Tang, G. Xue, and W. Zhang, "Interference-aware topology control and QoS routing in multi-channel wireless mesh networks," in *Proceedings of the 6th ACM International Symposium on Mobile Ad Hoc Networking and Computing (MOBIHOC '05)*, pp. 68–77, ACM, Urbana-Champaign, Ill, USA, May 2005.

[24] H. Skalli, S. Ghosh, S. K. Das, L. Lenzini, and M. Conti, "Channel assignment strategies for multiradio wireless mesh networks: issues and solutions," *IEEE Communications Magazine*, vol. 45, no. 11, pp. 86–95, 2007.

[25] X. Hong, B. Gu, M. Hoque, and L. Tang, "Exploring multiple radios and multiple channels in wireless mesh networks," *IEEE Wireless Communications*, vol. 17, no. 3, pp. 76–85, 2010.

[26] P. H. Pathak and R. Dutta, "A survey of network design problems and joint design approaches in wireless mesh networks," *IEEE Communications Surveys and Tutorials*, vol. 13, no. 3, pp. 396–428, 2011.

[27] A. Musaddiq, F. Hashim, C. A. B. C. Ujang, and B. M. Ali, "Survey of channel assignment algorithms for multi-radio multi-channel wireless mesh networks," *IETE Technical Review*, vol. 32, no. 3, pp. 164–182, 2015.

[28] J. J. Galvez, P. M. Ruiz, and A. Gomez-Skarmeta, *Responsive Online Load-Balancing Routing and Load-Aware Channel Re-Assignment in Multi-Radio Multi-Channel Wireless Mesh Networks*, University of Murcia, Murcia, Spain, 2011.

[29] A. A. Franklin, A. Balachandran, and C. S. R. Murthy, "Online reconfiguration of channel assignment in multi-channel multi-radio wireless mesh networks," *Computer Communications*, vol. 35, no. 16, pp. 2004–2013, 2012.

[30] M. Nekoui, A. Ghiamatyoun, S. N. Esfahani, and M. Soltan, "Iterative cross layer schemes for throughput maximization in multi-channel wireless mesh networks," in *Proceedings of the 16th International Conference on Computer Communications and Networks (ICCCN '07)*, pp. 1088–1092, IEEE, Honolulu, Hawaii, USA, August 2007.

[31] X.-Y. Li, A. Nusairat, Y. Wu et al., "Joint throughput optimization for wireless mesh networks," *IEEE Transactions on Mobile Computing*, vol. 8, no. 7, pp. 895–909, 2009.

[32] C. Cicconetti, V. Gardellin, L. Lenzini, and E. Mingozzi, "PaMeLA: a joint channel assignment and routing algorithm for multi-radio multi-channel wireless mesh networks with grid topology," in *Proceedings of the IEEE 6th International Conference on Mobile Adhoc and Sensor Systems (MASS '09)*, pp. 199–207, Macau, China, October 2009.

[33] T.-Y. Lin, K.-C. Hsieh, and H.-C. Huang, "Applying genetic algorithms for multiradio wireless mesh network planning," *IEEE Transactions on Vehicular Technology*, vol. 61, no. 5, pp. 2256–2270, 2012.

[34] B. Claise, B. Trammell, and P. Aitken, *Specification of the Ip Flow Information Export (Ipfix) Protocol for the Exchange of Flow Information*, 2013.

[35] A. A. Kanagasabapathy, A. A. Franklin, and C. S. R. Murthy, "An adaptive channel reconfiguration algorithm for multi-channel

multi-radio wireless mesh networks," *IEEE Transactions on Wireless Communications*, vol. 9, no. 10, pp. 3064–3071, 2010.

[36] X. Meng, K. Tan, and Q. Zhang, "Joint routing and channel assignment in multi-radio wireless mesh networks," in *Proceedings of the IEEE International Conference on Communications (ICC '06)*, pp. 3596–3601, Instanbul, Turkey, July 2006.

[37] J. J. Gálvez and P. M. Ruiz, "Efficient rate allocation, routing and channel assignment in wireless mesh networks supporting dynamic traffic flows," *Ad Hoc Networks*, vol. 11, no. 6, pp. 1765–1781, 2013.

[38] T. Clausen and P. Jacquet, *Optimized link state routing protocol (olsr)*; 2070-1721; 2003.

[39] Z. Wang, Y. Chen, and C. Li, "PSR: a lightweight proactive source routing protocol for mobile ad hoc networks," *IEEE Transactions on Vehicular Technology*, vol. 63, no. 2, pp. 859–868, 2014.

[40] H. Le Minh, G. Sexton, and N. Aslam, "Self-adaptive proactive routing scheme for mobile ad-hoc networks," *IET Networks*, vol. 4, pp. 128–136, 2014.

[41] J. A. N. Cordero, J. Yi, and T. Clausen, "An adaptive jitter mechanism for reactive route discovery in sensor networks," *Sensors*, vol. 14, no. 8, pp. 14440–14471, 2014.

[42] J. Niu, L. Cheng, Y. Gu, L. Shu, and S. K. Das, "R3E: reliable reactive routing enhancement for wireless sensor networks," *IEEE Transactions on Industrial Informatics*, vol. 10, no. 1, pp. 784–794, 2014.

[43] S. K. Singh, R. Duvvuru, and J. P. Singh, "TCP and UDP-based performance evaluation of proactive and reactive routing protocols using mobility models in MANETS," *International Journal of Information and Communication Technology*, vol. 7, no. 6, pp. 632–644, 2015.

[44] J. Duan, X. Wang, S. Wang, and S. Xu, "HHR: hierarchical hybrid routing scheme for information-centric network," *China Communications*, vol. 12, no. 6, Article ID 7122472, pp. 141–153, 2015.

[45] C. M. S. Figueiredo, E. F. Nakamura, and A. A. F. Loureiro, "A hybrid adaptive routing algorithm for event-driven wireless sensor networks," *Sensors*, vol. 9, no. 9, pp. 7287–7307, 2009.

[46] J. A. Guerrero Ibanez, L. A. Garcia Morales, J. J. Contreras Castillo, R. Buenrostro Mariscal, and M. Cosio Leon, "HYRMA: a hybrid routing protocol for monitoring of marine environments," *IEEE Latin America Transactions*, vol. 13, no. 5, pp. 1562–1568, 2015.

[47] N. Kojić, I. Reljin, and B. Reljin, "A neural networks-based hybrid routing protocol for wireless mesh networks," *Sensors*, vol. 12, no. 6, pp. 7548–7575, 2012.

[48] X. Chen, Z. Zhang, and H. Luo, "Joint optimization of power control, channel assignment and scheduling in wireless mesh network," in *Proceedings of the 3rd International Conference on Communications and Networking in China (ChinaCom '08)*, pp. 606–611, IEEE, Hangzhou, China, August 2008.

[49] A. U. Chaudhry, N. Ahmad, and R. H. M. Hafez, "Improving throughput and fairness by improved channel assignment using topology control based on power control for multi-radio multichannel wireless mesh networks," *EURASIP Journal on Wireless Communications and Networking*, vol. 2012, article 155, pp. 1–25, 2012.

[50] L. Yang and L. Quan, "A topology control algorithm using power control for wireless mesh network," in *Proceedings of the 3rd International Conference on Multimedia Information Networking and Security (MINES '11)*, pp. 141–145, Shanghai, China, November 2011.

[51] Q. Liu, X. Jia, and Y. Zhou, "Topology control for multichannel multi-radio wireless mesh networks using directional antennas," *Wireless Networks*, vol. 17, no. 1, pp. 41–51, 2011.

[52] A. Ali, M. E. Ahmed, M. J. Piran, and D. Y. Suh, "Resource optimization scheme for multimedia-enabled wireless mesh networks," *Sensors*, vol. 14, no. 8, pp. 14500–14525, 2014.

[53] T. Zhang, K. Yang, and H.-H. Chen, "Topology control for service-oriented wireless mesh networks," *IEEE Wireless Communications*, vol. 16, no. 4, pp. 64–71, 2009.

[54] H. Zhang and D. H. K. Tsang, "Traffic oriented topology formation and load-balancing routing in wireless mesh networks," in *Proceedings of the 16th International Conference on Computer Communications and Networks (ICCCN '07)*, pp. 1046–1052, IEEE, Honolulu, Hawaii, USA, August 2007.

[55] F. Liu and Y. Bai, "An overview of topology control mechanisms in multi-radio multi-channel wireless mesh networks," *EURASIP Journal on Wireless Communications and Networking*, vol. 2012, article 324, 2012.

[56] M. Kodialam and T. Nandagopal, "Characterizing the capacity region in multi-radio multi-channel wireless mesh networks," in *Proceedings of the 11th Annual International Conference on Mobile Computing and Networking (MobiCom '05)*, pp. 73–87, ACM, Cologne, Germany, September 2005.

[57] A. H. Mohsenian-Rad and V. W. S. Wong, "Joint logical topology design, interface assignment, channel allocation, and routing for multi-channel wireless mesh networks," *IEEE Transactions on Wireless Communications*, vol. 6, no. 12, pp. 4432–4440, 2007.

[58] Y. Zhou, S.-H. Chung, and H.-Y. Jeong, "Reconfiguring multirate wi-fi mesh networks with flow disruption constraints," in *Dynamics in Logistics*, pp. 383–393, Springer, New York, NY, USA, 2013.

[59] A. Iyer, C. Rosenberg, and A. Karnik, "What is the right model for wireless channel interference?" *IEEE Transactions on Wireless Communications*, vol. 8, no. 5, pp. 2662–2671, 2009.

[60] A. U. Chaudhry, R. H. M. Hafez, and J. W. Chinneck, "On the impact of interference models on channel assignment in multiradio multi-channel wireless mesh networks," *Ad Hoc Networks*, vol. 27, pp. 68–80, 2015.

[61] H. Li, Y. Cheng, C. Zhou, and P. Wan, "Multi-dimensional conflict graph based computing for optimal capacity in MR-MC wireless networks," in *Proceedings of the 30th IEEE International Conference on Distributed Computing Systems (ICDCS '10)*, pp. 774–783, IEEE, Genova, Italy, June 2010.

[62] M. Al-Ayyoub and H. Gupta, "Joint routing, channel assignment, and scheduling for throughput maximization in general interference models," *IEEE Transactions on Mobile Computing*, vol. 9, no. 4, pp. 553–565, 2010.

[63] J. Wellons and Y. Xue, "The robust joint solution for channel assignment and routing for wireless mesh networks with time partitioning," *Ad Hoc Networks*, vol. 13, pp. 210–221, 2014.

[64] V. Gardellin, S. K. Das, L. Lenzini, C. Cicconetti, and E. Mingozzi, "G-PaMeLA: a divide-and-conquer approach for joint channel assignment and routing in multi-radio multi-channel wireless mesh networks," *Journal of Parallel and Distributed Computing*, vol. 71, no. 3, pp. 381–396, 2011.

[65] O. Goussevskaia, Y. A. Oswald, and R. Wattenhofer, "Complexity in geometric SINR," in *Proceedings of the 8th ACM International Symposium on Mobile Ad Hoc Networking and Computing (MobiHoc '07)*, pp. 100–109, Montreal, Canada, September 2007.

[66] V. Kumar, M. V. Marathe, S. Parthasarathy, and A. Srinivasan, "End-to-end packet-scheduling in wireless ad-hoc networks,"

in *Proceedings of the 15th Annual ACM-SIAM Symposium on Discrete Algorithms (SODA '04)*, pp. 1021–1030, Society for Industrial and Applied Mathematics, 2004.

[67] CPLEX, *V12. 1: User's Manual for CPLEX*, International Business Machines Corporation, 2009.

[68] X. Huang, S.-L. Feng, and H.-C. Zhuang, "Cross-layer fair resources allocation for multi-radio multi-channel wireless mesh networks," in *Proceedings of the 5th International Conference on Wireless Communications, Networking and Mobile Computing (WiCOM '09)*, pp. 1–5, IEEE, Beijing, China, September 2009.

[69] N. Sadeghianpour, T. C. Chuah, and S. W. Tan, "Joint channel assignment and routing in multiradio multichannel wireless mesh networks with directional antennas," *International Journal of Communication Systems*, vol. 28, no. 9, pp. 1521–1536, 2015.

[70] S. Avallone, I. F. Akyildiz, and G. Ventre, "A channel and rate assignment algorithm and a layer-2.5 forwarding paradigm for multi-radio wireless mesh networks," *IEEE/ACM Transactions on Networking*, vol. 17, no. 1, pp. 267–280, 2009.

[71] J. J. Gálvez and P. M. Ruiz, "Joint link rate allocation, routing and channel assignment in multi-rate multi-channel wireless networks," *Ad Hoc Networks*, vol. 29, pp. 78–98, 2015.

[72] R. Kikuchi, K. Hosaki, and M. Hasegawa, "Implementation and evaluation of a combined optimization scheme for routing and channel assignment in wireless mesh networks," in *Proceedings of the 12th Annual IEEE Consumer Communications and Networking Conference (CCNC '15)*, pp. 619–624, IEEE, Las Vegas, Nev, USA, January 2015.

[73] K.-M. Liu, T. Ma, Y.-A. Liu, and K.-H. Kou, "Fairness-oriented routing algorithm joint with power control and channel assignment for multi-radio multi-channel wireless mesh networks," *The Journal of China Universities of Posts and Telecommunications*, vol. 21, no. 5, pp. 55–60, 2014.

[74] M. Sharifi Jebeli and M. Dehghan, "Joint multicast routing and channel assignment in Multiradio Multichannel Wireless Mesh Networks using a multi objective algorithm," in *Proceedings of the 6th Conference on Information and Knowledge Technology (IKT '14)*, pp. 163–170, IEEE, Shahrud, Iran, May 2014.

[75] E. Vaezpour and M. Dehghan, "A multi-objective optimization approach for joint channel assignment and multicast routing in multi-radio multi-channel wireless mesh networks," *Wireless Personal Communications*, vol. 77, no. 2, pp. 1055–1076, 2014.

[76] P. Raghavan and C. D. Tompson, "Randomized rounding: a technique for provably good algorithms and algorithmic proofs," *Combinatorica*, vol. 7, no. 4, pp. 365–374, 1987.

[77] M. R. Garey and D. S. Johnson, *Computers and Intractability: A Guide to the Theory of NP-Completeness*, Freeman, San Francisco, La, USA, 1979.

[78] X. Shao, C. Hua, and A. Huang, "Robust resource allocation for multi-hop wireless mesh networks with end-to-end traffic specifications," *Ad Hoc Networks*, vol. 13, pp. 123–133, 2014.

[79] S. Avallone, F. P. D'Elia, and G. Ventre, "A traffic-aware channel re-assignment algorithm for wireless mesh networks," in *Proceedings of the European Wireless Conference (EW '10)*, pp. 683–688, IEEE, Lucca, Italy, April 2010.

[80] P. Kyasanur and N. H. Vaidya, "Routing and interface assignment in multi-channel multi-interface wireless networks," in *Proceedings of the IEEE Wireless Communications and Networking Conference (WCNC '05)*, pp. 2051–2056, IEEE, New Orleans, La, USA, March 2005.

[81] F. Herzel, G. Fischer, and H. Gustat, "An integrated CMOS RF synthesizer for 802.11a wireless LAN," *IEEE Journal of Solid-State Circuits*, vol. 38, no. 10, pp. 1767–1770, 2003.

[82] M. Yun, Y. Zhou, A. Arora, and H.-A. Choi, "Channel-assignment and scheduling in wireless mesh networks considering switching overhead," in *Proceedings of the IEEE International Conference on Communications (ICC '09)*, pp. 1–6, IEEE, Dresden, Germany, June 2009.

[83] P. Li, N. Scalabrino, Y. Fang, E. Gregori, and I. Chlamtac, "How to effectively use multiple channels in wireless mesh networks," *IEEE Transactions on Parallel and Distributed Systems*, vol. 20, no. 11, pp. 1641–1652, 2009.

[84] S. Avallone, G. Di Stasi, and A. Kassler, "A traffic-aware channel and rate reassignment algorithm for wireless mesh networks," *IEEE Transactions on Mobile Computing*, vol. 12, no. 7, pp. 1335–1348, 2013.

[85] J. J. Galvez, P. M. Ruiz, and A. F. G. Skarmeta, "TCP flow-aware channel re-assignment in multi-radio multi-channel wireless mesh networks," in *Proceedings of the 8th IEEE International Conference on Mobile Ad-hoc and Sensor Systems (MASS '11)*, pp. 262–271, Valencia, Spain, October 2011.

[86] S. Arkoulis, E. Anifantis, V. Karyotis, S. Papavassiliou, and N. Mitrou, "On the optimal, fair and channel-aware cognitive radio network reconfiguration," *Computer Networks*, vol. 57, no. 8, pp. 1739–1757, 2013.

[87] W. Fu, B. Xie, X. Wang, and D. P. Agrawal, "Flow-based channel assignment in channel constrained wireless mesh networks," in *Proceedings of the 17th International Conference on Computer Communications and Networks (ICCCN '08)*, pp. 1–6, IEEE, St. Thomas, Virgin Islands, USA, August 2008.

[88] P. Dely, M. Castro, S. Soukhakian, A. Moldsvor, and A. Kassler, "Practical considerations for channel assignment in wireless mesh networks," in *Proceedings of the IEEE Globecom Workshops (GC Wkshps '10)*, pp. 763–767, IEEE, Miami, Fla, USA, December 2010.

[89] B. Blywis, M. Guenes, F. Juraschek, and J. H. Schiller, "Trends, advances, and challenges in testbed-based wireless mesh network research," *Mobile Networks and Applications*, vol. 15, no. 3, pp. 315–329, 2010.

[90] P. Dely and A. Kassler, "Kaumesh a multi-radio multi-channel mesh testbed," in *Proceedings of 9th Scandinavian Workshop on Wireless Ad-hoc & Sensor Networks (ADHOC '09)*, Niagara Falls, Canada, 2009.

[91] M. C. Castro, P. Dely, A. J. Kassler, F. P. D'Elia, and S. Avallone, "Olsr and net-X as a framework for channel assignment experiments," in *Proceedings of the 4th ACM International Workshop on Experimental Evaluation and Characterization (WINTECH '09)*, pp. 79–80, ACM, Beijing, China, 2009.

[92] G. Di Stasi, R. Bifulco, S. Avallone et al., "Interconnection of geographically distributed wireless mesh testbeds: resource sharing on a large scale," *Ad Hoc Networks*, vol. 9, no. 8, pp. 1389–1403, 2011.

[93] D. Zhu, X. Yang, P. Zhao, and W. Yu, "Towards effective intra-flow network coding in software defined wireless mesh networks," in *Proceedings of the 24th International Conference on Computer Communication and Networks (ICCCN '15)*, pp. 1–8, IEEE, Las Vegas, Nev, USA, 2015.

[94] P. Dely, "Towards an architecture for openflow and wireless mesh networks," in *Proceedings of the Ofelia Summer School*, November 2011.

[95] P. Dely, A. Kassler, and N. Bayer, "OpenFlow for wireless mesh networks," in *Proceedings of the 20th International Conference on*

Computer Communications and Networks (ICCCN '11), pp. 1–6, Maui, Hawaii, USA, August 2011.

[96] V. Angelakis, A. Capone, A. Fragkiadakis et al., "Experience from testbeds and management platforms towards mesh networking with heterogeneous wireless access," in *Proceedings of the IEEE 14th International Symposium and Workshops on a World of Wireless, Mobile and Multimedia Networks (WoWMoM '13)*, pp. 1–6, Madrid, Spain, June 2013.

[97] Redcomm project, April 2016, http://www.redcomm-project .eu/description.html.

[98] P. Kyasanur, C. Chereddi, and N. H. Vaidya, "Net-x: system extensions for supporting multiple channels, multiple interfaces, and other interface capabilities," Tech. Rep., University of Illinois at Urbana-Champaign, Wireless Networking Group, Urbana, Ill, USA, 2006.

[99] A. Adya, P. Bahl, J. Padhye, A. Wolman, and L. Zhou, "A multi-radio unification protocol for IEEE 802.11 wireless networks," in *Proceedings of the 1st International Conference on Broadband Networks (BroadNets '04)*, pp. 344–354, IEEE, San Jose, Calif, USA, October 2004.

[100] S. Kukliński, P. Radziszewski, and J. Wytrębowicz, "WARF: component based platform for wireless mesh networks," *Smart CR*, vol. 1, no. 2, pp. 125–138, 2011.

[101] S. Ortiz Jr., "Software-defined networking: on the verge of a breakthrough?" *IEEE Computer*, vol. 46, no. 7, pp. 10–12, 2013.

[102] N. McKeown, T. Anderson, H. Balakrishnan et al., "OpenFlow: enabling innovation in campus networks," *ACM SIGCOMM Computer Communication Review*, vol. 38, no. 2, pp. 69–74, 2008.

15

Frequency Diverse Array Antennas: From their Origin to their Application in Wireless Communication Systems

Shaddrack Yaw Nusenu[1,2] and **Abdul Basit**[1,3]

[1]*University of Electronic Science and Technology of China, Chengdu, China*
[2]*Koforidua Technical University (KTU), Koforidua, Ghana*
[3]*Department of Electrical Engineering, International Islamic University, Islamabad, Pakistan*

Correspondence should be addressed to Shaddrack Yaw Nusenu; nusenu2012gh@yahoo.com

Academic Editor: Gianluigi Ferrari

Wireless communication systems have gained considerable growth rate nowadays, with the anticipation that communications will be available everywhere and anywhere in the near future. Phased array antenna whose beam steering is fixed in an angle for all range cells has been utilized for wireless communications. To mitigate this problem, a new array concept, namely, frequency diverse array (FDA), was proposed. This paper presents how FDA technology could be useful in today's wireless communication technology. FDA is distinct from phased array in a sense that it employs frequency increment across array elements. The use of a frequency increment creates a beam steering that is a function of angle, time, and range which allows the FDA antenna to transmit the energy along the prespecified range and angle direction. In addition, we consider the time-variant beampattern aspect of an FDA, which has normally been ignored in the literature. In this study, we present the mathematical fundamentals of FDA antenna and why it could be exploited for wireless communication systems. Furthermore, FDA using Butler matrix for communication has been discussed. Performance analysis in terms of transmit beampattern, signal-to-interference-and-noise ratio (SINR), and direction of arrival has been presented and compared with that of phased array antenna.

1. Introduction

Wireless communication systems have become very promising than their counterpart wired communication due to their merits [1], and this has attracted a huge demand on wireless technology, hence the explosive rate in many technical fields. The proposed fifth generation (5G) of wireless cellular communication systems is envisaged to be available by 2020 [2]. Besides, antenna array applications have been put forward in recent years for wireless communications systems. The array antennas' advantages can be summarized as (1) increasing channel capacity and spectrum efficiency, (2) extending range coverage, (3) tailoring beam shape, (4) steering multiple beams to track many mobiles, and (5) compensating aperture distortion electronically. In addition, they reduce multipath fading and cancel cochannel interferences, BER, and outage probability [3, 4].

An array of antennas works on the principle that the desired signal and unwanted signal (cochannel interferences) arrive from diverse directions. Therefore, the beampattern could be adjusted by combining signals from the array antennas with appropriate weighting factor to suit the requirements. Antennas can be classified as omnidirectional, directional, phased array, and frequency diverse array. Phased array antennas have been employed in many applications, for example, in radar systems, electronic warfare, radio astronomy, and airport safety and communications [5]. Phased array antennas have the capability to steer the beam electronically with high directivity. The offered directional gain is beneficial for detecting mobile users, tracking users, and suppressing sidelobe interferences from other directions [6]. Although phased arrays have several advantages, some of their drawbacks in many applications are as follows: (1) One of the major disadvantage is their high manufacturing cost. A more directed beam requires a greater number of antenna elements and electronic phase shifters, which are quite expensive [7]. (2) In phased arrays, exceeding interelement distance beyond half wavelength results in the appearance of grating lobes in the visible regions that deteriorates the communication user(s) tracking performance [8]. (3) Phased array antenna produces a power maximum at a fixed angle for all ranges. Therefore, to suppress range-dependent interferences and to localize multiple targets with the same direction but distinct ranges using phased arrays is very difficult.

In order to circumvent this problem, recently, a flexible beam scanning array, namely, frequency diverse array (FDA), was proposed by [9, 10] to overcome the limitation of beam steering which is fixed at an angle for all the range cells [6] in phased array and FDA has no phase shifters. In FDA, a small frequency increment is applied across the array elements, and this frequency increment results in a range-angle-dependent beampattern [9]. The FDA is quite different from multiple-input multiple-output (MIMO) [11] radar as it transmits overlapped signals closely spaced in frequencies, while MIMO, in some cases, employs orthogonal signals from widely separated antennas (i.e., widely spaced MIMO) over multiple independent paths to provide spatial diversity [12] and in some cases, uses multiple waveforms to provide waveform diversity from closely located antennas (i.e., colocated MIMO) [13]. Likewise, FDA is also different from orthogonal frequency division multiplexing (OFDM) [14]. The latter uses orthogonal subcarriers [15]. Moreover, an FDA is also different from the conventional frequency scanning arrays [16], where each element uses the same frequency at a given time [17]. Different from phased arrays, the FDA beampattern provides a global maximum, as well as, a number of local maxima at diverse angle and ranges values [18]. This ability can be utilized for detecting multiple targets having same directions, but different range values. Note that the introduction of frequency offsets, the apparent scan angle, is not equal to its nominal scan angle as well as the actual beam-steering direction cannot be effectively predicted as phased arrays. Furthermore, since the phases of the FDA transmitted signals add constructively in certain regions, while destructively in others, this property can be utilized to suppress interferences or avoid transmitting the signals to some undesired regions [19]. In [20–23], discussed about the applications of FDA and recently, FDA antennas have been utilized in wireless communications for security applications [14, 24–28].

In this paper, we give a review (i.e., origin) on the development of FDA antenna technology that is from phased array antenna to FDA antenna. We also highlight the potential applications of using FDA in communication areas. Additionally, we appeal to the antenna and wireless communication research communities to contribute in terms of more publications on FDA antenna research and development. Performance analysis in terms of transmit beampattern, SINR, and direction of arriving is then evaluated, and we give example of FDA using 4×4 Butler matrix for communication application.

The rest of this paper is organized as follows: Section 2 presents an overview and some necessary details about the data model of frequency diverse array (FDA) antenna. Section 3 explains why the FDA antenna could be used for wireless communication systems. Section 4 presents FDA antenna architecture schemes. Section 5 presents FDA and Butler matrix scheme for communication. Next, performance

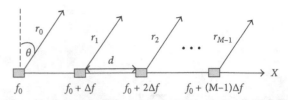

FIGURE 1: Illustration of linear Frequency diverse array.

analysis is presented in Section 6, followed by numerical results in Section 7. Finally, concluding summaries are drawn in Section 8.

2. Mathematical Formulation of FDA Antenna

In a standard phased array, it is assumed that identical transmitted signal is emitted from the individual array element, excluding the amplitudes and phases. The FDA antenna, which is different from phased arrays, can be excited by the same signal or different signals. For simplicity and without loss of validity, we assume that the waveforms radiated from each FDA antenna element are identical with a frequency increment or offsets Δf and element spacing d.

Consider a number of FDA antenna elements, M, as shown in Figure 1, and the radiation frequency of each element can be given by [19].

$$f_m = f_0 + (m-1) \cdot \Delta f, \quad m = 1, 2, 3, \ldots, M, \quad (1)$$

where f_0 denotes the radar operating carrier frequency.

And the phase of the signal transmitted by the first antenna element can be written as

$$\phi_1 = \frac{2\pi f_0 r_1}{c}, \quad (2)$$

where c is the speed of light, r_1 denotes the distance between the first element and the observed point target. Similarly, the phase of the signal transmitted by the second element can be expressed as

$$\phi_2 = \frac{2\pi f_2 r_2}{c} = \frac{2\pi (f_0 + \Delta f) r_2}{c}. \quad (3)$$

The phase difference between the signals arriving at the first and second elements, respectively, is given in (4)

$$\Delta \phi_1 = \phi_2 - \phi_1 = -\frac{2\pi f_0 d \sin \theta}{c} - \frac{2\pi \Delta f d \sin \theta}{c} + \frac{2\pi \Delta f r_1}{c}. \quad (4)$$

Similarly, (5) is the phase difference between the first and the mth element;

$$\Delta \phi_{m-1} = \phi_m - \phi_1 = -\frac{2\pi f_0 (m-1) d \sin \theta}{c} + \frac{2\pi (m-1) \Delta f r_1}{c} - \frac{2\pi (m-1)^2 \Delta f d \sin \theta}{c}, \quad (5)$$

where θ denotes the angle direction of the target, $r_m \approx r - (m-1) d \sin \theta$ is the difference between individual elements approximation with $r = r_1$ being the slant range of

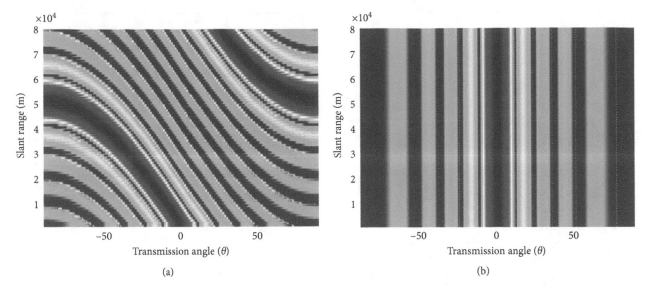

FIGURE 2: Transmit beampattern: (a) conventional FDA antenna and (b) phased array antenna.

the first element. Note that the first term in (5) is simply the conventional array factor seen in the array theory. The last term is of significance since it shows that the radiation beampattern of the array depends on both the range and frequency increment. It should be noted that the FDA antenna is different from conventional frequency scanning arrays. Frequency scanned arrays employ the frequency increment as a function of time for all elements, while the FDA antenna applies the frequency increment as a function of the elements.

Taking the first element as the reference for the array, the steering vector of the FDA antenna is expressed as in (6), with r denoting the slant range of the first element,

$$\mathbf{a}(\theta, r, t) = \mathbf{a}_\theta(\theta) \odot \mathbf{a}_r(r) \odot \mathbf{a}_t(t), \qquad (6)$$

where

$$\mathbf{a}_\theta(\theta) = \left(1, \ \exp\left(\frac{j2\pi md \sin \theta}{\lambda}\right), \ \ldots, \ \exp\left(\frac{j2\pi Md \sin \theta}{\lambda}\right)\right)^T,$$

$$\mathbf{a}_r(r) = \left(1, \ \exp\left(\frac{j2\pi \Delta fr}{c}\right), \ \ldots, \ \exp\left(\frac{j2\pi M\Delta fr}{c}\right)\right)^T, \qquad (7)$$

$$\mathbf{a}_t(t) = \left(1, \ \exp\left(j2\pi \Delta ft\right), \ \ldots, \ \exp\left(j2\pi M\Delta ft\right)\right)^T,$$

with $\odot$ denoting the Hadamard product and $(\cdot)^T$ being the transpose operator.

The following summarized FDA antenna characteristics [19, 21]:

(1) If the frequency increment Δf is fixed, the beam direction is a function of range r dependent.

(2) If the range r is fixed, the beam direction is a function of Δf dependent.

(3) If the frequency increment Δf is not employed ($\Delta f = 0$), it simplified to phased array antenna.

(4) As the frequency increment Δf influences the beamwidth, a higher resolution may be achieved for the FDA as compared to the phased array antenna.

Hence, the FDA antenna is rather different from phased arrays. It is a new array concept and novel beam scanning technique. The range-dependent and frequency offset-dependent beamforming is of great importance because it can achieve local maxima at different ranges as this may provide many promising application potentials in wireless communication systems in future.

Assume the following parameters: $M = 10$, $\Delta f = 30$ kHz, $f_0 = 10$ GHz, and $d = (1/2)\lambda$, in Figure 2, we show the transmit beampattern of the conventional FDA antenna, and phased array antenna.

It can be noticed that in Figure 2(a), the conventional FDA yields range-angle-dependent beampattern, and Figure 2(b) depicts the phased array antenna which yields only angle-dependent beampattern with no range-dependent capability.

3. Why FDA Could Be Used for Wireless Communication Systems

According [19], the maximum field can be obtained as

$$\Delta ft - \frac{\Delta fr}{c} + \frac{df_0 \sin \theta}{c} + \frac{\Delta fd \sin \theta}{c} = z, \quad z = 0, \ \pm 1, \ \ldots. \qquad (8)$$

From (8), it is clear that there are multiple solutions for the unfixed variables, when only one variable is fixed. Moreover, when two variables are fixed, the periodicity array pattern depends on the unfixed variable. For instance, if (8) is solved for the following variables t, r, and θ, we can express as follows:

$$t = \frac{z}{\Delta f} + \frac{r}{c} - \frac{df_0 \sin \theta}{cf_0 \Delta f} + \frac{d \sin \theta}{c},$$

$$r = ct + \frac{df_0 \sin \theta}{\Delta f} - \frac{zc}{\Delta f} + d \sin \theta, \qquad (9)$$

$$\theta = \sin^{-1}\left[\frac{zc - \Delta f(ct - r)}{df_0 + \Delta fd}\right].$$

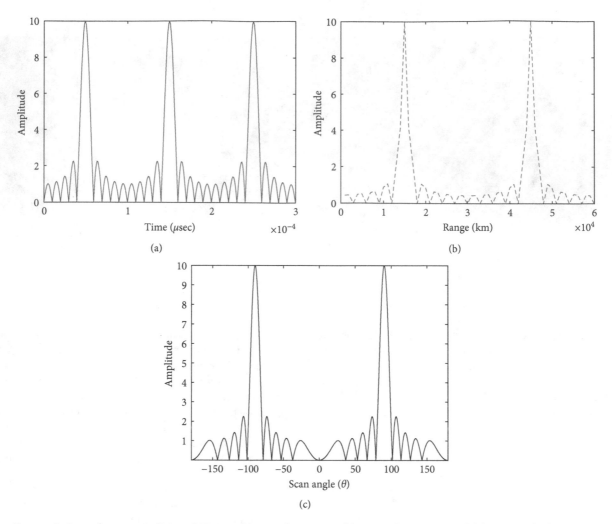

FIGURE 3: Array factor periodicity of FDA in (a) time dimension, (b) range dimension, and (c) scan angle dimension.

Figure 3 illustrates the array factor periodicity of FDA antenna using (9).

Now it is evident that FDA antenna has autoscanning property [29] which is a unique property that could be exploited for wireless communication systems application, for instance at the base station and communication devices.

3.1. Range and Angle Estimation of Mobile Targets/Users. As noted already, FDA provides range-dependent beampattern. Therefore, it has the capability of suppressing range-dependent interferences. For instance, Figure 4 shows comparative transmit beampattern in suppressing range-dependent interferences. It can be noticed that in Figure 4(a), the FDA beampattern can identify the target (30 km, 40°) and suppress the interferences, for example, (50 km, 40°) and (20 km, 40°), effectively due to the frequency offsets employed, whereas the phased array beampattern (Figure 4(b)) cannot effectively identify the target and interferences. Nevertheless, due to coupling range and angle peaks in the beamformer output, FDA antenna cannot estimate the range and angle of a target solely. It should be noted that

the range–angle response can be decoupled as depicted in Figure 5.

3.2. Security for Wireless Communication Systems. One of the major issues in wireless communication systems is security, because of the broadcasting nature of wireless signals. Therefore, any receiver is able to have a copy of the transmitted signal, making the activities of the eavesdroppers much easier compared to wired communication [32]. The work done by Wyner [33] created the concept of physical-layer security. The fundamental principle behind physical-layer security is to exploit the normal randomness of wireless communication channels to ensure that the information to the desired destination is secured, and at the same time, this information cannot be extracted by an undesired receiver [34]. Physical-layer security can be implemented by employing various techniques [35] such as beam-steering and jamming. In beam-steering techniques, the transmitter steers the mainlobe along the desired direction, and steer the null towards the undesired direction [36–38]. As stated before, by employing the frequency offsets, the apparent scan angle is not equal to its nominal

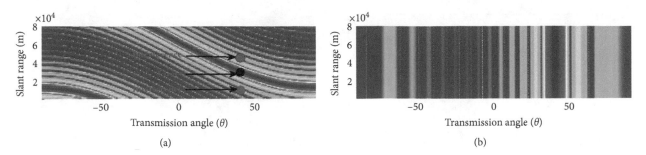

FIGURE 4: Comparative performance of transmit beampattern in suppressing range-dependent interferences: (a) FDA antenna (top) and (b) phased array antenna (bottom).

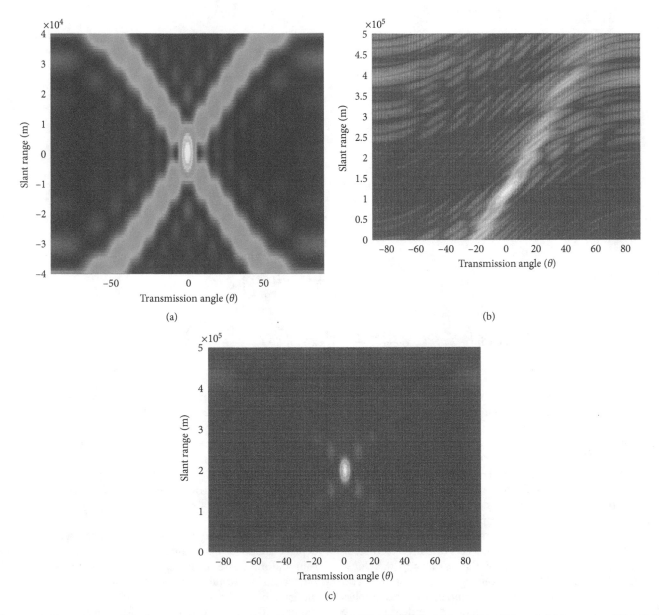

FIGURE 5: Comparison of the beampattern generated by (a) symmetrical FDA [19, 28], (b) log FDA [30], and (c) hamming FDA [31].

scan angle as well as the actual beam-steering direction cannot be effectively predicted as phased array antenna; hence, this property can be utilized to suppress interferences, avoid transmitting the signals to some undesired regions, and design low probability of interception required for physical-layer security in wireless communication systems [27]. Figure 6 shows the illustration of FDA antenna's apparent direction angle and physical direction angle.

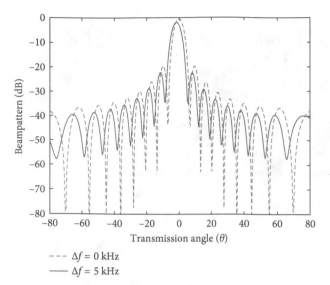

--- $\Delta f = 0$ kHz
—— $\Delta f = 5$ kHz

FIGURE 6: FDA antenna apparent direction angle and physical direction angle.

4. FDA Antenna Architecture Schemes

4.1. FDA Antenna Architecture. In the FDA antenna, we have uniform amplitude weightings and/or nonuniform weightings and uniform frequency offsets and nonuniform frequency offset. The antenna sidelobes can be decreased by

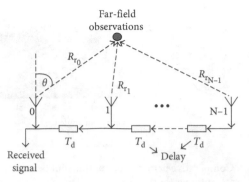

FIGURE 7: FDA antenna receiving architecture.

applying nonuniform weightings but at the expense of the beamwidth. At the transmitting side, the far-field of the FDA beampattern can be expressed as [39, 40],

$$\text{FDA}_T = \sum_{m=1}^{M} \frac{a_m}{r_m} f_e(f_m) \exp\left\{ j2\pi f_m t - j\frac{2\pi f_m r_m}{c} - jm\phi \right\},$$

(10)

where a_m is the transmitting weightings and ϕ denotes the phase difference between two elements.

At the receiving side, suppose the incoming signal is a continuous signal, $s(t) = \exp(j2\pi f_0 t)$, then FDA far-field array pattern is expressed as in (11) [40].

$$\text{FDA}_R = \sum_{n=1}^{N} \frac{a_n}{R_{r_n}} s(t - \tau_n) \exp\left\{ -j\frac{2\pi f_0(t - \tau_n)}{c} R_{r_n} \right\} \exp\left(j2\pi \frac{v_r f_0}{c} t \right),$$

(11)

$$\simeq \frac{a_n}{R_{r_0}} \sum_{n=1}^{N} \exp\left\{ jn\left(-2\pi f_0 T_d + \frac{2\pi f_0 d \sin\theta}{c} \right) \right\} \exp\left\{ j\left(2\pi f_0 t - \frac{2\pi f_0 R_{r_0}}{c} \right) \right\} \exp\left(j2\pi \frac{v_r f_0}{c} t \right),$$

where a_n is the receiving weightings, $\tau_n = nT_d$, where T_d is the interelement delay. It should be noted that, in communication systems, two moving platforms with relative velocity v_r, the Doppler frequency shift f_d at the receiver is $f_d = v_r f_0 / c$. Note that herein, equal Doppler frequency shift is adopted for the individual array element. Based on approximation, the distance from the far-field observation point to the nth array element is $R_{r_n} \simeq R_{r_0} - nd\sin\theta$ with R_{r_0} denoting the distance from the point to the first receiving element. Also in amplitude sense, we can have $R_{r_n} \simeq R_{r_0}$. Figure 7 shows the FDA antenna receiving architecture.

By inspection, it can be seen that, similar to the transmitting FDA antenna (10), the receiving FDA antenna (11) also creates a range-angle-dependent beampattern. This implies that at the receiver, beamforming range-dependent nulls are possible. It should be noted that in the FDA antenna, changing the carrier frequency and frequency increment, every point in space can be scanned in a discrete way. Moreover, if the total frequency increments are increased, some points in space can be scanned with more than one frequency component and this diversity has advantages in terms of multipath interferences.

From the literature [41], we can jointly employ transmitting FDA and receiving FDA antennas. In addition, the concepts of combining transmitting FDA antenna and omnidirectional receiving antenna or omnidirectional transmitting antenna and receiving FDA antenna are also possible implementation. Table 1, compares the FDA antenna and phased array antenna. And Table 2, compares distinct FDA antenna configuration.

4.2. Adaptive/Optimal FDA Antenna Architecture. Figure 8 depicts adaptive FDA antenna architecture whereby the gain and the phase of the signals which are induced at each array element are altered before combining in order to adjust the gain of the array in a dynamic fashion, as the system required. The adaptive system provides a way for the antenna arrays to adapt to the situation, and the adaption process is generally influenced by the control of the system. On the other hand, an optimal FDA antenna can be exploited in such a way that the gain and phase of each antenna element are adjusted to provide an optimal performance. For instance, maximum output signal-to-interference-and-noise ratio (SINR) can be

TABLE 1: Antenna array comparisons: FDA and phased array.

Antenna array	Transmitted signals	Gain (array)	Transmit capabilities
FDA	Coherent	Yes	Range-angle-dependent
Phased array	Coherent	Yes	Angle-dependent only

TABLE 2: Comparison among distinct FDA antenna configuration.

Antenna configuration	Range and angle	Computation complexity	Interference suppression	User detection capability
Conventional FDA	Coupled beampattern	Reasonable	Good	Good
FDA with nonuniform frequency offset	Decoupled beampattern	Less	Improved	Improved

obtained by canceling unwanted interferences and receiving the desired signal without distortion by adjusting the gains and phases of each FDA antenna element.

5. FDA Transmitter Scheme Using Butler Matrix for Wireless Communication

Figure 9 shows a block diagram of two-dimensional (2-D) (i.e., range and angle) half wavelength spaced FDA antenna using a 4×4 Butler matrix [42–44] for wireless communication. We employ four FDA elements with carrier frequencies connected at the outport of a 4×4 Butler matrix, namely, f_0, $f_0 + \Delta f$, $f_0 + 2\Delta f$, and $f_0 + 3\Delta f$, respectively, where f_0 is the carrier frequency and Δf being the frequency increment across the array element.

The basic principle is that, when Port 1 is excited, it goes through the signal path, A-B-C-D to f_0, with phase shift of 135°. Similarly, a phase shift of 90° is obtained between Port 1 and $f_0 + \Delta f$ using the signal path A-B-C-E and so forth. Note that, since we employ a 4×4 Butler matrix, the FDA elements has been set to four. The phase differences of a 4×4 Butler matrix are $\pm 45°$ for the output ports 1 and 4, and $\pm 135°$ for the output ports 2 and 3, respectively [45].

Here, we adopt a uniform linear frequency offset FDA antenna as depicted in Figure 1. The transfer function from

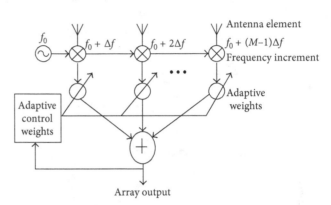

FIGURE 8: Adaptive FDA antenna architecture.

the nth input port to the mth output port of the 4×4 Butler matrix is given as [46].

$$T_{mn} = \frac{1}{\sqrt{N}} e^{-j(2\pi/N)(m-(N+1/2))(n-(N+1/2))},$$

$$m, n = 1, 2, \ldots, N.$$

(12)

And the far-field radiation pattern of the nth Butler matrix input port excitation can be obtained by (13).

$$F_n(\theta, r) = \sum_{m=1}^{N} \left[\left(\frac{1}{\sqrt{N}} e^{-j(2\pi/N)(m-(N+1/2))(n-(N+1/2))} \right) e^{j\left[(m-(N+1/2))\pi \sin(\theta) - (2\pi\Delta f r/c_0) \right]} \right].$$

(13)

This implies that the main beam pointing direction depends on not only the angle θ but also the range r and frequency increment Δf. From (13), the beampattern peak corresponds to

$$\frac{2\pi}{N} \left(m - \frac{N+1}{2} \right) \left(n - \frac{N+1}{2} \right) = \pi \left[\left(m - \frac{N+1}{2} \right) \sin \theta - \frac{2\Delta f r}{c_0} \right].$$

(14)

And the corresponding instantaneous main beam pointing direction angle θ_n can be calculated by

$$\theta_n = \sin^{-1} \left[\frac{2n - N - 1}{N} + \frac{4\Delta f r_n}{c_0(2m - N - 1)} \right].$$

(15)

Therefore, the instantaneous main beam pointing direction angle θ_n depends on both the range r_n and the frequency increment Δf, which characteristics can be exploited for directional secure communications.

Similarly, by replacing n in (13) and (15), with q, the far-field $F_q(\theta, r)$ generated by the qth Butler matrix input port excitation with the instantaneous main beam pointing direction angle θ_q can be acquired. It is easily verified that $F_n(\theta_q) = 0$ when $n \neq q$. This implies that $F_q(\theta, r)$'s main beam is projected along the null radiation direction of $F_n(\theta, r)$. It should be noted that because of beam orthogonality property of a Butler matrix, we can have $F_n(\theta, r)$'s main beam and $F_q(\theta, r)$'s null direction.

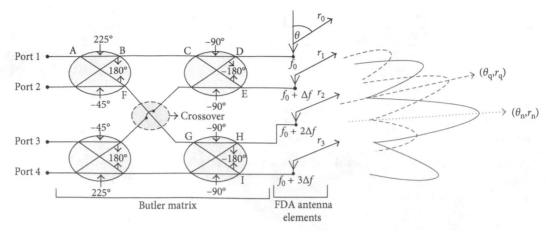

FIGURE 9: FDA using a 4×4 Butler matrix for wireless communications.

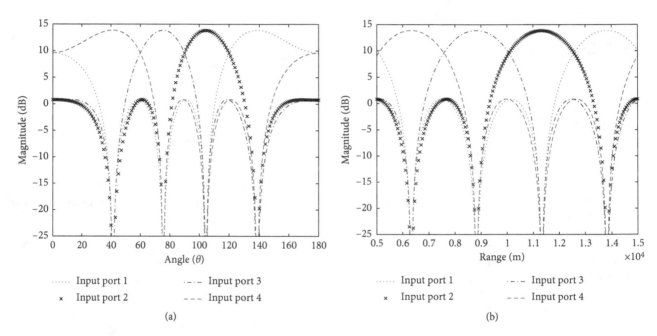

(a)

(b)

FIGURE 10: FDA 4×4 Butler matrix input ports excited radiation power pattern when $\Delta f = 30$ kHz is adopted (a) in angle dimension and (b) in range dimension.

In Figure 10, we simulate the far-field radiation power pattern in angle and range dimensions for each of the four input port excitations, namely, "1," "2," "3," and "4," respectively. It is evident that the four main beams are orthogonal to each other, pointing along 41°, 76°, 104°, and 139°, respectively, in angle dimension (Figure 10(a)), whereas in range dimension (Figure 10(b)), the beams point along 6.2 km, 8.9 km, 11.2 km, and 13.9 km, respectively.

6. Performance Analysis of FDA Antenna

6.1. Signal-to-Interference-and-Noise Ratio (SINR). In this section, we discuss the output SINR of the FDA antenna beamformer with respect to its spatial resolution (mainlobe) and interference rejection capability (sidelobe level and

spectral nulls). According to [19], the output SINR can be expressed as

$$\text{SINR} \triangleq \frac{\sigma_s^2 \left| \mathbf{w}^H \mathbf{a}(t - \tau, \ \theta, \ r) \right|^2}{\mathbf{w}^H \left(\sum_i \sigma_i^2 \mathbf{a}(t - \tau, \ \theta_i, \ r_i) \, \mathbf{a}^H(t - \tau, \ \theta_i, \ r_i) + \sigma_n^2 \right) \mathbf{w}}, \tag{16}$$

where σ_s^2 denotes the variance of the intended user/target signal. In case, the user (target) is being observed in the background of few weak interferences, (16) is simplified to (17):

$$\text{SINR} \simeq \frac{\sigma_s^2 M^2}{\sigma_n^2}. \tag{17}$$

On the contrary, if the user (target) is observed in the background of strong interferences, then we have

$$\text{SINR} \simeq \frac{\sigma_s^2 M^2}{\sum_i \sigma_i^2 \left| \mathbf{w}^H \mathbf{a}\left(t - \tau, \ \theta_i, \ r_i\right) \right|^2 \left| \mathbf{w}^H \mathbf{a}\left(t - \tau, \ \theta_i, \ r_i\right) \right|^2}. \tag{18}$$

6.2. Direction of Arrival (DOA). In array signal processing, direction of arrival (DOA) estimation, also known as angle of arrival (AOA) detection is an important concept [47]. The main objective of direction of arrival (DOA) estimation is to utilize the data received on the uplink at the base-station antenna array in order to estimate the directions of the signals from the desired mobile users and the directions of interference signals. For instance, suppose several transmitters are employed simultaneously to work, hence each source will process the potential multipath components at the receivers. Therefore, it is essential for the receiving antennas to able to estimate those angles of arrival to know the possible location of transmitters and/or users.

In this paper, we resort to the classical DOA algorithm, namely, multiple signal classification (MUSIC) to resolve multipath signals DOA estimation. The MUSIC algorithm employs the covariance matrix of the received data to separate the signal subspace and noise subspace. And then it creates space scanning spectrum to search the peaks in the whole region by utilizing orthogonality between the signal directional vector and noise subspace, in order to estimate signals' DOA [47]. The MUSIC for FDA antenna can be expressed as

$$P(\theta, \ r) = \frac{1}{\mathbf{a}_r^H(\theta, \ r) \mathbf{V}_n \mathbf{V}_n^H \mathbf{a}_r(\theta, \ r)}, \tag{19}$$

where $\mathbf{V}_n$ denotes the noise subspace and $\mathbf{a}_r(\theta, r)$ is given as

$$\mathbf{a}_r(\theta, \ r) = \left[1 \exp\left(j\psi_{r_1}\right) \cdots \exp\left(j\psi_{r_n}\right) \cdots \exp\left(j\psi_{r_{N-1}}\right)\right] \tag{20}$$

with ψ_{r_n} being expressed as

$$\psi_{r_n} = 2\pi\left(f_0 \frac{nd \sin\theta}{c} + \frac{\Delta F_n r}{c} + \frac{n\Delta F_n d \sin\theta}{c}\right). \tag{21}$$

7. Numerical Results

In this section, we use (17) and (18) to show the results of SINR as a function of SNR. Figure 11 depicts comparative performance of FDA antenna and phased array antenna in noise dominant. It can be seen that both antenna systems exhibited the same performance.

But in Figure 12, the FDA antenna shows a better SINR performance compared to phased array antenna because the FDA antenna has the capability to suppress range-dependent interferences, especially, where there are strong interferences with angle being the same but different range form the intended user.

Finally, we assume the following parameters: $M = 10$, SNR = 10, and number of snapshots = 100. Figure 13(a), shows the DOA performance between the FDA antenna and

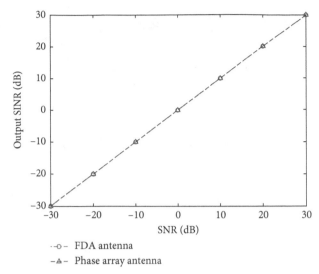

--o-- FDA antenna
--△-- Phase array antenna

FIGURE 11: SINR as a function of SNR in noise dominant.

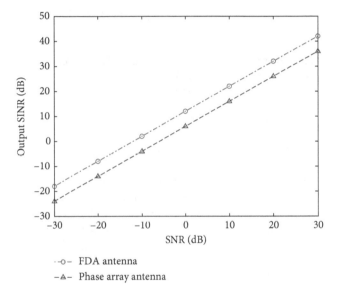

--o-- FDA antenna
--△-- Phase array antenna

FIGURE 12: SINR as a function of SNR in interference dominant.

phased array antenna in angle dimension. It can be observed that both FDA antenna and phased array antenna have the same DOA performances towards angle directions, such as [40°60°]. In Figure 13(b), that is range dimension, phased array antenna lack range resolution. In contrast, the FDA antenna still has DOA performance towards the range directions, such as 8 km and 10 km which is unavailable to phased array antenna. Therefore, the FDA antenna has range-dependent capability, and it can effectively identify signal sources.

7.1. Hardware/Software Complexity Discussions. Antenna Configuration: Apart from linear array antenna configuration, different antenna geometry can be adopted in designing FDA such as planar and circular. In phased array antenna, the cost of using phase shifters is very high. In FDA, no phase shifters are required. The most important difference of FDA

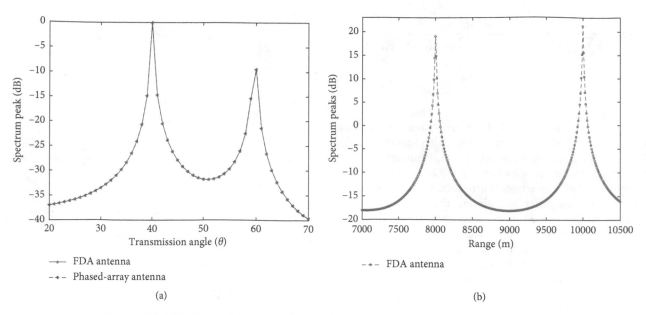

FIGURE 13: MUSIC pseudospectra: (a) in angle dimension and (b) in range dimension.

antenna from a phased array antenna is that a small amount of frequency increment compared to the carrier frequency is used across the array elements.

Hardware/software complexity: FDA with constant element spacing may not be an ideal configuration due to the frequency diversity. We can employ larger element spacing to reduce the array complexity. Implementation of FDA concept on array hardware may require agile local oscillators and mixers to change the frequency for each element of the array. The complex transmit-receive weighting functions of FDA depends on the baseband frequency and frequency increment. We can relax this weighting function's frequency increment dependence. This means that spatial weighting can be factored out from the summation and applied once to the entire signal, thus reducing computation complexity.

8. Conclusion

In this paper, we have shown the capability of FDA antenna from its origin to the potential applications in wireless communication systems. The range-angle-dependent array factor permits the FDA antenna to transmit energy over a desired range dimension and angle dimension. Because of the range-angle-dependent property, the FDA has the potential to suppress range-dependent interference. Thus, this provides an extra degree of freedom unavailable to the phased array antennas. In addition, we have discussed application scenario of using FDA and Butler matrix for communication. Numerical example shows that the FDA antenna is a promising array concept for wireless communication systems. Certainly, there may be more problems to be investigated by employing FDA antenna in communication applications. We also call for more support on the research and development of FDA antenna for future wireless communication systems.

References

[1] N. N. Alotaibi and K. A. Hamdi, "Switched phased-array transmission architecture for secure millimeter-wave wireless communication," *IEEE Transactions On Communications*, vol. 64, no. 3, pp. 1303–1312, 2016.

[2] W. Roh, J.-Y. Seol, J. Park et al., "Millimeter-wave beam-forming as an enabling technology for 5g cellular communications: theoretical feasibility and prototype results," *IEEE Communications Magazine*, vol. 52, no. 2, pp. 106–113, 2014.

[3] L. C. Godara, "Applications of antenna arrays to mobile communications, part I: performance improvement, feasibility, and system considerations," *Proceedings of the IEEE*, vol. 85, no. 7, pp. 1031–1060, 1997.

[4] L. C. Godara, "Application of antenna arrays to mobile communications, part II: beam-forming and direction-of-arrival considerations," *Proceedings of the IEEE*, vol. 85, no. 8, pp. 1195–1245, 1997.

[5] P. F. McManamon, P. J. Bos, M. J. Escuti et al., "A review of phased array steering for narrow-band electrooptical systems," *Proceedings of the IEEE*, vol. 97, no. 6, pp. 1078–1096, 2009.

[6] J. Li and P. Stoica, "The phased array is the maximum SNR active array," *IEEE Signal Processing Magazine*, vol. 27, no. 2, pp. 143-144, 2010.

[7] E. Brookner, "Phased array radars-past, present and future," in *2002 International Radar Conference (Radar 2002)*, pp. 104–113, Santa Barbara, CA, USA, April 2002.

[8] J. H. G. Ender, H. Wilden, U. Nickel et al., "Progress in phased-array radar applications," in *Proceedings of the IEEE First European Radar Conference, EURAD*, pp. 113–116, October 2004.

[9] P. Antonik, *An investigation of a frequency diverse array*, Ph.D. dissertation, University College London, London, UK, 2009.

[10] P. Antonik, M. C. Wicks, H. D. Griffiths et al., "Frequency diverse array radars," in *2006 IEEE Conference on Radar*, pp. 215–217, Verona, NY, USA, April 2006.

[11] W. Q. Wang and J. Cai, "MIMO SAR using chirp diverse waveform for wideswath remote sensing," *IEEE Transactions*

on *Aerospace and Electronic Systems*, vol. 48, no. 4, pp. 3171–3185, 2012.

[12] A. M. Haimovich, R. Blum, and L. Cimini, "MIMO radar with widely separated antennas," *IEEE Signal Processing Magazine*, vol. 25, no. 1, pp. 116–129, 2008.

[13] J. Li and P. Stoica, "MIMO radar with colocated antennas," *IEEE Signal Processing Magazine*, vol. 24, no. 5, pp. 106–114, 2007.

[14] Y. Ding, J. Zhang, and V. Fusco, "Frequency diverse array OFDM transmitter for secure wireless communication," *Electronics Letters*, vol. 51, no. 17, pp. 1374–1376, 2015.

[15] W. Q. Wang, "Mitigating range ambiguities in high-PRF SAR with OFDM waveform diversity," *IEEE Geoscience and Remote Sensing Letters*, vol. 10, no. 1, pp. 101–105, 2013.

[16] F. S. Johansson, L. G. Josefsson, and T. Lorentzon, "A novel frequency-scanned reflector antenna," *IEEE Transactions on Antennas and Propagatio*, vol. 37, no. 8, pp. 984–989, 1989.

[17] C. Vazquez, C. Garcia, Y. Alvarez et al., "Near field characterization of an imaging system based on a frequency scanning antenna array," *IEEE Transactions on Antennas and Propagation IEEE Transactions on Antennas and Propagation*, vol. 61, no. 5, pp. 2874–2879, 2013.

[18] W. Q. Wang, "Range-angle dependent transmit beampattern synthesis for linear frequency diverse arrays," *IEEE Transactions on Antennas and Propagation*, vol. 61, no. 8, pp. 4073–4081, 2014.

[19] W. Q. Wang, "Overview of frequency diverse array in radar and navigation applications," *IET Radar, Sonar and Navigation*, vol. 10, no. 6, pp. 1001–1012, 2016.

[20] H. Shao, J. Li, H. Chen et al., "Adaptive frequency offset selection in frequency diverse array radar," *IEEE Antennas and Wireless Propagation Letters*, vol. 13, no. 1, pp. 1405–1408, 2014.

[21] W. Q. Wang and H. C. So, "Transmit subaperturing for range and angle estimation in frequency diverse array radar," *IEEE Transactions on Signal Processing*, vol. 62, no. 8, pp. 2000–2011, 2014.

[22] Y. Wang, W. Q. Wang, H. Chen et al., "Optimal frequency diverse subarray design with Cramer–Rao lower bound minimization," *IEEE Antennas and Wireless Propagation Letters*, vol. 14, no. 1, pp. 1188–1191, 2015.

[23] B. Abdul, W. Khan, S. Khan, and I. M. Qureshi, "Development of frequency diverse array radar technology: a review," *IET Radar, Sonar and Navigation*, vol. 12, no. 2, pp. 165–175, 2018.

[24] J. Xiong, S. Y. Nusenu, and W. Q. Wang, "Directional modulation using frequency diverse array for secure communications," *Wireless Personal Communications*, vol. 95, no. 3, pp. 2979–2689, 2017.

[25] J. Hu, S. Yan, F. Shu et al., "Artificial-noise-aided secure transmission with directional modulation based on random frequency diverse arrays," *IEEE Access*, vol. 5, pp. 1658–1667, 2017.

[26] S. Y. Nusenu, W. Q. Wang, and J. Xiong, "Time-modulated frequency diverse array for physical-layer security," *IET Microwaves Antenna and Propagation*, vol. 11, no. 9, pp. 1274–1279, 2017.

[27] S. Y. Nusenu, W.-Q. Wang, and S. Ji, "Secure directional modulation using frequency diverse array antenna," in *2017 IEEE Radar Conference*, pp. 378–382, Seattle, WA, USA, May 2017.

[28] W. Q. Wang, "DM using FDA antenna for secure transmission," *IET Microwaves Antenna and Propagation*, vol. 11, no. 3, pp. 336–345, 2017.

[29] L. Zhuang and X. Z. Liu, "Precisely beam steering for frequency diverse arrays based on frequency offset selection," in

[30] W. Khan, I. M. Qureshi, and S. Sarah, "Frequency diverse array radar with logarithmically increasing frequency offset," *IEEE Antennas And Wireless Propagation Letters*, vol. 14, pp. 499–502, 2015.

[31] B. Abdul, I. M. Qureshi, W. Khan et al., "Beam pattern synthesis for an FDA radar with Hamming window-based nonuniform frequency offset," *IEEE Antennas and Wireless Propagation Letters*, vol. 16, pp. 2283–2286, 2017.

[32] A. Mukherjee, S. A. A. Fakoorian, J. Huang, and A. L. Swindlehurst, "Principles of physical layer security in multiuser wireless networks: a survey," *IEEE Communications Surveys and Tutorials*, vol. 16, no. 3, pp. 1550–1573, 2014.

[33] A. D. Wyner, "The wire-tap channel," *Bell System Technical Journal*, vol. 54, no. 8, pp. 1355–1387, 1975.

[34] P. K. Gopala, L. Lai, and H. El-Gamal, "On the secrecy capacity of fading channels," *IEEE Transactions on Information Theory*, vol. 54, no. 10, pp. 4687–4698, 2008.

[35] H.-M. Wang, M. Luo, Q. Yin, and X.-G. Xia, "Hybrid cooperative beamforming and jamming for physical-layer security of two-way relay networks," *IEEE Transactions on Information Forensics and Security*, vol. 8, no. 12, pp. 2007–2020, 2013.

[36] N. Valliappan, A. Lozano, and R. W. Heath, "Antenna subset modulation for secure millimeter-wave wireless communication," *IEEE Transactions on Communications*, vol. 61, no. 8, pp. 3231–3245, 2013.

[37] J. Kim, A. Ikhlef, and R. Schober, "Combined relay selection and cooperative beamforming for physical layer security," *Journal of Communications and Networks*, vol. 14, no. 4, pp. 364–373, 2012.

[38] H. Ma and P. Ma, "Beamforming design of decode-and-forward cooperation for improving wireless physical layer security," in *15th International Conference on Advanced Communications Technology*, pp. 41–49, Pyeongchang, Republic of Korea, January 2013.

[39] C.A. Balanis, *Antenna Theory Analysis and Design*, John Wiley and Sons, New York, NY, USA, 1997.

[40] T. Eker, S. Demir, and A. Hizal, "Exploitation of linear frequency modulated continuous waveform (LFMCW) for frequency diverse arrays," *IEEE Transactions on Antennas and Propagation*, vol. 61, no. 7, pp. 3546–3553, 2013.

[41] A. Jones and B. Rigling, "Planar frequency diverse array receiver architecture," in *2012 IEEE Radar Conference*, pp. 145–150, Atlanta, GA, USA, May 2012.

[42] M. Campo, W. Simon, and R. Baggen, "Steerable antenna array at 24 GHz using Butler matrices and MEMS-switches," in *Proceedings of the IEEE International Symposium on Antennas and Propagation*, pp. 1-2, Kamp-Lintfort, Germany, July 2012.

[43] W. Bhowmik and S. Srivastava, "Optimum design of a 4x4 planar Butler matrix array for WLAN application," *Journal of Telecommunications*, vol. 2, no. 1, pp. 68–74, 2010.

[44] M. Ueno, "A systematic design formulation for Butler matrix applied FFT algorithm," *IEEE Transactions on Antennas and Propagation*, vol. 29, no. 3, pp. 496–501, 1981.

[45] R. J. Mailloux, *Phased Array Antenna Handbook*, Artech House Inc., Boston, MA, USA, 2005.

IEEE International Radar Conference, pp. 1–4, Bordeaux, France, 2009.

Permissions

The contributors of this book come from diverse backgrounds, making this book a truly international effort. This book will bring forth new frontiers with its revolutionizing research information and detailed analysis of the nascent developments around the world.

We would like to thank all the contributing authors for lending their expertise to make the book truly unique. They have played a crucial role in the development of this book. Without their invaluable contributions this book wouldn't have been possible. They have made vital efforts to compile up to date information on the varied aspects of this subject to make this book a valuable addition to the collection of many professionals and students.

This book was conceptualized with the vision of imparting up-to-date information and advanced data in this field. To ensure the same, a matchless editorial board was set up. Every individual on the board went through rigorous rounds of assessment to prove their worth. After which they invested a large part of their time researching and compiling the most relevant data for our readers.

The editorial board has been involved in producing this book since its inception. They have spent rigorous hours researching and exploring the diverse topics which have resulted in the successful publishing of this book. They have passed on their knowledge of decades through this book. To expedite this challenging task, the publisher supported the team at every step. A small team of assistant editors was also appointed to further simplify the editing procedure and attain best results for the readers.

Apart from the editorial board, the designing team has also invested a significant amount of their time in understanding the subject and creating the most relevant covers. They scrutinized every image to scout for the most suitable representation of the subject and create an appropriate cover for the book.

The publishing team has been an ardent support to the editorial, designing and production team. Their endless efforts to recruit the best for this project, has resulted in the accomplishment of this book. They are a veteran in the field of academics and their pool of knowledge is as vast as their experience in printing. Their expertise and guidance has proved useful at every step. Their uncompromising quality standards have made this book an exceptional effort. Their encouragement from time to time has been an inspiration for everyone.

The publisher and the editorial board hope that this book will prove to be a valuable piece of knowledge for researchers, students, practitioners and scholars across the globe.

List of Contributors

Taimur Bakhshi and Bogdan Ghita
Center for Security, Communications and Network Research, University of Plymouth, Plymouth PL4 8AA, UK

Juha Partala
Physiological Signal Analysis Team, The Center for Machine Vision and Signal Analysis, University of Oulu, Oulu, Finland

Luiz Carlos Pessoa Albini
Department of Informatics, Federal University of Parana (UFPR), 81531970 Curitiba, Brazil

Eduardo da Silva
Department of Informatics, Federal University of Parana (UFPR), 81531970 Curitiba, Brazil
Department of Informatics, Catarinense Federal Institute (IFC), 89245000 Araquari, Brazil

BipunMan Pati and Attaphongse Taparugssanagorn
Telecommunications, Asian Institute of Technology, Klong Luang, Pathumthani 12120, Thailand

Amrit Lal Sangal
Department of Computer Science and Engineering, National Institute of Technology, Jalandhar, Punjab, India

Ramanpreet Kaur
Department of Computer Science and Engineering, National Institute of Technology, Jalandhar, Punjab, India
Department of Information Technology, Jaypee University of Information Technology, Solan, Himachal Pradesh, India

Krishan Kumar
Department of Computer Science and Engineering, Shaheed Bhagat Singh State Technical Campus, Ferozepur, Punjab, India

Timothy T. Adeliyi and Oludayo O. Olugbara
ICT and Society Research Group, Durban University of Technology, Durban, South Africa

Selahattin Gokceli, Nikolay Zhmurov, Gunes Karabulut Kurt and Berna Ors
Department of Electronics and Communication Engineering, Istanbul Technical University, Istanbul, Turkey

Ayotuyi Tosin Akinola and Matthew Olusegun Adigun
Department of Computer Science, Centre of Excellence at University of Zululand, Private Bag X1001, Ongoye, KwaDlangezwa 3886, South Africa

Abhishek Joshi, Sarang Dhongdi, Rishabh Sethunathan, Pritish Nahar and K. R. Anupama
BITS Pilani, K K Birla Goa Campus, Goa, India

Huda Saleh Abbas, Mark A. Gregory and Michael W. Austin
RMIT University, Melbourne, Australia

S. J. Sheela and K. V. Suresh
Department of E and C, Siddaganga Institute of Technology, Visvesvaraya Technological University, Tumakuru, India

Deepaknath Tandur
Corporate Research India, ABB, Bengaluru, India

Zelalem Hailu Gebeyehu
Institute of Science, Technology and Innovation, Pan African University, Nairobi, Kenya

Philip Kibet Langat
Jomo Kenyatta University of Agriculture and Technology, Nairobi, Kenya

Ciira Wa Maina
Dedan Kimathi University of Technology, Nyeri, Kenya

René Rietz, Radoslaw Cwalinski and Hartmut König
Brandenburg University of Technology, Department of Computer Science, Group Computer Networks, PF 101344, Cottbus, Germany

Andreas Brinner
Genua GmbH, Domagkstraße 7, 85551 Kirchheim Near Munich, Germany

Aisha-Hassan A. Hashim, Othman O. Khalifa, M. Azram and Mistura L. Sanni
Department of Electrical and Computer Engineering, International Islamic University Malaysia, 50728 Kuala Lumpur, Malaysia

Omar M. Zakaria
Department of Electrical and Computer Engineering, International Islamic University Malaysia, 50728 Kuala Lumpur, Malaysia

Malaysia-Japan International Institute of Technology (MJIIT), Department of Electronic Systems Engineering, Universiti Teknologi Malaysia, 54100 Kuala Lumpur, Jalan Semarak, Malaysia

Wan H. Hassan, Lalitha B. Jivanadham and Mahdi Zareei
Malaysia-Japan International Institute of Technology (MJIIT), Department of Electronic Systems Engineering, Universiti Teknologi Malaysia, 54100 Kuala Lumpur, Jalan Semarak, Malaysia

Shaddrack Yaw Nusenu
University of Electronic Science and Technology of China, Chengdu, China
Koforidua Technical University (KTU), Koforidua, Ghana

Abdul Basit
University of Electronic Science and Technology of China, Chengdu, China
Department of Electrical Engineering, International Islamic University, Islamabad, Pakistan

Index

CPSIA information can be obtained
at www.ICGtesting.com
Printed in the USA
BVHW011739260820
587403BV00002B/10